Modern Verse in English
1900-1950

Edited by

DAVID CECIL *and* ALLEN TATE

With critical introductions on
British and American poetry and
biographical notes on the poets included

THE MACMILLAN COMPANY · NEW YORK

Printed in the United States of America

First Printing

Professor Tate's Introduction previously published in the Sewanee Review *under the title: "Reflections on American Poetry, 1900–1950,"* *© The Macmillan Company, 1956.*

Library of Congress catalog card number: 58–13621

CONTENTS

INTRODUCTION TO BRITISH POETRY, 1900-1950

THIS ANTHOLOGY covers the years 1900–1950. It is not a period of which it is easy to give an ordered survey. For one thing, it is so close to us that it is difficult to see it in perspective; and for another, it is less a complete period than part of a phase of English letters which began more than a hundred and fifty years ago. Unromantic though we may feel, the romantic age is not over yet. The poets of today are still in what may be called the romantic situation.

The romantic situation is the result of that disintegration of orthodoxy which took place towards the end of the eighteenth century. During that century the standards of belief and taste, of which Augustan poetry was the expression, had begun to crumble. The consequence was that poets felt at sea in a way that the poets of previous ages had not done. They were conscious of a compelling urge to write poetry and of an instinctive feeling that in so doing they were fulfilling an important human function. But there was no one whom they trusted to tell them what that function was and what their poetry should be like. Each poet had to decide these things for himself. This was the romantic situation.

The fact they were in it made the first romantic poets turn to their own private experience to discover an answer to their questions. This affected their work in various ways. First of all it made it much more deliberately and avowedly individualistic than that of older writers had been. Each built up a theory of life and art founded on those elements in his own personal experience which he felt most precious and significant: Wordsworth's was founded on his mystical apprehension of an indwelling spirit in nature, Keats's on his response to the beautiful, and so on. Their styles too, created as they were to suit the particular subject-matter of each author, were more consciously idiosyncratic and experimental than the styles of the previous generation. The idea of the "correct" went out to be replaced by the idea of the "original".

Poetry, too, tended to become more subjective than before,

more concerned with the inner life of the author, his private unspoken dreams and fears and aspirations. The typical long serious poems of the past had dealt with character and idea and action in an ostensibly impersonal fashion; the poet seldom openly brought himself in. The outstanding long poem of the romantic age, Wordsworth's *Prelude*, is accurately described by its author as "a history of the poet's mind".

Finally, romantic poetry represents man as of his nature at odds with his environment. Examining experience as he did with a fresh and unprejudiced eye, the poet was struck by the fact that while instinctively he desired beauty, harmony and order, he found himself in a world chaotic and dissonant and, largely, ugly. Sometimes, like Wordsworth, he evolved a philosophy that purported to reconcile these discords. Sometimes, like Byron, he judged them to be irreconcilable. But either way he started off aware of discord as a primary basic fact of experience. This awareness is a distinguishing mark of the romantic poet; and the mingled sense of aspiration and disillusionment which it inspired in him is the characteristic romantic emotion.

During the nineteenth century no new orthodoxy arose to win general acceptance. The nineteenth century was a period of mental disorder in which progressives and neo-medievalists, rationalists and mystics, joined their voices in a confused clamour. Poets remained inextricably caught in the romantic situation. Indeed as the century progressed two factors appeared to render it even more acute. The scientific discoveries of Darwin and others shook men's faith not only in Christian orthodoxy but also in any ideal interpretation of the nature of existence. Man was looked on less and less as an immortal spirit, the master of created things, and more and more as an alien victim living in a universe controlled by mechanical forces that moved on their ruthless and mysterious way with no regard for his feelings or his ideals. Further, the industrial revolution was creating a society, at once materialistic and puritanical, which set no serious value on art. Art was at best a harmless amusement, at worst a frivolous distraction from the serious business of life. Since poets are artists and since their work is largely the expression of their ideal feelings, all this made them feel more at odds with their environment than ever.

More and more were they conscious of a discrepancy between the realities they saw around them and the dreams which commanded the allegiance of their hearts. They began to see themselves as rebels and outcasts, glorious, defiant and wistful, following the call of their genius amid an unsympathetic society and an indifferent universe.

They reacted in various ways. A few found salvation in faith founded on personal, spiritual experience. It might be orthodox Christian faith, as it was for Hopkins or Patmore; it might be some private home-made creed, as it was for Browning or Meredith. Others deliberately turned their backs on the world of contemporary action and took refuge in a citadel of art constructed from those elements in their own imaginative life which did give them satisfaction: natural beauty, classic myth, medieval and fairy legend. If they did comment on life, it was more often than not in a spirit of tragic pessimism. Arnold and Swinburne melodiously lament the incurable inadequacy of existence to satisfy the desires of the soul. But every line they took, and every mood they wrote in, confirmed the romantic tendency. Poets remained individualistic, subjective, and more than ever convinced of the incurable discrepancy between real and ideal.

When this anthology begins, this second phase of romanticism is still in full swing. The great writers who had already established themselves and were, as it were, in full production, exhibited one or more of the tendencies described above. Yeats had made his name as a sort of Celtic Pre-Raphaelite, scornfully repudiating the world of progress and science to take up his abode in the haunted Isle of Innisfree. Hardy and Housman were eloquent romantic pessimists. For them

> The troubles of our proud and angry dust
> Are from eternity and shall not fail.

They also drew inspiration and solace from the beauty of the natural world. So did Bridges, though he differed from them in outlook. Temperamentally happy but too clear-sighted to be optimistically progressive, his cool Olympian spirit found satisfaction in an Oxonian brand of Christian Platonism devised by himself.

Other noteworthy poets of this and the next generation range themselves into similar groups. Mary Coleridge was a delicate chip of the old Samuel Taylor block; without his mastery but with her own strain of haunted, Gothic strangeness. Binyon sings in Keatsian mood of Tristan and Iseult or of flashes of beauty glimpsed in street and woodland; Kipling, when most truly a poet, explores the romance of foreign lands or past ages or of a soldier's life. The writers that came to maturity soon after 1900 followed a like trend. Those associated with the Georgian books edited by Sir Edward Marsh made themselves at home in little citadels of natural and fanciful beauty, for the most part English and rural, but sometimes exotic or elfin. Two greater names fall into the same categories. Edward Thomas was a townsman who left the town to carry on a lifelong love affair with the English countryside; Walter de la Mare created a world of his own compounded of fairy-tale and childhood memory and twilit dream, through which to express his personal vision of spiritual reality.

Both writers memorably achieved their aims. Yet their achievement is slighter than that of those first romantics from whom they are descended. Edward Thomas's clear vision of nature is fragmentary compared to that of Wordsworth; de la Mare's elf-land, though as subtly imagined as that of Coleridge, is on a smaller scale. The fact was that the original romantic impulse was slackening. Its energy had weakened: several of its traditional modes of expression showed signs of wearing thin. It is not surprising that in a few years poetry took an abrupt and sensational turn in a new direction. This move was led by two distinguished writers, Yeats in a later phase of his development, and Mr. T. S. Eliot. There was no question, indeed, of their extricating themselves from the romantic situation. They were still individualistic, still absorbed in the inner life, still acutely conscious of the discrepancy between the real and the ideal. But the mood in which they approached these facts was different. They were not content lyrically to lament their lot as Housman had been, nor did they feel inclined to try to rise above it on the wings of imagination. Rather they wished to define and analyse it and also themselves; and to chart their relationship to the world around them and to past ages in clear-cut intellectual terms and realistic unsentimental tones. The two poets were led to this approach by different roads. Yeats's was curiosity; no longer content merely to enjoy his daydreams, he wished to trace their origin and examine their significance. Mr. Eliot–and here he was far more typical of his generation–was impelled by disillusion. The first romantics, though often sceptical and pessimistic about the world round them, believed passionately in themselves and in the value and significance of their own emotional responses. Mr. Eliot looked on his own inner life with the same sceptical eye as he turned on the outer world. Viewed honestly, was it not in fact an equally unimpressive spectacle? He presented the poet to the public not as a Byronic Childe Harold splendidly defying the ignoble universe, but as J. Alfred Prufrock, the comical, pathetic, prosaic sport of circumstances:

> I grow old . . . I grow old . . .
> I shall wear the bottoms of my trousers rolled.
> Shall I part my hair behind? Do I dare to eat a
>   peach?
> I shall wear white flannel trousers, and walk upon
>   the beach.
> I have heard the mermaids singing, each to each.
> I do not think that they will sing to me.

Such a figure was not possessed of emotions appropriately to be expressed in rapturous lyric verse: nor were his imaginative flights powerful enough to transport him up to a region immune from mundane troubles.

Mr. Eliot and Yeats soon found followers. The War of 1914–18 produced a number. Not, indeed, while hostilities were going on; the war-time atmosphere was too highly charged with emotion for that. At the very beginning it was an enthusiastic emotion. Rupert Brooke welcomed war as a means of escape from the romantic situation into a life of heroic action. The painful facts of twentieth-century warfare soon dispelled this pleasant idea. The two most memorable poets of the later war years, Wilfred Owen and Siegfried Sassoon, passionately protested against war as an outstandingly dreadful manifestation of the horror of the contemporary world. With the coming of peace this hot fit was succeeded by a cold fit: and it was a cold fit in which young writers felt less than ever able to rise above the discord of the romantic situation. What was the use of building citadels of imagination into which to retire from the onslaught of the hideous world? The world simply invaded them and broke them up. No good talking about escape while there was nowhere to escape to! The romantic situation had become the romantic predicament. All the poet could do was to confront it, examine it, expose it. A mood of wry, unhopeful curiosity pervaded the mental atmosphere. To find words for it the poets turned to the new modes of expression devised by Mr. Eliot and Yeats.

They were also disposed to do so by recent advances in psychological science. This was the period when Freud and Jung became generally known. Their ideas were inevitably interesting to the inheritors of the romantic tradition; for they were concerned with the inner life which had always been a principal romantic subject. But psychology treated the inner life in a most un-Wordsworthian spirit; for it suggested that all human sentiments, even the most exalted ones, were largely the unconscious expression of irrational impulses and animal instincts. Man's spirit, looked at in the cold light of the psychologist's laboratory, became less an object of veneration than of unrespectful curiosity. His inner life lost some of its mystery and more of its dignity. In order to describe it in the right terms poets turned once more to Mr. Eliot and Yeats for guidance.

Not that the new poetry excluded fancy and dream altogether. One of its most eminent exponents, Dame Edith Sitwell, created a world of fairy-tale and childhood memory as vivid as that of de la Mare. But to compare the two worlds is to realize the change that had taken place in the mental atmosphere. De la Mare's imaginative world is for him the home of ultimate reality. The fable and the child's fancy show us the truth about the universe in a way that we are not able to see it in the streets around us. Dame Edith Sitwell makes no such claim. The worlds of *Troy Park* and *The Sleeping Beauty* touch us with a poignancy that comes from the fact that we and the author know that so far from being true they are exquisite fabrications symbolizing those lost paradises of the innocent imagination which the bitter experience of maturity all too soon proves to be illusory. Anyway, this strain in Dame Edith Sitwell's work is rare in her generation. The great typical poem of the 1920s is Mr. Eliot's *Waste Land*, sceptical, ironical, tragic; the typical lines of the period are those which end Mr. Eliot's *Hollow Men*:

> This is the way the world ends,
> Not with a bang but a whimper.

The 1930s introduced a change of tone. The phase of ironical doubt was followed by a phase of faith-searching. Mr. Eliot came out as a practising Anglo-Catholic Christian; and a younger group led by Messrs. Auden, Day-Lewis and Spender turned to politics as a way of salvation. The slump had come, the war was coming. Their world seemed likely to end soon, and not with a whimper but with a disagreeably loud bang. So it was no use, they felt, to try and maintain an attitude of detachment. The old civilization was collapsing; ought they not to throw in their lot with those who were trying to create a new and better civilization to take its place? The romantic predicament was the consequence of a decaying order, and the sooner this order was done away with the better. Perhaps there was something to be said for Communism. Certainly capitalism was the enemy of the spirit of man. These poets preached this gospel emphatically and sometimes with a poignant eloquence. But there was something fevered and uncertain in their tone. They were more convincing when they attacked the old than when they professed hope in the new. It was as though they wanted to believe in the future rather than that they did believe in it. Indeed, as it proved, the realities of Communism as exhibited in Soviet Russia soon disenchanted its poetical followers in England. By the beginning of the War of 1939 the fashion for political poetry was past. The romantic discord remained unresolved.

In consequence, since then poetry has been as subjective and individualist as ever. So individualist, indeed, that it is even more misleading than usual to try and impose an order upon it. For the last fifteen years or so the poetical landscape has been a confused scene of shifting groups and independent experimentalists. Because the predicament still prevails, those masters who best expressed it have not lost their influence. Yeats and Mr. Eliot still dominate the poetic scene, but other figures have their special following: Dame Edith Sitwell, Mr. Robert Graves, Mr. Auden, Mr. Empson and Dylan Thomas. These last two made their reputations more recently. Though both are extremely "modern" in the sense of being experimental, they represent divergent tendencies. Mr. Empson and his disciples carry the intellectualist tendency of the Eliot movement to its furthest point. Ingenious, academic and, at their best, extremely accomplished, they seek to state a situation personal or intellectual, in a sort of compressed streamlined version of the metaphysical conceit. The other trend as exemplified by Dylan Thomas or Mr. Vernon Watkins, though using a modern technique of expression, is in reaction against the cerebral, and is dithyrambic, fanciful and sensuous. Which, if either, of these two schools is likely to attract many followers, it is impossible to say. Indeed, it is more futile even than usual to prophesy what course poetry is likely to take in the future. The art of letters, like other arts today, is in a state of flux. All we can see is that the romantic situation is still with us and that until a coherent and stable culture appears to supersede the present chaos, it is likely to remain.

Meanwhile style has followed a course of development similar to that of the spirit which it is its function to express. Up till 1914 most poets wrote in a manner derived from the first romantics, in particular Wordsworth and Keats. Some like Wordsworth sought to express themselves directly and poignantly in the "ordinary language of men", some like Keats desired to convey the impressions of the senses and the movements of the imagination, subtly, vividly, precisely. Many strove to do both at once. One cannot talk of a "typical" style of the period, for it is the essence of romantic poetry to be individual; and in fact the poetry of the first ten years of the century varies from the studied grace of Bridges to the conversational simplicity of Edward Thomas and the Georgians, from the Gothic ruggedness of Hardy to the Attic polish of Housman. Yet it is true to say that these diverse styles were all designed to convey feeling and sensuous impression rather than facts and intellectual distinctions.

Yeats and Mr. Eliot changed all this. Their more cerebral

approach required a more cerebral style of expression. Ezra Pound, who influenced them, said that poetry should be as well written as prose. This is a muddle-headed way of saying that poetry should have the merits of good expository prose. Mr. Eliot praised Dryden, for he himself was as much concerned with the expression of ideas as Dryden had been. There was a difference between them, though. Dryden's Augustan manner was too generalized and abstract a mode appropriately to convey the new individual and subjective vision. Yeats and Mr. Eliot sought a language that conveyed ideas, not as impersonal abstractions but shaped and coloured by the cloud of associations sensuous, imaginative, emotional, that had collected round them as they floated through the mind of the individual thinker. They wanted to give, as it were, "the feel of a thought"; they were intellectual impressionists as Keats and Rossetti were sensuous and imaginative impressionists. Other poets had preceded them in this ambition, notably Browning and Meredith. As a matter of fact Browning may be looked on as the original English ancestor of the "modernist" school of English poetry. But the specifically new style introduced by Yeats and Mr. Eliot was formed on another model, that of the French Symbolists. The stylistic ideal of these writers has been so accurately summed up by Mr. Edmund Wilson that I shall beg leave to quote his words:

"The assumptions which underlay Symbolism lead us to formulate some such doctrine as the following: Every feeling or sensation we have, every moment of consciousness, is different from every other; and it is, in consequence, impossible to render our sensations as we actually experience them through the conventional and universal language of ordinary literature. Each poet has his unique personality; each of his moments has its special tone, its special combination of elements. And it is the poet's task to find, to invent, the special language which will alone be capable of expressing his personality and feelings. Such a language must make use of symbols: what is so special, so fleeting and so vague cannot be conveyed by direct statement or description, but only by a succession of words, of images, which will serve to suggest it to the reader. The Symbolists themselves, full of the idea of producing with poetry effects like those of music, tended to think of these images as possessing an abstract value like musical notes and chords. But the words of our speech are not musical notation, and what the symbols of Symbolism really were, were metaphors detached from their subjects–for one cannot, beyond a certain point, in poetry, merely enjoy colour and sound for their own sake: one has to guess what the images are being applied to. And Symbolism may be defined as an attempt by carefully studied means – a complicated association of ideas represented by a medley of metaphors – to communicate unique personal feelings."

These words are true of the style of Mr. Eliot and the later Yeats and even truer of their followers. For they it is who have been influenced by modern psychological theory; and this holds that all our mental processes are made articulate to ourselves in symbols, unmodified by the discipline of a conscious reason. To write as the Symbolists do, therefore, is for them the only possible way to convey a true impression of man's inner life. As a matter of fact other influences can be traced in the style of the English modern school, notably those of Donne, Blake and Hopkins. But these are secondary and confined to certain specific literary devices. The basic character of the new style is derived directly or indirectly from the Symbolists.

It is its use of the symbolist mode which, far more than rhythm or diction or content, has come to differentiate the post-nineteen-fourteen "modern" school of poets from its predecessors. The moderns do indeed set out to employ a contemporary diction, avoiding anachronisms or fancy romantic terms. But so did many of the Georgian school: Edward Thomas's language is nearer the run of today's ordinary colloquial speech than is that of Mr. Eliot and his followers. And, though during the twenties there was a fashion for free and rhymeless verse, it has passed. Most young poets today write in strictly regular forms. The content of modern poetry has been too diverse to provide a distinguishing characteristic. Mr. Eliot's and Yeats's type of intellectual approach was new, but it only pervaded the modern movement in the years of its inception. Dylan Thomas is no more intellectualist than Christina Rossetti. As for the disillusioned view of modern society sometimes spoken of as the typical characteristic of today's poetry, that has existed, potentially at least, since the romantic situation arose. In this respect *The Waste Land* is not very different from *The Scholar Gipsy*; there is a hint of Mr. Prufrock in the hero of Clough's *Amours de Voyage*.

The new style has not been universally adopted by good poets. Critics sometimes talk glibly of the literary "revolution" made by Yeats and Mr. Eliot. This metaphor is inept. A political revolution is one in which the established system of government is completely overthrown and its supporters silenced if not liquidated. Parliamentary government will give us a better analogy of what has happened in literature. After 1918 the new poetry, as it were, took office with Yeats and Mr. Eliot as joint Prime Ministers. But the school that had been ejected has been no more silenced than are the members of a defeated parliamentary government. There were and still are a number of gifted poets more extroverted in their outlook than the new school and with no special taste for technical experiment, who have gone on writing in the manner of an earlier tradition; Mr. Blunden, Roy Campbell, Miss Ruth Pitter, Mr. Andrew Young and Mr. Betjeman, to name only a few of them. It is noteworthy that the majority of these are descriptive writers in that topographical and pastoral tradition that stretches back over two hundred years to the days of Lady Winchelsea and James Thompson. Schools of literature may come and go, but it seems that there are always poets to write well about the English landscape. The symbolist mode is unsuitable for descriptive purposes; it is too abstract and subjective. Those who wish to paint verbal pictures generally go back to earlier models.

This does not mean that their work is out-of-date. No living poet has evoked both the appearance and the spirit of the modern English scene more accurately than Mr. Betjeman; yet Mr. Eliot and his master Laforgue might never have lived so far as his mode of expression reveals their influence. The truth is that styles are as various as are the authors who employ them. Reviewers talk loosely of the author's duty to write in a truly "contemporary" style. The phrase betrays a confused mind. Any style is contemporary that convincingly expresses the mind and sentiment of a man alive at the present time. Such styles may be as diverse as are those of Mr. Betjeman, Mr. Empson and Dylan Thomas. On the other hand, the man, who has no live and individual vision of reality to express, produces lifeless work whether he seeks to speak with the tongue of Housman or of Mr. Eliot.

One word more about my principle of selection. The number of poets I could choose from was limited by the size of the book. I was thus faced with a decision. I might confine myself to the handful of outstandingly distinguished authors whose claims no one would dispute. But these were so few that the anthology would not then have been generally representative of the period, as it was intended to be. I therefore chose to draw from a wider field. But this inevitably meant leaving out some authors whose best work might well have justified their inclusion. I can only plead that I have included nothing that does not seem to me in itself genuinely interesting or delightful, or both.

I add that it has not been possible to observe the time limit 1900–1950 with absolute rigidity. One or two poems have been put in which were written before or after the period covered by these dates. However, I have kept within the limit so far as I could, and have therefore had to omit the earlier poems of such eminent authors as Yeats or Bridges; and also the work of writers who have made their reputation since 1950, for example, Miss Audrey Beecham, Mr. Philip Larkin and Mr. Thom Gunn, and whose work otherwise I should have been pleased to include. I should add there are one or two other authors who have preferred not to be included.

Finally, I must express my gratitude to those who have helped me by their advice; especially Miss Audrey Beecham, Mr. John Bayley and Mr. Alfred Alvarez.

David Cecil

INTRODUCTION TO AMERICAN POETRY, 1900–1950

THE RANGE of this anthology, 1900–1950, may well strike the reader as arbitrary, or worse; for when he is warned that he will not find the verse of any poet who had not published a book after 1900 or before the end of 1950, he may also think it wilful. I can only suggest (I do not speak for my collaborator) that although a neat envelope of a half-century may look irrelevant, any other beginning, such as 1917, the year of *Prufrock and Other Observations*, or even 1913, when Robert Frost's first book appeared, would satisfy only a minority. There is also Edwin Arlington Robinson, four-fifths of whose verse was written after 1900 but whose first book was published in 1897. A round half-century has allowed us a freedom that we should have lost had we decided to represent schools and tendencies. I could not, for example, have included Trumbull Stickney, a fine poet who has no relation to modernist verse; but his work was published in 1904, after his death; and so he is here. The inclusion of Dickinson and Hopkins has, from an American point of view, its obvious explanations and defence.

There is still another reason, I think, for the round numbers with which we have enclosed the period. Presently I shall notice a particular phase of our obsession with contemporary literary history. Besides 1913 and 1917, there was a time, some thirty-five years ago, when to many persons on both sides of the Atlantic 1911 seemed to have witnessed a revolution in poetry: for in that year John Masefield shocked the Anglo-American literary world with *The Everlasting Mercy*, a poem of plain people in plain language. It prompted, I believe it was Sir William Watson, to remark that the "language of Shakespeare was good enough" for him. But yet another revolution had already begun. Pound's first verse had been published in 1908 (very quietly in Venice); Eliot's came out only a little later. This poetic revolution, which has dominated poetry in English for almost a half-century, and which has sharpened our critical scrutiny of poets like Robinson and Frost, who were outside it, was brought about by two young men who were convinced that the language of Shakespeare was not merely good enough for them, but far too good.

These revolutionaries were bent upon poetic reform quite as radically as Coleridge and Wordsworth had been more than a century earlier: they vigorously set about the work of cutting down to size the post-Victorian rhetoric–to the size of what they could in that time know *as poets*, and so make actual in language. Mr. Eliot has written movingly of the plight of the young American poet before the First World War: there was literally nobody to talk to, no older living poet to take off from; there were only Moody and Woodberry, poets perhaps neither better nor worse than Watson and Sir Stephen Phillips, across the sea. That this situation shortly improved no observer of the period can doubt. The early reception in England of Robert Frost and the enormous international influence of Pound and Eliot and, later, of W. H. Auden, have at last produced an Anglo-American poetry that only by convention can be separated, as Lord David Cecil and I have separated it by writing two introductions to the period.

It is no part of my purpose to describe in detail the role Americans have played in the international poetic revolution; I cannot imagine a reader who might want to go over this ground again. Like a football field played on through weeks of dry weather, it has been trampled down to a flinty hardness by the historians of contemporaneity, and never a green spot, not even Whitman's spear of summer grass, remains to invite the roving eye. A modern poem becomes history for the fewer before the few, a handful of unprofessional readers, can read it, or read it long enough to dry the ink. Our critics, since Mr. Richards started them off with *The Principles of Literary Criticism* in 1924, have been perfecting an apparatus for "explicating" poems (not a bad thing to do), innocent of the permanently larger ends of criticism. They give us not only a "close reading" but the history of the sources of a new poem by Eliot or Stevens (or of an old one by Hart Crane or Dylan Thomas) before it is able to walk. Within five years of the appearance of *Four Quartets*, we knew more about the poem than Mr. Eliot knew–and quite predictably, for if a poet knew all *that*, he wouldn't have to write the poem and mankind would not need poetry. But what must strike the reader of the commentators on Eliot–on the *corpus* of Eliot, as I have seen his poetry, like Chaucer's, designated–is that they know more than anybody can know about anything. I am second to none in my admiration of the fine passages in the Quartets; I like to think of the speech, in "Little Gidding", of the composite shade of Mr. Eliot's teachers as the high-water mark of modern poetry. But that is not quite the point. One doubts a little more all the time, the use, to say nothing of the propriety, of writing memoirs and glosses on one's friends; and a friend is any person who is alive and whom one might conceivably meet. I know a little boy who, having asked if his grandmother was very old and would soon die, said, "Let's play like she's dead now."

In talking so much about Mr. Eliot I am poaching on the ground staked out by my collaborator; but Mr. Eliot is amphibian and, if "neither living nor dead", is likewise neither American nor English; he is both. He has borne the brunt of most of this anticipatory history; yet nobody has been safe, not even a comparatively private person like myself. The critics of our time not only have known "all about poetry": they have of late turned to fiction and examined its cannier techniques; so that one wonders why they have not considered critically the relation of their points of view to what they are looking at. In writing criticism they forget that they occupy "posts of observation", that they themselves are "trapped spectators"–these technical revelations having been delivered to us canonically two generations ago by a person lately described by Mr. Glenway Wescott as "that effete old hypocrite, Henry James". If what the novelist knows–or the Jamesian novelist, at any rate–is limited to what his characters see, hear, do and think, why is the critic not similarly confined to place and moment? The answer is that he *is*. But the critic does not see himself, *his* point of view, as a variable in the historical situation that he undertakes to explain: as one motion of the history that he is writing.

I am not repudiating the immense, and immensely resourceful, critical activity that began in England with Hulme, Eliot, Richards, and Read thirty to forty years ago, and, in the United States at about the same time, with the Crocean aesthetics of the late Joel Spingarn, and with the *Prefaces* of Henry James. There were also the formidable books, now languishing, of a great critic of ideas (not of literature), Irving

Babbitt: nor should we forget the early literary essays of Ezra Pound, until recently buried beneath the lyrical "economies" of his later writings, but now exhumed, with an introduction, by T. S. Eliot. A second wave of this Anglo-American criticism (I must ignore its French affiliations) brought forward in America men as different as Wilson, Ransom, and Blackmur; yet they were all from the beginning committed, in their several ways, to the aesthetic-historical reading of literature. We have been concerned in this country with the language of the literary work at its particular moment in time.

This glance at forty years of criticism is not, I must repeat, meant to dismiss it: I have been getting round to the American poetry that, from this fifty-year period, and in the fixed limits of an anthology, I could hope to include. A glance at the criticism is by no means irrelevant to a selection of the poetry. For the poetry of our time, as I began to see it after nearly a year of new reading and re-reading–by turns reluctant, desultory and concentrated–is also well within the aesthetic-historical mode. I shall do something with this phrase presently. (Towards the end of my reading it would not be denied; and I could consider no other.) Never have poetry and criticism in English been so close together, so mutually sensitive, the one so knowing about the other. This has been partly but not altogether the result of their appearing so often in the same person: many of our best poets, Eliot, Ransom, Auden, R. P. Warren, Jarrell, are among the most useful critics; and even that least professional of the best American poets, the late Wallace Stevens, tried his hand at criticism in a volume of meditations and *obiter dicta* on poetry, entitled *The Necessary Angel*. In another age, would these men have been critics at all? It is an unreal question; yet that so many poets have turned critics points to an historically unique self-conciousness among men of letters, which must inevitably reflect the more elusive conditions of the individual and society.

If poetry and criticism have been conducting a dialogue, the reasons for it are not very different from those that have brought about an isolated community of critics and poets. This state of affairs is frequently reprehended by the common man, a person of our age who can be either "educated" or merely arrogant. Reflections on the last half-century of American poetry ought,

I think, to include some notice of this question, not because it has been the subject of literary polemics and of historical speculation, but because it has got into the poetry itself. The isolation of the literary community was known first by Poe, as one phase of the alienation of the contemplative man that we have been talking about in England and America with increasing metaphysical cunning since the publication of *Ulysses* in 1922. Alienation as a subject for poetry seems to take two directions: first, the relation of the poet to the world–and this ranges all the way from a quasi-religious sense of man's isolation in the decentralized universe, down to the crass question of the poet's "contribution to society"; and, secondly, poems about the meaning of poetry itself. I suppose never before in the history of poetry in any language have so many poems been written, as in the American English of this century, *about* poetry.

Wallace Stevens's justly admired "Sunday Morning" ties up the entire subject in one package: the passive and alienated heroine (significantly, not a hero) meditates on the interior darkness of the soul, which has a brief exterior life in the intensity, not of passion, which would be active and humanly committed, but of refined sense-perception, which is passive, and which at last can be aware only of its own ultimate extinction. This poem is one of Stevens's many parables of the poet's relation to the modern world. If our common man (in his less arrogant phase) tends to look at the fastidious diction of "Sunday Morning" as a sort of Frenchified mannerism, I can only invite him to read, along with Stevens's poem, Mr. Frost's "Birches": these worlds are not so far apart as he may imagine. For what seems at first sight the sentimentality, or even bathos, of asking us to take second thought about a boy swinging on a birch sapling, turns out (on second thought) to be not only a self-contained image but an emblem of the meaning of poetry: if we have got to be doing something, then let's do something disinterested that has its end in itself. I should guess that more than half of Mr. Frost's poems are little essays on the poetic imagination. He is just as sophisticated and modern as anybody, and his way of being sophisticated and modern is to pretend in his diction that he is not: he is quite as self-conscious, in his grasp of the aesthetic-historic mode of perception, as the late Hart Crane, or Stevens himself.

Readers of this collection will have bought or borrowed it in order to read the poetry, not to discover the explicit opinions of the editors. My own opinions may not be entirely consistent with the kind of judgement that I had to exercise in deciding what poets and poems to include. A few poems in the American section are there not because I like them but because other people (1) liked them thirty years ago, or (2) would like to see what was liked by still other people thirty years ago, or (3) may want to be reminded of the poetic variety and vitality of the twentieth century. Having put poems in, to which at best he is indifferent, may an editor justify the omission of poems that he admires? I have included only three rather longish poems by Miss Marianne Moore, which take up about half the space given to Mr. Auden; I hope that this discrepancy will not convince the reader that I think Mr. Auden is twice as "good" as Miss Moore. Mr. Auden has great resources of subject and attack; one must read a large number of his poems to find out what he is up to; whereas Miss Moore's particular gift lies in her astonishing invention in a single mode; one may get a distinct, if not complete, impression of her virtuosity from the discreet reading of a few poems. Although this is equally true of Mr. Yvor Winters, I have given him a large representation, not merely because he is one of the best American poets, but to correct a balance: he has not been fashionable, and he has been grossly neglected by the school of Eliot and Pound.

The anthologist will apply absolute standards at the risk of boring the educated common reader, of confessing himself a prig, and of ending up perhaps without an anthology. Nor may he apportion space to the poets, the most to the best, a little less than most to the least good (if, to these, any at all), in the belief that his own hierarchy has been ordained on high. If he sets up for God he will resemble Swift's mathematical tailor on the flying island of Laputa.

Nevertheless, pragmatical doubt is not the only consideration back of my choice of poems. My interests in the past thirty years having been not aloof but committed, a certain compound of philosophical bias, common loyalty, and obscure prejudice must insensibly have affected my views of the entire half-century. It was not possible that I should think Stephen Benét, an amiable and patriotic rhymester, as important as Hart Crane, an imperfect genius whose profound honesty drove him to suicide after years of debauchery had stultified his mind. I have, in short, been concerned not with a group or school, but with a certain high contemporary tradition. It is not a tradition of the grand style or of the great subject. But it has resisted the strong political pressures which ask the poet to "communicate" to passively conditioned persons what a servile society expects them to feel. The best American poets (Crane is one of a handful) have tried to discover new and precise languages by which poetry now as always must give us knowledge of the human condition–knowledge that seems to reach us partly in the delight that one gets from rhythms and insights that one has not already heard and known. What particular qualities go to make up an original poet now or at any time, I shall attempt to describe. It has seemed to me that the best American poets of our age have used a certain mode of perception, that I have named the aesthetic-historical.

What poets know and how they know it are questions that go beyond the usual scope of criticism, for what a poet of the past knows is viewed historically, not for what it is, and we take it for granted. But with a poetry which is near us in time, or contemporaneous, much of the difficulty that appears to be in the language as such, is actually in the unfamiliar focus of feeling, belief, and experience which directs the language from the concealed depths that we must try laboriously to enter. The difference between Pound's "Mauberley" and Arnold's "Obermann" is not merely a difference of diction or of subject; it is the subtle difference between two ways of trying to get out of history what Herbert or Crashaw would have expected only from God. Both Arnold and Pound are asking history to make them whole–Arnold through philosophy, Pound through art, or aesthetic sensibility; and unless this difference is grasped the critic will pull himself up short at the mere differences of "style". How far into the past a poetry must recede before we can understand it in depth it is difficult to decide. I have used the word aesthetic not to point to a philosophy of art, but to indicate the way in which American poets have seemed to me to understand their world; nor by aesthetic do I mean art for its own sake. I mean a mode of perception, a heightened sensitivity, that began with Poe and Baudelaire and that produced in our generation concentrated metaphors like Crane's

> O thou steeled Cognizance whose leap commits
> The agile precincts of the lark's return

or Stevens's

> The pale intrusions into blue
> Are corrupting pallors . . . ay di mi,
>
> Blue buds or pitchy blooms. Be content–
> Expansions, diffusions–contents to be
>
> The unspotted imbecile revery,
> The heraldic center of the world
>
> Of blue, blue sleek with a hundred chins,
> The amorist Adjective aflame . . .

This controlled disorder of perception has been the means of rendering a direct impression of the poets' historical situation.

We are indebted to an English critic, the late Michael Roberts, for a clearer understanding of the American development of the aesthetic-historical mode. In his introduction to *The Faber Book of Modern Verse* (1936), Roberts pointed out that American poets are less firmly rooted in a settled poetic tradition than the British; they are thus able to seize and digest traditions and influences from many languages and periods. Roberts paradoxically described the American poet as "European", cosmopolitan, and far-ranging into the past; the British–in the Georgian period, before the "European" influence of T. S. Eliot–as national or even insular. The English insularity of a fine poet like Ralph Hodgson, who can assume that the language of his moment in British culture needs no further development, is very different from the aggressive provincialism, which he calls American nationalism, of Mr. Carl Sandburg. This self-conscious Mid-Westernism posits a *new* world, with a deliberately anti-historical glance at a corrupt Europe; but even in the Middle West, Europe, like Everest, is always *there*. The sense of likeness, or of difference from Europe, and the poet's alienation from the secularized community (not uniquely but acutely American), have brought about a self-consciousness that perhaps cannot be matched by any earlier poetry of the West. Mr. Stephen Spender, in a review of Wallace Stevens's first book under an English imprint, observed that a modern American poem is frequently a "cultural act", a conscious affirmation of an international culture above the commercialized mass culture of the United States at large.

My neighbour cannot understand or even try to read my poems, but I am expressing something about him that he himself doesn't know. This is what American poets say to themselves if they are influenced by Walt Whitman. I suspect that Dr. William Carlos Williams says it every morning, and it can issue in still another version of the aesthetic-historical mode. Dr. Williams is one of its most interesting specimens: his exaltation of the common man, in the common rhythm and the common word, asserts the doctrine that all Americans are common, except T. S. Eliot, who has "betrayed his class". This rhetorical Rousseauism may be a little too sophisticated to pass indefinitely for American primitivism. One cannot think it less highbrow than Stevens's and Mr. Ransom's serene neglect of everything common. Our British friends occasionally tell us that Mr. Ransom is a very good poet who but for the unhappy agitation of 1776 would be English.

The common man in a servile society is everybody; the modern society is everywhere servile; everybody must accept the servile destruction of leisure and of the contemplative life if he would live without alienation. On this subject I suppose that there has been more complicated nonsense written by literary critics in the past thirty years than on all other matters connected with literature combined. The liberal, utopian, "totalitarian" mind assumes that one must give up alienation at any cost. High on the list of costs would be poetry; and if we would sacrifice it, in the illusion that its sacrifice alone would propitiate the powers of darkness, we should forfeit along with it the centre of consciousness in which free and disinterested men must live. There are some things from which man, if he is to remain human, must remain permanently alienated. One of these is the idolatry of the means as the end.

Modern American poetry exhibits, often with power and distinction, its own infection by idolatry, and by the ritual of idolatry which is the language of magic. Frost and Stevens at the beginning, Hart Crane in the middle, and Robert Lowell towards the end of our period, once more confirm the commonplace that good poets are both above and of their age. The verbal shock, the violent metaphor, as a technique of magic, forces into *linguistic existence* subjective meanings and insights that poets can no longer discover in the common world.

This is the aesthetic consciousness, aware of its isolation at a moment of time. Whether this special stance of the modern poet will shift (or merely collapse) in the second half of the century, nobody can know or ought to think that he knows. One looks in vain at the work of the brilliant young poets of the fifth decade for the signs of a new poetry such as Pound, Eliot, Stevens, Miss Moore, Ransom, Cummings, and Crane gave us thirty-five years ago. The only distinguished American poet, the magnitude and precision of whose work might conceivably have attracted a younger generation, was Robinson; but his origins were in the nineteenth century; and although at his death in 1935 he had admirers, there were no first-rate poets who could be said to have derived from him, in the sense that Crane came out of Eliot and Pound. Mr. Frost is likewise an end, not a beginning. But poetry has its own way of surprising us. If we suppose that we are at the end of a period, or of a period style (I think we are), we must nevertheless be ready for something entirely new from a poet whose work may seem to be complete, or, from a new poet expect a style altogether new, which persons who have reached middle age would probably dislike. But the future of American or any other poetry we may leave to the puritans who cannot look at the world as it is; the future is at any rate no proper subject for criticism. Modern American poetry, limited in scope to the perceiving, as distinguished from the seeing, eye, has given us images of the present condition of man that we cannot find elsewhere; and we ought to have them. We should be grateful that we have got them.

ALLEN TATE

THE POETS

Emily Dickinson (*Am. 1830–1886*)

I like to see it lap the Miles

I like to see it lap the Miles–
And lick the Valleys up–
And stop to feed itself at Tanks–
And then–prodigious step

Around a Pile of Mountains–
And supercilious peer
In Shanties–by the sides of Roads–
And then a Quarry pare

To fit it's sides
And crawl between
Complaining all the while
In horrid–hooting stanza–
Then chase itself down Hill–

And neigh like Boanerges–
Then–prompter than a Star
Stop–docile and omnipotent
At it's own stable door–

My life closed twice before its close

My life closed twice before its close;
It yet remains to see
If Immortality unveil
A third event to me,

So huge, so hopeless to conceive
As these that twice befel.
Parting is all we know of heaven,
And all we need of hell.

A Bird came down the Walk

A Bird came down the Walk–
He did not know I saw–
He bit an Angleworm in halves
And ate the fellow, raw,

And then he drank a Dew
From a convenient Grass–
And then hopped sidewise to the Wall
To let a Beetle pass–

He glanced with rapid eyes
That hurried all around–
They looked like frightened Beads, I thought–
He stirred his Velvet Head

Like one in danger, Cautious,
I offered him a Crumb
And he unrolled his feathers
And rowed him softer home–

Than Oars divide the Ocean,
Too silver for a seam–
Or Butterflies, off Banks of Noon
Leap, plashless as they swim.

I died for Beauty–but was scarce

I died for Beauty–but was scarce
Adjusted in the Tomb
When One who died for Truth, was lain
In an adjoining Room–

He questioned softly "Why I failed"?
"For Beauty", I replied–
"And I–for Truth–Themself are One–
We Bretheren, are", He said–

And so, as Kinsmen, met a Night–
We talked between the Rooms–
Until the Moss had reached our lips–
And covered up–our names–

Because I could not stop for Death–

Because I could not stop for Death–
He kindly stopped for me–
The Carriage held but just Ourselves–
And Immortality.

We slowly drove–He knew no haste
And I had put away
My labor and my leisure too,
For His Civility–

We passed the School, where Children strove
At Recess–in the Ring–
We passed the Fields of Gazing Grain–
We passed the Setting Sun–

Or rather–He passed Us–
The Dews drew quivering and chill–
For only Gossamer, my Gown–
My Tippet–only Tulle–

We paused before a House that seemed
A Swelling of the Ground–
The Roof was scarcely visible–
The Cornice–in the Ground–

Since then–'tis Centuries–and yet
Feels shorter than the Day
I first surmised the Horses Heads
Were toward Eternity–

I heard a Fly buzz–when I died–

I heard a Fly buzz–when I died–
The Stillness in the Room
Was like the Stillness in the Air–
Between the Heaves of Storm–

The Eyes around–had wrung them dry–
And Breaths were gathering firm
For that last Onset–when the King
Be witnessed–in the Room–

I willed my Keepsakes–Signed away
What portion of me be
Assignable–and then it was
There interposed a Fly–

With Blue–uncertain stumbling Buzz–
Between the light–and me–
And then the Windows failed–and then
I could not see to see–

After great pain, a formal feeling comes–

After great pain, a formal feeling comes–
The Nerves sit ceremonious, like Tombs–
The stiff Heart questions was it He, that bore,
And Yesterday, or Centuries before?

The Feet, mechanical, go round–
Of Ground, or Air, or Ought–
A Wooden way
Regardless grown,
A Quartz contentment, like a stone–

This is the Hour of Lead–
Remembered, if outlived,
As Freezing persons, recollect the Snow–
First–Chill–then Stupor–then the letting go–

They called me to the Window, for

They called me to the Window, for
"'Twas Sunset," Some one said–
I only saw a Sapphire Farm–
And just a Single Herd–

Of Opal Cattle–feeding far
Upon so vain a Hill–
As even while I looked–dissolved–
Nor Cattle were–nor Soil–

But in their Room–a Sea–displayed–
And Ships–of such a size
As Crew of Mountains–could afford–
And Decks–to seat the skies–

This–too–the Showman rubbed away–
And when I looked again–
Nor Farm–nor Opal Herd–was there–
Nor Mediterranean–

We do not play on Graves–

We do not play on Graves–
Because there isn't Room–
Besides–it isn't even–it slants
And People come–

And put a Flower on it–
And hang their faces so–
We're fearing that their Hearts will drop–
And crush our pretty play–

And so we move as far
As Enemies–away–
Just looking round to see how far
It is–Occasionally–

It would have starved a Gnat–

It would have starved a Gnat–
To live so small as I–
And yet I was a living Child–
With Food's necessity

Upon me–like a Claw–
I could no more remove
Than I could coax a Leech away–
Or make a Dragon–move–

Nor like the Gnat–had I–
The privilege to fly
And seek a Dinner for myself–
How mightier He–than I–

Nor like Himself–the Art
Upon the Window Pane
To gad my little Being out–
And not begin–again–

Finding is the first Act

Finding is the first Act
The second, loss,
Third, Expedition for
the "Golden Fleece"

Fourth, no Discovery–
Fifth, no Crew–
Finally, no Golden Fleece–
Jason–sham–too.

Jesus! thy Crucifix

Jesus! thy Crucifix
Enable thee to guess
The smaller size!

Jesus! thy second face
Mind thee in Paradise
Of our's!

Some Wretched creature, savior take

Some Wretched creature, savior take
Who would exult to die
And leave for thy sweet mercy's sake
Another Hour to me

Said Death to Passion

Said Death to Passion
"Give of thine an Acre unto me."
Said Passion, through contracting Breaths
"A Thousand Times Thee Nay."

Bore Death from Passion
All His East
He–sovereign as the Sun
Resituated in the West
And the Debate was done.

Some we see no more, Tenements of Wonder

Some we see no more, Tenements of Wonder
Occupy to us though perhaps to them
Simpler are the Days than the Supposition
Their removing Manners
Leave us to presume

That oblique Belief which we call Conjecture
Grapples with a Theme stubborn as Sublime
Able as the Dust to equip its feature
Adequate as Drums
To enlist the Tomb.

No Passenger was known to flee–

No Passenger was known to flee–
That lodged a night in memory–
That wily–subterranean Inn
Contrives that none go out again–

I never hear that one is dead

I never hear that one is dead
Without the chance of Life
Afresh annihilating me
That mightiest Belief,

Too mighty for the Daily mind
That tilling its abyss,
Had Madness, had it once or twice
The yawning Consciousness,

Beliefs are Bandaged, like the Tongue
When Terror were it told
In any Tone commensurate
Would strike us instant Dead

I do not know the man so bold
He dare in lonely Place
That awful stranger Consciousness
Deliberately face–

Thomas Hardy (*Br. 1840–1928*)

The Voice

Woman much missed, how you call to me, call to me,
Saying that now you are not as you were
When you had changed from the one who was all to me,
But as at first, when our day was fair.

Can it be you that I hear? Let me view you, then,
Standing as when I drew near to the town
Where you would wait for me: yes, as I knew you then,
Even to the original air-blue gown!

Or is it only the breeze, in its listlessness
Travelling across the wet mead to me here,
You being ever dissolved to wan wistlessness,
Heard no more again far or near?

Thus I; faltering forward,
Leaves around me falling,
Wind oozing thin through the thorn from norward,
And the woman calling.

After a Journey

Hereto I come to view a voiceless ghost;
Whither, O whither will its whim now draw me?
Up the cliff, down, till I'm lonely, lost,
And the unseen waters' ejaculations awe me.
Where you will next be there's no knowing,
Facing round about me everywhere,
With your nut-coloured hair,
And gray eyes, and rose-flush coming and going.

Yes: I have re-entered your olden haunts at last;
Through the years, through the dead scenes I have tracked you;
What have you now found to say of our past–
Scanned across the dark space wherein I have lacked you?
Summer gave us sweets, but autumn wrought division?
Things were not lastly as firstly well
With us twain, you tell?
But all's closed now, despite Time's derision.

I see what you are doing: you are leading me on
To the spots we knew when we haunted here together,
The waterfall, above which the mist-bow shone
At the then fair hour in the then fair weather,
And the cave just under, with a voice still so hollow
That it seems to call out to me from forty years ago,
When you were all aglow,
And not the thin ghost that I now frailly follow!

Ignorant of what there is flitting here to see,
The waked birds preen and the seals flop lazily;
Soon you will have, Dear, to vanish from me,
For the stars close their shutters and the dawn whitens hazily.
Trust me, I mind not, though Life lours,
The bringing me here; nay, bring me here again!
I am just the same as when
Our days were a joy, and our paths through flowers.

I found her out there

I found her out there
On a slope few see,
That falls westwardly
To the salt-edged air,
Where the ocean breaks
On the purple strand,
And the hurricane shakes
The solid land.

I brought her here,
And have laid her to rest
In a noiseless nest
No sea beats near.
She will never be stirred
In her loamy cell
By the waves long heard
And loved so well.

So she does not sleep
By those haunted heights
The Atlantic smites
And the blind gales sweep,
Whence she often would gaze
At Dundagel's famed head,
While the dipping blaze
Dyed her face fire-red;

And would sigh at the tale
Of sunk Lyonnesse,
As a wind-tugged tress
Flapped her cheek like a flail;
Or listen at whiles
With a thought-bound brow
To the murmuring miles
She is far from now.

Yet her shade, maybe,
Will creep underground
Till it catch the sound
Of that western sea
As it swells and sobs
Where she once domiciled,
And joy in its throbs
With the heart of a child.

At Castle Boterel

As I drive to the junction of lane and highway,
  And the drizzle bedrenches the waggonette,
I look behind at the fading byway,
  And see on its slope, now glistening wet,
    Distinctly yet

Myself and a girlish form benighted
  In dry March weather. We climb the road
Beside a chaise. We had just alighted
  To ease the sturdy pony's load
    When he sighed and slowed.

What we did as we climbed, and what we talked of
  Matters not much, nor to what it led,–
Something that life will not be balked of
  Without rude reason till hope is dead,
    And feeling fled.

It filled but a minute. But was there ever
  A time of such quality, since or before,
In that hill's story? To one mind never,
  Though it has been climbed, foot-swift, foot-sore,
    By thousands more.

Primaeval rocks form the road's steep border,
  And much have they faced there, first and last,
Of the transitory in Earth's long order;
  But what they record in colour and cast
    Is–that we two passed.

And to me, though Time's unflinching rigour,
  In mindless rote, has ruled from sight
The substance now, one phantom figure
  Remains on the slope, as when that night
    Saw us alight.

I look and see it there, shrinking, shrinking,
  I look back at it amid the rain
For the very last time; for my sand is sinking,
  And I shall traverse old love's domain
    Never again.

A Trampwoman's Tragedy

(182–)

I

From Wynyard's Gap the livelong day,
    The livelong day,
We beat afoot the northward way
  We had travelled times before.
The sun-blaze burning on our backs,
Our shoulders sticking to our packs,
By fosseway, fields, and turnpike tracks
  We skirted sad Sedge-Moor.

II

Full twenty miles we jaunted on,
 We jaunted on,–
My fancy-man, and jeering John,
 And Mother Lee, and I.
And, as the sun drew down to west,
We climbed the toilsome Poldon crest,
And saw, of landskip sights the best,
 The inn that beamed thereby.

III

For months we had padded side by side,
 Ay, side by side
Through the Great Forest, Blackmoor wide,
 And where the Parret ran.
We'd faced the gusts on Mendip ridge,
Had crossed the Yeo unhelped by bridge,
Been stung by every Marshwood midge,
 I and my fancy-man.

IV

Lone inns we loved, my man and I,
 My man and I;
"King's Stag," "Windwhistle" high and dry,
 "The Horse" on Hintock Green,
The cosy house at Wynyard's Gap,
"The Hut" renowned on Bredy Knap,
And many another wayside tap
 Where folk might sit unseen.

V

Now as we trudged–O deadly day,
 O deadly day!–
I teased my fancy-man in play
 And wanton idleness.
I walked alongside jeering John,
I laid his hand my waist upon;
I would not bend my glances on
 My lover's dark distress.

VI

Thus Poldon top at last we won,
  At last we won,
And gained the inn at sink of sun
  Far-famed as "Marshal's Elm."
Beneath us figured tor and lea,
From Mendip to the western sea–
I doubt if finer sight there be
  Within this royal realm.

VII

Inside the settle all a-row–
  All four a-row
We sat, I next to John, to show
  That he had wooed and won.
And then he took me on his knee,
And swore it was his turn to be
My favoured mate, and Mother Lee
  Passed to my former one.

VIII

Then in a voice I had never heard,
  I had never heard,
My only Love to me: "One word,
  My lady, if you please!
Whose is the child you are like to bear?–
His? After all my months o' care?"
God knows 'twas not! But, O despair!
  I nodded–still to tease.

IX

Then up he sprung, and with his knife–
  And with his knife
He let out jeering Johnny's life,
  Yes; there, at set of sun.
The slant ray through the window nigh
Gilded John's blood and glazing eye,
Ere scarcely Mother Lee and I
  Knew that the deed was done.

X

The taverns tell the gloomy tale,
    The gloomy tale,
How that at Ivel-chester jail
  My Love, my sweetheart swung;
Though stained till now by no misdeed
Save one horse ta'en in time o' need;
(Blue Jimmy stole right many a steed
  Ere his last fling he flung.)

XI

Thereaft I walked the world alone,
    Alone, alone!
On his death-day I gave my groan
  And dropt his dead-born child.
'Twas nigh the jail, beneath a tree,
None tending me; for Mother Lee
Had died at Glaston, leaving me
  Unfriended on the wild.

XII

And in the night as I lay weak,
    As I lay weak,
The leaves a-falling on my cheek,
  The red moon low declined–
The ghost of him I'd die to kiss
Rose up and said: "Ah, tell me this!
Was the child mine, or was it his?
  Speak, that I rest may find!"

XIII

O doubt not but I told him then,
    I told him then,
That I had kept me from all men
  Since we joined lips and swore.
Whereat he smiled, and thinned away
As the wind stirred to call up day . . .
–'Tis past! And here alone I stray
  Haunting the Western Moor.

Julie-Jane

Sing; how 'a would sing!
How 'a would raise the tune
When we rode in the waggon from harvesting
By the light o' the moon!

Dance; how 'a would dance!
If a fiddlestring did but sound
She would hold out her coats, give a slanting glance,
And go round and round.

Laugh; how 'a would laugh!
Her peony lips would part
As if none such a place for a lover to quaff
At the deeps of a heart.

Julie, O girl of joy,
Soon, soon that lover he came.
Ah, yes; and gave thee a baby-boy,
But never his name. . . .

–Tolling for her, as you guess;
And the baby too. . . . 'Tis well.
You knew her in maidhood likewise?–Yes,
That's her burial bell.

"I suppose," with a laugh, she said,
"I should blush that I'm not a wife;
But how can it matter, so soon to be dead,
What one does in life!"

When we sat making the mourning
By her death-bed side, said she,
"Dears, how can you keep from your lovers, adorning
In honour of me!"

Bubbling and brightsome eyed!
But now–O never again.
She chose her bearers before she died
From her fancy-men.

Nobody Comes

Tree-leaves labour up and down,
And through them the fainting light
Succumbs to the crawl of night.
Outside in the road the telegraph wire
To the town from the darkening land
Intones to travellers like a spectral lyre
Swept by a spectral hand.

A car comes up, with lamps full-glare,
That flash upon a tree:
It has nothing to do with me,
And whangs along in a world of its own,
Leaving a blacker air;
And mute by the gate I stand again alone,
And nobody pulls up there.

Budmouth Dears

When we lay where Budmouth Beach is,
O, the girls were fresh as peaches,
With their tall and tossing figures and their eyes of blue and brown!
And our hearts would ache with longing
As we paced from our sing-songing,
With a smart *Clink! Clink!* up the Esplanade and down.

They distracted and delayed us
By the pleasant pranks they played us,
And what marvel, then, if troopers, even of regiments of renown,
On whom flashed those eyes divine, O,
Should forget the countersign, O,
As we tore *Clink! Clink!* back to camp above the town.

Do they miss us much, I wonder,
Now that war has swept us sunder,
And we roam from where the faces smile to where the faces frown?
And no more behold the features
Of the fair fantastic creatures,
And no more *Clink! Clink!* past the parlours of the town?

Shall we once again there meet them?
Falter fond attempts to greet them?
Will the gay sling-jacket glow again beside the muslin gown?
Will they archly quiz and con us
With a sideway glance upon us,
While our spurs *Clink! Clink!* up the Esplanade and down?

Afterwards

When the Present has latched its postern behind my tremulous stay,
And the May month flaps its glad green leaves like wings,
Delicate-filmed as new-spun silk, will the neighbours say,
"He was a man who used to notice such things"?

If it be in the dusk when, like an eyelid's soundless blink,
The dewfall-hawk comes crossing the shades to alight
Upon the wind-warped upland thorn, a gazer may think,
"To him this must have been a familiar sight."

If I pass during some nocturnal blackness, mothy and warm,
When the hedgehog travels furtively over the lawn,
One may say, "He strove that such innocent creatures should come to no harm,
But he could do little for them; and now he is gone."

If, when hearing that I have been stilled at last, they stand at the door,
Watching the full-starred heavens that winter sees,
Will this thought rise on those who will meet my face no more,
"He was one who had an eye for such mysteries"?

And will any say when my bell of quittance is heard in the gloom,
And a crossing breeze cuts a pause in its outrollings,
Till they rise again, as they were a new bell's boom,
"He hears it not now, but used to notice such things"?

The Fallow Deer at the Lonely House

One without looks in to-night
  Through the curtain-chink
From the sheet of glistening white;
One without looks in to-night
  As we sit and think
  By the fender-brink.

We do not discern those eyes
  Watching in the snow;
Lit by lamps of rosy dyes
We do not discern those eyes
  Wondering, aglow,
  Fourfooted, tiptoe.

On the Doorstep

The rain imprinted the step's wet shine
With target-circles that quivered and crossed
As I was leaving this porch of mine;
When from within there swelled and paused
    A song's sweet note;
  And back I turned, and thought,
    "Here I'll abide."

The step shines wet beneath the rain,
Which prints its circles as heretofore;
I watch them from the porch again,
But no song-notes within the door
    Now call to me
  To shun the dripping lea;
    And forth I stride.

The Convergence of the Twain
(Lines on the loss of the *Titanic*)

I

In a solitude of the sea
Deep from human vanity,
And the Pride of Life that planned her, stilly couches she.

II

Steel chambers, late the pyres
Of her salamandrine fires,
Cold currents thrid, and turn to rhythmic tidal lyres.

III

Over the mirrors meant
To glass the opulent
The sea-worm crawls – grotesque, slimed, dumb, indifferent.

IV

Jewels in joy designed
To ravish the sensuous mind
Lie lightless, all their sparkles bleared and black and blind.

V

Dim moon-eyed fishes near
Gaze at the gilded gear
And query: "What does this vaingloriousness down here?" . . .

VI

Well: while was fashioning
This creature of cleaving wing,
The Immanent Will that stirs and urges everything

VII

Prepared a sinister mate
For her – so gaily great –
A Shape of Ice, for the time far and dissociate.

VIII

And as the smart ship grew
In stature, grace, and hue,
In shadowy silent distance grew the Iceberg too.

IX

Alien they seemed to be:
No mortal eye could see
The intimate welding of their later history,

X

Or sign that they were bent
By paths coincident
On being anon twin halves of one august event,

XI

Till the Spinner of the Years
Said "Now!" And each one hears,
And consummation comes, and jars two hemispheres.

Regret not me

Regret not me;
Beneath the sunny tree
I lie uncaring, slumbering peacefully.

Swift as the light
I flew my faery flight;
Ecstatically I moved, and feared no night.

I did not know
That heydays fade and go,
But deemed that what was would be always so.

I skipped at morn
Between the yellowing corn,
Thinking it good and glorious to be born.

I ran at eves
Among the piled-up sheaves,
Dreaming, "I grieve not, therefore nothing grieves."

Now soon will come
The apple, pear, and plum,
And hinds will sing, and autumn insects hum.

Again you will fare
To cider-makings rare,
And junketings; but I shall not be there.

Yet gaily sing
Until the pewter ring
Those songs we sang when we went gipsying.

And lightly dance
Some triple-timed romance
In coupled figures, and forget mischance;

And mourn not me
Beneath the yellowing tree;
For I shall mind not, slumbering peacefully.

Beyond the Last Lamp
(Near Tooting Common)

I

While rain, with eve in partnership,
Descended darkly, drip, drip, drip,
Beyond the last lone lamp I passed
Walking slowly, whispering sadly,
Two linked loiterers, wan, downcast:
Some heavy thought constrained each face,
And blinded them to time and place.

II

The pair seemed lovers, yet absorbed
In mental scenes no longer orbed
By love's young rays. Each countenance
As it slowly, as it sadly
Caught the lamplight's yellow glance,
Held in suspense a misery
At things which had been or might be.

III

When I retrod that watery way
Some hours beyond the droop of day,
Still I found pacing there the twain
Just as slowly, just as sadly,
Heedless of the night and rain.
One could but wonder who they were,
And what wild woe detained them there.

IV

Though thirty years of blur and blot
Have slid since I beheld that spot,
And saw in curious converse there
  Moving slowly, moving sadly
  That mysterious tragic pair,
Its olden look may linger on–
All but the couple; they have gone.

V

Whither? Who knows, indeed. . . . And yet
To me, when nights are weird and wet,
Without those comrades there at tryst
  Creeping slowly, creeping sadly,
  That lone lane does not exist.
There they seem brooding on their pain,
And will, while such a lane remain.

Great Things

Sweet cyder is a great thing,
  A great thing to me,
Spinning down to Weymouth town
  By Ridgway thirstily,
And maid and mistress summoning
  Who tend the hostelry:
O cyder is a great thing,
  A great thing to me!

The dance it is a great thing,
  A great thing to me,
With candles lit and partners fit
  For night-long revelry;
And going home when day-dawning
  Peeps pale upon the lea:
O dancing is a great thing,
  A great thing to me!

Love is, yea, a great thing,
  A great thing to me,
When, having drawn across the lawn
  In darkness silently,

A figure flits like one a-wing
  Out from the nearest tree:
O love is, yes, a great thing,
  A great thing to me!

Will these be always great things,
  Great things to me? . . .
Let it befall that One will call,
  "Soul, I have need of thee":
What then? Joy-jaunts, impassioned flings,
  Love, and its ecstasy,
Will always have been great things,
  Great things to me!

Reminiscences of a Dancing Man

I

Who now remembers Almack's balls–
  Willis's sometime named–
In those two smooth-floored upper halls
  For faded ones so famed?
Where as we trod to trilling sound
The fancied phantoms stood around,
  Or joined us in the maze,
Of the powdered Dears from Georgian years,
Whose dust lay in sightless sealed-up biers,
  The fairest of former days.

II

Who now remembers gay Cremorne,
  And all its jaunty jills,
And those wild whirling figures born
  Of Jullien's grand quadrilles?
With hats on head and morning coats
There footed to his prancing notes
  Our partner-girls and we;
And the gas-jets winked, and the lustres clinked,
And the platform throbbed as with arms enlinked
  We moved to the minstrelsy.

III

Who now recalls those crowded rooms
  Of old yclept "The Argyle,"
Where to the deep Drum-polka's booms
  We hopped in standard style?
Whither have danced those damsels now!
Is Death the partner who doth moue
  Their wormy chaps and bare?
Do their spectres spin like sparks within
The smoky halls of the Prince of Sin
  To a thunderous Jullien air?

Old Furniture

I know not how it may be with others
  Who sit amid relics of householdry
That date from the days of their mothers' mothers,
  But well I know how it is with me
    Continually.

I see the hands of the generations
  That owned each shiny familiar thing
In play on its knobs and indentations,
  And with its ancient fashioning
    Still dallying:

Hands behind hands, growing paler and paler,
  As in a mirror a candle-flame
Shows images of itself, each frailer
  As it recedes, though the eye may frame
    Its shape the same.

On the clock's dull dial a foggy finger,
  Moving to set the minutes right
With tentative touches that lift and linger
  In the wont of a moth on a summer night,
    Creeps to my sight.

On this old viol, too, fingers are dancing–
  As whilom–just over the strings by the nut,
The tip of a bow receding, advancing
  In airy quivers, as if it would cut
    The plaintive gut.

And I see a face by that box for tinder,
  Glowing forth in fits from the dark,
And fading again, as the linten cinder
  Kindles to red at the flinty spark,
    Or goes out stark.

Well, well. It is best to be up and doing,
  The world has no use for one to-day
Who eyes things thus–no aim pursuing!
  He should not continue in this stay,
    But sink away.

Shut out that Moon

Close up the casement, draw the blind,
  Shut out that stealing moon,
She wears too much the guise she wore
  Before our lutes were strewn
With years-deep dust, and names we read
  On a white stone were hewn.

Step not out on the dew-dashed lawn
  To view the Lady's Chair,
Immense Orion's glittering form,
  The Less and Greater Bear:
Stay in; to such sights we were drawn
  When faded ones were fair.

Brush not the bough for midnight scents
  That come forth lingeringly,
And wake the same sweet sentiments
  They breathed to you and me
When living seemed a laugh, and love
  All it was said to be.

Within the common lamp-lit room
  Prison my eyes and thought;
Let dingy details crudely loom,
  Mechanic speech be wrought:
Too fragrant was Life's early bloom,
  Too tart the fruit it brought!

An Ancient to Ancients

Where once we danced, where once we sang,
Gentlemen,
The floors are sunken, cobwebs hang,
And cracks creep; worms have fed upon
The doors. Yea, sprightlier times were then
Than now, with harps and tabrets gone,
Gentlemen!

Where once we rowed, where once we sailed,
Gentlemen,
And damsels took the tiller, veiled
Against too strong a stare (God wot
Their fancy, then or anywhen!)
Upon that shore we are clean forgot,
Gentlemen!

We have lost somewhat, afar and near,
Gentlemen,
The thinning of our ranks each year
Affords a hint we are nigh undone,
That we shall not be ever again
The marked of many, loved of one,
Gentlemen.

In dance the polka hit our wish,
Gentlemen,
The paced quadrille, the spry schottische,
"Sir Roger."–And in opera spheres
The "Girl" (the famed "Bohemian"),
And "Trovatore," held the ears,
Gentlemen.

This season's paintings do not please,
Gentlemen,
Like Etty, Mulready, Maclise;
Throbbing romance has waned and wanned;
No wizard wields the witching pen
Of Bulwer, Scott, Dumas, and Sand,
Gentlemen.

The bower we shrined to Tennyson,
Gentlemen,
Is roof-wrecked; damps there drip upon
Sagged seats, the creeper-nails are rust,
The spider is sole denizen;
Even she who voiced those rhymes is dust,
Gentlemen!

We who met sunrise sanguine-souled,
Gentlemen,
Are wearing weary. We are old;
These younger press; we feel our rout
Is imminent to Aïdes' den,–
That evening shades are stretching out,
Gentlemen!

And yet, though ours be failing frames,
Gentlemen,
So were some others' history names,
Who trode their track light-limbed and fast
As these youth, and not alien
From enterprise, to their long last,
Gentlemen.

Sophocles, Plato, Socrates,
Gentlemen,
Pythagoras, Thucydides,
Herodotus, and Homer,–yea,
Clement, Augustin, Origen,
Burnt brightlier towards their setting-day,
Gentlemen.

And ye, red-lipped and smooth-browed; list,
Gentlemen;
Much is there waits you we have missed;
Much lore we leave you worth the knowing,
Much, much has lain outside our ken:
Nay, rush not: time serves: we are going,
Gentlemen.

Gerard Manley Hopkins (*Br. 1844–1889*)

The Wreck of the 'Deutschland'

To the
happy memory of five Franciscan Nuns
exiles by the Falk Laws
drowned between midnight and morning of
7 December 1875

PART THE FIRST

1

Thou mastering me
God! giver of breath and bread;
World's strand, sway of the sea;
Lord of living and dead;
Thou hast bound bones and veins in me, fastened me flesh,
And after it almost unmade, what with dread,
Thy doing: and dost thou touch me afresh?
Over again I feel thy finger and find thee.

2

I did say yes
O at lightning and lashed rod;
Thou heardst me truer than tongue confess
Thy terror, O Christ, O God;
Thou knowest the walls, altar and hour and night:
The swoon of a heart that the sweep and the hurl of thee trod
Hard down with a horror of height:
And the midriff astrain with leaning of, laced with fire of stress.

3

The frown of his face
Before me, the hurtle of hell
Behind, where, where was a, where was a place?
I whirled out wings that spell
And fled with a fling of the heart to the heart of the Host.
My heart, but you were dove-winged, I can tell,
Carrier-witted, I am bold to boast,
To flash from the flame to the flame then, tower from the grace
to the grace.

4

I am soft sift
In an hourglass–at the wall
Fast, but mined with a motion, a drift,
And it crowds and it combs to the fall;
I steady as a water in a well, to a poise, to a pane,
But roped with, always, all the way down from the tall
Fells or flanks of the voel, a vein
Of the gospel proffer, a pressure, a principle, Christ's gift.

5

I kiss my hand
To the stars, lovely-asunder
Starlight, wafting him out of it; and
Glow, glory in thunder;
Kiss my hand to the dappled-with-damson west:
Since, tho' he is under the world's splendour and wonder,
His mystery must be instressed, stressed;
For I greet him the days I meet him, and bless when I understand.

6

Not out of his bliss
Springs the stress felt
Nor first from heaven (and few know this)
Swings the stroke dealt–
Stroke and a stress that stars and storms deliver,
That guilt is hushed by, hearts are flushed by and melt–
But it rides time like riding a river
(And here the faithful waver, the faithless fable and miss).

7

It dates from day
Of his going in Galilee;
Warm-laid grave of a womb-life grey;
Manger, maiden's knee;
The dense and the driven Passion, and frightful sweat;
Thence the discharge of it, there its swelling to be,
Though felt before, though in high flood yet–
What none would have known of it, only the heart, being hard at bay,

8

Is out with it! Oh,
We lash with the best or worst
Word last! How a lush-kept plush-capped sloe
Will, mouthed to flesh-burst,
Gush!–flush the man, the being with it, sour or sweet,
Brim, in a flash, full!–Hither then, last or first,
To hero of Calvary, Christ's feet–
Never ask if meaning it, wanting it, warned of it–men go.

9

Be adored among men,
God, three-numberèd form;
Wring thy rebel, dogged in den,
Man's malice, with wrecking and storm.
Beyond saying sweet, past telling of tongue,
Thou art lightning and love, I found it, a winter and warm;
Father and fondler of heart thou hast wrung:
Hast thy dark descending and most art merciful then.

10

With an anvil-ding
And with fire in him forge thy will
Or rather, rather then, stealing as Spring
Through him, melt him but master him still:
Whether at once, as once at a crash Paul,
Or as Austin, a lingering-out sweet skill,
Make mercy in all of us, out of us all
Mastery, but be adored, but be adored King.

PART THE SECOND

11

"Some find me a sword; some
The flange and the rail; flame,
Fang, or flood" goes Death on drum,
And storms bugle his fame.
But wé dream we are rooted in earth–Dust!
Flesh falls within sight of us, we, though our flower the same,
Wave with the meadow, forget that there must
The sour scythe cringe, and the blear share come.

12

On Saturday sailed from Bremen,
American-outward-bound,
Take settler and seamen, tell men with women,
Two hundred souls in the round–
O Father, not under thy feathers nor ever as guessing
The goal was a shoal, of a fourth the doom to be drowned;
Yet did the dark side of the bay of thy blessing
Not vault them, the millions of rounds of thy mercy not reeve even them in?

13

Into the snows she sweeps,
Hurling the haven behind,
The *Deutschland*, on Sunday; and so the sky keeps,
For the infinite air is unkind,
And the sea flint-flake, black-backed in the regular blow,
Sitting Eastnortheast, in cursed quarter, the wind;
Wiry and white-fiery and whirlwind-swivellèd snow
Spins to the widow-making unchilding unfathering deeps.

14

She drove in the dark to leeward,
She struck–not a reef or a rock
But the combs of a smother of sand: night drew her
Dead to the Kentish Knock;
And she beat the bank down with her bows and the ride of her keel:
The breakers rolled on her beam with ruinous shock;
And canvas and compass, the whorl and the wheel
Idle for ever to waft her or wind her with, these she endured.

15

Hope had grown grey hairs,
Hope had mourning on,
Trenched with tears, carved with cares,
Hope was twelve hours gone;
And frightful a nightfall folded rueful a day
Nor rescue, only rocket and lightship, shone,
And lives at last were washing away:
To the shrouds they took,–they shook in the hurling and horrible airs.

16

One stirred from the rigging to save
The wild woman-kind below,
With a rope's end round the man, handy and brave–
He was pitched to his death at a blow,
For all his dreadnought breast and braids of thew:
They could tell him for hours, dandled the to and fro
Through the cobbled foam-fleece, what could he do
With the burl of the fountains of air, buck and the flood of the wave?

17

They fought with God's cold–
And they could not and fell to the deck
(Crushed them) or water (and drowned them) or rolled
With the sea-romp over the wreck.
Night roared, with the heart-break hearing a heart-broke rabble,
The woman's wailing, the crying of child without check–
Till a lioness arose breasting the babble,
A prophetess towered in the tumult, a virginal tongue told.

18

Ah, touched in your bower of bone
Are you! turned for an exquisite smart,
Have you! make words break from me here all alone,
Do you!–mother of being in me, heart.
O unteachably after evil, but uttering truth,
Why, tears! is it? tears; such a melting, a madrigal start!
Never-eldering revel and river of youth,
What can it be, this glee? the good you have there of your own?

19

Sister, a sister calling
A master, her master and mine!–
And the inboard seas run swirling and hawling;
The rash smart sloggering brine
Blinds her; but she that weather sees one thing, one;
Has one fetch in her: she rears herself to divine
Ears, and the call of the tall nun
To the men in the tops and the tackle rode over the storm's brawling.

20

She was first of a five and came
Of a coifèd sisterhood.
(O *Deutschland*, double a desperate name!
O world wide of its good!
But Gertrude, lily, and Luther, are two of a town,
Christ's lily and beast of the waste wood:
From life's dawn it is drawn down,
Abel is Cain's brother and breasts they have sucked the same.)

21

Loathed for a love men knew in them,
Banned by the land of their birth,
Rhine refused them. Thames would ruin them;
Surf, snow, river and earth
Gnashed: but thou art above, thou Orion of light;
Thy unchancelling poising palms were weighing the worth,
Thou martyr-master: in thy sight
Storm flakes were scroll-leaved flowers, lily showers–sweet heaven was astrew in them.

22

Five! the finding and sake
And cipher of suffering Christ.
Mark, the mark is of man's make
And the word of it Sacrificed.
But he scores it in scarlet himself on his own bespoken,
Before-time-taken, dearest prizèd and priced–
Stigma, signal, cinquefoil token
For lettering of the lamb's fleece, ruddying of the rose-flake.

23

Joy fall to thee, father Francis,
Drawn to the Life that died;
With the gnarls of the nails in thee, niche of the lance, his
Lovescape crucified
And seal of his seraph-arrival! and these thy daughters
And five-livèd and leavèd favour and pride,
Are sisterly sealed in wild waters,
To bathe in his fall-gold mercies, to breathe in his all-fire glances.

24

Away in the loveable west,
On a pastoral forehead of Wales,
I was under a roof here, I was at rest,
And they the prey of the gales;
She to the black-about air, to the breaker, the thickly
Falling flakes, to the throng that catches and quails
Was calling "O Christ, Christ, come quickly":
The cross to her she calls Christ to her, christens her wild-
worst Best.

25

The majesty! what did she mean?
Breathe, arch and original Breath.
Is it love in her of the being as her lover had been?
Breathe, body of lovely Death.
They were else-minded then, altogether, the men
Woke thee with a *we are perishing* in the weather of Gen-
nesareth.
Or is it that she cried for the crown then,
The keener to come at the comfort for feeling the combating
keen?

26

For how to the heart's cheering
The down-dugged ground-hugged grey
Hovers off, the jay-blue heavens appearing
Of pied and peeled May!
Blue-beating and hoary-glow height; or night, still higher,
With belled fire and the moth-soft Milky Way,
What by your measure is the heaven of desire,
The treasure never eyesight got, nor was ever guessed what for
the hearing?

27

No, but it was not these.
The jading and jar of the cart,
Time's tasking, it is fathers that asking for ease
Of the sodden-with-its-sorrowing heart,
Not danger, electrical horror; then further it finds
The appealing of the Passion is tenderer in prayer apart:
Other, I gather, in measure her mind's
Burden, in wind's burly and beat of endragonèd seas.

28

But how shall I . . . make me room there:
Reach me a . . . Fancy, come faster–
Strike you the sight of it? look at it loom there,
Thing that she . . . there then! the Master,
Ipse, the only one, Christ, King, Head:
He was to cure the extremity where he had cast her;
Do, deal, lord it with living and dead;
Let him ride, her pride, in his triumph, despatch and have done
with his doom there.

29

Ah! there was a heart right!
There was single eye!
Read the unshapeable shock night
And knew the who and the why;
Wording it how but by him that present and past,
Heaven and earth are word of, worded by?–
The Simon Peter of a soul! to the blast
Tarpeian-fast, but a blown beacon of light.

30

Jesu, heart's light,
Jesu, maid's son
What was the feast followed the night
Thou hadst glory of this nun?–
Feast of the one woman without stain.
For so conceivèd, so to conceive thee is done;
But here was heart-throe, birth of a brain,
Word, that heard and kept thee and uttered thee outright.

31

Well, she has thee for the pain, for the
Patience; but pity of the rest of them!
Heart, go and bleed at a bitterer vein for the
Comfortless unconfessed of them–
No not uncomforted: lovely-felicitous Providence
Finger of a tender of, O of a feathery delicacy, the breast
of the
Maiden could obey so, be a bell to, ring of it, and
Startle the poor sheep back! is the shipwrack then a harvest,
does tempest carry the grain for thee?

32

I admire thee, master of the tides,
Of the Yore-flood, of the year's fall;
The recurb and the recovery of the gulf's sides,
The girth of it and the wharf of it and the wall;
Stanching, quenching ocean of a motionable mind;
Ground of being, and granite of it: past all
Grasp God, throned behind
Death with a sovereignty that heeds but hides, bodes but abides;

33

With a mercy that outrides
The all of water, an ark
For the listener; for the lingerer, with a love glides
Lower than death and the dark;
A vein for the visiting of the past-prayer, pent in prison,
The-last-breath penitent spirits–the uttermost mark
Our passion-plungèd giant risen,
The Christ of the Father compassionate, fetched in the storm of his strides.

34

Now burn, new born to the world,
Doubled-naturèd name,
The heaven-flung, heart-fleshed, maiden-furled
Miracle-in-Mary-of-flame,
Mid-numbered He in three of the thunder-throne!
Not a dooms-day dazzle in his coming nor dark as he came;
Kind, but royally reclaiming his own;
A released shower, let flash to the shire, not a lightning of fire hard-hurled.

35

Dame, at our door
Drowned, and among our shoals,
Remember us in the roads, the heaven-haven of the Reward:
Our King back, oh, upon English souls!
Let him easter in us, be a dayspring to the dimness of us, be a crimson-cresseted east,

More brightening her, rare-dear Britain, as his reign rolls,
Pride, rose, prince, hero of us, high-priest,
Our hearts' charity's hearth's fire, our thoughts' chivalry's throng's Lord.

The Starlight Night

Look at the stars! look, look up at the skies!
O look at all the fire-folk sitting in the air!
The bright boroughs, the circle-citadels there!
Down in dim woods the diamond delves! the elves'-eyes!
The grey lawns cold where gold, where quickgold lies!
Wind-beat whitebeam! airy abeles set on a flare!
Flake-doves sent floating forth at a farmyard scare!–
Ah well! it is all a purchase, all is a prize.

Buy then! bid then!–What?–Prayer, patience, alms, vows.
Look, look: a May-mess, like on orchard boughs!
Look! March-bloom, like on mealed-with-yellow sallows!
These are indeed the barn; withindoors house
The shocks. This piece-bright paling shuts the spouse
Christ home, Christ and his mother and all his hallows.

Spring

Nothing is so beautiful as spring–
When weeds, in wheels, shoot long and lovely and lush;
Thrush's eggs look little low heavens, and thrush
Through the echoing timber does so rinse and wring
The ear, it strikes like lightnings to hear him sing;
The glassy peartree leaves and blooms, they brush
The descending blue; that blue is all in a rush
With richness; the racing lambs too have fair their fling.

What is all this juice and all this joy?
A strain of the earth's sweet being in the beginning
In Eden garden.–Have, get, before it cloy,
Before it cloud, Christ, lord, and sour with sinning,
Innocent mind and Mayday in girl and boy,
Most, O maid's child, thy choice and worthy the winning.

Pied Beauty

Glory be to God for dappled things–
For skies of couple-colour as a brinded cow;
For rose-moles all in stipple upon trout that swim;
Fresh-firecoal chestnut-falls; finches' wings;
Landscape plotted and pieced–fold, fallow, and plough;
And áll trádes, their gear and tackle and trim.

All things counter, original, spare, strange;
Whatever is fickle, freckled (who knows how?)
With swift, slow; sweet, sour; adazzle, dim;
He fathers-forth whose beauty is past change:
Praise him.

Hurrahing in Harvest

Summer ends now; now, barbarous in beauty, the stooks arise
Around; up above, what wind-walks! what lovely behaviour
Of silk-sack clouds! has wilder, wilful-wavier
Meal-drift moulded ever and melted across skies?

I walk, I lift up, I lift up heart, eyes,
Down all that glory in the heavens to glean our Saviour;
And, éyes, heárt, what looks, what lips yet gave you a
Rapturous love's greeting of realer, of rounder replies?

And the azurous hung hills are his world-wielding shoulder
Majestic–as a stallion stalwart, very-violet-sweet!–
These things, these things were here and but the beholder
Wanting; which two when they once meet,
The heart rears wings bold and bolder
And hurls for him, O half hurls earth for him off under his feet.

Spring and Fall

(to a Young Child)

Márgarét, are you gríeving
Over Goldengrove unleaving?
Leáves, líke the things of man, you
With your fresh thoughts care for, can you?
Áh! ás the heart grows older
It will come to such sights colder

By and by, nor spare a sigh
Though worlds of wanwood leafmeal lie;
And yet you wíll weep and know why.
Now no matter, child, the name:
Sórrow's spríngs áre the same.
Nor mouth had, no nor mind, expressed
What heart heard of, ghost guessed:
It ís the blight man was born for,
It is Margaret you mourn for.

God's Grandeur

The world is charged with the grandeur of God.
It will flame out, like shining from shook foil;
It gathers to a greatness, like the ooze of oil
Crushed. Why do men then now not reck his rod?
Generations have trod, have trod, have trod;
And all is seared with trade; bleared, smeared with toil;
And wears man's smudge and shares man's smell: the soil
Is bare now, nor can foot feel, being shod.

And for all this, nature is never spent;
There lives the dearest freshness deep down things;
And though the last lights off the black West went
Oh, morning, at the brown brink eastward, springs–
Because the Holy Ghost over the bent
World broods with warm breast and with ah! bright wings.

Binsey Poplars

(Felled 1879)

My aspens dear, whose airy cages quelled,
Quelled or quenched in leaves the leaping sun,
All felled, felled, are all felled;
Of a fresh and following folded rank
Not spared, not one
That dandled a sandalled
Shadow that swam or sank
On meadow and river and wind-wandering weed-winding bank.

O if we but knew what we do
When we delve or hew–
Hack and rack the growing green!
Since country is so tender
To touch, her being só slender,
That, like this sleek and seeing ball
But a prick will make no eye at all,
Where we, even where we mean
To mend her we end her,
When we hew or delve:
After-comers cannot guess the beauty been.
Ten or twelve, only ten or twelve
Strokes of havoc únselve
The sweet especial scene,
Rural scene, a rural scene,
Sweet especial rural scene.

The Windhover

(to Christ our Lord)

I caught this morning morning's minion, king-
dom of daylight's dauphin, dapple-dawn-drawn Fal-
con, in his riding
Of the rolling level underneath him steady air, and
striding
High there, how he rung upon the rein of a wimpling wing
In his ecstasy! then off, off forth on swing,
As a skate's heel sweeps smooth on a bow-bend: the hurl and
gliding
Rebuffed the big wind. My heart in hiding
Stirred for a bird,–the achieve of, the mastery of the thing!

Brute beauty and valour and act, oh, air, pride, plume, here
Buckle! AND the fire that breaks from thee then, a
billion
Times told lovelier, more dangerous, O my chevalier!

No wonder of it: shéer plód makes plough down sillion
Shine, and blue-bleak embers, ah my dear,
Fall, gall themselves, and gash gold-vermilion.

The Leaden Echo and the Golden Echo
(Maidens' song from St. Winefred's Well)

THE LEADEN ECHO

How to kéep—is there ány any, is there none such, nowhere known some, bow or brooch or braid or brace, láce, latch or catch or key to keep
Back beauty, keep it, beauty, beauty, beauty, . . . from vanishing away?
Ó is there no frowning of these wrinkles, rankèd wrinkles deep,
Dówn? no waving off of these most mournful messengers, still messengers, sad and stealing messengers of grey?
No there's none, there's none, O no there's none,
Nor can you long be, what you now are, called fair,
Do what you may do, what, do what you may,
And wisdom is early to despair:
Be beginning; since, no, nothing can be done
To keep at bay
Age and age's evils, hoar hair,
Ruck and wrinkle, drooping, dying, death's worst, winding sheets, tombs and worms and tumbling to decay;
So be beginning, be beginning to despair.
O there's none; no no no there's none:
Be beginning to despair, to despair,
Despair, despair, despair, despair.

THE GOLDEN ECHO

Spare!
There ís one, yes I have one (Hush there!);
Only not within seeing of the sun,
Not within the singeing of the strong sun,
Tall sun's tingeing, or treacherous the tainting of the earth's air,
Somewhere elsewhere there is ah well where! one,
Óne. Yes I can tell such a key, I do know such a place,
Where whatever's prized and passes of us, everything that's fresh and fast flying of us, seems to us sweet of us and swiftly away with, done away with, undone,
Undone, done with, soon done with, and yet dearly and dangerously sweet

Of us, the wimpled-water-dimpled, not-by-morning-matchèd face,
The flower of beauty, fleece of beauty, too too apt to, ah! to fleet,
Never fleets móre, fastened with the tenderest truth
To its own best being and its loveliness of youth: it is an everlastingness of, O it is an all youth!
Come then, your ways and airs and looks, locks, maiden gear, gallantry and gaiety and grace,
Winning ways, airs innocent, maiden manners, sweet looks, loose locks, long locks, lovelocks, gaygear, going gallant, girlgrace–
Resign them, sign them, seal them, send them, motion them with breath,
And with sighs soaring, soaring síghs deliver
Them; beauty-in-the-ghost, deliver it, early now, long before death
Give beauty back, beauty, beauty, beauty, back to God, beauty's self and beauty's giver.
See; not a hair is, not an eyelash, not the least lash lost; every hair
Is, hair of the head, numbered.
Nay, what we had lighthanded left in surly the mere mould
Will have waked and have waxed and have walked with the wind what while we slept,
This side, that side hurling a heavyheaded hundredfold
What while we, while we slumbered.
O then, weary then why should we tread? O why are we so haggard at the heart, so care-coiled, care-killed, so fagged, so fashed, so cogged, so cumbered,
When the thing we freely fórfeit is kept with fonder a care,
Fonder a care kept than we could have kept it, kept
Far with fonder a care (and we, we should have lost it) finer, fonder
A care kept.–Where kept? Do but tell us where kept, where.–
Yonder.–What high as that! We follow, now we follow.–Yonder, yes yonder, yonder,
Yonder.

That Nature is a Heraclitean Fire and of the Comfort of the Resurrection

Cloud-puffball, torn tufts, tossed pillows flaunt forth, then
chevy on an air-
built thoroughfare: heaven-roysterers, in gay-gangs they
throng; they glitter in marches.
Down roughcast, down dazzling whitewash, wherever an elm
arches,
Shivelights and shadowtackle in long lashes lace, lance, and
pair.
Delightfully the bright wind boisterous ropes, wrestles, beats
earth bare
Of yestertempest's creases; in pool and rut peel parches
Squandering ooze to squeezed dough, crust, dust; stanches,
starches
Squadroned masks and manmarks treadmire toil there
Footfretted in it. Million-fuelèd, nature's bonfire burns
on.
But quench her bonniest, dearest to her, her clearest-selvèd
spark
Man, how fast his firedint, his mark on mind, is gone!
Both are in an unfathomable, all is in an enormous dark
Drowned. O pity and indignation! Manshape, that shone
Sheer off, disseveral, a star, death blots black out; nor
mark
Is any of him at all so stark
But vastness blurs and time beats level. Enough! the Resur-
rection,
A heart's clarion! Away grief's gasping, joyless days, dejec-
tion.
Across my foundering deck shone
A beacon, an eternal beam. Flesh fade, and mortal trash
Fall to the residuary worm; world's wildfire, leave but
ash:
In a flash, at a trumpet crash,
I am all at once what Christ is, since he was what I am, and
This Jack, joke, poor potsherd, patch, matchwood, immortal
diamond,
Is immortal diamond.

Sonnets

No worst, there is none. Pitched past pitch of grief,
More pangs will, schooled at forepangs, wilder wring.
Comforter, where, where is your comforting?
Mary, mother of us, where is your relief?
My cries heave, herds-long; huddle in a main, a chief
Woe, world-sorrow; on an age-old anvil wince and sing–
Then lull, then leave off. Fury had shrieked "No ling-
ering! Let me be fell: force I must be brief."

O the mind, mind has mountains; cliffs of fall
Frightful, sheer, no-man-fathomed. Hold them cheap
May who ne'er hung there. Nor does long our small
Durance deal with that steep or deep. Here! creep,
Wretch, under a comfort serves in a whirlwind: all
Life death does end and each day dies with sleep.

Justus quidem tu es, Domine, si disputem tecum: verumtamen justa loquar ad te: Quare via impiorum prosperatur? etc.

Thou art indeed just, Lord, if I contend
With thee; but, sir, so what I plead is just.
Why do sinners' ways prosper? and why must
Disappointment all I endeavour end?
Wert thou my enemy, O thou my friend,
How wouldst thou worse, I wonder, than thou dost
Defeat, thwart me? Oh, the sots and thralls of lust
Do in spare hours more thrive than I that spend,
Sir, life upon thy cause. See, banks and brakes
Now, leavèd how thick! lacèd they are again
With fretty chervil, look, and fresh wind shakes
Them; birds build–but not I build; no, but strain,
Time's eunuch, and not breed one work that wakes.
Mine, O thou Lord of life, send my roots rain.

Carrion Comfort

Not, I'll not, carrion comfort, Despair, not feast on thee;
Not untwist–slack they may be–these last strands of man
In me ór, most weary, cry *I can no more*. I can;
Can something, hope, wish day come, not choose not to be.

But ah, but O thou terrible, why wouldst thou rude on me
Thy wring-world right foot rock? lay a lionlimb against me? scan
With darksome devouring eyes my bruisèd bones? and fan,
O in turns of tempest, me heaped there; me frantic to avoid thee and flee?
Why? That my chaff might fly; my grain lie, sheer and clear.
Nay in all that toil, that coil, since (seems) I kissed the rod,
Hand rather, my heart lo! lapped strength, stole joy, would laugh, chéer.
Cheer whom though? the hero whose heaven-handling flung me, fóot tród.
Me? or me that fought him? O which one? is it each one? That night, that year
Of now done darkness I wretch lay wrestling with (my God!) my God.

Robert Bridges (*Br. 1844–1930*)

Noel: Christmas Eve, 1913

Pax hominibus bonae voluntatis

A frosty Christmas Eve
when the stars were shining
Fared I forth alone
where westward falls the hill,
And from many a village
in the water'd valley
Distant music reach'd me
peals of bells aringing:
The constellated sounds
ran sprinkling on earth's floor
As the dark vault above
with stars was spangled o'er.

Then sped my thought to keep
  that first Christmas of all
When the shepherds watching
  by their folds ere the dawn
Heard music in the fields
  and marveling could not tell
Whether it were angels
  or the bright stars singing.

Now blessed be the tow'rs
  that crown England so fair
That stand up strong in prayer
  unto God for our souls:
Blessed be their founders
  (said I) an' our country folk
Who are ringing for Christ
  in the belfries to-night
With arms lifted to clutch
  the rattling ropes that race
Into the dark above
  and the mad romping din.

But to me heard afar
  it was starry music
Angels' song, comforting
  as the comfort of Christ
When he spake tenderly
  to his sorrowful flock:
The old words came to me
  by the riches of time
Mellow'd and transfigured
  as I stood on the hill
Heark'ning in the aspect
  of th' eternal silence.

Flycatchers

Sweet pretty fledgelings, perched on the rail arow,
Expectantly happy, where ye can watch below
Your parents a-hunting i' the meadow grasses
All the gay morning to feed you with flies;

Ye recall me a time sixty summers ago,
When, a young chubby chap, I sat just so
With others on a school-form rank'd in a row,
Not less eager and hungry than you, I trow,
With intelligences agape and eyes aglow,
While an authoritative old wise-acre
Stood over us and from a desk fed us with flies.

Dead flies–such as litter the library south-window,
That buzzed at the panes until they fell stiff-baked on the sill,
Or are roll'd up asleep i' the blinds at sunrise,
Or wafer'd flat in a shrunken folio.

A dry biped he was, nurtured likewise
On skins and skeletons, stale from top to toe
With all manner of rubbish and all manner of lies.

Cheddar Pinks

Mid the squander'd colour
  idling as I lay
Reading the Odyssey
  in my rock-garden
I espied the cluster'd
  tufts of Cheddar pinks
Burgeoning with promise
  of their scented bloom
All the modish motley
  of their bloom to-be
Thrust up in narrow buds
  on the slender stalks
Thronging springing urgent
  hasting (so I thought)
As if they fear'd to be
  too late for summer–
Like schoolgirls overslept
  waken'd by the bell
Leaping from bed to don
  their muslin dresses
    on a May morning:

Then felt I like to one
  indulging in sin
(Whereto Nature is oft
  a blind accomplice)
Because my aged bones
  so enjoyed the sun
There as I lay along
  idling with my thoughts
Reading an old poet
  while the busy world
Toil'd moil'd fuss'd and scurried
  worried bought and sold
Plotted stole and quarrel'd
  fought and God knows what.
I had forgotten Homer
  dallying with my thoughts
Till I fell to making
  these little verses
Communing with the flowers
  in my rock-garden
    On a May morning.

From *The Testament of Beauty*

Introduction

'Twas late in my long journey, when I had clomb to where
the path was narrowing and the company few,
a glow of childlike wonder enthral'd me, as if my sense
had come to a new birth purified, my mind enrapt
re-awakening to a fresh initiation of life;
with like surprise of joy as any man may know
who rambling wide hath turn'd, resting on some hill-top
to view the plain he has left, and see'th it now out-spredd
mapp'd at his feet, a landscape so by beauty estranged
he scarce wil ken familiar haunts, nor his own home,
maybe, where far it lieth, small as a faded thought.
  Or as I well remember one highday in June
bright on the seaward South-downs, where I had come afar
on a wild garden planted years agone, and fenced
thickly within live-beechen walls: the season it was

of prodigal gay blossom, and man's skill had made
a fair-order'd husbandry of thatt nativ pleasaunce:
But had ther been no more than earth's wild loveliness,
the blue sky and soft air and the unmown flowersprent lawns,
I would hav lain me down and long'd, as then I did,
to lie there ever indolently undisturb'd, and watch
the common flowers that starr'd the fine grass of the wold,
waving in gay display their gold-heads to the sun,
each telling of its own inconscient happiness,
each type a faultless essence of God's will, such gems
as magic master-minds in painting or music
threw aside once for man's regard or disregard;
things supreme in themselves, eternal, unnumber'd
in the unexplored necessities of Life and Love.

To such a mood I had come, by what charm I know not,
where on thatt upland path I was pacing alone;
and yet was nothing new to me, only all was vivid
and significant that had been dormant or dead:
as if in a museum the fossils on their shelves
should come to life suddenly, or a winter rose-bed
burst into crowded holiday of scent and bloom.
I felt the domination of Nature's secret urge,
and happy escape therein; as when in boyhood once
from the rattling workshops of a great factory
conducted into the engine-room I stood in face
of the quiet driving power, that fast in nether cave
seated, set all the floors a-quiver, a thousand looms
throbbing and jennies dancing; and I felt at heart
a kinship with it and sympathy, as children wil
with amicable monsters: for in truth the mind
is indissociable from what it contemplates,
as thirst and generous wine are to a man that drinketh
nor kenneth whether his pleasur is more in his desire
or in the savor of the rich grape that allays it.

Man's Reason is in such deep insolvency to sense,
that tho' she guide his highest flight heav'nward, and teach him
dignity morals manners and human comfort,
she can delicatly and dangerously bedizen
the rioting joys that fringe the sad pathways of Hell.

Nor without alliance of the animal senses
hath she any miracle: Lov'st thou in the blithe hour
of April dawns–nay marvelest thou not–to hear
the ravishing music that the small birdës make
in garden or woodland, rapturously heralding
the break of day; when the first lark on high hath warn'd
the vigilant robin already of the sun's approach,
and he on slender pipe calleth the nesting tribes
to awake and fill and thrill their myriad-warbling throats
praising life's God, untill the blisful revel grow
in wild profusion unfeign'd to such a hymn as man
hath never in temple or grove pour'd to the Lord of heav'n?
Hast thou then thought that all this ravishing music,
that stirreth so thy heart, making thee dream of things
illimitable unsearchable and of heavenly import,
is but a light disturbance of the atoms of air,
whose jostling ripples, gather'd within the ear, are tuned
to resonant scale, and thence by the enthron'd mind received
on the spiral stairway of her audience chamber
as heralds of high spiritual significance?
and that without thine ear, sound would hav no report.
Nature hav no music; nor would ther be for thee
any better melody in the April woods at dawn
than what an old stone-deaf labourer, lying awake
o' night in his comfortless attic, might perchance
be aware of, when the rats run amok in his thatch?
Now since the thoughtless birds not only act and enjoy
this music, but to their offspring teach it with care,
handing on those small folk-songs from father to son
in such faithful tradition that they are familiar
unchanging to the changeful generations of men–
and year by year, listening to himself the nightingale
as amorous of his art as of his brooding mate
practiseth every phrase of his espousal lay,
and still provoketh envy of the lesser songsters
with the same notes that woke poetic eloquence
alike in Sophocles and the sick heart of Keats–
see then how deeply seated is the urgence whereto
Bach and Mozart obey'd, or those other minstels
who pioneer'd for us on the marches of heav'n

and paid no heed to wars that swept the world around,
nor in their homes wer more troubled by cannon-roar
than late the small birds wer, that nested and carol'd
upon the devastated battlefields of France.

Birds are of all animals the nearest to men
for that they take delight in both music and dance,
and gracefully schooling leisure to enliven life
wer the earlier artists: moreover in their airy flight
(which in its swiftness symboleth man's soaring thought)
they hav no rival but man, and easily surpass
in their free voyaging his most desperate daring,
altho' he hath fed and sped his ocean-ships with fire;
and now, disturbing me as I write, I hear on high
his roaring airplanes, and idly raising my head
see them there; like a migratory flock of birds
that rustle southward from the cold fall of the year
in order'd phalanx–so the thin-rankt squadrons ply,
til sound and sight failing me they are lost in the clouds.

From *The Testament of Beauty* (1)

The sky's unresting cloudland, that with varying play
sifteth the sunlight thru' its figured shades, that now
stand in massiv range, cumulated stupendous
mountainous snowbillowy up-piled in dazzling sheen,
Now like sailing ships on a calm ocean drifting,
Now scatter'd wispy waifs, that neath the eager blaze
disperse in air; Or now parcelling the icy inane
highspredd in fine diaper of silver and mother-of-pearl
freaking the intense azure; Now scurrying close o'erhead,
wild ink-hued random racers that fling sheeted rain
gustily, and with garish bows laughing o'erarch the land:
Or, if the spirit of storm be abroad, huge molten glooms
mount on the horizon stealthily, and gathering as they climb
deep-freighted with live lightning, thunder and drenching flood
rebuff the winds, and with black-purpling terror impend
til they be driven away, when grave Night peacefully

clearing her heav'nly rondure of its turbid veils
layeth bare the playthings of Creation's babyhood;
and the immortal fireballs of her uttermost space
twinkle like friendly rushlights on the countryside.
Them soon the jealous Day o'errideth to display
Earth's green robe, which the sun fostereth for shelter and shower
The dance of young trees that in a wild birch-spinney
toss to and fro the cluster of their flickering crests,
as rye curtseying in array to the breeze of May;
The ancestral trunks that mightily in the forest choirs
rear stedfast colonnade, or imperceptibly
sway in tall pinewoods to their whispering spires;
The woodland's alternating hues, the vaporous bloom
of the first blushings and tender flushings of spring;
The slumbrous foliage of high midsummer's wealth;
Rich Autumn's golden quittance, to the bankruptcy
of the black shapely skeletons standing in snow:
Or, in gay months of swelling pomp, the luxury
of leisur'd gardens teeming with affection'd thought;
the heartfelt secrecy of rustic nooks, and valleys
vocal with angelic rilling of rocky streams,
by rambling country-lanes, with hazel and thorn embower'd
woodbine, bryony and wild roses; the landscape lure
of rural England, that held glory in native art
untill our painters took their new fashion from France.

From *The Testament of Beauty* (2)

How was November's melancholy endear'd to me
in the effigy of plowteams following and recrossing
patiently the desolat landscape from dawn to dusk,
as the slow-creeping ripple of their single furrow
submerged the sodden litter of summer's festival!
They are fled, those gracious teams; high on the headland now
squatted, a roaring engin toweth to itself
a beam of bolted shares, that glideth to and fro
combing the stubbled glebe: and agriculture here,
blotting out with such daub so rich a pictur of grace,
hath lost as much of beauty as it hath saved in toil.

Again where reapers, bending to the ripen'd corn,
were wont to scythe in rank and step with measured stroke,
a shark-tooth'd chariot rampeth biting a broad way,
and, jerking its high swindging arms around in the air,
swoopeth the swath. Yet this queer Pterodactyl is well,
that in the sinister torpor of the blazing day
clicketeth in heartless mockery of swoon and sweat,
as 'twer the salamandrine voice of all parch'd things:
and the dry grasshopper wondering knoweth his God.
Or what man feeleth not a new poetry of toil,
whenas on frosty evenings neath its clouding smoke
the engin hath huddled-up its clumsy threshing-coach
against the ricks, wherefrom laborers standing aloft
toss the sheaves on its tongue; while the grain runneth out,
and in the whirr of its multitudinous hurry
it hummeth like the bee, a warm industrious boom
that comforteth the farm, and spreadeth far afield
with throbbing power; as when in a cathedral awhile
the great diapason speaketh, and the painted saints
feel their glass canopies flutter in the heav'nward prayer.

From *The Testament of Beauty* (3)

'TWAS at thatt hour of beauty when the setting sun
squandereth his cloudy bed with rosy hues, to flood
his lov'd works as in turn he biddeth them Good-night;
and all the towers and temples and mansions of men
face him in bright farewell, ere they creep from their pomp
naked beneath the darkness;–while to mortal eyes
'tis given, ifso thcy closc not of fatigue, nor strain
at lamplit tasks–'tis given, as for a royal boon
to beggarly outcasts in homeless vigil, to watch
where uncurtain'd behind the great windows of space
Heav'n's jewel'd company circleth unapproachably–
'Twas at sunset that I, fleeing to hide my soul
in refuge of beauty from a mortal distress,
walk'd alone with the Muse in her garden of thought,
discoursing at liberty with the mazy dreams

that came wavering pertinaciously about me; as when
the small bats, issued from their hangings, flitter o'erhead
thru' the summer twilight, with thin cries to and fro
hunting in muffled flight atween the stars and flowers.
Then fell I in strange delusion, illusion strange to tell;
for as a man who lyeth fast asleep in his bed
may dream he waketh, and that he walketh upright
pursuing some endeavour in full conscience–so 'twas
with me; but contrawise; for being in truth awake
methought I slept and dreamt; and in thatt dream methought
I was telling a dream; nor telling was I as one
who, truly awaked from a true sleep, thinketh to tell
his dream to a friend, but for his scant remembrances
findeth no token of speech–it was not so with me;
for my tale was my dream and my dream the telling,
and I remember wondring the while I told it
how I told it so tellingly. And yet now 'twould seem
that Reason inveigled me with her old orderings;
as once when she took thought to adjust theology,
peopling the inane that vex'd her between God and man
with a hierarchy of angels; like those asteroids
wherewith she later fill'd the gap 'twixt Jove and Mars.
Verily by Beauty it is that we come at WISDOM,
yet not by Reason at Beauty: and now with many words
pleasing myself betimes I am fearing lest in the end
I play the tedious orator who maundereth on
for lack of heart to make an end of his nothings.
Wherefor as when a runner who hath run his round
handeth his staff away, and is glad of his rest,
here break I off, knowing the goal was not for me
the while I ran on telling of what cannot be told.

For not the Muse herself can tell of Goddes love;
which cometh to the child from the Mother's embrace,
an Idea spacious as the starry firmament's
inescapable infinity of radiant gaze,
that fadeth only as it outpasseth mortal sight:
and this direct contact is't with eternities,
this springtide miracle of the soul's nativity
that oft hath set philosophers adrift in dream;

which thing Christ taught, when he set up a little child
to teach his first Apostles and to accuse their pride,
saying, *Unless ye shall receive it as a child,*
ye cannot enter into the kingdom of heaven.
So thru'out all his young mental apprenticehood
the child of very simplicity, and in the grace
and beauteous attitude of infantine wonder,
is apt to absorb Ideas in primal purity,
and by the assimilation of thatt immortal food
may build immortal life; but ever with the growth
of understanding, as the sensible images
are more and more corrupt, troubled by questioning thought,
or with vainglory alloy'd, 'tis like enough the boy
in prospect of his manhood wil hav cast to th' winds
his Baptism with his Babyhood; nor might he escape
the fall of Ev'ryman, did not a second call
of nature's Love await him to confirm his Faith
or to revoke him if he is wholly lapsed therefrom.
And so mighty is this second vision, which cometh
in puberty of body and adolescence of mind
that, forgetting his Mother, he calleth it 'first Love';
for it mocketh at suasion or stubbornness of heart,
as the oceantide of the omnipotent Pleasur of God,
flushing all avenues of life, and unawares
by thousandfold approach forestalling its full flood
with divination of the secret contacts of Love,–
of faintest ecstacies aslumber in Nature's calm,
like thought in a closed book, where some poet long since
sang his throbbing passion to immortal sleep–with coy
tendernesses delicat as the shifting hues
that sanctify the silent dawn with wonder-gleams,
whose evanescence is the seal of their glory,
consumed in self-becoming of eternity;
til every moment as it flyeth, cryeth "Seize!
Seize me ere I die! I am the Life of Life."

Alice Meynell (*Br. 1847–1922*)

The Rainy Summer

There's much afoot in heaven and earth this year;
  The winds hunt up the sun, hunt up the moon,
Trouble the dubious dawn, hasten the drear
  Height of a threatening noon.

No breath of boughs, no breath of leaves, of fronds
  May linger or grow warm; the trees are loud;
The forest, rooted, tosses in her bonds,
  And strains against the cloud.

No scents may pause within the garden-fold;
  The rifled flowers are cold as ocean-shells;
Bees, humming in the storm, carry their cold
  Wild honey to cold cells.

A Dead Harvest

(In Kensington Gardens)

Along the graceless grass of town
They rake the rows of red and brown,–
Dead leaves, unlike the rows of hay
Delicate, touched with gold and grey,
Raked long ago and far away.

A narrow silence in the park,
Between the lights a narrow dark.
One street rolls on the north; and one,
Muffled, upon the south doth run;
Amid the mist the work is done.

A futile crop!–for it the fire
Smoulders, and, for a stack, a pyre.
So go the town's lives on the breeze,
Even as the sheddings of the trees;
Bosom nor barn is filled with these.

A. E. Housman (*Br. 1859–1936*)

The fairies break their dances

The fairies break their dances
  And leave the printed lawn,
And up from India glances
  The silver sail of dawn.

The candles burn their sockets,
  The blinds let through the day,
The young man feels his pockets
  And wonders what's to pay.

The sigh that heaves the grasses

The sigh that heaves the grasses
  Whence thou wilt never rise
Is of the air that passes
  And knows not if it sighs.

The diamond tears adorning
  Thy low mound on the lea,
Those are the tears of morning,
  That weeps, but not for thee.

Epitaph

Here dead lie we because we did not choose
  To live and shame the land from which we sprung.
Life, to be sure, is nothing much to lose;
  But young men think it is, and we were young.

Epitaph on an Army of Mercenaries

These, in the day when heaven was falling,
  The hour when earth's foundations fled,
Followed their mercenary calling
  And took their wages and are dead.

Their shoulders held the sky suspended;
  They stood, and earth's foundations stay;
What God abandoned, these defended,
  And saved the sum of things for pay.

When summer's end is nighing

When summer's end is nighing
  And skies at evening cloud,
I muse on change and fortune
  And all the feats I vowed
  When I was young and proud.

The weathercock at sunset
  Would lose the slanted ray,
And I would climb the beacon
  That looked to Wales away
  And saw the last of day.

From hill and cloud and heaven
  The hues of evening died;
Night welled through lane and hollow
  And hushed the countryside,
  But I had youth and pride.

And I with earth and nightfall
  In converse high would stand,
Late, till the west was ashen
  And darkness hard at hand,
  And the eye lost the land.

The year might age, and cloudy
  The lessening day might close,
But air of other summers
  Breathed from beyond the snows,
  And I had hope of those.

They came and were and are not
  And come no more anew;
And all the years and seasons
  That ever can ensue
  Must now be worse and few.

So here's an end of roaming
  On eves when autumn nighs:
The ear too fondly listens
  For summer's parting sighs,
  And then the heart replies.

Tell me not here, it needs not saying

Tell me not here, it needs not saying,
  What tune the enchantress plays
In aftermaths of soft September
  Or under blanching mays,
For she and I were long acquainted
  And I knew all her ways.

On russet floors, by waters idle,
  The pine lets fall its cone;
The cuckoo shouts all day at nothing
  In leafy dells alone;
And traveller's joy beguiles in autumn
  Hearts that have lost their own.

On acres of the seeded grasses
  The changing burnish heaves;
Or marshalled under moon of harvest
  Stand still all night the sheaves;
Or beeches strip in storms for winter
  And stain the wind with leaves.

Possess, as I possessed a season,
  The countries I resign,
Where over elmy plains the highway
  Would mount the hills and shine,
And full of shade the pillared forest
  Would murmur and be mine.

For nature, heartless, witless nature,
  Will neither care nor know
What stranger's feet may find the meadow
  And trespass there and go,
Nor ask amid the dews of morning
  If they are mine or no.

Mary Coleridge (*Br. 1861–1907*)

On Such a Day

Some hang above the tombs,
Some weep in empty rooms,
I, when the iris blooms,
Remember.

I, when the cyclamen
Opens her buds again,
Rejoice a moment–then
Remember.

Gibberish

Many a flower have I seen blossom,
Many a bird for me will sing.
Never heard I so sweet a singer,
Never saw I so fair a thing.

She is a bird, a bird that blossoms,
She is a flower, a flower that sings;
And I a flower when I behold her,
And when I hear her, I have wings.

The Deserted House

There's no smoke in the chimney,
And the rain beats on the floor;
There's no glass in the window,
There's no wood in the door;
The heather grows behind the house,
And the sand lies before.

No hand hath trained the ivy,
The walls are grey and bare;
The boats upon the sea sail by,
Nor ever tarry there.
No beast of the field comes nigh,
Nor any bird of the air.

Change

Ah, there is no abiding!
  Signs from heaven are sent.
Over the grass the wind went gliding,
  And the green grass grew silver as he went.

Ah, there is no remaining!
  Ever the tide of ocean ebbs and flows.
Over the blue sea goes the wind complaining,
  And the blue sea turns emerald as he goes.

Cut it Down

By a dim road, o'ergrown with dry thin grass,
  A little straggling, wild, wind-beaten tree
Stood, like a sentry, where no feet might pass,
  And storm-swept by the sea.

What was the secret of that lonely place?
  Had some accursèd thing gone by this way,
Leaving the horror of his evil face
  On leaf and bough and spray?

I know not. But the very sunbeams took
  The darkness of the gnarled and twisted stem;
The summer air those wrinkled leaves forsook
  Nor ever played in them.

Rudyard Kipling (*Br. 1865–1936*)

Cities and Thrones and Powers

('A Centurion of the Thirtieth'–*Puck of Pook's Hill*)

Cities and Thrones and Powers
  Stand in Time's eye,
Almost as long as flowers,
  Which daily die:
But, as new buds put forth
  To glad new men,
Out of the spent and unconsidered Earth
  The Cities rise again.

This season's Daffodil,
  She never hears
What change, what chance, what chill,
  Cut down last year's;
But with bold countenance,
  And knowledge small,
Esteems her seven days' continuance
  To be perpetual.

So Time that is o'er-kind
  To all that be,
Ordains us e'en as blind,
  As bold as she:
That in our very death,
  And burial sure,
Shadow to shadow, well persuaded, saith,
  "See how our works endure!"

The Way through the Woods

('Marklake Witches'–*Rewards and Fairies*)

They shut the road through the woods
Seventy years ago.
Weather and rain have undone it again,
And now you would never know
There was once a road through the woods
Before they planted the trees.
It is underneath the coppice and heath
And the thin anemones.
Only the keeper sees
That, where the ring-dove broods,
And the badgers roll at ease,
There was once a road through the woods.

Yet, if you enter the woods
Of a summer evening late,
When the night-air cools on the trout-ringed pools
Where the otter whistles his mate,
(They fear not men in the woods,
Because they see so few.)

You will hear the beat of a horse's feet,
And the swish of a skirt in the dew,
Steadily cantering through
The misty solitudes,
As though they perfectly knew
The old lost road through the woods. . . .
But there is no road through the woods.

A St. Helena Lullaby

('A Priest in spite of Himself'–*Rewards and Fairies*)

"How far is St. Helena from a little child at play?"
What makes you want to wander there with all the world between?
Oh, Mother, call your son again or else he'll run away.
(*No one thinks of winter when the grass is green!*)

"How far is St. Helena from a fight in Paris Street?"
I haven't time to answer now–the men are falling fast.
The guns begin to thunder, and the drums begin to beat.
(*If you take the first step, you will take the last!*)

"How far is St. Helena from the field of Austerlitz?"
You couldn't hear me if I told–so loud the cannon roar.
But not so far for people who are living by their wits.
('*Gay go up*' *means* '*Gay go down*' *the wide world o'er!*)

"How far is St. Helena from an Emperor of France?"
I cannot see–I cannot tell–the Crowns they dazzle so.
The Kings sit down to dinner, and the Queens stand up to dance.
(*After open weather you may look for snow!*)

"How far is St. Helena from the Capes of Trafalgar?"
A longish way–a longish way–with ten year more to run.
It's south across the water underneath a falling star.
(*What you cannot finish you must leave undone!*)

"How far is St. Helena from the Beresina ice?"
An ill way–a chill way–the ice begins to crack.
But not so far for gentlemen who never took advice.
(*When you can't go forward you must e'en come back!*)

"How far is St. Helena from the field of Waterloo?"
A near way–a clear way–the ship will take you soon.
A pleasant place for gentlemen with little left to do.
(*Morning never tries you till the afternoon!*)

"How far from St. Helena to the Gate of Heaven's Grace?"
That no one knows–that no one knows–and no one ever will.
But fold your hands across your heart and cover up your face,
And after all your trapesings, child, lie still!

W. B. Yeats (*Br. 1865–1939*)

The Wild Swans at Coole

The trees are in their autumn beauty,
The woodland paths are dry,
Under the October twilight the water
Mirrors a still sky;
Upon the brimming water among the stones
Are nine-and-fifty swans.

The nineteenth autumn has come upon me
Since I first made my count;
I saw, before I had well finished,
All suddenly mount
And scatter wheeling in great broken rings
Upon their clamorous wings.

I have looked upon those brilliant creatures,
And now my heart is sore.
All's changed since I, hearing at twilight,
The first time on this shore,
The bell-beat of their wings above my head,
Trod with a lighter tread.

Unwearied still, lover by lover,
They paddle in the cold
Companionable streams or climb the air;
Their hearts have not grown old;
Passion or conquest, wander where they will,
Attend upon them still.

But now they drift on the still water,
Mysterious, beautiful;
Among what rushes will they build,
By what lake's edge or pool
Delight men's eyes when I awake some day
To find they have flown away?

The Dawn

I would be ignorant as the dawn
That has looked down
On that old queen measuring a town
With the pin of a brooch,
Or on the withered men that saw
From their pedantic Babylon
The careless planets in their courses,
The stars fade out where the moon comes,
And took their tablets and did sums;
I would be ignorant as the dawn
That merely stood, rocking the glittering coach
Above the cloudy shoulders of the horses;
I would be–for no knowledge is worth a straw–
Ignorant and wanton as the dawn.

On being asked for a War Poem

I think it better that in times like these
A poet's mouth be silent, for in truth
We have no gift to set a statesman right;
He has had enough of meddling who can please
A young girl in the indolence of her youth,
Or an old man upon a winter's night.

The Cold Heaven

Suddenly I saw the cold and rook-delighting heaven
That seemed as though ice burned and was but the
more ice,
And thereupon imagination and heart were driven
So wild that every casual thought of that and this
Vanished, and left but memories, that should be out
of season

With the hot blood of youth, of love crossed long ago;
And I took all the blame out of all sense and reason,
Until I cried and trembled and rocked to and fro,
Riddled with light. Ah! when the ghost begins to quicken,
Confusion of the death-bed over, is it sent
Out naked on the roads, as the books say, and stricken
By the injustice of the skies for punishment?

The Fool by the Roadside

When all works that have
From cradle run to grave
From grave to cradle run instead;
When thoughts that a fool
Has wound upon a spool
Are but loose thread, are but loose thread;

When cradle and spool are past
And I mere shade at last
Coagulate of stuff
Transparent like the wind,
I think that I may find
A faithful love, a faithful love.

Leda and the Swan

A sudden blow: the great wings beating still
Above the staggering girl, her thighs caressed
By the dark webs, her nape caught in his bill,
He holds her helpless breast upon his breast.

How can those terrified vague fingers push
The feathered glory from her loosening thighs?
And how can body, laid in that white rush,
But feel the strange heart beating where it lies?

A shudder in the loins engenders there
The broken wall, the burning roof and tower
And Agamemnon dead.
Being so caught up,
So mastered by the brute blood of the air,
Did she put on his knowledge with his power
Before the indifferent beak could let her drop?

The Second Coming

Turning and turning in the widening gyre
The falcon cannot hear the falconer;
Things fall apart; the centre cannot hold;
Mere anarchy is loosed upon the world,
The blood-dimmed tide is loosed, and everywhere
The ceremony of innocence is drowned;
The best lack all conviction, while the worst
Are full of passionate intensity.

Surely some revelation is at hand;
Surely the Second Coming is at hand.
The Second Coming! Hardly are those words out
When a vast image out of *Spiritus Mundi*
Troubles my sight: somewhere in sands of the desert
A shape with lion body and the head of a man,
A gaze blank and pitiless as the sun,
Is moving its slow thighs, while all about it
Reel shadows of the indignant desert birds.
The darkness drops again; but now I know
That twenty centuries of stony sleep
Were vexed to nightmare by a rocking cradle,
And what rough beast, its hour come round at last,
Slouches towards Bethlehem to be born?

The New Faces

If you, that have grown old, were the first dead,
Neither catalpa-tree nor scented lime
Should hear my living feet, nor would I tread
Where we wrought that shall break the teeth of Time.
Let the new faces play what tricks they will
In the old rooms; night can outbalance day,
Our shadows rove the garden gravel still,
The living seem more shadowy than they.

From *Meditations in Time of Civil War:*
Ancestral Houses

Surely among a rich man's flowering lawns,
Amid the rustle of his planted hills,
Life overflows without ambitious pains;

And rains down life until the basin spills,
And mounts more dizzy high the more it rains
As though to choose whatever shape it wills
And never stoop to a mechanical
Or servile shape, at others' beck and call.

Mere dreams, mere dreams! Yet Homer had not sung
Had he not found it certain beyond dreams
That out of life's own self-delight had sprung
The abounding glittering jet; though now it seems
As if some marvellous empty sea-shell flung
Out of the obscure dark of the rich streams,
And not a fountain, were the symbol which
Shadows the inherited glory of the rich.

Some violent bitter man, some powerful man
Called architect and artist in, that they,
Bitter and violent men, might rear in stone
The sweetness that all longed for night and day,
The gentleness none there had ever known;
But when the master's buried mice can play,
And maybe the great-grandson of that house,
For all its bronze and marble, 's but a mouse.

O what if gardens where the peacock strays
With delicate feet upon old terraces,
Or else all Juno from an urn displays
Before the indifferent garden deities;
O what if levelled lawns and gravelled ways
Where slippered Contemplation finds his ease
And Childhood a delight for every sense,
But take our greatness with our violence?

What if the glory of escutcheoned doors,
And buildings that a haughtier age designed,
The pacing to and fro on polished floors
Amid great chambers and long galleries, lined
With famous portraits of our ancestors;
What if those things the greatest of mankind
Consider most to magnify, or to bless,
But take our greatness with our bitterness?

Vacillation

I

Between extremities
Man runs his course;
A brand, or flaming breath,
Comes to destroy
All those antinomies
Of day and night;
The body calls it death,
The heart remorse.
But if these be right
What is joy?

II

A tree there is that from its topmost bough
Is half all glittering flame and half all green
Abounding foliage moistened with the dew;
And half is half and yet is all the scene;
And half and half consume what they renew,
And he that Attis' image hangs between
That staring fury and the blind lush leaf
May know not what he knows, but knows not grief.

III

Get all the gold and silver that you can,
Satisfy ambition, animate
The trivial days and ram them with the sun,
And yet upon these maxims meditate:
All women dote upon an idle man
Although their children need a rich estate;
No man has ever lived that had enough
Of children's gratitude or woman's love.

No longer in Lethean foliage caught
Begin the preparation for your death
And from the fortieth winter by that thought
Test every work of intellect or faith,
And everything that your own hands have wrought,
And call those works extravagance of breath
That are not suited for such men as come
Proud, open-eyed and laughing to the tomb.

IV

My fiftieth year had come and gone,
I sat, a solitary man,
In a crowded London shop,
An open book and empty cup
On the marble table-top.

While on the shop and street I gazed
My body of a sudden blazed;
And twenty minutes more or less
It seemed, so great my happiness,
That I was blessèd and could bless.

V

Although the summer sunlight gild
Cloudy leafage of the sky,
Or wintry moonlight sink the field
In storm-scattered intricacy,
I cannot look thereon,
Responsibility so weighs me down.

Things said or done long years ago,
Or things I did not do or say
But thought that I might say or do,
Weigh me down, and not a day
But something is recalled,
My conscience or my vanity appalled.

VI

A rivery field spread out below,
An odour of the new-mown hay
In his nostrils, the great lord of Chou
Cried, casting off the mountain snow,
'Let all things pass away.'

Wheels by milk-white asses drawn
Where Babylon or Nineveh
Rose; some conqueror drew rein
And cried to battle-weary men,
'Let all things pass away.'

From man's blood-sodden heart are sprung
Those branches of the night and day
Where the gaudy moon is hung.
What's the meaning of all song?
'Let all things pass away.'

VII

The Soul. Seek out reality, leave things that seem.
The Heart. What, be a singer born and lack a theme?
The Soul. Isaiah's coal, what more can man desire?
The Heart. Struck dumb in the simplicity of fire!
The Soul. Look on that fire, salvation walks within.
The Heart. What theme had Homer but original sin?

VIII

Must we part, Von Hügel, though much alike, for we
Accept the miracles of the saints and honour sanctity?
The body of Saint Teresa lies undecayed in tomb,
Bathed in miraculous oil, sweet odours from it come,
Healing from its lettered slab. Those self-same hands perchance
Eternalised the body of a modern saint that once
Had scooped out Pharaoh's mummy. I–though heart might find relief
Did I become a Christian man and choose for my belief
What seems most welcome in the tomb–play a predestined part.
Homer is my example and his unchristened heart.
The lion and the honeycomb, what has Scripture said?
So get you gone, Von Hügel, though with blessings on your head.

The Tower: Part III

It is time that I wrote my will;
I choose upstanding men
That climb the streams until
The fountain leap, and at dawn
Drop their cast at the side
Of dripping stone; I declare
They shall inherit my pride,
The pride of people that were

Bound neither to Cause nor to State,
Neither to slaves that were spat on,
Nor to the tyrants that spat,
The people of Burke and of Grattan
That gave, though free to refuse—
Pride, like that of the morn,
When the headlong light is loose,
Or that of the fabulous horn,
Or that of the sudden shower
When all streams are dry,
Or that of the hour
When the swan must fix his eye
Upon a fading gleam,
Float out upon a long
Last reach of glittering stream
And there sing his last song.
And I declare my faith:
I mock Plotinus' thought
And cry in Plato's teeth,
Death and life were not
Till man made up the whole,
Made lock, stock and barrel
Out of his bitter soul,
Aye, sun and moon and star, all,
And further add to that
That, being dead, we rise,
Dream and so create
Translunar Paradise.
I have prepared my peace
With learned Italian things
And the proud stones of Greece,
Poet's imaginings
And memories of love,
Memories of the words of women,
All those things whereof
Man makes a superhuman
Mirror-resembling dream.

As at the loophole there
The daws chatter and scream,
And drop twigs layer upon layer.

When they have mounted up,
The mother bird will rest
On their hollow top,
And so warm her wild nest.

I leave both faith and pride
To young upstanding men
Climbing the mountain-side,
That under bursting dawn
They may drop a fly;
Being of that metal made
Till it was broken by
This sedentary trade.

Now shall I make my soul,
Compelling it to study
In a learned school
Till the wreck of body,
Slow decay of blood,
Testy delirium
Or dull decrepitude,
Or what worse evil come–
The death of friends, or death
Of every brilliant eye
That made a catch in the breath–
Seem but the clouds of the sky
When the horizon fades,
Or a bird's sleepy cry
Among the deepening shades.

Sailing to Byzantium

I

That is no country for old men. The young
In one another's arms, birds in the trees,
–Those dying generations–at their song,
The salmon-falls, the mackerel-crowded seas,
Fish, flesh, or fowl, commend all summer long
Whatever is begotten, born, and dies.
Caught in that sensual music all neglect
Monuments of unageing intellect.

II

An aged man is but a paltry thing,
A tattered coat upon a stick, unless
Soul clap its hands and sing, and louder sing
For every tatter in its mortal dress,
Nor is there singing school but studying
Monuments of its own magnificence;
And therefore I have sailed the seas and come
To the holy city of Byzantium.

III

O sages standing in God's holy fire
As in the gold mosaic of a wall,
Come from the holy fire, perne in a gyre,
And be the singing-masters of my soul.
Consume my heart away; sick with desire
And fastened to a dying animal
It knows not what it is; and gather me
Into the artifice of eternity.

IV

Once out of nature I shall never take
My bodily form from any natural thing,
But such a form as Grecian goldsmiths make
Of hammered gold and gold enamelling
To keep a drowsy Emperor awake;
Or set upon a golden bough to sing
To lords and ladies of Byzantium
Of what is past, or passing, or to come.

Among School Children

I

I walk through the long schoolroom questioning;
A kind old nun in a white hood replies;
The children learn to cipher and to sing,
To study reading-books and histories,
To cut and sew, be neat in everything
In the best modern way–the children's eyes
In momentary wonder stare upon
A sixty-year-old smiling public man.

II

I dream of a Ledaean body, bent
Above a sinking fire, a tale that she
Told of a harsh reproof, or trivial event
That changed some childish day to tragedy–
Told, and it seemed that our two natures blent
Into a sphere from youthful sympathy,
Or else, to alter Plato's parable,
Into the yolk and white of the one shell.

III

And thinking of that fit of grief or rage
I look upon one child or t'other there
And wonder if she stood so at that age–
For even daughters of the swan can share
Something of every paddler's heritage–
And had that colour upon cheek or hair,
And thereupon my heart is driven wild:
She stands before me as a living child.

IV

Her present image floats into the mind–
Did Quattrocento finger fashion it
Hollow of cheek as though it drank the wind
And took a mess of shadows for its meat?
And I though never of Ledaean kind
Had pretty plumage once–enough of that,
Better to smile on all that smile, and show
There is a comfortable kind of old scarecrow.

V

What youthful mother, a shape upon her lap
Honey of generation had betrayed,
And that must sleep, shriek, struggle to escape
As recollection or the drug decide,
Would think her son, did she but see that shape
With sixty or more winters on its head,
A compensation for the pang of his birth,
Or the uncertainty of his setting forth?

VI

Plato thought nature but a spume that plays
Upon a ghostly paradigm of things;
Solider Aristotle played the taws
Upon the bottom of a king of kings;
World-famous golden-thighed Pythagoras
Fingered upon a fiddle-stick or strings
What a star sang and careless Muses heard:
Old clothes upon old sticks to scare a bird.

VII

Both nuns and mothers worship images,
But those the candles light are not as those
That animate a mother's reveries,
But keep a marble or a bronze repose.
And yet they too break hearts–O Presences
That passion, piety or affection knows,
And that all heavenly glory symbolise–
O self-born mockers of man's enterprise;

VIII

Labour is blossoming or dancing where
The body is not bruised to pleasure soul,
Nor beauty born out of its own despair,
Nor blear-eyed wisdom out of midnight oil.
O chestnut-tree, great-rooted blossomer,
Are you the leaf, the blossom or the bole?
O body swayed to music, O brightening glance,
How can we know the dancer from the dance?

All Souls' Night

(Epilogue to *A Vision*)

Midnight has come, and the great Christ Church Bell
And many a lesser bell sound through the room;
And it is All Souls' Night,
And two long glasses brimmed with muscatel
Bubble upon the table. A ghost may come;
For it is a ghost's right,
His element is so fine
Being sharpened by his death,

To drink from the wine-breath
While our gross palates drink from the whole wine.

I need some mind that, if the cannon sound
From every quarter of the world, can stay
Wound in mind's pondering
As mummies in the mummy-cloth are wound;
Because I have a marvellous thing to say,
A certain marvellous thing
None but the living mock,
Though not for sober ear;
It may be all that hear
Should laugh and weep an hour upon the clock.

Horton's the first I call. He loved strange thought
And knew that sweet extremity of pride
That's called platonic love,
And that to such a pitch of passion wrought
Nothing could bring him, when his lady died,
Anodyne for his love.
Words were but wasted breath;
One dear hope had he:
The inclemency
Of that or the next winter would be death.

Two thoughts were so mixed up I could not tell
Whether of her or God he thought the most,
But think that his mind's eye,
When upward turned, on one sole image fell;
And that a slight companionable ghost,
Wild with divinity,
Had so lit up the whole
Immense miraculous house
The Bible promised us,
It seemed a gold-fish swimming in a bowl.

On Florence Emery I call the next,
Who finding the first wrinkles on a face
Admired and beautiful,
And knowing that the future would be vexed
With 'minished beauty, multiplied commonplace,
Preferred to teach a school

Away from neighbour or friend,
Among dark skins, and there
Permit foul years to wear
Hidden from eyesight to the unnoticed end.

Before that end much had she ravelled out
From a discourse in figurative speech
By some learned Indian
On the soul's journey. How it is whirled about,
Wherever the orbit of the moon can reach,
Until it plunge into the sun;
And there, free and yet fast,
Being both Chance and Choice,
Forget its broken toys
And sink into its own delight at last.

And I call up MacGregor from the grave,
For in my first hard springtime we were friends,
Although of late estranged.
I thought him half a lunatic, half knave,
And told him so, but friendship never ends;
And what if mind seem changed,
And it seem changed with the mind,
When thoughts rise up unbid
On generous things that he did
And I grow half contented to be blind!

He had much industry at setting out,
Much boisterous courage, before loneliness
Had driven him crazed;
For meditations upon unknown thought
Make human intercourse grow less and less;
They are neither paid nor praised.
But he'd object to the host,
The glass because my glass;
A ghost-lover he was
And may have grown more arrogant being a ghost.

But names are nothing. What matter who it be,
So that his elements have grown so fine
The fume of muscatel
Can give his sharpened palate ecstasy.

No living man can drink from the whole wine.
I have mummy truths to tell
Whereat the living mock,
Though not for sober ear,
For maybe all that hear
Should laugh and weep an hour upon the clock.

Such thought–such thought have I that hold it tight
Till meditation master all its parts,
Nothing can stay my glance
Until that glance run in the world's despite
To where the damned have howled away their hearts,
And where the blessed dance;
Such thought, that in it bound
I need no other thing,
Wound in mind's wandering
As mummies in the mummy-cloth are wound.

Lapis Lazuli

(for Harry Clifton)

I have heard that hysterical women say
They are sick of the palette and fiddle-bow,
Of poets that are always gay,
For everybody knows or else should know
That if nothing drastic is done
Aeroplane and Zeppelin will come out,
Pitch like King Billy bomb-balls in
Until the town lie beaten flat.

All perform their tragic play,
There struts Hamlet, there is Lear,
That's Ophelia, that Cordelia;
Yet they, should the last scene be there,
The great stage curtain about to drop,
If worthy their prominent part in the play,
Do not break up their lines to weep.
They know that Hamlet and Lear are gay;
Gaiety transfiguring all that dread.
All men have aimed at, found and lost;

Black out; Heaven blazing into the head:
Tragedy wrought to its uttermost.
Though Hamlet rambles and Lear rages,
And all the drop-scenes drop at once
Upon a hundred thousand stages,
It cannot grow by an inch or an ounce.

On their own feet they came, or on shipboard,
Camel-back, horse-back, ass-back, mule-back,
Old civilizations put to the sword.
Then they and their wisdom went to rack:
No handiwork of Callimachus,
Who handled marble as if it were bronze,
Made draperies that seemed to rise
When sea-wind swept the corner, stands;
His long lamp-chimney shaped like the stem
Of a slender palm, stood but a day;
All things fall and are built again,
And those that build them again are gay.

Two Chinamen, behind them a third,
Are carved in lapis lazuli,
Over them flies a long-legged bird,
A symbol of longevity;
The third, doubtless a serving-man,
Carries a musical instrument.

Every discoloration of the stone,
Every accidental crack or dent,
Seems a water-course or an avalanche,
Or lofty slope where it still snows
Though doubtless plum or cherry-branch
Sweetens the little half-way house
Those Chinamen climb towards, and I
Delight to imagine them seated there;
There, on the mountain and the sky,
On all the tragic scene they stare.
One asks for mournful melodies;
Accomplished fingers begin to play.
Their eyes mid many wrinkles, their eyes,
Their ancient, glittering eyes, are gay.

The Wheel

Through winter-time we call on spring,
And through the spring on summer call,
And when abounding hedges ring
Declare that winter's best of all;
And after that there's nothing good
Because the spring-time has not come–
Nor know that what disturbs our blood
Is but its longing for the tomb.

Laurence Binyon (*Br. 1869–1943*)

Bab-Lock-Hythe

In the time of wild roses
As up Thames we travelled
Where 'mid water-weeds ravelled
The lily uncloses,

To his old shores the river
A new song was singing,
And young shoots were springing
On old roots for ever.

Dog-daisies were dancing,
And flags flamed in cluster,
On the dark stream a lustre
Now blurred and now glancing.

A tall reed down-weighing,
The sedge-warbler fluttered;
One sweet note he uttered,
Then left it soft-swaying.

By the bank's sandy hollow
My dipt oars went beating,
And past our bows fleeting
Blue-backed shone the swallow.

High woods, heron-haunted,
Rose, changed, as we rounded
Old hills greenly mounded,
To meadows enchanted;

A dream ever moulded
Afresh for our wonder,
Still opening asunder
For the stream many-folded;

Till sunset was rimming
The west with pale flushes;
Behind the black rushes
The last light was dimming;

And the lonely stream, hiding
Shy birds, grew more lonely,
And with us was only
The noise of our gliding.

In clouds of gray weather
The evening o'erdarkened,
In the stillness we hearkened;
Our hearts sang together.

The Little Dancers

Lonely, save for a few faint stars, the sky
Dreams; and lonely, below, the little street
Into its gloom retires, secluded and shy.
Scarcely the dumb roar enters this soft retreat;
And all is dark, save where come flooding rays
From a tavern-window; there, to the brisk measure
Of an organ that down in an alley merrily plays,
Two children, all alone and no one by,
Holding their tattered frocks, thro' an airy maze
Of motion lightly threaded with nimble feet
Dance sedately; face to face they gaze,
Their eyes shining, grave with a perfect pleasure.

Lament

Fall now, my cold thoughts, frozen fall
My sad thoughts, over my heart
To be the tender burial
Of sweetness and of smart.

Fall soft as the snow, when all men sleep,
On copse and on bank forlorn,
That tenderly buries, yet buries deep
Frail violets, freshly born.

The Burning of the Leaves

Now is the time for the burning of the leaves.
They go to the fire; the nostril pricks with smoke
Wandering slowly into a weeping mist.
Brittle and blotched, ragged and rotten sheaves!
A flame seizes the smouldering ruin and bites
On stubborn stalks that crackle as they resist.

The last hollyhock's fallen tower is dust;
All the spices of June are a bitter reek,
All the extravagant riches spent and mean.
All burns! The reddest rose is a ghost;
Sparks whirl up, to expire in the mist: the wild
Fingers of fire are making corruption clean.

Now is the time for stripping the spirit bare,
Time for the burning of days ended and done,
Idle solace of things that have gone before:
Rootless hope and fruitless desire are there;
Let them go to the fire, with never a look behind.
The world that was ours is a world that is ours no more.

They will come again, the leaf and the flower, to arise
From squalor of rottenness into the old splendour,
And magical scents to a wondering memory bring;
The same glory, to shine upon different eyes.
Earth cares for her own ruins, naught for ours.
Nothing is certain, only the certain spring.

Edgar Lee Masters (*Am. 1869–1950*)

Petit, the Poet

Seeds in a dry pod, tick, tick, tick,
Tick, tick, tick, like mites in a quarrel–
Faint iambics that the full breeze wakens–
But the pine tree makes a symphony thereof.
Triolets, villanelles, rondels, rondeaus,
Ballades by the score with the same old thought:
The snows and the roses of yesterday are vanished;
And what is love but a rose that fades?
Life all around me here in the village:
Tragedy, comedy, valor and truth,
Courage, constancy, heroism, failure–
All in the loom, and oh what patterns!
Woodlands, meadows, streams and rivers–
Blind to all of it all my life long.
Triolets, villanelles, rondels, rondeaus,
Seeds in a dry pod, tick, tick, tick,
Tick, tick, tick, what little iambics,
While Homer and Whitman roared in the pines!

Anne Rutledge

Out of me unworthy and unknown
The vibrations of deathless music;
"With malice toward none, with charity for all."
Out of me the forgiveness of millions toward millions,
And the beneficent face of a nation
Shining with justice and truth.

I am Anne Rutledge who sleep beneath these weeds,
Beloved in life of Abraham Lincoln,
Wedded to him, not through union,
But through separation.
Bloom forever, O Republic,
From the dust of my bosom!

Lucinda Matlock

I went to the dances at Chandlerville,
And played snap-out at Winchester.
One time we changed partners,
Driving home in the moonlight of middle June,
And then I found Davis.
We were married and lived together for seventy years,
Enjoying, working, raising the twelve children,
Eight of whom we lost
Ere I had reached the age of sixty.
I spun, I wove, I kept the house, I nursed the sick,
I made the garden, and for holiday
Rambled over the fields where sang the larks,
And by Spoon River gathering many a shell,
And many a flower and medicinal weed–
Shouting to the wooded hills, singing to the green valleys.
At ninety-six I had lived enough, that is all,
And passed to a sweet repose.
What is this I hear of sorrow and weariness,
Anger, discontent and drooping hopes?
Degenerate sons and daughters,
Life is too strong for you–
It takes life to love Life.

Daisy Fraser

Did you ever hear of Editor Whedon
Giving to the public treasury any of the money he received
For supporting candidates for office?
Or for writing up the canning factory
To get people to invest?
Or for suppressing the facts about the bank,
When it was rotten and ready to break?
Did you ever hear of the Circuit Judge
Helping anyone except the "Q" railroad,
Or the bankers? Or did Rev. Peet or Rev. Sibley
Give any part of their salary, earned by keeping still,
Or speaking out as the leaders wished them to do,
To the building of the water works?

But I, Daisy Fraser, who always passed
Along the streets through rows of nods and smiles,
And coughs and words such as "there she goes,"
Never was taken before Justice Arnett
Without contributing ten dollars and costs
To the school fund of Spoon River!

Julia Miller

We quarreled that morning,
For he was sixty-five, and I was thirty,
And I was nervous and heavy with the child
Whose birth I dreaded.
I thought over the last letter written me
By that estranged young soul
Whose betrayal of me I had concealed
By marrying the old man.
Then I took morphine and sat down to read.
Across the blackness that came over my eyes
I see the flickering light of these words even now:
"And Jesus said unto him, Verily
I say unto thee, To-day thou shalt
Be with me in paradise."

Edwin Arlington Robinson (*Am. 1869–1935*)

George Crabbe

Give him the darkest inch your shelf allows,
Hide him in lonely garrets, if you will,–
But his hard, human pulse is throbbing still
With the sure strength that fearless truth
endows.
In spite of all fine science disavows,
Of his plain excellence and stubborn skill
There yet remains what fashion cannot kill,
Though years have thinned the laurel from
his brows.

Whether or not we read him, we can feel
From time to time the vigor of his name
Against us like a finger for the shame
And emptiness of what our souls reveal
In books that are as altars where we kneel
To consecrate the flicker, not the flame.

Many Are Called

The Lord Apollo, who has never died,
Still holds alone his immemorial reign,
Supreme in an impregnable domain
That with his magic he has fortified;
And though melodious multitudes have tried
In ecstasy, in anguish, and in vain,
With invocation sacred and profane
To lure him, even the loudest are outside.

Only at unconjectured intervals,
By will of him on whom no man may gaze,
By word of him whose law no man has read,
A questing light may rift the sullen walls,
To cling where mostly its infrequent rays
Fall golden on the patience of the dead.

The Clerks

I did not think that I should find them there
When I came back again; but there they stood,
As in the days they dreamed of when young blood
Was in their cheeks and women called them fair.
Be sure, they met me with an ancient air,-
And yes, there was a shop-worn brotherhood
About them; but the men were just as good,
And just as human as they ever were.

And you that ache so much to be sublime,
And you that feed yourselves with your descent,
What comes of all your visions and your fears?
Poets and kings are but the clerks of Time,
Tiering the same dull webs of discontent,
Clipping the same sad alnage of the years.

Zola

Because he puts the compromising chart
Of hell before your eyes, you are afraid;
Because he counts the price that you have paid
For innocence, and counts it from the start,
You loathe him. But he sees the human heart
Of God meanwhile, and in His hand was weighed
Your squeamish and emasculate crusade
Against the grim dominion of his art.

Never until we conquer the uncouth
Connivings of our shamed indifference
(We call it Christian faith) are we to scan
The racked and shrieking hideousness of Truth
To find, in hate's polluted self-defence
Throbbing, the pulse, the divine heart of man.

New England

Here where the wind is always north-north-east
And children learn to walk on frozen toes,
Wonder begets an envy of all those
Who boil elsewhere with such a lyric yeast
Of love that you will hear them at a feast
Where demons would appeal for some repose,
Still clamoring where the chalice overflows
And crying wildest who have drunk the least.

Passion is here a soilure of the wits,
We're told, and Love a cross for them to bear;
Joy shivers in the corner where she knits
And Conscience always has the rocking-chair,
Cheerful as when she tortured into fits
The first cat that was ever killed by Care.

Luke Havergal

Go to the western gate, Luke Havergal,
There where the vines cling crimson on the wall,
And in the twilight wait for what will come.
The leaves will whisper there of her, and some,

Like flying words, will strike you as they fall;
But go, and if you listen she will call.
Go to the western gate, Luke Havergal–
Luke Havergal.

No, there is not a dawn in eastern skies
To rift the fiery night that's in your eyes;
But there, where western glooms are gathering,
The dark will end the dark, if anything:
God slays Himself with every leaf that flies.
And hell is more than half of paradise.
No, there is not a dawn in eastern skies–
In eastern skies.

Out of a grave I come to tell you this,
Out of a grave I come to quench the kiss
That flames upon your forehead with a glow
That blinds you to the way that you must go.
Yes, there is yet one way to where she is,
Bitter, but one that faith may never miss.
Out of a grave I come to tell you this–
To tell you this.

There is the western gate, Luke Havergal,
There are the crimson leaves upon the wall.
Go, for the winds are tearing them away,–
Nor think to riddle the dead words they say,
Nor any more to feel them as they fall;
But go, and if you trust her she will call.
There is the western gate, Luke Havergal–
Luke Havergal.

Eros Turannos

She fears him, and will always ask
  What fated her to choose him;
She meets in his engaging mask
  All reasons to refuse him;
But what she meets and what she fears
Are less than are the downward years,
Drawn slowly to the foamless weirs
  Of age, were she to lose him.

Between a blurred sagacity
  That once had power to sound him,
And Love, that will not let him be
  The Judas that she found him,
Her pride assuages her almost,
As if it were alone the cost.—
He sees that he will not be lost.
  And waits and looks around him.

A sense of ocean and old trees
  Envelops and allures him;
Tradition, touching all he sees,
  Beguiles and reassures him;
And all her doubts of what he says
Are dimmed with what she knows of days—
Till even prejudice delays
  And fades, and she secures him.

The falling leaf inaugurates
  The reign of her confusion;
The pounding wave reverberates
  The dirge of her illusion;
And home, where passion lived and died,
Becomes a place where she can hide,
While all the town and harbor side
  Vibrate with her seclusion.

We tell you, tapping on our brows,
  The story as it should be,—
As if the story of a house
  Were told, or ever could be;
We'll have no kindly veil between
Her visions and those we have seen,—
As if we guessed what hers have been,
  Or what they are or would be.

Meanwhile we do no harm; for they
  That with a god have striven,
Not hearing much of what we say,
  Take what the god has given;

Though like waves breaking it may be,
Or like a changed familiar tree,
Or like a stairway to the sea
Where down the blind are driven.

Richard Cory

Whenever Richard Cory went down town,
We people on the pavement looked at him:
He was a gentleman from sole to crown,
Clean favored, and imperially slim.

And he was always quietly arrayed,
And he was always human when he talked;
But still he fluttered pulses when he said,
"Good morning," and he glittered when he walked.

And he was rich–yes, richer than a king–
And admirably schooled in every grace:
In fine, we thought that he was everything
To make us wish that we were in his place.

So on we worked, and waited for the light,
And went without the meat, and cursed the bread;
And Richard Cory, one calm summer night,
Went home and put a bullet through his head.

The Mill

The miller's wife had waited long,
The tea was cold, the fire was dead;
And there might yet be nothing wrong
In how he went and what he said:
"There are no millers any more,"
Was all that she had heard him say;
And he had lingered at the door
So long that it seemed yesterday.

Sick with a fear that had no form
She knew that she was there at last;
And in the mill there was a warm
And mealy fragrance of the past.

What else there was would only seem
To say again what he had meant;
And what was hanging from a beam
Would not have heeded where she went.

And if she thought it followed her,
She may have reasoned in the dark
That one way of the few there were
Would hide her and would leave no mark:
Black water, smooth above the weir
Like starry velvet in the night,
Though ruffled once, would soon appear
The same as ever to the sight.

The Man Against the Sky

Between me and the sunset, like a dome
Against the glory of a world on fire,
Now burned a sudden hill,
Bleak, round, and high, by flame-lit height made higher,
With nothing on it for the flame to kill
Save one who moved and was alone up there
To loom before the chaos and the glare
As if he were the last god going home
Unto his last desire.

Dark, marvelous, and inscrutable he moved on
Till down the fiery distance he was gone,
Like one of those eternal, remote things
That range across a man's imaginings
When a sure music fills him and he knows
What he may say thereafter to few men,–
The touch of ages having wrought
An echo and a glimpse of what he thought
A phantom or a legend until then;
For whether lighted over ways that save,
Or lured from all repose,
If he go on too far to find a grave,
Mostly alone he goes.

Even he, who stood where I had found him,
On high with fire all round him,
Who moved along the molten west,
And over the round hill's crest
That seemed half ready with him to go down,
Flame-bitten and flame-cleft,
As if there were to be no last thing left
Of a nameless unimaginable town,–
Even he who climbed and vanished may have
taken
Down to the perils of a depth not known,
From death defended though by men forsaken,
The bread that every man must eat alone;
He may have walked while others hardly dared
Look on to see him stand where many fell;
And upward out of that, as out of hell,
He may have sung and striven
To mount where more of him shall yet be
given,
Bereft of all retreat,
To sevenfold heat,–
As on a day when three in Dura shared
The furnace, and were spared
For glory by that king of Babylon
Who made himself so great that God, who heard,
Covered him with long feathers, like a bird.

Again, he may have gone down easily,
By comfortable altitudes, and found,
As always, underneath him solid ground
Whereon to be sufficient and to stand
Possessed already of the promised land,
Far stretched and fair to see:
A good sight, verily,
And one to make the eyes of her who bore him
Shine glad with hidden tears.
Why question of his ease of who before him,
In one place or another where they left
Their names as far behind them as their bones,
And yet by dint of slaughter toil and theft,

And shrewdly sharpened stones,
Carved hard the way for his ascendency
Through deserts of lost years?
Why trouble him now who sees and hears
No more than what his innocence requires,
And therefore to no other height aspires
Than one at which he neither quails nor tires?
He may do more by seeing what he sees
Than others eager for iniquities;
He may, by seeing all things for the best,
Incite futurity to do the rest.

Or with an even likelihood,
He may have met with atrabilious eyes
The fires of time on equal terms and passed
Indifferently down, until at last
His only kind of grandeur would have been,
Apparently, in being seen.
He may have had for evil or for good
No argument; he may have had no care
For what without himself went anywhere
To failure or to glory, and least of all
For such a stale, flamboyant miracle;
He may have been the prophet of an art
Immovable to old idolatries;
He may have been a player without a part,
Annoyed that even the sun should have the skies
For such a flaming way to advertise;
He may have been a painter sick at heart
With Nature's toiling for a new surprise;
He may have been a cynic, who now, for all
Of anything divine that his effete
Negation may have tasted,
Saw truth in his own image, rather small,
Forbore to fever the ephemeral,
Found any barren height a good retreat
From any swarming street,
And in the sun saw power superbly wasted;
And when the primitive old-fashioned stars
Came out again to shine on joys and wars

More primitive, and all arrayed for doom,
He may have proved a world a sorry thing
In his imagining,
And life a lighted highway to the tomb.

Or, mounting with infirm unsearching tread,
His hopes to chaos led,
He may have stumbled up there from the past,
And with an aching strangeness viewed the last
Abysmal conflagration of his dreams,–
A flame where nothing seems
To burn but flame itself, by nothing fed;
And while it all went out,
Not even the faint anodyne of doubt
May then have eased a painful going down
From pictured heights of power and lost renown,
Revealed at length to his outlived endeavor
Remote and unapproachable forever;
And at his heart there may have gnawed
Sick memories of a dead faith foiled and flawed
And long dishonored by the living death
Assigned alike by chance
To brutes and hierophants;
And anguish fallen on those he loved around him
May once have dealt the last blow to confound
him,
And so have left him as death leaves a child,
Who sees it all too near;
And he who knows no young way to forget
May struggle to the tomb unreconciled.
Whatever suns may rise or set
There may be nothing kinder for him here
Than shafts and agonies;
And under these
He may cry out and stay on horribly;
Or, seeing in death too small a thing to fear,
He may go forward like a stoic Roman
Where pangs and terrors in his pathway lie,–
Or, seizing the swift logic of a woman,
Curse God and die.

Or maybe there, like many another one
Who might have stood aloft and looked ahead,
Black-drawn against wild red,
He may have built, unawed by fiery gules
That in him no commotion stirred,
A living reason out of molecules
Why molecules occurred,
And one for smiling when he might have sighed
Had he seen far enough,
And in the same inevitable stuff
Discovered an odd reason too for pride
In being what he must have been by laws
Infrangible and for no kind of cause.
Deterred by no confusion or surprise
He may have seen with his mechanic eyes
A world without a meaning, and had room,
Alone amid magnificence and doom,
To build himself an airy monument
That should, or fail him in his vague intent,
Outlast an accidental universe–
To call it nothing worse–
Or, by the burrowing guile
Of Time disintegrated and effaced,
Like once-remembered mighty trees go down
To ruin, of which by man may now be traced
No part sufficient even to be rotten,
And in the book of things that are forgotten
Is entered as a thing not quite worth while.
He may have been so great
That satraps would have shivered at his frown,
And all he prized alive may rule a state
No larger than a grave that holds a clown;
He may have been a master of his fate,
And of his atoms,–ready as another
In his emergence to exonerate
His father and his mother;
He may have been a captain of a host,
Self-eloquent and ripe for prodigies,
Doomed here to swell by dangerous degrees,
And then give up the ghost.

Nahum's great grasshoppers were such as these,
Sun-scattered and soon lost.

Whatever the dark road he may have taken,
This man who stood on high
And faced alone the sky,
Whatever drove or lured or guided him,–
A vision answering a faith unshaken,
An easy trust assumed of easy trials,
A sick negation born of weak denials,
A crazed abhorrence of an old condition,
A blind attendance on a brief ambition,–
Whatever stayed him or derided him,
His way was even as ours;
And we, with all our wounds and all our powers,
Must each await alone at his own height
Another darkness or another light;
And there, of our poor self dominion reft,
If inference and reason shun
Hell, Heaven, and Oblivion,
May thwarted will (perforce precarious,
But for our conservation better thus)
Have no misgiving left
Of doing yet what here we leave undone?
Or if unto the last of these we cleave,
Believing or protesting we believe
In such an idle and ephemeral
Florescence of the diabolical,–
If, robbed of two fond old enormities,
Our being had no onward auguries,
What then were this great love of ours to say
For launching other lives to voyage again
A little farther into time and pain,
A little faster in a futile chase
For a kingdom and a power and a Race
That would have still in sight
A manifest end of ashes and eternal night?
Is this the music of the toys we shake
So loud,–as if there might be no mistake
Somewhere in our indomitable will?

Are we no greater than the noise we make
Along one blind atomic pilgrimage
Whereon by crass chance billeted we go
Because our brains and bones and cartilage
Will have it so?
If this we say, then let us all be still
About our share in it, and live and die
More quietly thereby.

Where was he going, this man against the sky?
You know not, nor do I.
But this we know, if we know anything:
That we may laugh and fight and sing
And of our transience here make offering
To an orient Word that will not be erased,
Or, save in incommunicable gleams
Too permanent for dreams,
Be found or known.
No tonic and ambitious irritant
Of increase or of want
Has made an otherwise insensate waste
Of ages overthrown
A ruthless, veiled, implacable foretaste
Of other ages that are still to be
Depleted and rewarded variously
Because a few, by fate's economy,
Shall seem to move the world the way it goes;
No soft evangel of equality,
Safe-cradled in a communal repose
That huddles into death and may at last
Be covered well with equatorial snows–
And all for what, the devil only knows–
Will aggregate an inkling to confirm
The credit of a sage or of a worm,
Or tell us why one man in five
Should have a care to stay alive
While in his heart he feels no violence
Laid on his humor and intelligence
When infant Science makes a pleasant face
And waves again that hollow toy, the Race;

No planetary trap where souls are wrought
For nothing but the sake of being caught
And sent again to nothing will attune
Itself to any key of any reason
Why man should hunger through another season
To find out why 'twere better late than soon
To go away and let the sun and moon
And all the silly stars illuminate
A place for creeping things,
And those that root and trumpet and have wings,
And herd and ruminate,
Or dive and flash and poise in rivers and seas,
Or by their loyal tails in lofty trees
Hang screeching lewd victorious derision
Of man's immortal vision.

Shall we, because Eternity records
Too vast an answer for the time-born words
We spell, whereof so many are dead that once
In our capricious lexicons
Were so alive and final, hear no more
The Word itself, the living word
That none alive has ever heard
Or ever spelt,
And few have ever felt
Without the fears and old surrenderings
And terrors that began
When Death let fall a feather from his wings
And humbled the first man?
Because the weight of our humility,
Wherefrom we gain
A little wisdom and much pain,
Falls here too sore and there too tedious,
Are we in anguish or complacency,
Not looking far enough ahead
To see by what mad couriers we are led
Along the roads of the ridiculous,
To pity ourselves and laugh at faith
And while we curse life bear it?
And if we see the soul's dead end in death,
Are we to fear it?

What folly is here that has not yet a name
Unless we say outright that we are liars?
What have we seen beyond our sunset fires
That lights again the way by which we came?
Why pay we such a price, and one we give
So clamoringly, for each racked empty day
That leads one more last human hope away,
As quiet fiends would lead past our crazed eyes
Our children to an unseen sacrifice?
If after all that we have lived and thought,
All comes to Nought,–
If there be nothing after now,
And we be nothing anyhow,
And we know that,–why live?
'Twere sure but weaklings' vain distress
To suffer dungeons where so many doors
Will open on the cold eternal shores
That look sheer down
To the dark tideless floods of Nothingness
Where all who know may drown.

Hilaire Belloc (*Br. 1870–1953*)

Ballade of Hell and of Mrs. Roebeck

I

I'm going out to dine at Gray's
  With Bertie Morden, Charles and Kit,
And Manderly who never pays,
  And Jane who wins in spite of it,
  And Algernon who won't admit
The truth about his curious hair
  And teeth that very nearly fit:–
And Mrs. Roebeck will be there.

II

And then to-morrow someone says
  That someone else has made a hit
In one of Mister Twister's plays.
  And off we go to yawn at it;
  And when it's petered out we quit
For number 20, Taunton Square,
  And smoke, and drink, and dance a bit:–
And Mrs. Roebeck will be there.

III

And so through each declining phase
  Of emptied effort, jaded wit,
And day by day of London days
  Obscurely, more obscurely, lit;
  Until the uncertain shadows flit
Announcing to the shuddering air
  A Darkening, and the end of it:–
And Mrs. Roebeck will be there.

Envoi

Prince, on their iron thrones they sit,
  Impassible to our despair,
The dreadful Guardians of the Pit:–
  And Mrs. Roebeck will be there.

Ballade of the Heresiarchs

I

John Calvin whose peculiar fad
  It was to call God murderous,
Which further led that feverish cad
  To burn alive the Servetus.
The horrible Bohemian Huss,
  The tedious Wycliffe, where are they?
But where is old Nestorius?
  The wind has blown them all away.

II

The Kohen out of Novdograd
Who argued from the Roman Jus
"*Privata fasta nihil ad*
Rem nisi sint de sacribus."
And Hume, who made a dreadful fuss
About the Resurrection Day
And said it was ridiculous–
The wind has blown them all away.

III

Of Smith the gallant Mormon lad
That took of wives an over-plus:
Johanna Southcott who was mad
And nasty Nietzsche, who was worse.
Of Tolstoy, the Eccentric Russ,
Our strong Posterity shall say:
"Lord Jesus! What are these to us?
The wind has blown them all away!"

Envoi

Prince, should you meet upon a bus
A man who makes a great display
Of Dr. Haeckel, argue thus:–
The wind has blown them all away.

The Garden Party

The Rich arrived in pairs
And also in Rolls Royces;
They talked of their affairs
In loud and strident voices.

(The Husbands and the Wives
Of this select society
Lead independent lives
Of infinite variety.)

The Poor arrived in Fords,
Whose features they resembled;
They laughed to see so many Lords
And Ladies all assembled.

The People in Between
Looked underdone and harassed
And out of place and mean,
And horribly embarrassed.

For the hoary social curse
Gets hoarier and hoarier,
And it stinks a trifle worse
Than in the days of Queen Victoria,
When they married and gave in marriage,
They danced at the County Ball,
And some of them kept a carriage.
And the flood destroyed them all.

Cuckoo!

In woods so long time bare.
  Cuckoo!
Up and in the wood, I know not where
Two notes fall.
Yet I do not envy him at all
His phantasy.
Cuckoo!
I too,
Somewhere,
I have sung as merrily as he
Who can dare,
Small and careless lover, so to laugh at care,
And who
Can call
Cuckoo!
In woods of winter weary,
In scented woods, of winter weary, call
Cuckoo!
In woods so long time bare.

EPIGRAMS

The Telephone

To-night in million-voicèd London I
Was lonely as the million-pointed sky
Until your single voice. Ah! So the sun
Peoples all heaven, although he be but one.

The Statue

When we are dead, some Hunting-boy will pass
And find a stone half-hidden in tall grass
And grey with age: but having seen that stone
(Which was your image), ride more slowly on.

On a Dead Hostess

Of this bad world the loveliest and the best
Has smiled and said "Good Night", and gone to rest.

On a Sundial

Stealthy the silent hours advance, and still;
And each may wound you, and the last shall kill.

On Mundane Acquaintances

Good morning, Algernon: Good morning, Percy.
Good morning, Mrs. Roebeck. Christ have mercy!

On a General Election

The accursèd power which stands on Privilege
(And goes with Women, and Champagne and Bridge)
Broke–and Democracy resumed her reign:
(Which goes with Bridge, and Women and Champagne).

The Pacifist

Pale Ebenezer thought it wrong to fight,
But Roaring Bill (who killed him) thought it right.

Fatigue

I'm tired of Love: I'm still more tired of Rhyme.
But Money gives me pleasure all the time.

W. H. Davies (*Br. 1871–1940*)

The Moon

Thy beauty haunts me heart and soul,
  Oh thou fair moon, so close and bright;
Thy beauty makes me like the child,
  That cries aloud to own thy light:
The little child that lifts each arm,
To press thee to her bosom warm.

Though there are birds that sing this night
  With thy white beams across their throats,
Let my deep silence speak for me
  More than for them their sweetest notes:
Who worships thee till music fails,
Is greater than thy nightingales.

A Great Time

Sweet Chance, that led my steps abroad,
  Beyond the town, where wild flowers grow–
A rainbow and a cuckoo, Lord,
  How rich and great the times are now!
    Know, all ye sheep
    And cows, that keep
On staring that I stand so long
  In grass that's wet from heavy rain–
A rainbow and a cuckoo's song
  May never come together again;
    May never come
    This side the tomb.

The Bird of Paradise

Here comes Kate Summers who, for gold,
  Takes any man to bed:
"You knew my friend, Nell Barnes," said she;
  "You knew Nell Barnes–she's dead.

"Nell Barnes was bad on all you men,
Unclean, a thief as well;
Yet all my life I have not found
A better friend than Nell.

"So I sat at her side at last,
For hours, till she was dead;
And yet she had no sense at all
Of any word I said.

"For all her cry but came to this–
'Not for the world! Take care:
Don't touch that bird of paradise,
Perched on the bedpost there!'

"I asked her would she like some grapes,
Some damsons ripe and sweet;
A custard made with new-laid eggs,
Or tender fowl to eat.

"I promised I would follow her,
To see her in her grave;
And buy a wreath with borrowed pence,
If nothing I could save.

"Yet still her cry but came to this–
'Not for the world! Take care:
Don't touch that bird of paradise,
Perched on the bedpost there!'"

The Kingfisher

It was the Rainbow gave thee birth,
And left thee all her lovely hues;
And, as her mother's name was Tears,
So runs it in thy blood to choose
For haunts the lonely pools, and keep
In company with trees that weep.

Go you and, with such glorious hues,
Live with proud Peacocks in green parks;
On lawns as smooth as shining glass,
Let every feather show its marks;
Get thee on boughs and clap thy wings
Before the windows of proud kings.

Nay, lovely Bird, thou art not vain;
  Thou hast no proud ambitious mind;
I also love a quiet place
  That's green, away from all mankind;
A lonely pool, and let a tree
Sigh with her bosom over me.

Ralph Hodgson (*Br. 1871–1940*)

The Bull

See an old unhappy bull,
Sick in soul and body both,
Slouching in the undergrowth
Of the forest beautiful,
Banished from the herd he led,
Bulls and cows a thousand head.

Cranes and gaudy parrots go
Up and down the burning sky;
Tree-top cats purr drowsily
In the dim-day green below;
And troops of monkeys, nutting, some,
All disputing, go and come;

And things abominable sit
Picking offal buck or swine,
On the mess and over it
Burnished flies and beetles shine,
And spiders big as bladders lie
Under hemlocks ten foot high;

And a dotted serpent curled
Round and round and round a tree,
Yellowing its greenery,
Keeps a watch on all the world,
All the world and this old bull
In the forest beautiful.

Bravely by his fall he came:
One he led, a bull of blood
Newly come to lustihood,
Fought and put his prince to shame,
Snuffed and pawed the prostrate head
Tameless even while it bled.

There they left him, every one,
Left him there without a lick,
Left him for the birds to pick,
Left him there for carrion,
Vilely from their bosom cast
Wisdom, worth and love at last.

When the lion left his lair
And roared his beauty through the hills,
And the vultures pecked their quills
And flew into the middle air,
Then this prince no more to reign
Came to life and lived again.

He snuffed the herd in far retreat,
He saw the blood upon the ground,
And snuffed the burning airs around
Still with beevish odours sweet,
While the blood ran down his head
And his mouth ran slaver red.

Pity him, this fallen chief,
All his splendour, all his strength,
All his body's breadth and length
Dwindled down with shame and grief,
Half the bull he was before,
Bones and leather, nothing more.

See him standing dewlap-deep
In the rushes at the lake,
Surly, stupid, half asleep,
Waiting for his heart to break
And the birds to join the flies
Feasting at his bloodshot eyes;

Standing with his head hung down
In a stupor, dreaming things:
Green savannas, jungles brown,
Battlefields and bellowings,
Bulls undone and lions dead
And vultures flapping overhead.

Dreaming things: of days he spent
With his mother gaunt and lean
In the valley warm and green,
Full of baby wonderment,
Blinking out of silly eyes
At a hundred mysteries;

Dreaming over once again
How he wandered with a throng
Of bulls and cows a thousand strong,
Wandered on from plain to plain,
Up the hill and down the dale,
Always at his mother's tail;

How he lagged behind the herd,
Lagged and tottered, weak of limb,
And she turned and ran to him
Blaring at the loathly bird
Stationed always in the skies,
Waiting for the flesh that dies.

Dreaming maybe of a day
When her drained and drying paps
Turned him to the sweets and saps,
Richer fountains by the way,
And she left the bull she bore
And he looked to her no more;

And his little frame grew stout,
And his little legs grew strong,
And the way was not so long;
And his little horns came out,
And he played at butting trees
And boulder-stones and tortoises,

Joined a game of knobby skulls
With the youngsters of his year,
All the other little bulls,
Learning both to bruise and bear,
Learning how to stand a shock
Like a little bull of rock.

Dreaming of a day less dim,
Dreaming of a time less far,
When the faint but certain star
Of destiny burned clear for him,
And a fierce and wild unrest
Broke the quiet of his breast,

And the gristles of his youth
Hardened in his comely pow,
And he came to fighting growth,
Beat his bull and won his cow,
And flew his tail and trampled off
Past the tallest, vain enough,

And curved about in splendour full
And curved again and snuffed the airs
As who should say Come out who dares!
And all beheld a bull, a Bull,
And knew that here was surely one
That backed for no bull, fearing none.

And the leader of the herd
Looked and saw, and beat the ground,
And shook the forest with his sound,
Bellowed at the loathly bird
Stationed always in the skies,
Waiting for the flesh that dies,

Dreaming, this old bull forlorn,
Surely dreaming of the hour
When he came to sultan power,
And they owned him master-horn,
Chiefest bull of all among
Bulls and cows a thousand strong;

And in all the tramping herd
Not a bull that barred his way,
Not a cow that said him nay,
Not a bull or cow that erred
In the furnace of his look
Dared a second, worse rebuke;

Not in all the forest wide,
Jungle, thicket, pasture, fen,
Not another dared him then,
Dared him and again defied;
Not a sovereign buck or boar
Came a second time for more;

Not a serpent that survived
Once the terrors of his hoof
Risked a second time reproof,
Came a second time and lived,
Not a serpent in its skin
Came again for discipline;

Not a leopard bright as flame,
Flashing fingerhooks of steel
That a wooden tree might feel,
Met his fury once and came
For a second reprimand,
Not a leopard in the land;

Not a lion of them all,
Not a lion of the hills,
Hero of a thousand kills,
Dared a second fight and fall,
Dared that ram terrific twice,
Paid a second time the price.

Pity him, this dupe of dream,
Leader of the herd again
Only in his daft old brain,
Once again the bull supreme
And bull enough to bear the part
Only in his tameless heart.

Pity him that he must wake;
Even now the swarm of flies
Blackening his bloodshot eyes
Bursts and blusters round the lake,
Scattered from the feast half-fed,
By great shadows overhead;

And the dreamer turns away
From his visionary herds
And his splendid yesterday,
Turns to meet the loathly birds
Flocking round him from the skies,
Waiting for the flesh that dies.

Reason has Moons

Reason has moons, but moons not hers
  Lie mirror'd on her sea,
Confounding her astronomers,
  But, O! delighting me.

* * * *

Babylon–where I go dreaming
When I weary of to-day,
Weary of a world grown grey.

God loves an idle rainbow,
No less than labouring seas.

Walter de la Mare (*Br. 1873–1956*)

The Listeners

"Is there anybody there?" said the Traveller,
  Knocking on the moonlit door;
And his horse in the silence champed the grasses
  Of the forest's ferny floor:
And a bird flew up out of the turret,
  Above the Traveller's head:
And he smote upon the door again a second time;
  "Is there anybody there?" he said.

But no one descended to the Traveller;
  No head from the leaf-fringed sill
Leaned over and looked into his grey eyes,
  Where he stood perplexed and still.
But only a host of phantom listeners
  That dwelt in the lone house then
Stood listening in the quiet of the moonlight
  To that voice from the world of men:
Stood thronging the faint moonbeams on the dark stair,
  That goes down to the empty hall,
Hearkening in an air stirred and shaken
  By the lonely Traveller's call.
And he felt in his heart their strangeness,
  Their stillness answering his cry,
While his horse moved, cropping the dark turf,
  'Neath the starred and leafy sky;
For he suddenly smote on the door, even
  Louder, and lifted his head:–
"Tell them I came, and no one answered,
  That I kept my word," he said.
Never the least stir made the listeners,
  Though every word he spake
Fell echoing through the shadowiness of the still house
  From the one man left awake:
Ay, they heard his foot upon the stirrup,
  And the sound of iron on stone,
And how the silence surged softly backward,
  When the plunging hoofs were gone.

The Moth

Isled in the midnight air,
Musked with the dark's faint bloom,
Out into glooming and secret haunts
  The flame cries, "Come!"

Lovely in dye and fan,
A-tremble in shimmering grace,
A moth from her winter swoon
  Uplifts her face:

Stares from her glamorous eyes;
Wafts her on plumes like mist;
In ecstasy swirls and sways
To her strange tryst.

Napoleon

"What is the world, O soldiers?
It is I:
I, this incessant snow,
This northern sky;
Soldiers, this solitude
Through which we go
Is I."

An Epitaph

Here lies a most beautiful lady,
Light of step and heart was she;
I think she was the most beautiful lady
That ever was in the West Country.

But beauty vanishes; beauty passes;
However rare–rare it be;
And when I crumble, who will remember
This lady of the West Country?

The Stranger

Half-hidden in a graveyard,
In the blackness of a yew,
Where never living creature stirs,
Nor sunbeam pierces through,

Is a tomb-stone, green and crooked–
Its faded legend gone–
With one rain-worn cherub's head
To sing of the unknown.

There, when the dusk is falling,
Silence broods so deep
It seems that every air that breathes
Sighs from the fields of sleep.

Day breaks in heedless beauty,
  Kindling each drop of dew,
But unforsaking shadow dwells
  Beneath this lonely yew.

And, all else lost and faded,
  Only this listening head
Keeps with a strange unanswering smile
  Its secret with the dead.

Alulvan

The sun is clear of bird and cloud,
The grass shines windless, grey, and still,
In dusky ruin the owl dreams on,
The cuckoo echoes on the hill;
  Yet soft along Alulvan's walks
    The ghost at noonday stalks.

His eyes in shadow of his hat
Stare on the ruins of his house;
His cloak, up-fastened with a brooch,
Of faded velvet, grey as mouse,
  Brushes the roses as he goes:
    Yet wavers not one rose.

The wild birds in a cloud fly up
From their sweet feeding in the fruit;
The droning of the bees and flies
Rises gradual as a lute;
  Is it for fear the birds are flown,
    And shrills the insect-drone?

Thick is the ivy o'er Alulvan,
And crisp with summer-heat its turf;
Far, far across its empty pastures
Alulvan's sands are white with surf:
  And he himself is grey as the sea,
    Watching beneath an elder-tree.

All night the fretful, shrill Banshee
Lurks in the chambers' dark festoons,
Calling for ever, o'er garden and river,
Through magpie changing of the moons:
"Alulvan, O, alas! Alulvan,
The doom of lone Alulvan!"

The Keys of Morning

While at her bedroom window once,
Learning her task for school,
Little Louisa lonely sat
In the morning clear and cool,
She slanted her small, bead-brown eyes
Across the empty street,
And saw Death softly watching her
In the sunshine pale and sweet.

His was a long lean sallow face;
He sat with half-shut eyes,
Like an old sailor in a ship
Becalmed 'neath tropic skies.
Beside him in the dust he had set
His staff and shady hat;
These, peeping small, Louisa saw
Quite clearly where she sat–
The thinness of his coal-black locks,
His hands so long and lean
They scarcely seemed to grasp at all
The keys that hung between:
Both were of gold, but one was small,
And with this last did he
Wag in the air, as if to say,
"Come hither, child, to me!"

Louisa laid her lesson book
On the cold window-sill;
And in the sleepy sunshine house
Went softly down, until
She stood in the half-opened door,
And peeped. But strange to say,

Where Death just now had sunning sat
 Only a shadow lay:
Just the tall chimney's round-topped cowl,
 And the small sun behind,
Had with its shadow in the dust
 Called sleepy Death to mind.
But most she thought how strange it was
 Two keys that he should bear,
And that, when beckoning, he should wag
 The littlest in the air.

The Ghost

"Who knocks?" "I, who was beautiful,
 Beyond all dreams to restore,
I, from the roots of the dark thorn am hither.
 And knock on the door."
"Who speaks?" "I–once was my speech
 Sweet as the bird's on the air,
When echo lurks by the waters to heed;
 'Tis I speak thee fair."
"Dark is the hour!" "Ay, and cold."
 "Lone is my house." "Ah, but mine?"
"Sight, touch, lips, eyes yearned in vain."
 "Long dead these to thine. . . ."
Silence. Still faint on the porch
 Brake the flames of the stars.
In gloom groped a hope-wearied hand
 Over keys, bolts, and bars.
A face peered. All the grey night
 In chaos of vacancy shone;
Nought but vast sorrow was there–
 The sweet cheat gone.

Lovelocks

I watched the Lady Caroline
Bind up her dark and beauteous hair;
Her face was rosy in the glass,
And 'twixt the coils her hands would pass,
 White in the candleshine.

Her bottles on the table lay,
Stoppered, yet sweet of violet;
Her image in the mirror stooped
To view those locks as lightly looped
  As cherry-boughs in May.

The snowy night lay dim without,
I heard the Waits their sweet song sing;
The window smouldered keen with frost;
Yet still she twisted, sleeked and tossed
  Her beauteous hair about.

Echo

"Who called?" I said, and the words
  Through the whispering glades,
Hither, thither, baffled the birds–
  "Who called? Who called?"

The leafy boughs on high
  Hissed in the sun;
The dark air carried my cry
  Fainitngly on:

Eyes in the green, in the shade,
  In the motionless brake,
Voices that said what I said,
  For mockery's sake:

"Who cares?" I bawled through my tears;
  The wind fell low:
In the silence, "Who cares? Who cares?"
  Wailed to and fro.

Winter

Green mistletoe!
Oh, I remember now
A dell of snow,
Frost on the bough;
None there but I:
Snow, snow, and a wintry sky.

None there but I,
And footprints one by one,
Zigzaggedly,
Where I had run;
Where shrill and powdery
A robin sat in the tree.

And he whistled sweet;
And I in the crusted snow
With snow-clubbed feet
Jigged to and fro,
Till, from the day,
The rose-light ebbed away.

And the robin flew
Into the air, the air,
The white mist through;
And small and rare
The night-frost fell
Into the calm and misty dell.

And the dusk gathered low,
And the silver moon and stars
On the frozen snow
Drew taper bars,
Kindled winking fires
In the hooded briers.

And the sprawling Bear
Growled deep in the sky;
And Orion's hair
Streamed sparkling by:
But the North sighed low:
"*Snow, snow, more snow!*"

The Funeral

They dressed us up in black,
Susan and Tom and me;
And, walking through the fields
All beautiful to see,

With branches high in the air
And daisy and buttercup,
We heard the lark in the clouds,–
In black dressed up.

They took us to the graves,
Susan and Tom and me,
Where the long grasses grow
And the funeral tree:
We stood and watched; and the wind
Came softly out of the sky
And blew in Susan's hair,
As I stood close by.

Back through the fields we came,
Tom and Susan and me,
And we sat in the nursery together,
And had our tea.
And, looking out of the window,
I heard the thrushes sing;
But Tom fell asleep in his chair.
He was so tired, poor thing.

The Song of the Mad Prince

Who said, "Peacock Pie"?
  The old King to the sparrow:
Who said, "Crops are ripe"?
  Rust to the harrow:
Who said, "Where sleeps she now?
  Where rests she now her head,
Bathed in eve's loveliness"?–
  That's what I said.

Who said, "Ay, mum's the word"?
  Sexton to willow:
Who said, "Green dusk for dreams,
  Moss for a pillow"?
Who said, "All Time's delight
  Hath she for narrow bed;
Life's troubled bubble broken"?–
  That's what I said.

Vain Questioning

What needest thou?–a few brief hours of rest
Wherein to seek thyself in thine own breast;
A transient silence wherein truth could say
Such was thy constant hope, and this thy way?–
  O burden of life that is
  A livelong tangle of perplexities!

What seekest thou?–a truce from that thou art;
Some steadfast refuge from a fickle heart;
Still to be thou, and yet no thing of scorn,
To find no stay here, and yet not forlorn?–
  O riddle of life that is
  An endless war 'twixt contrarieties.

Leave this vain questioning. Is not sweet the rose?
Sings not the wild bird ere to rest he goes?
Hath not in miracle brave June returned?
Burns not her beauty as of old it burned?
  O foolish one to roam
  So far in thine own mind away from home!

Where blooms the flower when her petals fade,
Where sleepeth echo by earth's music made,
Where all things transient to the changeless win,
There waits the peace thy spirit dwelleth in.

Clear Eyes

Clear eyes do dim at last,
  And cheeks outlive their rose.
Time, heedless of the past,
  No loving-kindness knows;
Chill unto mortal lip
  Still Lethe flows.

Griefs, too, but brief while stay,
  And sorrow, being o'er,
Its salt tears shed away,
  Woundeth the heart no more.
Stealthily lave those waters
  That solemn shore.

Ah, then, sweet face, burn on,
While yet quick memory lives!
And Sorrow, ere thou art gone,
Know that my heart forgives–
Ere yet, grown cold in peace,
It loves not, nor grieves.

Fare Well

When I lie where shades of darkness
Shall no more assail mine eyes,
Nor the rain make lamentation
When the wind sighs;
How will fare the world whose wonder
Was the very proof of me?
Memory fades, must the remembered
Perishing be?

Oh, when this my dust surrenders
Hand, foot, lip, to dust again,
May these loved and loving faces
Please other men!
May the rusting harvest hedgerow
Still the Traveller's Joy entwine,
And as happy children gather
Posies once mine.

Look thy last on all things lovely,
Every hour. Let no night
Seal thy sense in deathly slumber
Till to delight
Thou have paid thy utmost blessing;
Since that all things thou wouldst praise
Beauty took from those who loved them
In other days.

Amy Lowell (*Am. 1874–1925*)

Lilacs

Lilacs,
False blue,
White,
Purple,
Colour of lilac,
Your great puffs of flowers
Are everywhere in this my New England.
Among your heart-shaped leaves
Orange orioles hop like music-box birds and sing
Their little weak soft songs;
In the crooks of your branches
The bright eyes of song sparrows sitting on spotted eggs
Peer restlessly through the light and shadow
Of all Springs.
Lilacs in dooryards
Holding quiet conversations with an early moon;
Lilacs watching a deserted house
Settling sideways into the grass of an old road;
Lilacs, wind-beaten, staggering under a lopsided shock of bloom
Above a cellar dug into a hill.
You are everywhere.
You were everywhere.
You tapped the window when the preacher preached his sermon,
And ran along the road beside the boy going to school.
You stood by pasture-bars to give the cows good milking,
You persuaded the housewife that her dish pan was of silver
And her husband an image of pure gold.
You flaunted the fragrance of your blossoms
Through the wide doors of Custom Houses–
You, and sandalwood, and tea,
Charging the noses of quill-driving clerks
When a ship was in from China.
You called to them: "Goose-quill men, goose-quill men,
May is a month for flitting,"
Until they writhed on their high stools
And wrote poetry on their letter-sheets behind the propped-up
ledgers.

Paradoxical New England clerks,
Writing inventories in ledgers, reading the "Song of Solomon" at night,
So many verses before bed time,
Because it was the Bible.
The dead fed you
Amid the slant stones of graveyards.
Pale ghosts who planted you
Came in the night time
And let their thin hair blow through your clustered stems.
You are of the green sea,
And of the stone hills which reach a long distance.
You are of elm-shaded streets with little shops where they sell kites and marbles,
You are of great parks where everyone walks and nobody is at home.
You cover the blind sides of greenhouses
And lean over the top to say a hurry-word through the glass
To your friends, the grapes, inside.

Lilacs,
False blue,
White,
Purple,
Colour of lilac,
You have forgotten your Eastern origin,
The veiled women with eyes like panthers,
The swollen, aggressive turbans of jewelled Pashas.
Now you are a very decent flower,
A reticent flower,
A curiously clear-cut, candid flower,
Standing beside clean doorways,
Friendly to a house-cat and a pair of spectacles,
Making poetry out of a bit of moonlight
And a hundred or two sharp blossoms.

Maine knows you,
Has for years and years;
New Hampshire knows you,
And Massachusetts
And Vermont.

Cape Cod starts you along the beaches to Rhode Island;
Connecticut takes you from a river to the sea.
You are brighter than apples,
Sweeter than tulips,
You are the great flood of our souls
Bursting above the leaf-shapes of our hearts,
You are the smell of all Summers,
The love of wives and children,
The recollection of the gardens of little children,
You are State Houses and Charters
And the familiar treading of the foot to and fro on a road it knows.
May is lilac here in New England,
May is a thrush singing "Sun up!" on a tip-top ash-tree,
May is white clouds behind pine-trees
Puffed out and marching upon a blue sky.
May is a green as no other,
May is much sun through small leaves,
May is soft earth,
And apple-blossoms,
And windows open to a South wind.
May is a full light wind of lilac
From Canada to Narragansett Bay.

Lilacs,
False blue,
White,
Purple,
Colour of lilac.
Heart-leaves of lilac all over New England,
Roots of lilac under all the soil of New England.
Lilac in me because I am New England,
Because my roots are in it,
Because my leaves are of it,
Because my flowers are for it,
Because it is my country
And I speak to it of itself
And sing of it with my own voice
Since certainly it is mine.

Gordon Bottomley (*Br. 1874–1948*)

The End of the World

The snow had fallen many nights and days;
The sky was come upon the earth at last,
Sifting thinly down as endlessly
As though within the system of blind planets
Something had been forgot or overdriven.
The dawn now seemed neglected in the grey
Where mountains were unbuilt and shadowless trees
Rootlessly paused or hung upon the air.
There was no wind, but now and then a sigh
Crossed that dry falling dust and rifted it
Through crevices of slate and door and casement.
Perhaps the new moon's time was even past.
Outside, the first white twilights were too void
Until a sheep called once, as to a lamb,
And tenderness crept everywhere from it;
But now the flock must have strayed far away.
The lights across the valley must be veiled,
The smoke lost in the greyness or the dusk,
For more than three days now the snow had thatched
That cow-house roof where it had ever melted
With yellow stains from the beasts' breath inside;
But yet a dog howled there, though not quite lately.
Someone passed down the valley swift and singing,
Yes, with locks spreaded like a son of morning;
But if he seemed too tall to be a man
It was that men had been so long unseen,
Or shapes loom larger through a moving snow.
And he was gone and food had not been given him.
When snow slid from an overweighted leaf,
Shaking the tree, it might have been a bird
Slipping in sleep or shelter, whirring wings;
Yet never bird fell out, save once a dead one–
And in two days the snow had covered it.
The dog had howled again–or thus it seemed
Until a lean fox passed and cried no more.
All was so safe indoors where life went on
Glad of the close, enfolding snow–O glad

To be safe and secret at its heart,
Watching the strangeness of familiar things.
They knew not what dim hours went on, went by,
For while they slept the clock stopt newly wound
As the cold hardened. Once they watched the road,
Thinking to be remembered. Once they doubted
If they had kept the sequence of the days,
Because they heard not any sound of bells.
A butterfly, that hid until the Spring
Under a ceiling's shadow, dropt, was dead.
The coldness seemed more nigh, the coldness deepened
As a sound deepens into silences;
It was of earth and came not by the air;
The earth was cooling and drew down the sky.
The air was crumbling. There was no more sky.
Rails of a broken bed charred in the grate,
And when he touched the bars he thought the sting
Came from their heat–he could not feel such cold . . .
She said, "O, do not sleep,
Heart, heart of mine, keep near me. No, no; sleep.
I will not lift his fallen, quiet eyelids,
Although I know he would awaken then–
He closed them thus but now of his own will.
He can stay with me while I do not lift them."

G. K. Chesterton (*Br. 1874–1936*)

From *The Ballad of the White Horse: The Harp of Alfred*

Blue-eyed was Elf the minstrel,
  With womanish hair and ring,
Yet heavy was his hand on sword,
  Though light upon the string.

And as he stirred the strings of the harp
  To notes but four or five,
The heart of each man moved in him
  Like a babe buried alive.

And they felt the land of the folk-songs
  Spread southward of the Dane,
And they heard the good Rhine flowing
  In the heart of all Allemagne.

They felt the land of the folk-songs,
  Where the gifts hang on the tree,
Where the girls give ale at morning
  And the tears come easily.

The mighty people, womanlike,
  That have pleasure in their pain
As he sang of Balder beautiful,
  Whom the heavens loved in vain.

As he sang of Balder beautiful,
  Whom the heavens could not save,
Till the world was like a sea of tears
  And every soul a wave.

"There is always a thing forgotten
  When all the world goes well;
A thing forgotten, as long ago
When the gods forgot the mistletoe,
And soundless as an arrow of snow
  The arrow of anguish fell.

"The thing on the blind side of the heart,
  On the wrong side of the door,
The green plant groweth, menacing
Almighty lovers in the spring;
There is always a forgotten thing,
  And love is not secure."

And all that sat by the fire were sad,
  Save Ogier, who was stern,
And his eyes hardened, even to stones,
  As he took the harp in turn;

Earl Ogier of the Stone and Sling
  Was odd to ear and sight,
Old he was, but his locks were red,
And jests were all the words he said,
Yet he was sad at board and bed
  And savage in the fight.

"You sing of the young gods easily
  In the days when you are young;
But I go smelling yew and sods,
And I know there are gods behind the gods,
  Gods that are best unsung.

"And a man grows ugly for women,
  And a man grows dull with ale,
Well if he find in his soul at last
  Fury, that does not fail.

"The wrath of the gods behind the gods
  Who would rend all gods and men,
Well if the old man's heart hath still
Wheels sped of rage and roaring will,
Like cataracts to break down and kill,
  Well for the old man then–

"While there is one tall shrine to shake,
  Or one live man to rend;
For the wrath of the gods behind the gods
  Who are weary to make an end.

"There lives one moment for a man
  When the door at his shoulder shakes,
When the taut rope parts under the pull,
And the barest branch is beautiful
  One moment, while it breaks.

"So rides my soul upon the sea
  That drinks the howling ships,
Though in black jest it bows and nods
Under the moons with silver rods,
I know it is roaring at the gods,
  Waiting the last eclipse.

"And in the last eclipse the sea
  Shall stand up like a tower,
Above all moons made dark and riven,
Hold up its foaming head in heaven,
  And laugh, knowing its hour.

"And the high ones in the happy town
Propped of the planets seven,
Shall know a new light in the mind,
A noise about them and behind,
Shall hear an awful voice, and find
Foam in the courts of heaven.

"And you that sit by the fire are young,
And true loves wait for you;
But the King and I grow old, grow old,
And hate alone is true."

And Guthrum shook his head but smiled,
For he was a mighty clerk,
And had read lines in the Latin books
When all the north was dark.

He said, "I am older than you, Ogier;
Not all things would I rend,
For whether life be bad or good
It is best to abide the end."

He took the great harp wearily,
Even Guthrum of the Danes,
With wide eyes bright as the one long day
On the long polar plains.

For he sang of a wheel returning,
And the mire trod back to mire,
And how red hells and golden heavens
Are castles in the fire.

"It is good to sit where the good tales go,
To sit as our fathers sat;
But the hour shall come after his youth,
When a man shall know not tales but truth,
And his heart fail thereat.

"When he shall read what is written
So plain in clouds and clods,
When he shall hunger without hope
Even for evil gods.

"For this is a heavy matter,
And the truth is cold to tell;
Do we not know, have we not heard,
The soul is like a lost bird,
The body a broken shell.

"And a man hopes, being ignorant,
Till in white woods apart
He finds at last the lost bird dead:
And a man may still lift up his head
But never more his heart.

"There comes no noise but weeping
Out of the ancient sky,
And a tear is in the tiniest flower
Because the gods must die.

"The little brooks are very sweet,
Like a girl's ribbons curled,
But the great sea is bitter
That washes all the world.

"Strong are the Roman roses,
Or the free flowers of the heath,
But every flower, like a flower of the sea,
Smelleth with the salt of death.

"And the heart of the locked battle
Is the happiest place for men;
When shrieking souls as shafts go by
And many have died and all may die;
Though this word be a mystery,
Death is most distant then.

"Death blazes bright above the cup,
 And clear above the crown;
But in that dream of battle
 We seem to tread it down.

"Wherefore I am a great king,
 And waste the world in vain,
Because man hath not other power,
Save that in dealing death for dower,
He may forget it for an hour
 To remember it again."

And slowly his hands and thoughtfully
 Fell from the lifted lyre,
And the owls moaned from the mighty trees
Till Alfred caught it to his knees
 And smote it as in ire.

He heaved the head of the harp on high
 And swept the framework barred,
And his stroke had all the rattle and spark
 Of horses flying hard.

"When God put man in a garden
 He girt him with a sword,
And sent him forth a free knight
 That might betray his lord;

"He brake Him and betrayed Him,
 And fast and far he fell,
Till you and I may stretch our necks
 And burn our beards in hell.

"But though I lie on the floor of the world,
 With the seven sins for rods,
I would rather fall with Adam
 Than rise with all your gods.

"What have the strong gods given?
 Where have the glad gods led?
When Guthrum sits on a hero's throne
 And asks if he is dead?

"Sirs, I am but a nameless man,
  A rhymester without home,
Yet since I come of the Wessex clay
  And carry the cross of Rome,

"I will even answer the mighty earl
  That asked of Wessex men
Why they be meek and monkish folk,
And bow to the White Lord's broken yoke;
What sign have we save blood and smoke?
  Here is my answer then.

"That on you is fallen the shadow,
  And not upon the Name;
That though we scatter and though we fly,
And you hang over us like the sky,
You are more tired of victory,
  Than we are tired of shame.

"That though you hunt the Christian man
  Like a hare on the hill-side,
The hare has still more heart to run
  Than you have heart to ride.

"That though all lances split on you,
  All swords be heaved in vain,
We have more lust again to lose
  Than you to win again.

"Your lord sits high in the saddle,
  A broken-hearted king,
But our King Alfred, lost from fame,
Fallen among foes or bonds of shame,
In I know not what mean trade or name,
  Has still some song to sing;

"Our monks go robed in rain and snow,
  But the heart of flame therein,
But you go clothed in feasts and flames,
  When all is ice within;

"Nor shall all iron dooms make dumb
  Men wondering ceaselessly,
If it be not better to fast for joy
  Than feast for misery.

"Nor monkish order only
  Slides down, as field to fen,
All things achieved and chosen pass,
As the White Horse fades in the grass,
  No work of Christian men.

"Ere the sad gods that made your gods
  Saw their sad sunrise pass,
The White Horse of the White Horse Vale,
That you have left to darken and fail,
  Was cut out of the grass.

"Therefore your end is on you,
  Is on you and your kings,
Not for a fire in Ely fen,
Not that your gods are nine or ten,
But because it is only Christian men
  Guard even heathen things.

"For our God hath blessed creation,
  Calling it good. I know
What spirit with whom you blindly band
Hath blessed destruction with his hand;
Yet by God's death the stars shall stand
  And the small apples grow."

And the King, with harp on shoulder,
  Stood up and ceased his song;
And the owls moaned from the mighty trees,
  And the Danes laughed loud and long.

Trumbull Stickney (*Am. 1874–1904*)

At Sainte-Marguerite

The gray tide flows and flounders in the rocks
Along the crannies up the swollen sand.
Far out the reefs lie naked–dunes and blocks
Low in the watery wind. A shaft of land
Going to sea thins out the western strand.

It rains, and all along and always gulls
Career sea-screaming in and weather-glossed.
It blows here, pushing round the cliff; in lulls
Within the humid stone a motion lost
Ekes out the flurried heart-beat of the coast.

It blows and rains a pale and whirling mist
This summer morning. I that hither came–
Was it to pluck this savage from the schist,
This crazy yellowish bloom without a name,
With leathern blade and tortured wiry frame?

Why here alone, away, the forehead pricked
With dripping salt and fingers damp with brine,
Before the offal and the derelict
And where the hungry sea-wolves howl and whine,
Live human hours? now that the columbine

Stands somewhere shaded near the fields that fall
Great starry sheaves of the delighted year,
And globing rosy on the garden wall
The peach and apricot and soon the pear
Drip in the teasing hand their sugared tear.

Inland a little way the summer lies.
Inland a little and but yesterday
I saw the weary teams, I heard the cries
Of sicklemen across the fallen hay,
And buried in the sunburned stacks I lay

Tasting the straws and tossing, laughing soft
Into the sky's great eyes of gold and blue
And nodding to the breezy leaves aloft
Over the harvest's mellow residue.
But sudden then—then strangely dark it grew.

How good it is, before the dreary flow
Of cloud and water, here to lie alone
And in this desolation to let go
Down the ravine one with another, down
Across the surf to linger or to drown

The loves that none can give and none receive,
The fearful asking and the small retort,
The life to dream of and the dream to live!
Very much more is nothing than a part,
Nothing at all and darkness in the heart.

I would my manhood now were like the sea.—
Thou at high-tide, when compassing the land
Thou find'st the issue short, questioningly
A moment poised, thy floods then down the strand
Sink without rancour, sink without command,

Sink of themselves in peace without despair,
And turn as still the calm horizon turns,
Till they repose little by little nowhere
And the long light unfathomable burns
Clear from the zenith stars to the sea-ferns.

Thou art thy Priest, thy Victim and thy God.
Thy life is bulwarked with a thread of foam,
And of the sky, the mountains and the sod
Thou askest nothing, evermore at home
In thy own self's perennial masterdom.

Mt. Lykaion

Alone on Lykaion since man hath been
Stand on the height two columns, where at rest
Two eagles hewn of gold sit looking East
Forever; and the sun goes up between.
Far down around the mountain's oval green
An order keeps the falling stones abreast.
Below within the chaos last and least
A river like a curl of light is seen.
Beyond the river lies the even sea,
Beyond the sea another ghost of sky–
O God, support the sickness of my eye
Lest the far space and long antiquity
Suck out my heart, and on this awful ground
The great wind kill my little shell with sound.

Robert Frost (*Am. b. 1875*)

My November Guest

My Sorrow, when she's here with me,
  Thinks these dark days of autumn rain
Are beautiful as days can be;
She loves the bare, the withered tree;
  She walks the sodden pasture lane.

Her pleasure will not let me stay.
  She talks and I am fain to list:
She's glad the birds are gone away,
She's glad her simple worsted gray
  Is silver now with clinging mist.

The desolate, deserted trees,
   The faded earth, the heavy sky,
The beauties she so truly sees,
She thinks I have no eye for these,
   And vexes me for reason why.

Not yesterday I learned to know
   The love of bare November days
Before the coming of the snow,
But it were vain to tell her so,
   And they are better for her praise.

Mending Wall

Something there is that doesn't love a wall,
That sends the frozen-ground-swell under it,
And spills the upper boulders in the sun;
And makes gaps even two can pass abreast.
The work of hunters is another thing:
I have come after them and made repair
Where they have left not one stone on a stone,
But they would have the rabbit out of hiding,
To please the yelping dogs. The gaps I mean,
No one has seen them made or heard them made,
But at spring mending-time we find them there.
I let my neighbor know beyond the hill;
And on a day we meet to walk the line
And set the wall between us once again.
We keep the wall between us as we go.
To each the boulders that have fallen to each.
And some are loaves and some so nearly balls
We have to use a spell to make them balance:
"Stay where you are until our backs are turned."
We wear our fingers rough with handling them.
Oh, just another kind of outdoor game,
One on a side. It comes to little more:
There where it is we do not need the wall:
He is all pine and I am apple orchard.

My apple trees will never get across
And eat the cones under his pines, I tell him.
He only says, "Good fences make good neighbors."
Spring is the mischief in me, and I wonder
If I could put a notion in his head:
"*Why* do they make good neighbors? Isn't it
Where there are cows? But here there are no cows.
Before I built a wall I'd ask to know
What I was walling in or walling out,
And to whom I was like to give offence.
Something there is that doesn't love a wall,
That wants it down." I could say 'Elves' to him,
But it's not elves exactly, and I'd rather
He said it for himself. I see him there
Bringing a stone grasped firmly by the top
In each hand, like an old-stone savage armed.
He moves in darkness as it seems to me,
Not of woods only and the shade of trees,
He will not go behind his father's saying,
And he likes having thought of it so well
He says again, "Good fences make good neighbors."

After Apple-Picking

My long two-pointed ladder's sticking through a tree
Toward heaven still,
And there's a barrel that I didn't fill
Beside it, and there may be two or three
Apples I didn't pick upon some bough.
But I am done with apple-picking now.
Essence of winter sleep is on the night,
The scent of apples: I am drowsing off.
I cannot rub the strangeness from my sight
I got from looking through a pane of glass
I skimmed this morning from the drinking trough
And held against the world of hoary grass.
It melted, and I let it fall and break.
But I was well
Upon my way to sleep before it fell,
And I could tell

What form my dreaming was about to take.
Magnified apples appear and disappear,
Stem end and blossom end,
And every fleck of russet showing clear.
My instep arch not only keeps the ache,
It keeps the pressure of a ladder-round.
I feel the ladder sway as the boughs bend.
And I keep hearing from the cellar bin
The rumbling sound
Of load on load of apples coming in.
For I have had too much
Of apple-picking: I am overtired
Of the great harvest I myself desired.
There were ten thousand thousand fruit to touch,
Cherish in hand, lift down, and not let fall.
For all
That struck the earth,
No matter if not bruised or spiked with stubble,
Went surely to the cider-apple heap
As of no worth.
One can see what will trouble
This sleep of mine, whatever sleep it is.
Were he not gone,
The woodchuck could say whether it's like his
Long sleep, as I describe its coming on,
Or just some human sleep.

An Old Man's Winter Night

All out-of-doors looked darkly in at him
Through the thin frost, almost in separate stars,
That gathers on the pane in empty rooms.
What kept his eyes from giving back the gaze
Was the lamp tilted near them in his hand.
What kept him from remembering what it was
That brought him to that creaking room was age.
He stood with barrels round him–at a loss.
And having scared the cellar under him
In clomping there, he scared it once again
In clomping off;–and scared the outer night,

Which has its sounds, familiar, like the roar
Of trees and crack of branches, common things,
But nothing so like beating on a box.
A light he was to no one but himself
Where now he sat, concerned with he knew what,
A quiet light, and then not even that.
He consigned to the moon, such as she was,
So late-arising, to the broken moon
As better than the sun in any case
For such a charge, his snow upon the roof,
His icicles along the wall to keep;
And slept. The log that shifted with a jolt
Once in the stove, disturbed him and he shifted,
And eased his heavy breathing, but still slept.
One aged man–one man–can't keep a house,
A farm, a countryside, or if he can,
It's thus he does it of a winter night.

Birches

When I see birches bend to left and right
Across the lines of straighter darker trees,
I like to think some boy's been swinging them.
But swinging doesn't bend them down to stay
As ice-storms do. Often you must have seen them
Loaded with ice a sunny winter morning
After a rain. They click upon themselves
As the breeze rises, and turn many-colored
As the stir cracks and crazes their enamel.
Soon the sun's warmth makes them shed crystal shells
Shattering and avalanching on the snow-crust–
Such heaps of broken glass to sweep away
You'd think the inner dome of heaven had fallen.
They are dragged to the withered bracken by the load,
And they seem not to break; though once they are bowed
So low for long, they never right themselves:
You may see their trunks arching in the woods
Years afterwards, trailing their leaves on the ground
Like girls on hands and knees that throw their hair
Before them over their heads to dry in the sun.

But I was going to say when Truth broke in
With all her matter-of-fact about the ice-storm
I should prefer to have some boy bend them
As he went out and in to fetch the cows–
Some boy too far from town to learn baseball,
Whose only play was what he found himself,
Summer or winter, and could play alone.
One by one he subdued his father's trees
By riding them down over and over again
Until he took the stiffness out of them,
And not one but hung limp, not one was left
For him to conquer. He learned all there was
To learn about not launching out too soon
And so not carrying the tree away
Clear to the ground. He always kept his poise
To the top branches, climbing carefully
With the same pains you use to fill a cup
Up to the brim, and even above the brim.
Then he flung outward, feet first, with a swish,
Kicking his way down through the air to the ground.
So was I once myself a swinger of birches.
And so I dream of going back to be.
It's when I'm weary of considerations,
And life is too much like a pathless wood
Where your face burns and tickles with the cobwebs
Broken across it, and one eye is weeping
From a twig's having lashed across it open.
I'd like to get away from earth awhile
And then come back to it and begin over.
May no fate willfully misunderstand me
And half grant what I wish and snatch me away
Not to return. Earth's the right place for love:
I don't know where it's likely to go better.
I'd like to go by climbing a birch tree,
And climb black branches up a snow-white trunk
Toward heaven, till the tree could bear no more,
But dipped its top and set me down again.
That would be good both going and coming back.
One could do worse than be a swinger of birches.

Fire and Ice

Some say the world will end in fire,
Some say in ice.
From what I've tasted of desire
I hold with those who favor fire.
But if it had to perish twice,
I think I know enough of hate
To say that for destruction ice
Is also great
And would suffice.

Stopping by Woods on a Snowy Evening

Whose woods these are I think I know.
His house is in the village though;
He will not see me stopping here
To watch his woods fill up with snow.

My little horse must think it queer
To stop without a farmhouse near
Between the woods and frozen lake
The darkest evening of the year.

He gives his harness bells a shake
To ask if there is some mistake.
The only other sound's the sweep
Of easy wind and downy flake.

The woods are lovely, dark and deep,
But I have promises to keep,
And miles to go before I sleep,
And miles to go before I sleep.

To Earthward

Love at the lips was touch
As sweet as I could bear;
And once that seemed too much;
I lived on air

That crossed me from sweet things
The flow of–was it musk
From hidden grapevine springs
Down hill at dusk?

I had the swirl and ache
From sprays of honeysuckle
That when they're gathered shake
Dew on the knuckle.

I craved strong sweets, but those
Seemed strong when I was young;
The petal of the rose
It was that stung.

Now no joy but lacks salt
That is not dashed with pain
And weariness and fault;
I crave the stain

Of tears, the aftermark
Of almost too much love,
The sweet of bitter bark
And burning clove.

When stiff and sore and scarred
I take away my hand
From leaning on it hard
In grass and sand,

The hurt is not enough:
I long for weight and strength
To feel the earth as rough
To all my length.

Tree at My Window

Tree at my window, window tree,
My sash is lowered when night comes on;
But let there never be curtain drawn
Between you and me.

Vague dream-head lifted out of the ground,
And thing next most diffuse to cloud,
Not all your light tongues talking aloud
Could be profound.

But tree, I have seen you taken and tossed,
And if you have seen me when I slept,
You have seen me when I was taken and swept
And all but lost.

That day she put our heads together,
Fate had her imagination about her,
Your head so much concerned with outer,
Mine with inner, weather.

Desert Places

Snow falling and night falling fast, oh, fast
In a field I looked into going past,
And the ground almost covered smooth in snow,
But a few weeds and stubble showing last.

The woods around it have it–it is theirs.
All animals are smothered in their lairs.
I am too absent-spirited to count;
The loneliness includes me unawares.

And lonely as it is that loneliness
Will be more lonely ere it will be less–
A blanker whiteness of benighted snow
With no expression, nothing to express.

They cannot scare me with their empty spaces
Between stars–on stars where no human race is.
I have it in me so much nearer home
To scare myself with my own desert places.

Moon Compasses

I stole forth dimly in the dripping pause
Between two downpours to see what there was.
And a masked moon had spread down compass rays
To a cone mountain in the midnight haze,
As if the final estimate were hers,
And as it measured in her calipers,
The mountain stood exalted in its place.
So love will take between the hands a face. . . .

Carl Sandburg (*Am. b. 1878*)

Chicago

Hog Butcher for the World,
Tool Maker, Stacker of Wheat,
Player with Railroads and the Nation's Freight Handler;
Stormy, husky, brawling,
City of the Big Shoulders:

They tell me you are wicked and I believe them, for I have seen your painted women under the gas lamps luring the farm boys.
And they tell me you are crooked and I answer: Yes, it is true I have seen the gunman kill and go free to kill again.
And they tell me you are brutal and my reply is: On the faces of women and children I have seen the marks of wanton hunger.
And having answered so I turn once more to those who sneer at this my city, and I give them back the sneer and say to them:
Come and show me another city with lifted head singing so proud to be alive and coarse and strong and cunning.
Flinging magnetic curses amid the toil of piling job on job, here is a tall bold slugger set vivid against the little soft cities;
Fierce as a dog with tongue lapping for action, cunning as a savage pitted against the wilderness,
Bareheaded,
Shoveling,
Wrecking,
Planning,
Building, breaking, rebuilding.
Under the smoke, dust all over his mouth, laughing with white teeth,
Under the terrible burden of destiny laughing as a young man laughs,
Laughing even as an ignorant fighter laughs who has never lost a battle,
Bragging and laughing that under his wrist is the pulse, and under his ribs the heart of the people,
Laughing!

Laughing the stormy, husky, brawling laughter of Youth, half-naked, sweating, proud to be Hog Butcher, Tool Maker, Stacker of Wheat, Player with Railroads and Freight Handler to the Nation.

Losers

If I should pass the tomb of Jonah
I would stop there and sit for a while;
Because I was swallowed one time deep in the dark
And came out alive after all.

If I pass the burial spot of Nero
I shall say to the wind, "Well, well!"–
I who have fiddled in a world on fire,
I who have done so many stunts not worth doing.

I am looking for the grave of Sinbad too.
I want to shake his ghost-hand and say,
"Neither of us died very early, did we?"

And the last sleeping-place of Nebuchadnezzar–
When I arrive there I shall tell the wind:
"You ate grass; I have eaten crow–
Who is better off now or next year?"

Jake Cade, John Brown, Jesse James,
There too I could sit down and stop for a while.
I think I could tell their headstones:
"God, let me remember all good losers."

I could ask people to throw ashes on their heads
In the name of that sergeant at Belleau Woods,
Walking into the drumfires, calling his men,
"Come on, you . . . Do you want to live forever?"

Killers

I am put high over all others in the city today.
I am the killer who kills for those who wish a killing today.

Here is a strong young man who killed.
There was a driving wind of city dust and horse dung blowing and he stood at an intersection of five sewers and there pumped the bullets of an automatic pistol into another man, a fellow citizen.
Therefore, the prosecuting attorneys, fellow citizens, and a jury of his peers, also fellow citizens, listened to the testimony of other fellow citizens, policemen, doctors, and after a verdict of guilty, the judge, a fellow citizen, said: I sentence you to be hanged by the neck till you are dead.

So there is a killer to be killed and I am the killer of the killer for today.
I don't know why it beats in my head in the lines I read once in an old school reader: I'm to be queen of the May, mother, I'm to be queen of the May.
Anyhow it comes back in language just like that today.

I am the high honorable killer today.
There are five million people in the state, five million killers for whom I kill
I am the killer who kills today for five million killers who wish a killing.

Grass

Pile the bodies high at Austerlitz and Waterloo.
Shovel them under and let me work–
I am the grass; I cover all.

And pile them high at Gettysburg
And pile them high at Ypres and Verdun.
Shovel them under and let me work.
Two year, ten years, and passengers ask the conductor:
What place is this?
Where are we now?

I am the grass.
Let me work.

Cool Tombs

When Abraham Lincoln was shoveled into the tombs, he forgot the copperheads and the assassin . . . in the dust, in the cool tombs.

And Ulysses Grant lost all thought of con men and Wall Street, cash and collateral turned ashes . . . in the dust, in the cool tombs.

Pocahontas' body, lovely as a poplar, sweet as a red haw in November or a pawpaw in May, did she wonder? does she remember? . . . in the dust, in the cool tombs?

Take any streetful of people buying clothes and groceries, cheering a hero or throwing confetti and blowing tin horns . . . tell me if the lovers are losers . . . tell me if any get more than the lovers . . . in the dust . . . in the cool tombs.

Edward Thomas (*Br. 1878–1917*)

Early One Morning

Early one morning in May I set out,
And nobody I knew was about.
  I'm bound away for ever,
  Away somewhere, away for ever.

There was no wind to trouble the weathercocks.
I had burnt my letters and darned my socks.

No one knew I was going away,
I thought myself I should come back some day.

I heard the brook through the town gardens run.
O sweet was the mud turned to dust by the sun.

A gate banged in a fence and banged in my head.
"A fine morning, sir," a shepherd said.

I could not return from my liberty,
To my youth and my love and my misery.

The past is the only dead thing that smells sweet,
The only sweet thing that is not also fleet.
  I'm bound away for ever,
  Away somewhere, away for ever.

Out in the Dark

Out in the dark over the snow
The fallow fawns invisible go
With the fallow doe;
And the winds blow
Fast as the stars are slow.

Stealthily the dark haunts round
And, when the lamp goes, without sound
At a swifter bound
Than the swiftest hound,
Arrives, and all else is drowned;

And star and I and wind and deer,
Are in the dark together,–near,
Yet far,–and fear
Drums on my ear
In that sage company drear.

How weak and little is the light,
All the universe of sight,
Love and delight,
Before the might,
If you love it not, of night.

Snow

In the gloom of whiteness,
In the great silence of snow,
A child was sighing
And bitterly saying: "Oh,
They have killed a white bird up there on her nest,
The down is fluttering from her breast!"
And still it fell through that dusky brightness
On the child crying for the bird of the snow.

The Brook

Seated once by a brook, watching a child
Chiefly that paddled, I was thus beguiled.
Mellow the blackbird sang and sharp the thrush
Not far off in the oak and hazel brush,
Unseen. There was a scent like honeycomb
From mugwort dull. And down upon the dome
Of the stone the cart-horse kicks against so oft
A butterfly alighted. From aloft
He took the heat of the sun, and from below.
On the hot stone he perched contented so,
As if never a cart would pass again
That way; as if I were the last of men
And he the first of insects to have earth
And sun together and to know their worth.
I was divided between him and the gleam,
The motion, and the voices, of the stream,
The waters running frizzled over gravel,
That never vanish and for ever travel.
A grey flycatcher silent on a fence
And I sat as if we had been there since
The horseman and the horse lying beneath
The fir-tree-covered barrow on the heath,
The horseman and the horse with silver shoes,
Galloped the downs last. All that I could lose
I lost. And then the child's voice raised the dead.
"No one's been here before" was what she said
And what I felt, yet never should have found
A word for, while I gathered sight and sound.

Old Man

Old Man, or Lad's-love,–in the name there's nothing
To one that knows not Lad's-love, or Old Man,
The hoar-green feathery herb, almost a tree,
Growing with rosemary and lavender.
Even to one that knows it well, the names
Half decorate, half perplex, the thing it is:
At least, what that is clings not to the names
In spite of time. And yet I like the names.

The herb itself I like not, but for certain
I love it, as some day the child will love it
Who plucks a feather from the door-side bush
Whenever she goes in or out of the house.
Often she waits there, snipping the tips and shrivelling
The shreds at last on to the path, perhaps
Thinking, perhaps of nothing, till she sniffs
Her fingers and runs off. The bush is still
But half as tall as she, though it is as old;
So well she clips it. Not a word she says;
And I can only wonder how much hereafter
She will remember, with that bitter scent,
Of garden rows, and ancient damson trees
Topping a hedge, a bent path to a door,
A low thick bush beside the door, and me
Forbidding her to pick.
As for myself,
Where first I met the bitter scent is lost.
I, too, often shrivel the grey shreds,
Sniff them and think and sniff again and try
Once more to think what it is I am remembering,
Always in vain. I cannot like the scent,
Yet I would rather give up others more sweet,
With no meaning, than this bitter one.

I have mislaid the key. I sniff the spray
And think of nothing; I see and I hear nothing;
Yet seem, too, to be listening, lying in wait
For what I should, yet never can, remember:
No garden appears, no path, no hoar-green bush
Of Lad's-love, or Old Man, no child beside,
Neither father nor mother, nor any playmate;
Only an avenue, dark, nameless, without end.

The Path

Running along a bank, a parapet
That saves from the precipitous wood below
The level road, there is a path. It serves
Children for looking down the long smooth steep,
Between the legs of beech and yew, to where

A fallen tree checks the sight: while men and women
Content themselves with the road and what they see
Over the bank, and what the children tell.
The path, winding like silver, trickles on,
Bordered and even invaded by thinnest moss
That tries to cover roots and crumbling chalk
With gold, olive, and emerald, but in vain.
The children wear it. They have flattened the bank
On top, and silvered it between the moss
With the current of their feet, year after year.
But the road is houseless, and leads not to school.
To see a child is rare there, and the eye
Has but the road, the wood that overhangs
And underyawns it, and the path that looks
As if it led on to some legendary
Or fancied place where men have wished to go
And stay; till, sudden, it ends where the wood ends.

It Rains

It rains, and nothing stirs within the fence
Anywhere through the orchard's untrodden, dense
Forest of parsley. The great diamonds
Of rain on the grassblades there is none to break,
Or the fallen petals further down to shake.

And I am nearly as happy as possible
To search the wilderness in vain though well,
To think of two walking, kissing there,
Drenched, yet forgetting the kisses of the rain:
Sad, too, to think that never, never again,

Unless alone, so happy shall I walk
In the rain. When I turn away, on its fine stalk
Twilight has fined to naught, the parsley flower
Figures, suspended still and ghostly white,
The past hovering as it revisits the light.

October

The green elm with the one great bough of gold
Lets leaves into the grass slip, one by one,–
The short hill grass, the mushrooms small, milk-white,

Harebell and scabious and tormentil,
That blackberry and gorse, in dew and sun,
Bow down to; and the wind travels too light
To shake the fallen birch leaves from the fern;
The gossamers wander at their own will.
At heavier steps than birds' the squirrels scold.
The rich scene has grown fresh again and new
As Spring and to the touch is not more cool
Than it is warm to the gaze; and now I might
As happy be as earth is beautiful,
Were I some other or with earth could turn
In alternation of violet and rose,
Harebell and snowdrop, at their season due,
And gorse that has no time not to be gay.
But if this be not happiness, – who knows?
Some day I shall think this a happy day,
And this mood by the name of melancholy
Shall no more blackened and obscurèd be.

Swedes

They have taken the gable from the roof of clay
On the long swede pile. They have let in the sun
To the white and gold and purple of curled fronds
Unsunned. It is a sight more tender-gorgeous
At the wood-corner where Winter moans and drips
Than when, in the Valley of the Tombs of Kings,
A boy crawls down into a Pharaoh's tomb
And, first of Christian men, beholds the mummy,
God and monkey, chariot and throne and vase,
Blue pottery, alabaster, and gold.

But dreamless long-dead Amen-hotep lies.
This is a dream of Winter, sweet as Spring.

Melancholy

The rain and wind, the rain and wind, raved endlessly.
On me the Summer storm, and fever, and melancholy
Wrought magic, so that if I feared the solitude
Far more I feared all company: too sharp, too rude,

Had been the wisest or the dearest human voice.
What I desired I knew not, but whate'er my choice
Vain it must be, I knew. Yet naught did my despair
But sweeten the strange sweetness, while through the wild
  air
All day long I heard a distant cuckoo calling
And, soft as dulcimers, sounds of near water falling,
And, softer, and remote as if in history,
Rumours of what had touched my friends, my foes, or me

Lob

At hawthorn-time in Wiltshire travelling
In search of something chance would never bring,
An old man's face, by life and weather cut
And coloured, – rough, brown, sweet as any nut, –
A land face, sea-blue-eyed, – hung in my mind
When I had left him many a mile behind.
All he said was: "Nobody can't stop 'ee. It's
A footpath, right enough. You see those bits
Of mounds – that's where they opened up the barrows
Sixty years since, while I was scaring sparrows.
They thought as there was something to find there,
But couldn't find it, by digging, anywhere."

To turn back then and seek him, where was the use?
There were three Manningfords, – Abbots, Bohun, and Bruce:
And whether Alton, not Manningford, it was,
My memory could not decide, because
There was both Alton Barnes and Alton Priors.
All had their churches, graveyards, farms, and byres,
Lurking to one side up the paths and lanes,
Seldom well seen except by aeroplanes;
And when bells rang, or pigs squealed, or cocks crowed,
Then only heard. Ages ago the road
Approached. The people stood and looked and turned.
Nor asked it to come nearer, nor yet learned
To move out there and dwell in all men's dust.
And yet withal they shot the weathercock, just
Because 'twas he crowed out of tune, they said:
So now the copper weathercock is dead.

If they had reaped their dandelions and sold
Them fairly, they could have afforded gold.
Many years passed, and I went back again
Among those villages, and looked for men
Who might have known my ancient. He himself
Had long been dead or laid upon the shelf,
I thought. One man I asked about him roared
At my description: " 'Tis old Bottlesford
He means, Bill." But another said: "Of course,
It was Jack Button up at the White Horse.
He's dead, sir, these three years." This lasted till
A girl proposed Walker of Walker's Hill,
"Old Adam Walker. Adam's Point you'll see
Marked on the maps."

"That was her roguery,"
The next man said. He was a squire's son
Who loved wild bird and beast, and dog and gun
For killing them. He had loved them from his birth,
One with another, as he loved the earth.
"The man may be like Button, or Walker, or
Like Bottlesford, that you want, but far more
He sounds like one I saw when I was a child.
I could almost swear to him. The man was wild
And wandered. His home was where he was free.
Everybody has met one such man as he.
Does he keep clear old paths that no one uses
But once a lifetime when he loves or muses?
He is English as this gate, these flowers, this mire.
And when at eight years old Lob-lie-by-the-fire
Came in my books, this was the man I saw.
He has been in England as long as dove and daw,
Calling the wild cherry tree the merry tree,
The rose campion Bridget-in-her-bravery;
And in a tender mood he, as I guess,
Christened one flower Love-in-idleness,
And while he walked from Exeter to Leeds
One April called all cuckoo-flowers Milkmaids.
From him old herbal Gerard learnt, as a boy,
To name wild clematis the Traveller's-joy.

Our blackbirds sang no English till his ear
Told him they called his Jan Toy 'Pretty dear'.
(She was Jan Toy the Lucky, who, having lost
A shilling, and found a penny loaf, rejoiced.)
For reasons of his own to him the wren
Is Jenny Pooter. Before all other men
'Twas he first called the Hog's Back the Hog's Back.
That Mother Dunch's Buttocks should not lack
Their name was his care. He too could explain
Totteridge and Totterdown and Juggler's Lane:
He knows, if anyone. Why Tumbling Bay,
Inland in Kent, is called so, he might say.

" But little he says compared with what he does.
If ever a sage troubles him he will buzz
Like a beehive to conclude the tedious fray:
And the sage, who knows all languages, runs away.
Yet Lob has thirteen hundred names for a fool,
And though he never could spare time for school
To unteach what the fox so well expressed,
On biting the cock's head off, – Quietness is best, –
He can talk quite as well as anyone
After his thinking is forgot and done.
He first of all told someone else's wife,
For a farthing she'd skin a flint and spoil a knife
Worth sixpence skinning it. She heard him speak:
'She had a face as long as a wet week,'
Said he, telling the tale in after years.
With blue smock and with gold rings in his ears,
Sometimes he is a pedlar, not too poor
To keep his wit. This is tall Tom that bore
The logs in, and with Shakespeare in the hall
Once talked, when icicles hung by the wall.
As Herne the Hunter he has known hard times.
On sleepless nights he made up weather rhymes
Which others spoilt. And, Hob being then his name,
He kept the hog that thought the butcher came
To bring his breakfast. 'You thought wrong,' said Hob.
When there were kings in Kent this very Lob,

Whose sheep grew fat and he himself grew merry,
Wedded the king's daughter of Canterbury;
For he alone, unlike squire, lord, and king,
Watched a night by her without slumbering;
He kept both waking. When he was but a lad
He won a rich man's heiress, deaf, dumb, and sad,
By rousing her to laugh at him. He carried
His donkey on his back. So they were married.
And while he was a little cobbler's boy
He tricked the giant coming to destroy
Shrewsbury by flood. 'And how far is it yet?'
The giant asked in passing. 'I forget;
But see these shoes I've worn out on the road
And we're not there yet.' He emptied out his load
Of shoes for mending. The giant let fall from his spade
The earth for damming Severn, and thus made
The Wrekin hill; and little Ercall hill
Rose where the giant scraped his boots. While still
So young, our Jack was chief of Gotham's sages.
But long before he could have been wise, ages
Earlier than this, while he grew thick and strong
And ate his bacon, or, at times, sang a song
And merely smelt it, as Jack the giant-killer
He made a name. He too ground up the miller,
The Yorkshireman who ground men's bones for flour.

"Do you believe Jack dead before his hour?
Or that his name is Walker, or Bottlesford,
Or Button, a mere clown, or squire, or lord?
The man you saw,–Lob-lie-by-the-fire, Jack Cade,
Jack Smith, Jack Moon, poor Jack of every trade,
Young Jack, or old Jack, or Jack What-d'ye-call,
Jack-in-the-hedge, or Robin-run-by-the-wall,
Robin Hood, Ragged Robin, lazy Bob,
One of the lords of No Man's Land, good Lob,–
Although he was seen dying at Waterloo,
Hastings, Agincourt, and Sedgemoor too,–
Lives yet. He never will admit he is dead
Till millers cease to grind men's bones for bread,

Not till our weathercock crows once again
And I remove my house out of the lane
On to the road." With this he disappeared
In hazel and thorn tangled with old-man's-beard.
But one glimpse of his back, as there he stood,
Choosing his way, proved him of old Jack's blood,
Young Jack perhaps, and now a Wiltshireman
As he has oft been since his days began.

No one cares less than I

"No one cares less than I,
Nobody knows but God,
Whether I am destined to lie
Under a foreign clod,"
Were the words I made to the bugle call
in the morning.

But laughing, storming, scorning,
Only the bugles know
What the bugles say in the morning,
And they do not care, when they blow
The call that I heard and made words to
early this morning.

John Masefield (*Br. b. 1878*)

From *Reynard the Fox: The Fox Awakes*

On old Cold Crendon's windy tops
Grows wintrily Blown Hilcote Copse,
Wind-bitten beech with badger barrows,
Where brocks eat wasp-grubs with their marrows,
And foxes lie on short-grassed turf,
Nose between paws, to hear the surf
Of wind in the beeches drowsily.
There was our fox bred lustily
Three years before, and there he berthed,
Under the beech-roots snugly earthed,
With a roof of flint and a floor of chalk
And ten bitten hens' heads each on its stalk,

Some rabbits' paws, some fur from scuts,
A badger's corpse and a smell of guts.
And there on the night before my tale
He trotted out for a point in the vale.

* * * *

He saw, from the cover edge, the valley
Go trooping down with its droops of sally
To the brimming river's lipping bend,
And a light in the inn at Water's End.
He heard the owl go hunting by
And the shriek of the mouse the owl made die,
And the purr of the owl as he tore the red
Strings from between his claws and fed;
The smack of joy of the horny lips
Marbled green with the blobby strips.
He saw the farms where the dogs were barking,
Cold Crendon Court and Copsecote Larking;
The fault with the spring as bright as gleed,
Green-slash-laced with water-weed.
A glare in the sky still marked the town,
Though all folk slept and the blinds were down,
The street lamps watched the empty square,
The night-cat sang his evil there.

* * * *

The fox's nose tipped up and round,
Since smell is a part of sight and sound.
Delicate smells were drifting by,
The sharp nose flaired them heedfully;
Partridges in the clover stubble,
Crouched in a ring for the stoat to nubble.
Rabbit bucks beginning to box;
A scratching place for the pheasant cocks,
A hare in the dead grass near the drain,
And another smell like the spring again.

* * * *

A faint rank taint like April coming,
It cocked his ears and his blood went drumming,
For somewhere out by Ghost Heath Stubs
Was a roving vixen wanting cubs.

Over the valley, floating faint
On a warmth of windflaw, came the taint;
He cocked his ears, he upped his brush,
And he went upwind like an April thrush.

* * * *

By the Roman Road to Braiches Ridge,
Where the fallen willow makes a bridge,
Over the brook by White Hart's Thorn
To the acres thin with pricking corn,
Over the sparse green hair of the wheat,
By the Clench Brook Mill at Clench Brook Leat,
Through Cowfoot Pastures to Nonely Stevens,
And away to Poltrewood St. Jevons.
Past Tott Hill Down all snaked with meuses,
Past Clench St. Michael and Naunton Crucis,
Past Howle's Oak Farm where the raving brain
Of a dog who heard him foamed his chain;
Then off, as the farmer's window opened,
Past Stonepits Farm to Upton Hope End,
Over short sweet grass and worn flint arrows
And the three dumb hows of Tencombe Barrows.
And away and away with a rolling scramble,
Through the sally and up the bramble,
With a nose for the smells the night wind carried,
And his red fell clean for being married;
For clicketting time and Ghost Heath Wood
Had put the violet in his blood.

* * * *

At Tencombe Rings near the Manor Linney
His foot made the great black stallion whinny,
And the stallion's whinny aroused the stable
And the bloodhound bitches stretched their cable,
And the clink of the bloodhounds' chain aroused
The sweet-breathed kye as they chewed and drowsed,
And the stir of the cattle changed the dream
Of the cat in the loft to tense green gleam.
The red-wattled black cock hot from Spain
Crowed from his perch for dawn again,

His breast-pufft hens, one-legged on perch,
Gurgled, beak-down, like men in church,
They crooned in the dark, lifting one red eye
In the raftered roost as the fox went by.

* * * *

By Tencombe Regis and Slaughters Court,
Through the great grass square of Roman Fort,
By Nun's Wood Yews and the Hungry Hill,
And the Corpse Way Stones all standing still.
By Seven Springs Mead to Deerlip Brook,
And a lolloping leap to Water Hook.
Then with eyes like sparks and his blood awoken,
Over the grass to Water's Oaken,
And over the hedge and into ride
In Ghost Heath Wood for his roving bride.

Wilfrid Gibson (*Br. b. 1878*)

Flannan Isle

Though three men dwell on Flannan Isle
To keep the lamp alight,
As we steered under the lee we caught
No glimmer through the night.

A passing ship at dawn had brought
The news, and quickly we set sail
To find out what strange thing might ail
The keepers of the deep-sea light.

The winter day broke blue and bright
With glancing sun and glancing spray
While over the swell our boat made way,
As gallant as a gull in flight.

But as we neared the lonely Isle
And looked up at the naked height,
And saw the lighthouse towering white
With blinded lantern that all night

Had never shot a spark
Of comfort through the dark,
So ghostly in the cold sunlight
It seemed that we were struck the while
With wonder all too dread for words.
And, as into the tiny creek
We stole, beneath the hanging crag
We saw three queer black ugly birds–
Too big by far in my belief
For cormorant or shag–
Like seamen sitting bolt-upright
Upon a half-tide reef:
But as we neared they plunged from sight
Without a sound or spurt of white.

And still too mazed to speak,
We landed and made fast the boat
And climbed the track in single file,
Each wishing he were safe afloat
On any sea, however far,
So it be far from Flannan Isle:
And still we seemed to climb and climb
As though we'd lost all count of time
And so must climb for evermore;
Yet all too soon we reached the door–
The black sun-blistered lighthouse door
That gaped for us ajar.

As on the threshold for a spell
We paused, we seemed to breathe the smell
Of limewash and of tar,
Familiar as our daily breath,
As though 'twere some strange scent of death;
And so yet wondering side by side
We stood a moment still tongue-tied,
And each with black foreboding eyed
The door ere we should fling it wide
To leave the sunlight for the gloom:
Till, plucking courage up, at last
Hard on each other's heels we passed
Into the living-room.

Yet as we crowded through the door
We only saw a table spread
For dinner, meat and cheese and bread,
But all untouched and no one there;
As though when they sat down to eat,
Ere they could even taste,
Alarm had come and they in haste
Had risen and left the bread and meat,
For at the table-head a chair
Lay tumbled on the floor.

We listened, but we only heard
The feeble cheeping of a bird
That starved upon its perch;
And, listening still, without a word
We set about our hopeless search.
We hunted high, we hunted low,
And soon ransacked the empty house;
Then over the Island to and fro
We ranged, to listen and to look
In every cranny, cleft or nook
That might have hid a bird or mouse;
But though we searched from shore to shore
We found no sign in any place,
And soon again stood face to face
Before the gaping door,
And stole into the room once more
As frightened children steal.
Ay, though we hunted high and low
And hunted everywhere,
Of the three men's fate we found no trace
Of any kind in any place
But a door ajar and an untouched meal
And an overtoppled chair.

And as we listened in the gloom
Of that forsaken living-room–
A chill clutch on our breath–
We thought how ill-chance came to all
Who kept the Flannan Light,

And how the rock had been the death
Of many a likely lad–
How six had come to a sudden end
And three had gone stark mad,
And one, whom we'd all known as friend,
Had leapt from the lantern one still night
And fallen dead by the lighthouse wall–
And long we thought
On the three we sought,
And on what might yet befall.

Like curs a glance has brought to heel
We listened, flinching there,
And looked and looked on the untouched meal
And the overtoppled chair.

We seemed to stand for an endless while,
Though still no word was said,
Three men alive on Flannan Isle
Who thought on three men dead.

By the Weir

A scent of esparto grass–and again I recall
That hour we spent by the weir of the paper-mill,
Watching together the curving thunderous fall
Of frothing amber, bemused by the roar until
My mind was as blank as the speckless sheets that wound
On the hot steel ironing rollers perpetually turning
In the humming dark rooms of the mill–all sense and discerning
By the stunning and dazzling oblivion of hill-waters drowned.

And my heart was empty of memory, hope, and desire
Till, rousing, I looked afresh on your face as you gazed–
Behind you an old gnarled fruit-tree in one still fire
Of innumerable flame in the sun of October blazed,
Scarlet and gold that the first white frost would spill
With eddying flicker and patter of dead leaves falling–
I looked on your face as an outcast from Eden recalling
A vision of Eve as she dallied bewildered and still

By the serpent-encircled Tree of Knowledge that flamed
With gold and scarlet of good and evil, her eyes
Rapt on the river of life: then bright and untamed
By the labour and sorrow and fear of a world that dies,
Your ignorant eyes looked up into mine; and I knew
That never our hearts should be one till your young lips had tasted
The core of the bitter-sweet fruit, and, wise and toil-wasted,
You should stand at my shoulder an outcast from Eden too.

Wallace Stevens (*Am. 1879–1955*)

To the One of Fictive Music

Sister and mother and diviner love,
And of the sisterhood of the living dead
Most near, most clear, and of the clearest bloom,
And of the fragrant mothers the most dear
And queen, and of diviner love the day
And flame and summer and sweet fire, no thread
Of cloudy silver sprinkles in your gown
Its venom of renown, and on your head
No crown is simpler than the simple hair.

Now, of the music summoned by the birth
That separates us from the wind and sea,
Yet leaves us in them, until earth becomes,
By being so much of the things we are,
Gross effigy and simulacrum, none
Gives motion to perfection more serene
Than yours, out of our imperfections wrought,
Most rare, or ever of more kindred air
In the laborious weaving that you wear.

For so retentive of themselves are men
That music is intensest which proclaims
The near, the clear, and vaunts the clearest bloom,
And of all vigils musing the obscure,

That apprehends the most which sees and names,
As in your name, an image that is sure,
Among the arrant spices of the sun,
O bough and bush and scented vine, in whom
We give ourselves our likest issuance.

Yet not too like, yet not so like to be
Too near, too clear, saving a little to endow
Our feigning with the strange unlike, whence springs
The difference that heavenly pity brings.
For this, musician, in your girdle fixed
Bear other perfumes. On your pale head wear
A band entwining, set with fatal stones.
Unreal, give back to us what once you gave:
The imagination that we spurned and crave.

A High-Toned Old Christian Woman

Poetry is the supreme fiction, madame.
Take the moral law and make a nave of it
And from the nave build haunted heaven. Thus,
The conscience is converted into palms,
Like windy citherns hankering for hymns.
We agree in principle. That's clear. But take
The opposing law and make a peristyle,
And from the peristyle project a masque
Beyond the planets. Thus, our bawdiness,
Unpurged by epitaph, indulged at last,
Is equally converted into palms,
Squiggling like saxophones. And palm for palm,
Madame, we are where we began. Allow,
Therefore, that in the planetary scene
Your disaffected flagellants, well-stuffed,
Smacking their muzzy bellies in parade,
Proud of such novelties of the sublime,
Such tink and tank and tunk-a-tunk-tunk,
May, merely may, madame, whip from themselves
A jovial hullabaloo among the spheres.
This will make windows wince. But fictive things
Wink as they will. Wink most when widows wincc.

The Emperor of Ice-Cream

Call the roller of big cigars,
The muscular one, and bid him whip
In kitchen cups concupiscent curds.
Let the wenches dawdle in such dress
As they are used to wear, and let the boys
Bring flowers in last month's newspapers.
Let be be finale of seem.
The only emperor is the emperor of ice-cream.

Take from the dresser of deal,
Lacking the three glass knobs, that sheet
On which she embroidered fantails once
And spread it so as to cover her face.
If her horny feet protrude, they come
To show how cold she is, and dumb.
Let the lamp affix its beam.
The only emperor is the emperor of ice-cream.

Another Weeping Woman

Pour the unhappiness out
From your too bitter heart,
Which grieving will not sweeten.

Poison grows in this dark.
It is in the water of tears
Its black blooms rise.

The magnificent cause of being,
The imagination, the one reality
In this imagined world

Leaves you
With him for whom no phantasy moves,
And you are pierced by a death.

Bantams in Pine-Woods

Chieftain Iffucan of Azcan in caftan
Of tan with henna hackles, halt!

Damned universal cock, as if the sun
Was blackamoor to bear your blazing tail.

Fat! Fat! Fat! Fat! I am the personal.
Your world is you. I am my world.

You ten-foot poet among inchlings. Fat!
Begone! An inchling bristles in these pines,

Bristles, and points their Appalachian tangs,
And fears not portly Azcan nor his hoos.

Anecdote of the Jar

I placed a jar in Tennessee,
And round it was, upon a hill.
It made the slovenly wilderness
Surround that hill.

The wilderness rose up to it,
And sprawled around, no longer wild.
The jar was round upon the ground
And tall and of a port in air.

It took dominion everywhere.
The jar was gray and bare.
It did not give of bird or bush,
Like nothing else in Tennessee.

Sunday Morning

I

Complacencies of the peignoir, and late
Coffee and oranges in a sunny chair,
And the green freedom of a cockatoo
Upon a rug mingle to dissipate
The holy hush of ancient sacrifice.
She dreams a little, and she feels the dark
Encroachment of that old catastrophe,
As a calm darkens among water-lights.
The pungent oranges and bright, green wings
Seem things in some procession of the dead,
Winding across wide water, without sound.
The day is like wide water, without sound,
Stilled for the passing of her dreaming feet
Over the seas, to silent Palestine,
Dominion of the blood and sepulchre.

II

Why should she give her bounty to the dead?
What is divinity if it can come
Only in silent shadows and in dreams?
Shall she not find in comforts of the sun,
In pungent fruit and bright, green wings, or else
In any balm or beauty of the earth,
Things to be cherished like the thought of heaven?
Divinity must live within herself:
Passions of rain, or moods in falling snow;
Grievings in loneliness, or unsubdued
Elations when the forest blooms; gusty
Emotions on wet roads on autumn nights;
All pleasures and all pains, remembering
The bough of summer and the winter branch.
These are the measures destined for her soul.

III

Jove in the clouds had his inhuman birth.
No mother suckled him, no sweet land gave
Large-mannered motions to his mythy mind.
He moved among us, as a muttering king,
Magnificent, would move among his hinds,
Until our blood, commingling, virginal,
With heaven, brought such requital to desire
The very hinds discerned it, in a star.
Shall our blood fail? Or shall it come to be
The blood of paradise? And shall the earth
Seem all of paradise that we shall know?
The sky will be much friendlier then than now,
A part of labor and a part of pain,
And next in glory to enduring love,
Not this dividing and indifferent blue.

IV

She says, "I am content when wakened birds,
Before they fly, test the reality
Of misty fields, by their sweet questionings;
But when the birds are gone, and their warm fields
Return no more, where, then, is paradise?"

There is not any haunt of prophecy,
Nor any old chimera of the grave,
Neither the golden underground, nor isle
Melodious, where spirits gat them home,
Nor visionary south, nor cloudy palm
Remote on heaven's hill, that has endured
As April's green endures; or will endure
Like her remembrance of awakened birds,
Or her desire for June and evening, tipped
By the consummation of the swallow's wings.

V

She says, "But in contentment I still feel
The need of some imperishable bliss."
Death is the mother of beauty; hence from her,
Alone, shall come fulfilment to our dreams
And our desires. Although she strews the leaves
Of sure obliteration on our paths,
The path sick sorrow took, the many paths
Where triumph rang its brassy phrase, or love
Whispered a little out of tenderness,
She makes the willow shiver in the sun
For maidens who were wont to sit and gaze
Upon the grass, relinquished to their feet.
She causes boys to pile new plums and pears
On disregarded plate. The maidens taste
And stray impassioned in the littering leaves.

VI

Is there no change of death in paradise?
Does ripe fruit never fall? Or do the boughs
Hang always heavy in that perfect sky,
Unchanging, yet so like our perishing earth,
With rivers like our own that seek for seas
They never find, the same receding shores
That never touch with inarticulate pang?
Why set the pear upon those river-banks
Or spice the shores with odors of the plum?
Alas, that they should wear our colors there,

The silken weavings of our afternoons,
And pick the strings of our insipid lutes!
Death is the mother of beauty, mystical,
Within whose burning bosom we devise
Our earthly mothers waiting, sleeplessly.

VII

Supple and turbulent, a ring of men
Shall chant in orgy on a summer morn
Their boisterous devotion to the sun,
Not as a god, but as a god might be,
Naked among them, like a savage source.
Their chant shall be a chant of paradise,
Out of their blood, returning to the sky;
And in their chant shall enter, voice by voice,
The windy lake wherein their lord delights,
The trees, like serafin, and echoing hills,
That choir among themselves long afterward.
They shall know well the heavenly fellowship
Of men that perish and of summer morn.
And whence they came and whither they shall go
The dew upon their feet shall manifest.

VIII

She hears, upon that water without sound,
A voice that cries, "The tomb in Palestine
Is not the porch of spirits lingering.
It is the grave of Jesus, where he lay."
We live in an old chaos of the sun,
Or old dependency of day and night,
Or island solitude, unsponsored, free,
Of that wide water, inescapable.
Deer walk upon our mountains, and the quail
Whistle about us their spontaneous cries;
Sweet berries ripen in the wilderness;
And, in the isolation of the sky,
At evening, casual flocks of pigeons make
Ambiguous undulations as they sink,
Downward to darkness, on extended wings.

No Possum, No Sop, No Taters

He is not here, the old sun,
As absent as if we were asleep.

The field is frozen. The leaves are dry.
Bad is final in this light.

In this bleak air the broken stalks
Have arms without hands. They have trunks

Without legs or, for that, without heads.
They have heads in which a captive cry

Is merely the moving of a tongue.
Snow sparkles like eyesight falling to earth

Like seeing fallen brightly away.
The leaves hop, scraping on the ground.

It is deep January. The sky is hard.
The stalks are firmly rooted in ice.

It is in this solitude, a syllable,
Out of these gawky flitterings,

Intones its single emptiness,
The savagest hollow of winter-sound.

It is here, in this bad, that we reach
The last purity of the knowledge of good.

The crow looks rusty as he rises up.
Bright is the malice in his eye . . .

One joins him there for company,
But at a distance, in another tree.

The Woman in Sunshine

It is only that this warmth and movement are like
The warmth and movement of a woman.

It is not that there is any image in the air
Nor the beginning nor end of a form:

It is empty. But a woman in threadless gold
Burns us with brushings of her dress

And a dissociated abundance of being,
More definite for what she is–

Because she is disembodied,
Bearing the odors of the summer fields,
Confessing the taciturn and yet indifferent,
Invisibly clear, the only love.

Vachel Lindsay (*Am. 1879–1931*)

Simon Legree:–A Negro Sermon

To be read in your own variety of negro dialect

Legree's big house was white and green.
His cotton-fields were the best to be seen.
He had strong horses and opulent cattle,
And bloodhounds bold, with chains that would rattle.
His garret was full of curious things:
Books of magic, bags of gold,
And rabbits' feet on long twine strings.
But he went down to the Devil.

Legree he sported a brass-buttoned coat,
A snake-skin necktie, a blood-red shirt.
Legree he had a beard like a goat,
And a thick hairy neck, and eyes like dirt.
His puffed-out cheeks were fish-belly white,
He had great long teeth, and an appetite.
He ate raw meat, 'most every meal,
And rolled his eyes till the cat would squeal.

His fist was an enormous size
To mash poor niggers that told him lies:
He was surely a witch-man in disguise.
But he went down to the Devil.

He wore hip-boots, and would wade all day
To capture his slaves that had fled away.
But he went down to the Devil.

He beat poor Uncle Tom to death
Who prayed for Legree with his last breath.
Then Uncle Tom to Eva flew,
To the high sanctoriums bright and new;
And Simon Legree stared up beneath,

And cracked his heels, and ground his teeth:
And went down to the Devil.

He crossed the yard in the storm and gloom;
He went into his grand front room.
He said, "I killed him, and I don't care."
He kicked a hound, he gave a swear;
He tightened his belt, he took a lamp,
Went down cellar to the webs and damp.
There in the middle of the mouldy floor
He heaved up a slab, he found a door–
And went down to the Devil.

His lamp blew out, but his eyes burned bright.
Simon Legree stepped down all night–
Down, down to the Devil.
Simon Legree he reached the place,
He saw one half of the human race,
He saw the Devil on a wide green throne,
Gnawing the meat from a big ham-bone,
And he said to Mister Devil:

"I see that you have much to eat–
A red ham-bone is surely sweet.
I see that you have lion's feet;
I see your frame is fat and fine,
I see you drink your poison wine–
Blood and burning turpentine."

And the Devil said to Simon Legree:
"I like your style, so wicked and free.
Come sit and share my throne with me,
And let us bark and revel."
And there they sit and gnash their teeth,
And each one wears a hop-vine wreath.
They are matching pennies and shooting craps,
They are playing poker and taking naps.
And old Legree is fat and fine:
He eats the fire, he drinks the wine–
Blood and burning turpentine–
Down, down with the Devil;
Down, down with the Devil;
Down, down with the Devil.

Abraham Lincoln Walks at Midnight

(In Springfield, Illinois)

It is portentous, and a thing of state
That here at midnight, in our little town
A mourning figure walks, and will not rest,
Near the old court-house pacing up and down,

Or by his homestead, or in shadowed yards
He lingers where his children used to play,
Or through the market, on the well-worn stones
He stalks until the dawn-stars burn away.

A bronzed, lank man! His suit of ancient black,
A famous high top-hat and plain worn shawl
Make him the quaint great figure that men love,
The prairie-lawyer, master of us all.

He cannot sleep upon his hillside now.
He is among us: –as in times before!
And we who toss and lie awake for long
Breathe deep, and start, to see him pass the door.

His head is bowed. He thinks on men and kings.
Yea, when the sick world cries, how can he sleep?
Too many peasants fight, they know not why,
Too many homesteads in black terror weep.

The sins of all the war-lords burn his heart.
He sees the dreadnaughts scouring every main.
He carries on his shawl-wrapped shoulders now
The bitterness, the folly and the pain.

He cannot rest until a spirit-dawn
Shall come;– the shining hope of Europe free:
The league of sober folk, the Workers' Earth,
Bringing long peace to Cornland, Alp and Sea.

It breaks his heart that kings must murder still,
That all his hours of travail here for men
Seem yet in vain. And who will bring white peace
That he may sleep upon his hill again?

James Stephens (*Br. 1882–1950*)

The Shell

I

And then I pressed the shell
Close to my ear,
And listened well.

And straightway, like a bell,
Came low and clear
The slow, sad, murmur of far distant seas

Whipped by an icy breeze
Upon a shore
Wind-swept and desolate.

It was a sunless strand that never bore
The footprint of a man,
Nor felt the weight

Since time began
Of any human quality or stir,
Save what the dreary winds and wave incur.

II

And in the hush of waters was the sound
Of pebbles, rolling round;
For ever rolling, with a hollow sound:

And bubbling sea-weeds, as the waters go,
Swish to and fro
Their long cold tentacles of slimy grey:

There was no day;
Nor ever came a night
Setting the stars alight

To wonder at the moon:
Was twilight only, and the frightened croon,
Smitten to whimpers, of the dreary wind

And waves that journeyed blind. . . .
And then I loosed my ear–Oh, it was sweet
To hear a cart go jolting down the street.

The Rivals

I heard a bird at dawn
Singing sweetly on a tree,
That the dew was on the lawn,
And the wind was on the lea;
But I didn't listen to him,
For he didn't sing to me!

I didn't listen to him,
For he didn't sing to me
That the dew was on the lawn,
And the wind was on the lea!
I was singing at the time,
Just as prettily as he!

I was singing all the time,
Just as prettily as he,
About the dew upon the lawn,
And the wind upon the lea!
So I didn't listen to him,
As he sang upon a tree!

In Waste Places

As a naked man I go
Through the desert, sore afraid;
Holding high my head, although
I'm as frightened as a maid.

The lion couches there! I saw
In barren rocks his amber eye!
He parts the cactus with his paw!
He stares at me, as I go by!

He would pad upon my trace
If he thought I was afraid!
If he knew my hardy face
Veils the terrors of a maid.

He rises in the night-time, and
He stretches forth! He snuffs the air!
He roars! He leaps along the sand!
He creeps! He watches everywhere!

His burning eyes, his eyes of bale
Through the darkness I can see!
He lashes fiercely with his tail!
He makes again to spring at me!

I am the lion, and his lair!
I am the fear that frightens me!
I am the desert of despair!
And the night of agony!

Night or day, whate'er befall,
I must walk that desert land,
Until I dare my fear, and call
The lion out to lick my hand!

William Carlos Williams (*Am. b. 1883*)

Spring and All

By the road to the contagious hospital
under the surge of the blue
mottled clouds driven from the
north east–a cold wind. Beyond, the
waste of broad, muddy fields
brown with dried weeds, standing and fallen

patches of standing water
the scattering of tall trees

All along the road the reddish
purplish, forked, upstanding, twiggy
stuff of bushes and small trees
with dead, brown leaves under them
leafless vines–

Lifeless in appearance, sluggish
dazed spring approaches–

They enter the new world naked,
cold, uncertain of all
save that they enter. All about them
the cold, familiar wind–

Now the grass, tomorrow
the stiff curl of wild carrot leaf
One by one objects are defined–
It quickens: clarity, outline of leaf

But now the stark dignity of
entrance–Still, the profound change
has come upon them: rooted they
grip down and begin to awaken

The Right of Way

In passing with my mind
on nothing in the world

but the right of way
I enjoy on the road by

virtue of the law–
I saw

an elderly man who
smiled and looked away

to the north past a house–
a woman in blue

who was laughing and
leaning forward to look up

into the man's half
averted face

and a boy of eight who was
looking at the middle of

the man's belly
at a watch-chain–

The supreme importance
of this nameless spectacle

sped me by them
without a word–

Why bother where I went?
for I went spinning on the

four wheels of my car
along the wet road until

I saw a girl with one leg
over the rail of a balcony

Hemmed-in Males

The saloon is gone up the creek
with the black sand round its
mouth, it went floating like

a backhouse on the Mississippi in
flood time but it went up
the creek into Limbo from whence

only empty bottles ever return
and that's where George is
He's gone upstream to ask 'em

to let him in at the hole
in the wall where the W.C.T.U.
sits knitting elastic stockings

for varicose veins. Poor George
he's got a job now as janitor
in Lincoln School but the saloon

is gone forever with pictures
of Sullivan and Kilrain on
the walls and Pop Anson holding

a bat. Poor George, they've cut
out his pituitary gland and his
vas deferens is in the spitoon–

you can laugh at him without his
organs but that's the way with
a river when it wants to

drown you, it sucks you in and
you feel the old saloon sinking
under you and you say good-by

just as George did, good-by poetry
the black sand's got me, the old
days are over, there's no place

any more for me to go now
except home–

The Bull

It is in captivity–
ringed, haltered, chained
to a drag
the bull is godlike

Unlike the cows
he lives alone, nozzles
the sweet grass gingerly
to pass the time away

He kneels, lies down
and stretching out
a foreleg licks himself
about the hoof

then stays
with half-closed eyes,
Olympian commentary on
the bright passage of days.

–The round sun
smooths his lacquer
through
the glossy pine trees
his substance hard
as ivory or glass–
through which the wind
yet plays–
                    milkless

he nods
the hair between his horns
and eyes matted
with hyacinthine curls.

The Yachts

contend in a sea which the land partly encloses
shielding them from the too-heavy blows
of an ungoverned ocean which when it chooses

tortures the biggest hulls, the best man knows
to pit against its beatings, and sinks them pitilessly.
Mothlike in mists, scintillant in the minute

brilliance of cloudless days, with broad bellying sails
they glide to the wind tossing green water
from their sharp prows while over them the crew crawls

ant-like, solicitously grooming them, releasing,
making fast as they turn, lean far over and having
caught the wind again, side by side, head for the mark.

In a well-guarded arena of open water surrounded by
lesser and greater craft which, sycophant, lumbering
and flittering follow them, they appear youthful, rare

as the light of a happy eye, live with the grace
of all that in the mind is feckless, free and
naturally to be desired. Now the sea which holds them

is moody, lapping their glossy sides, as if feeling
for some slightest flaw but fails completely.
Today no race. Then the wind comes again. The yachts

move, jockeying for a start, the signal is set and they
are off. Now the waves strike at them but they are too
well made, they slip through, though they take in canvas.

Arms with hands grasping seek to clutch at the prows.
Bodies thrown recklessly in the way are cut aside.
It is a sea of faces about them in agony, in despair

until the horror of the race dawns staggering the mind,
the whole sea become an entanglement of watery bodies
lost to the world bearing what they cannot hold. Broken,

beaten, desolate, reaching from the dead to be taken up
they cry out, failing, failing! their cries rising
in waves still as the skillful yachts pass over.

Signs everywhere of birds nesting, while

Signs everywhere of birds nesting, while
in the air, slow, a crow zigzags
with heavy wings before the wasp-thrusts
of smaller birds circling about him
that dive from above stabbing for his eyes

Walking–

he leaves the path, finds hard going
across-field, stubble and matted brambles
seeming a pasture–but no pasture .
–old furrows, to say labour sweated or
had sweated here .

a flame,

spent.

The file-sharp grass .

When! from before his feet, half tripping,
picking a way, there starts

a flight of empurpled wings!

–invisibly created (their
jackets dust-grey) from the dust kindled
to sudden ardor!

They fly away, churring! until
their strength spent they plunge
to the coarse cover again and disappear
–but leave, livening the mind, a flashing
of wings and a churring song .

AND a grasshopper of red basalt, boot-long,
tumbles from the core of his mind,
a rubble-bank disintegrating beneath a
tropic downpour

Chapultepec! grasshopper hill!

–a matt stone solicitously instructed
to bear away some rumor
of the living presence that has preceded
it, out-precedented its breath .

These wings do not unfold for flight–
no need!
the weight (to the hand) finding
a counter-weight or counter buoyancy
by the mind's wings .

He is afraid! What then?

Before his feet, at each step, the flight
is renewed. A burst of wings, a quick
churring sound :

couriers to the ceremonial of love!

-aflame in flight!

-aflame only in flight!

No flesh but the caress!

He is led forward by their announcing wings.

James Elroy Flecker (*Br. 1884–1915*)

The Old Ships

I have seen old ships sail like swans asleep
Beyond the village which men still call Tyre,
With leaden age o'ercargoed, dipping deep
For Famagusta and the hidden sun
That rings black Cyprus with a lake of fire;
And all those ships were certainly so old
Who knows how oft with squat and noisy gun,
Questing brown slaves or Syrian oranges,
The pirate Genoese
Hell-raked them till they rolled
Blood, water, fruit and corpses up the hold.
But now through friendly seas they softly run,
Painted the mid-sea blue or shore-sea green,
Still patterned with the vine and grapes in gold.

But I have seen,
Pointing her shapely shadows from the dawn
An image tumbled on a rose-swept bay,
A drowsy ship of some yet older day;
And, wonder's breath indrawn,
Thought I–who knows–who knows–but in
that same
(Fished up beyond Ææa, patched up new
–Stern painted brighter blue–)
That talkative, bald-headed seaman came

(Twelve patient comrades sweating at the oar)
From Troy's doom-crimson shore,
And with great lies about his wooden horse
Set the crew laughing, and forgot his course.

It was so old a ship–who knows, who knows?
–And yet so beautiful, I watched in vain
To see the mast burst open with a rose,
And the whole deck put on its leaves again.

November Eves

November Evenings! Damp and still
They used to cloak Leckhampton hill,
And lie down close on the grey plain,
And dim the dripping window-pane,
And send queer winds like Harlequins
That seized our elms for violins
And struck a note so sharp and low
Even a child could feel the woe.

Now fire chased shadow round the room;
Tables and chairs grew vast in gloom:
We crept about like mice, while Nurse
Sat mending, solemn as a hearse,
And even our unlearned eyes
Half closed with choking memories.

Is it the mist or the dead leaves,
Or the dead men–November eves?

Andrew Young (*Br. b. 1885*)

Hard Frost

Frost called to water "Halt!"
And crusted the moist snow with sparkling salt;
Brooks, their own bridges, stop,
And icicles in long stalactites drop,
And tench in water-holes
Lurk under gluey glass like fish in bowls.

In the hard-rutted lane
At every footstep breaks a brittle pane,
And tinkling trees ice-bound,
Changed into weeping willows, sweep the ground;
Dead boughs take root in ponds
And ferns on windows shoot their ghostly fronds.

But vainly the fierce frost
Interns poor fish, ranks trees in an armed host,
Hangs daggers from house-eaves
And on the windows ferny ambush weaves;
In the long war grown warmer
The sun will strike him dead and strip his armour.

Late Autumn

The boy called to his team
And with blue-glancing share
Turned up the rape and turnip
With yellow charlock to spare.

The long lean thistles stood
Like beggars ragged and blind,
Half their white silken locks
Blown away on the wind.

But I thought not once of winter
Or summer that was past
Till I saw that slant-legged robin
With autumn on his chest.

March Hares

I made myself as a tree,
No withered leaf twirling on me;
No, not a bird that stirred my boughs,
As looking out from wizard brows
I watched those lithe and lovely forms
That raised the leaves in storms.

I watched them leap and run,
Their bodies hollowed in the sun
To thin transparency,
That I could clearly see
The shallow colour of their blood
Joyous in love's full flood.

I was content enough,
Watching that serious game of love,
That happy hunting in the wood
Where the pursuer was the more pursued,
To stand in breathless hush
With no more life myself than tree or bush.

Walking in Beech Leaves

I tread on many autumns here
  But with no pride,
For at the leaf-fall of each year
  I also died.

This is last autumn, crisp and brown,
  That my knees feel;
But through how many years sinks down
  My sullen heel.

Elinor Wylie (*Am. 1885–1929*)

Hymn to Earth

Farewell, incomparable element,
Whence man arose, where he shall not return;
And hail, imperfect urn
Of his last ashes, and his firstborn fruit;
Farewell, the long pursuit,
And all the adventures of his discontent;
The voyages which sent
His heart averse from home:
Metal of clay, permit him that he come
To thy slow-burning fire as to a hearth;
Accept him as a particle of earth.

Fire, being divided from the other three,
It lives removed, or secret at the core;
Most subtle of the four,
When air flies not, nor water flows,
It disembodied goes,
Being light, elixir of the first decree,
More volatile than he;
With strength and power to pass
Through space, where never his least atom
  was:
He has no part in it, save as his eyes
Have drawn its emanation from the skies.

A wingless creature heavier than air,
He is rejected of its quintessence;
Coming and going hence,
In the twin minutes of his birth and death,
He may inhale as breath,
As breath relinquish heaven's atmosphere,
Yet in it have no share,
Nor can survive therein
Where its outer edge is filtered pure and thin:
It doth but lend its crystal to his lungs
For his early crying, and his final songs.

The element of water has denied
Its child; it is no more his element;
It never will relent;
Its silver harvests are more sparsely given
Than the rewards of heaven,
And he shall drink cold comfort at its side:
The water is too wide:
The seamew and the gull
Feather a nest made soft and pitiful
Upon its foam; he has not any part
In the long swell of sorrow at its heart.

Hail and farewell, beloved element,
Whence he departed, and his parent once;
See where thy spirit runs
Which for so long hath had the moon to wife;
Shall this support his life

Until the arches of the waves be bent
And grow shallow and spent?
Wisely it cast him forth
With his dead weight of burdens nothing worth,
Leaving him, for the universal years,
A little sea water to make his tears.

Hail, element of earth, receive thy own,
And cherish, at thy charitable breast,
This man, this mongrel beast:
He ploughs the sand, and, at his hardest need,
He sows himself for seed;
He ploughs the furrow, and in this lies down
Before the corn is grown;
Between the apple bloom
And the ripe apple is sufficient room
In time, and matter, to consume his love
And make him parcel of a cypress grove.

Receive him as thy lover for an hour
Who will not weary, by a longer stay,
The kind embrace of clay;
Even within thine arms he is dispersed
To nothing, as at first;
The air flings downward from its four-quartered
  tower
Him whom the flames devour;
At the full tide, at the flood,
The sea is mingled with his salty blood:
The traveller dust, although the dust be vile,
Sleeps as thy lover for a little while.

D. H. Lawrence (*Br. 1885–1930*)

Ballad of Another Ophelia

O the green glimmer of apples in the orchard,
Lamps in a wash of rain!
O the wet walk of my brown hen through the stackyard!
O tears on the window-pane!

Nothing now will ripen the bright green apples
Full of disappointment and of rain;
Blackish they will taste, of tears, when the yellow dapples
Of autumn tell the withered tale again.

All round the yard it is cluck! my brown hen.
Cluck! and the rain-wet wings;
Cluck! my marigold bird, and again
Cluck! for your yellow darlings.

For a grey rat found the gold thirteen
Huddled away in the dark.
Flutter for a moment, oh, the beast is quick and keen,
Extinct one yellow-fluffy spark!

Once I had a lover bright like running water,
Once his face was open like the sky,
Open like the sky looking down in all its laughter
On the buttercups, and the buttercups was I.

What then is there hidden in the skirts of all the blossom?
What is peeping from your skirts, O mother hen?
'Tis the sun that asks the question, in a lovely haste for wisdom;
What a lovely haste for wisdom is in men!

Yea, but it is cruel when undressed is all the blossom
And her shift is lying white upon the floor,
That a grey one, like a shadow, like a rat, a thief, a rainstorm
Creeps upon her then and ravishes her store!

O the grey garner that is full of half-grown apples!
O the golden sparkles laid extinct!
And O, behind the cloud-leaves, like yellow autumn dapples,
Did you see the wicked sun that winked?

End of Another Home Holiday

When shall I see the half-moon sink again
Behind the black sycamore at the end of the garden?
When will the scent of the dim white phlox
Creep up the wall to me, and in at my open window?

Why is it, the long, slow stroke of the midnight bell
(Will it never finish the twelve?)
Falls again and again on my heart with a heavy reproach?

The moon-mist is over the village, out of the mist speaks the bell,
And all the little roofs of the village bow low, pitiful, beseeching, resigned.
–Speak, you my home! what is it I don't do well?

Ah home, suddenly I love you
As I hear the sharp clean trot of a pony down the road,
Succeeding sharp little sounds dropping into silence
Clear upon the long-drawn hoarseness of a train across the valley.

* * * *

The light has gone out, from under my mother's door.
That she should love me so!–
She, so lonely, greying now
And I leaving her,
Bent on my pursuits!

Love is the great Asker.
The sun and the rain do not ask the secret
Of the time when the grain struggles down in the dark.
The moon walks her lonely way without anguish,
Because no one grieves over her departure.

Forever, ever by my shoulder pitiful love will linger,
Crouching as little houses crouch under the mist when I turn.
Forever, out of the mist, the church lifts up a reproachful finger,
Pointing my eyes in wretched defiance where love hides her face to mourn.

Oh! but the rain creeps down to wet the grain
That struggles alone in the dark,
And asking nothing, patiently steals back again!
The moon sets forth o' nights
To walk the lonely, dusky heights
Serenely, with steps unswerving;
Pursued by no sigh of bereavement,
No tears of love unnerving
Her constant tread:

While ever at my side,
Frail and sad, with grey, bowed head,
The beggar-woman, the yearning-eyed
Inexorable love goes lagging.

The wild young heifer, glancing distraught,
With a strange new knocking of life at her side
Runs seeking a loneliness.
The little grain draws down the earth, to hide.
Nay, even the slumberous egg, as it labours under the shell
Patiently to divide and self-divide,
Asks to be hidden, and wishes nothing to tell.

But when I draw the scanty cloak of silence over my eyes
Piteous love comes peering under the hood;
Touches the clasp with trembling fingers, and tries
To put her ear to the painful sob of my blood;
While her tears soak through to my breast,
Where they burn and cauterise.

* * * *

The moon lies back and reddens.
In the valley a corncrake calls
Monotonously,
With a plaintive, unalterable voice, that deadens
My confident activity;
With a hoarse, insistent request that falls
Unweariedly, unweariedly,
Asking something more of me,
Yet more of me.

Snake

A snake came to my water-trough
On a hot, hot day, and I in pyjamas for the heat,
To drink there.

In the deep, strange-scented shade of the great dark carob-tree
I came down the steps with my pitcher
And must wait, must stand and wait, for there he was at the trough before me.

He reached down from a fissure in the earth-wall in the gloom
And trailed his yellow-brown slackness soft-bellied down, over
  the edge of the stone trough
And rested his throat upon the stone bottom,
And where the water had dripped from the tap, in a small
  clearness,
He sipped with his straight mouth,
Softly drank through his straight gums, into his slack long body,
Silently.

Someone was before me at my water-trough,
And I, like a second comer, waiting.

He lifted his head from his drinking, as cattle do,
And looked at me vaguely, as drinking cattle do,
And flickered his two-forked tongue from his lips, and mused
  a moment,
And stooped and drank a little more,
Being earth-brown, earth-golden from the burning bowels of
  the earth
On the day of Sicilian July, with Etna smoking.

The voice of my education said to me
He must be killed,
For in Sicily the black, black snakes are innocent, the gold are
  venomous.

And voices in me said, If you were a man
You would take a stick and break him now, and finish him off.

But must I confess how I liked him,
How glad I was he had come like a guest in quiet, to drink at
  my water-trough
And depart peaceful, pacified, and thankless,
Into the burning bowels of this earth?

Was it cowardice, that I dared not kill him?
Was it perversity, that I longed to talk to him?
Was it humility, to feel so honoured?
I felt so honoured.

And yet those voices:
If you were not afraid, you would kill him!

And truly I was afraid, I was most afraid,
But even so, honoured still more
That he should seek my hospitality
From out the dark door of the secret earth.

He drank enough
And lifted his head, dreamily, as one who has drunken,
And flickered his tongue like a forked night on the air, so
black,
Seeming to lick his lips,
And looked around like a god, unseeing, into the air,
And slowly turned his head,
And slowly, very slowly, as if thrice adream,
Proceeded to draw his slow length curving round
And climb again the broken bank of my wall-face.
And as he put his head into that dreadful hole,
And as he slowly drew up, snake-easing his shoulders, and
entered farther,
A sort of horror, a sort of protest against his withdrawing into
that horrid black hole,
Deliberately going into the blackness, and slowly drawing him-
self after,
Overcame me now his back was turned.

I looked round, I put down my pitcher,
I picked up a clumsy log
And threw it at the water-trough with a clatter.

I think it did not hit him,
But suddenly that part of him that was left behind convulsed in
undignified haste,
Writhed like lightning, and was gone
Into the black hole, the earth-lipped fissure in the wall-front,
At which, in the intense still noon, I stared with fascination.

And immediately I regretted it.
I thought how paltry, how vulgar, what a mean act!
I despised myself and the voices of my accursed human
education.

And I thought of the albatross,
And I wished he would come back, my snake.

For he seemed to me again like a king,
Like a king in exile, uncrowned in the underworld,
Now due to be crowned again.

And so, I missed my chance with one of the lords
Of life.
And I have something to expiate;
A pettiness.

Kangaroo

In the northern hemisphere
Life seems to leap at the air, or skim under the wind
Like stags on rocky ground, or pawing horses, or springy scut-tailed rabbits.

Or else rush horizontal to charge at the sky's horizon,
Like bulls or bisons or wild pigs.

Or slip like water slippery towards its ends,
As foxes, stoats, and wolves, and prairie dogs.

Only mice, and moles, and rats, and badgers, and beavers, and perhaps bears
Seem belly-plumbed to the earth's mid-navel.
Or frogs that when they leap come flop, and flop to the centre of the earth.

But the yellow antipodal Kangaroo, when she sits up,
Who can unseat her, like a liquid drop that is heavy, and just touches earth.

The downward drip.
The down-urge.
So much denser than cold-blooded frogs.

Delicate mother Kangaroo
Sitting up there rabbit-wise, but huge, plumb-weighted,
And lifting her beautiful slender face, oh! so much more gently and finely lined than a rabbit's, or than a hare's,
Lifting her face to nibble at a round white peppermint drop, which she loves, sensitive mother Kangaroo.

Her sensitive, long, pure-bred face.
Her full antipodal eyes, so dark,
So big and quiet and remote, having watched so many empty dawns in silent Australia.

Her little loose hands, and drooping Victorian shoulders.
And then her great weight below the waist, her vast pale belly
With a thin young yellow little paw hanging out, and straggle
  of a long thin ear, like ribbon,
Like a funny trimming to the middle of her belly, thin little
  dangle of an immature paw, and one thin ear.

Her belly, her big haunches
And, in addition, the great muscular python-stretch of her tail.

There, she shan't have any more peppermint drops.
So she wistfully, sensitively sniffs the air, and then turns, goes
  off in slow sad leaps
On the long flat skis of her legs,
Steered and propelled by that steel-strong snake of a tail.

Stops again, half turns, inquisitive to look back.
While something stirs quickly in her belly, and a lean little face
  comes out, as from a window,
Peaked and a bit dismayed,
Only to disappear again quickly away from the sight of the
  world, to snuggle down in the warmth,
Leaving the trail of a different paw hanging out.

Still she watches with eternal, cocked wistfulness!
How full her eyes are, like the full, fathomless, shining eyes of
  an Australian black-boy
Who has been lost so many centuries on the margins of existence!

She watches with insatiable wistfulness.
Untold centuries of watching for something to come,
For a new signal from life, in that silent lost land of the South.
Where nothing bites but insects and snakes and the sun, small life.
Where no bull roared, no cow ever lowed, no stag cried, no
  leopard screeched, no lion coughed, no dog barked,
But all was silent save for parrots occasionally, in the haunted
  blue bush.

Wistfully watching, with wonderful liquid eyes.
And all her weight, all her blood, dripping sack-wise down
  towards the earth's centre,
And the live little-one taking in its paw at the door of her belly.

Leap then, and come down on the line that draws to the earth's
  deep, heavy centre.

Sicilian Cyclamens

When he pushed his bush of black hair off his brow:
When she lifted her mop from her eyes, and screwed it in a knob behind
–O act of fearful temerity!
When they felt their foreheads bare, naked to heaven, their eyes revealed:
When they felt the light of heaven brandished like a knife at their defenceless eyes,
And the sea like a blade at their face,
Mediterranean savages:
When they came out, face-revealed, under heaven, from the shaggy undergrowth of their own hair
For the first time,
They saw tiny rose cyclamens between their toes, growing
Where the slow toads sat brooding on the past.

Slow toads, and cyclamen leaves
Stickily glistening with eternal shadow
Keeping to earth.
Cyclamen leaves
Toad-filmy, earth-iridescent
Beautiful
Frost-filigreed
Spumed with mud
Snail-nacreous
Low down.

The shaking aspect of the sea
And man's defenceless bare face
And cyclamens putting their ears back.
Long, pensive, slim-muzzled greyhound buds
Dreamy, not yet present,
Drawn out of earth
At his toes.

Dawn-rose
Sub-delighted, stone-engendered
Cyclamens, young cyclamens
Arching

Waking, pricking their ears
Like delicate very-young greyhound bitches
Half-yawning at the open, inexperienced
Vista of day,
Folding back their soundless petalled ears.

Greyhound bitches
Bending their rosy muzzles pensive down,
And breathing soft, unwilling to wake to the new day
Yet sub-delighted.

Ah Mediterranean morning, when our world began!
Far-off Mediterranean mornings,
Pelasgic faces uncovered,
And unbudding cyclamens.
The hare suddenly goes uphill
Laying back her long ears with unwinking bliss.

And up the pallid, sea-blenched Mediterranean stone-slopes
Rose cyclamen, ecstatic fore-runner!
Cyclamens, ruddy-muzzled cyclamens
In little bunches like bunches of wild hares
Muzzles together, ears-aprick,
Whispering witchcraft
Like women at a well, the dawn-fountain.
Greece, and the world's morning
Where all the Parthenon marbles still fostered the roots of the
cyclamen.
Violets
Pagan, rosy-muzzled violets
Autumnal
Dawn-pink,
Dawn-pale
Among squat toad-leaves sprinkling the unborn
Erechtheion marbles.

Ezra Pound (*Am. b. 1885*)

From Hugh Selwyn Mauberley (*Life and Contacts*) I-V

E.P. Ode Pour l'Election de Son Sepnlchre

For three years, out of key with his time,
He strove to resuscitate the dead art
Of poetry; to maintain "the sublime"
In the old sense. Wrong from the start–

No, hardly, but seeing he had been born
In a half savage country, out of date;
Bent resolutely on wringing lilies from the acorn;
Capaneus; trout for factitious bait;

Ἴδμεν γάρ τοι πάνθ', ὅσ' ἐνὶ Τροίῃ
Caught in the unstopped ear;
Giving the rocks small lee-way
The chopped seas held him, therefore, that year.

His true Penelope was Flaubert,
He fished by obstinate isles;
Observed the elegance of Circe's hair
Rather than the mottoes on sun-dials.

Unaffected by "the march of events,"
He passed from men's memory in *l'an trentiesme*
De son eage; the case presents
No adjunct to the Muses' diadem.

II

The age demanded an image
Of its accelerated grimace,
Something for the modern stage,
Not, at any rate, an Attic grace;

Not, not certainly, the obscure reveries
Of the inward gaze;
Better mendacities
Than the classics in paraphrase!

The "age demanded" chiefly a mould in plaster,
Made with no loss of time,
A prose kinema, not, not assuredly, alabaster
Or the "sculpture" of rhyme.

III

The tea-rose tea-gown, etc.
Supplants the mousseline of Cos,
The pianola "replaces"
Sappho's barbitos.

Christ follows Dionysus,
Phallic and ambrosial
Made way for macerations;
Caliban casts out Ariel.

All things are a flowing,
Sage Heracleitus says;
But a tawdry cheapness
Shall outlast our days.

Even the Christian beauty
Defects–after Samothrace;
We see τὸ καλὸν
Decreed in the market place.

Faun's flesh is not to us,
Nor the saint's vision.
We have the press for wafer;
Franchise for circumcision.

All men, in law, are equals.
Free of Pisistratus,
We choose a knave or an eunuch
To rule over us.

O bright Apollo,
τίν' ἄνδρα, τίν' ἥρωα, τίνα θεόν,
What god, man, or hero
Shall I place a tin wreath upon!

IV

These fought in any case,
and some believing,
pro domo, in any case . . .

Some quick to arm,
some for adventure,
some from fear of weakness,
some from fear of censure,
some for love of slaughter, in imagination,
learning later . . .
some in fear, learning love of slaughter;

Died some, pro patria,
non "dulce" non "et decor" . . .
walked eye-deep in hell
believing in old men's lies, then unbelieving
came home, home to a lie,
home to many deceits,
home to old lies and new infamy;
usury age-old and age-thick
and liars in public places.

Daring as never before, wastage as never before.
Young blood and high blood,
fair cheeks, and fine bodies;

fortitude as never before,

frankness as never before,
disillusions as never told in the old days,
hysterias, trench confessions,
laughter out of dead bellies.

V

There died a myriad,
And of the best, among them,
For an old bitch gone in the teeth,
For a botched civilization,

Charm, smiling at the good mouth,
Quick eyes gone under earth's lid,

For two gross of broken statues,
For a few thousand battered books.

Homage to Sextus Propertius, I

Shades of Callimachus, Coan ghosts of Philetas
It is in your grove I would walk,
I who come first from the clear font
Bringing the Grecian orgies into Italy,
and the dance into Italy.
Who hath taught you so subtle a measure,
in what hall have you heard it;
What foot beat out your time-bar,
what water has mellowed your whistles?

Out-weariers of Apollo will, as we know, continue their Martian generalities,
We have kept our erasers in order.
A new-fangled chariot follows the flower-hung horses;
A young Muse with young loves clustered about her
ascends with me into the aether, . . .
And there is no high-road to the Muses.

Annalists will continue to record Roman reputations,
Celebrities from the Trans-Caucasus will belaud Roman celebrities
And expound the distentions of Empire,
But for something to read in normal circumstances?
For a few pages brought down from the forked hill unsullied?
I ask a wreath which will not crush my head.
And there is no hurry about it;
I shall have, doubtless, a boom after my funeral,
Seeing that long standing increases all things
regardless of quality.

And who would have known the towers
pulled down by a deal-wood horse;
Or of Achilles withstaying waters by Simois
Or of Hector spattering wheel-rims,
Or of Polydmantus, by Scamander, or Helenus and Deiphoibos?
Their door-yards would scarcely know them, or Paris.
Small talk O Ilion, and O Troad
twice taken by Oetian gods,
If Homer had not stated your case!

And I also among the later nephews of this city
shall have my dog's day,
With no stone upon my contemptible sepulchre;
My vote coming from the temple of Phoebus in Lycia, at
Patara,
And in the meantime my songs will travel,
And the devirginated young ladies will enjoy them
when they have got over the strangeness,
For Orpheus tamed the wild beasts–
and held up the Threician river;
And Citharaon shook up the rocks by Thebes
and danced them into a bulwark at his pleasure,
And you, O Polyphemus? Did harsh Galatea almost
Turn to your dripping horses, because of a tune, under
Aetna?
We must look into the matter.
Bacchus and Apollo in favour of it,
There will be a crowd of young women doing homage to my
palaver,
Though my house is not propped up by Taenarian columns
from Laconia (associated with Neptune and Cerberus),
Though it is not stretched upon gilded beams;
My orchards do not lie level and wide
as the forests of Phaecia,
the luxurious and Ionian,
Nor are my caverns stuffed stiff with a Marcian vintage,
My cellar does not date from Numa Pompilius,
Nor bristle with wine jars,
Nor is it equipped with a frigidaire patent;
Yet the companions of the Muses
will keep their collective nose in my books,
And weary with historical data, they will turn to my dance
tune.

Happy who are mentioned in my pamphlets,
the songs shall be a fine tombstone over their beauty.
But against this?
Neither expensive pyramids scraping the stars in their route,
Nor houses modelled upon that of Jove in East Elis,
Nor the monumental effigies of Mausolus,
are a complete elucidation of death.

Flame burns, rain sinks into the cracks
And they all go to rack ruin beneath the thud of the years.
Stands genius a deathless adornment,
a name not to be worn out with the years.

Portrait d'Une Femme

Your mind and you are our Sargasso Sea,
London has swept about you this score years
And bright ships left you this or that in fee:
Ideas, old gossip, oddments of all things,
Strange spars of knowledge and dimmed wares of
price.
Great minds have sought you–lacking someone else.
You have been second always. Tragical?
No. You preferred it to the usual thing:
One dull man, dulling and uxorious,
One average mind–with one thought less each year.
Oh, you are patient, I have seen you sit
Hours, where something might have floated up.
And now you pay one. Yes, you richly pay.
You are a person of some interest, one comes to you
And takes strange gain away:
Trophies fished up; some curious suggestion;
Fact that leads nowhere; and a tale or two,
Pregnant with mandrakes, or with something else
That might prove useful and yet never proves,
That never fits a corner or shows use,
Or finds its hour upon the loom of days:
The tarnished, gaudy, wonderful old work;
Idols and ambergris and rare inlays,
These are your riches, your great store; and yet
For all this sea-hoard of deciduous things,
Strange woods half sodden, and new brighter stuff:
In the slow float of differing light and deep,
No! there is nothing! In the whole and all,
Nothing that's quite your own.
Yet this is you.

Δώρια

Be in me as the eternal moods
    of the bleak wind, and not
As transient things are–
    gaiety of flowers.
Have me in the strong loneliness
    of sunless cliffs
And of grey waters.
    Let the gods speak softly of us
In days hereafter,
    The shadowy flowers of Orcus
Remember thee.

Canto I

And then went down to the ship,
Set keel to breakers, forth on the godly sea, and
We set up mast and sail on that swart ship,
Bore sheep aboard her, and our bodies also
Heavy with weeping, and winds from sternward
Bore us out onward with bellying canvas,
Circe's this craft, the trim-coifed goddess.
Then sat we amidships, wind jamming the tiller,
Thus with stretched sail, we went over sea till day's end.
Sun to his slumber, shadows o'er all the ocean,
Came we then to the bounds of deepest water,
To the Kimmerian lands, and peopled cities
Covered with close-webbed mist, unpierced ever
With glitter of sun-rays
Nor with stars stretched, nor looking back from heaven
Swartest night stretched over wretched men there.
The ocean flowing backward, came we then to the place
Aforesaid by Circe.
Here did they rites, Perimedes and Eurylochus,
And drawing sword from my hip
I dug the ell-square pitkin;
Poured we libations unto each the dead,
First mead and then sweet wine, water mixed with white flour.
Then prayed I many a prayer to the sickly death's-heads;

As set in Ithaca, sterile bulls of the best
For sacrifice, heaping the pyre with goods,
A sheep to Tiresias only, black and a bell-sheep.
Dark blood flowed in the fosse,
Souls out of Erebus, cadaverous dead, of brides
Of youths and of the old who had borne much;
Souls stained with recent tears, girls tender,
Men many, mauled with bronze lance heads,
Battle spoil, bearing yet dreory arms,
These many crowded about me; with shouting,
Pallor upon me, cried to my men for more beasts;
Slaughtered the herds, sheep slain of bronze;
Poured ointment, cried to the gods,
To Pluto the strong, and praised Proserpine;
Unsheathed the narrow sword,
I sat to keep off the impetuous impotent dead,
Till I should hear Tiresias.
But first Elpenor came, our friend Elpenor,
Unburied, cast on the wide earth,
Limbs that we left in the house of Circe,
Unwept, unwrapped in sepulchre, since toils urged other.
Pitiful spirit. And I cried in hurried speech:
"Elpenor, how art thou come to this dark coast?
"Cam'st thou afoot, outstripping seamen?"
            And he in heavy speech:
"Ill fate and abundant wine. I slept in Circe's ingle.
"Going down the long ladder unguarded,
"I fell against the buttress,
"Shattered the nape-nerve, the soul sought Avernus.
"But thou, O King, I bid remember me, unwept, unburied,
"Heap up mine arms, be tomb by sea-bord, and inscribed:
"*A man of no fortune, and with a name to come.*
"And set my oar up, that I swung mid fellows."

And Anticlea came, whom I beat off, and then Tiresias
  Theban,
Holding his golden wand, knew me, and spoke first:
"A second time? why? man of ill star,
"Facing the sunless dead and this joyless region?
"Stand from the fosse, leave me my bloody bever

"For soothsay."
            And I stepped back,
And he strong with the blood, said then: "Odysseus
"Shalt return through spiteful Neptune, over dark seas,
"Lose all companions." And then Anticlea came.
Lie quiet Divus. I mean, that is Andreas Divus,
In officina Wecheli, 1538, out of Homer.
And he sailed, by Sirens and thence outward and away
And unto Circe.
            Venerandam,
In the Cretan's phrase, with the golden crown, Aphrodite,
Cypri munimenta sortita est, mirthful, oricalchi, with golden
Girdles and breast bands, thou with dark eyelids
Bearing the golden bough of Argicida. So that:

From *Canto LXXXI*

Yet
Ere the season died a-cold
Borne upon a zephyr's shoulder
I rose through the aureate sky
                        Lawes and Jenkyns guard thy rest
                        Dolmetsch ever be thy guest,
Has he tempered the viol's wood
To enforce   both the grave   and the acute?
Has he curved us the bowl of the lute?
                        Lawes and Jenkyns guard thy rest
                        Dolmetsch ever be thy guest
Hast 'ou fashioned so airy a mood
    To draw up leaf from the root?
Hast 'ou found   a cloud   so light
    As seemed neither mist nor shade?

                        Then resolve me, tell me aright
                        If Waller sang or Dowland played.

                Your eyen two wol sleye me sodenly
                I may the beauté of hem nat susteyne

And for 180 years almost nothing.

Ed ascoltando al leggier mormorio
        there came new subtlety of eyes into my tent,
whether of spirit or hypostasis,
        but what the blindfold hides
or at carneval
                                nor any pair showed anger
        Saw but the eyes and stance between the eyes,
colour, diastasis,
        careless or unaware it had not the
    whole tent's room
nor was place for the full Ειδὼς
interpass, penetrate
        casting but shade beyond the other lights
                sky's clear
                night's sea
                green of the mountain pool
                shone from the unmasked eyes in half-mask's space.
What thou lovest well remains,
                                                    the rest is dross
What thou lov'st well shall not be reft from thee
What thou lov'st well is thy true heritage
Whose world, or mine or theirs
                                            or is it of none?
First came the seen, then thus the palpable
        Elysium, though it were in the halls of hell,
What thou lovest well is thy true heritage

The ant's a centaur in his dragon world.
Pull down thy vanity, it is not man
Made courage, or made order, or made grace,
        Pull down thy vanity, I say pull down.
Learn of the green world what can be thy place
In scaled invention or true artistry,
Pull down thy vanity,
                                            Paquin pull down!
The green casque has outdone your elegance.

"Master thyself, then others shall thee beare"
        Pull down thy vanity
Thou art a beaten dog beneath the hail,
A swollen magpie in a fitful sun,

Half black half white
Nor knowst 'ou wing from tail
Pull down thy vanity
                How mean thy hates
Fostered in falsity,
                Pull down thy vanity,
Rathe to destroy, niggard in charity,
Pull down thy vanity,
                I say pull down.

But to have done instead of not doing
                this is not vanity
To have, with decency, knocked
That a Blunt should open
        To have gathered from the air a live tradition
or from a fine old eye the unconquered flame
This is not vanity.
    Here error is all in the not done,
all in the diffidence that faltered,

John Gould Fletcher (*Am. 1886–1950*)

Green Symphony

I

The glittering leaves of the rhododendrons
Balance and vibrate in the cool air;
While in the sky above them
White clouds chase each other.

Like scampering rabbits,
Flashes of sunlight sweep the lawn;
They fling in passing
Patterns of shadow,
Golden and green.

With long cascades of laughter,
The mating birds dart and swoop to the turf:
'Mid their mad trillings
Glints the gay sun behind the trees.

Down there are deep blue lakes:
Orange blossom droops in the water.

In the tower of the winds,
All the bells are set adrift:
Jingling
For the dawn.

Thin fluttering streamers
Of breeze lash through the swaying boughs;
Palely expectant
The earth receives the slanting rain.

I am a glittering raindrop
Hugged close by the cool rhododendron.
I am a daisy starring
The exquisite curves of the close-cropped turf.

The glittering leaves of the rhododendron
Are shaken like blue-green blades of grass,
Flickering, cracking, falling:
Splintering in a million fragments.

The wind runs laughing up the slope
Stripping off handfuls of wet green leaves,
To fling in people's faces.
Wallowing on the daisy-powdered turf,
Clutching at the sunlight,
Cavorting in the shadow.

Like baroque pearls,
Like cloudy emeralds,
The clouds and the trees clash together;
Whirling and swirling
In the tumult
Of the spring,
And the wind.

II

The trees splash the sky with their fingers,
A restless green rout of stars.

With whirling movement
They swing their boughs
About their stems:

Planes on planes of light and shadow
Pass among them,
Opening fanlike to fall.

The trees are like a sea;
Tossing,
Trembling,
Roaring,
Wallowing,
Darting their long green flickering fronds up at the sky,
Spotted with white blossom-spray.

The trees are roofs:
Hollow caverns of cool blue shadow,
Solemn arches
In the afternoons.
The whole vast horizon
In terrace beyond terrace,
Pinnacle above pinnacle,
Lifts to the sky
Serrated ranks of green on green.

They caress the roofs with their fingers,
They sprawl about the river to look into it;
Up the hill they come
Gesticulating challenge:
They cower together
In dark valleys;
They yearn out over the fields.

Enamelled domes
Tumble upon the grass,
Crashing in ruin
Quiet at last.

The trees lash the sky with their leaves,
Uneasily shaking their dark green manes.

III

Far let the voices of the mad wild birds be
calling me,
I will abide in this forest of pines.

When the wind blows,
Battling through the forest,
I hear it distantly,
The crash of a perpetual sea.

When the rain falls,
I watch silver spears slanting downwards
From pale river-pools of sky,
Enclosed in dark fronds.

When the sun shines,
I weave together far branches till they shape
  mighty circles,
I sway to the movement of hooded summits,
I swim leisurely in deep blue seas of air.

I hug the smooth bark of stately red pillars,
And with cones carefully scattered
I mark the progression of dark dial-shadows
Flung diagonally downwards through the afternoon.

This turf is not like turf:
It is a smooth dry carpet of velvet,
Embroidered with brown patterns of needles and cones.
These trees are not like trees:
They are innumerable feathery pagoda-umbrellas,
Stiffly ungracious to the wind,
Teetering on red-lacquered stems.

In the evening I listen to the winds' lisping,
While the conflagrations of the sunset flicker and clash
  behind me,
Flamboyant crenellations of glory amid the charred
  ebony boles.

In the night the fiery nightingales
Shall clash and trill through the silence:
Like the voices of mermaids crying
From the sea.

Long ago has the moon whelmed this uncompleted temple.
Stars swim like goldfish far above the black arches.

Far let the timid feet of dawn fly to catch me:
I will abide in this forest of pines:

For I have unveiled naked beauty,
And the things that she whispered to me in the darkness
Are buried deep in my heart.

Now let the black tops of the pine-trees break like a spent
wave,
Against the grey sky:
These are tombs and memorials and temples and altars
sun-kindled for me.

Frances Cornford (*Br. b. 1886*)

Autumn Morning at Cambridge

I ran out in the morning, when the air was clean and new
And all the grass was glittering and grey with autumn dew,
I ran out to an apple-tree and pulled an apple down,
And all the bells were ringing in the old grey town.

Down in the town off the bridges and the grass,
They are sweeping up the leaves to let the people pass,
Sweeping up the old leaves, golden-reds and browns,
Whilst the men go to lecture with the wind in their gowns.

Susan to Diana

Villanelle

Your youth is like a water-wetted stone,
A pebble by the living sea made rare,
Bright with a beauty that is not its own.

Behold it flushed like flowers newly-blown,
Miraculously fresh beyond compare,
Your youth is like a water-wetted stone.

For when the triumphing tide recedes, alone
The stone will stay, and shine no longer there
Bright with a beauty that is not its own.

But lie and dry as joyless as a bone,
Because the sorceress sea has gone elsewhere.
Your youth is like a water-wetted stone.

Then all your lovers will be children, shown
Their treasure only transitory-fair,
Bright with a beauty that is not its own.

Remember this before your hour is flown;
O you, who are so glorious, beware!
Your youth is like a water-wetted stone,
Bright with a beauty that is not its own.

Siegfried Sassoon (*Br. b. 1886*)

The Dug-out

Why do you lie with your legs ungainly huddled,
And one arm bent across your sullen, cold,
Exhausted face? It hurts my heart to watch you,
Deep-shadow'd from the candle's guttering gold;
And you wonder why I shake you by the shoulder;
Drowsy, you mumble and sigh and turn your head . . .
You are too young to fall asleep for ever;
And when you sleep you remind me of the dead.

The General

"Good-morning; good-morning!" the General said
When we met him last week on our way to the line.
Now the soldiers he smiled at are most of 'em dead,
And we're cursing his staff for incompetent swine.
"He's a cheery old card," grunted Harry to Jack
As they slogged up to Arras with rifle and pack.

* * * *

But he did for them both by his plan of attack.

'*Blighters*'

The House is crammed: tier beyond tier they grin
And cackle at the Show, while prancing ranks
Of harlots shrill the chorus, drunk with din;
"We're sure the Kaiser loves our dear old Tanks!"
I'd like to see a Tank come down the stalls,
Lurching to rag-time tunes, or "Home, sweet Home,"

And there'd be no more jokes in Music-halls
To mock the riddled corpses round Bapaume.

The Death-bed

He drowsed and was aware of silence heaped
Round him, unshaken as the steadfast walls;
Aqueous like floating rays of amber light,
Soaring and quivering in the wings of sleep.
Silence and safety; and his mortal shore
Lipped by the inward, moonless waves of death.

Someone was holding water to his mouth.
He swallowed, unresisting; moaned and dropped
Through crimson gloom to darkness; and forgot
The opiate throb and ache that was his wound.
  Water–calm, sliding green above the weir.
  Water–a sky-lit alley for his boat,
  Bird-voiced, and bordered with reflected flowers
  And shaken hues of summer; drifting down,
  He dipped contented oars, and sighed, and slept.

Night, with a gust of wind, was in the ward,
Blowing the curtain to a glimmering curve.
Night. He was blind; he could not see the stars
Glinting among the wraiths of wandering cloud;
Queer blots of colour, purple, scarlet, green,
Flickered and faded in his drowning eyes.

Rain–he could hear it rustling through the dark;
Fragrance and passionless music woven as one;
Warm rain on drooping roses; pattering showers
That soak the woods; not the harsh rain that sweeps
Behind the thunder, but a trickling peace,
Gently and slowly washing life away.

* * * *

He stirred, shifting his body; then the pain
Leapt like a prowling beast, and gripped and tore
His groping dreams with grinding claws and fangs.
  But someone was beside him; soon he lay
  Shuddering because that evil thing had passed.
  And death, who'd stepped toward him, paused and stared.

Light many lamps and gather round his bed.
Lend him your eyes, warm blood, and will to live.
Speak to him; rouse him; you may save him yet.
He's young; he hated War; how should he die
When cruel old campaigners win safe through?

But death replied: "I choose him." So he went,
And there was silence in the summer night;
Silence and safety; and the veils of sleep.
Then, far away, the thudding of the guns.

Fantasia on a Wittelsbach Atmosphere

Drab drugget paths protect these polished floors
From tourist-soled attrition. Guide-book phrases
Co-ordinate fatigued and baffled brains
With mute ex-regal affluence. Simpering faces
Exposed in state-saloons and corridors
Survive the modes of soporific reigns.

A baton, and a battle (was it Blenheim?)
Respectfully remote; the steed curvetting
Beneath his flushed Elector: what's the betting
He failed? . . . No gouty poet lives to pen him
Campaign-concluding odes. Mark, too, the mien
(Obese in ermine, sceptred and serene),
Of goggling Max Augustus! Where's the Court
That equerried his jinks down aisles of green
To chevy stags in sycophantic sport?

Nevertheless, while strolling past such glories
(Van Dyck to Winterhalter; stiff brocade
And powder, to frock-coats and whiskered smiles),
My spirit shares with monarchismal Tories
The fairy-tale of Flunkeydom, displayed
In feudal relicry of centuried styles.
My sympathy for Soviets notwithstanding–
(Dare one deplore the dullness of Democracy?)
I am touched, I am enticed, by super-lavish
Expense; half-cultured coxcomb Kings commanding
In palacefuls the trappings of Autocracy,
With all their country's coffers ripe to ravish.

Outside, sham Renaissance façades evade
Modernity; a melancholic air
Half-masks them, while the sun-warmed windows stare
Affronted on the purposeless parade
Of pygmy visitors. In postures glum,
Like exiled Counts the statues mope aloof.
No vultured banner flaps above the roof:
And loyal gardens, drowsing in the hum
And slant of lapsing afternoon, seem sad.
Fountains upheave pale plumes against the sky,
Murmuring, "*Their Majesties came sauntering by–*
Was it but yesterday?" . . . Proud fountains sigh
Toward the long glades in golden foliage clad,
"*Kurfürsts could do no wrong.*" . . . And the woods reply,
"*Take them for what they were, they weren't so bad!*"

Storm on Fifth Avenue

A sallow waiter brings me six huge oysters . . .
Gloom shutters up the sunset with a plague
Of unpropitious twilight jagged asunder
By flashlight demonstrations. *Gee, what a peach*
Of a climate! (Pardon slang: these sultry storms
Afflict me with neurosis: rumbling thunder
Shakes my belief in academic forms.)

An oyster-coloured atmospheric rumpus
Beats up to blot the sunken daylight's gildings.
Against the looming cloud-bank, ivory-pale,
Stand twenty-storied blocks of office-buildings.
Snatched upward on a gust, lost news-sheets sail
Forlorn in lone arena of mid-air;
Flapping like melancholy kites, they scare
My gaze, a note of wildness in the scene.

Out on the pattering side-walk, people hurry
For shelter, while the tempest swoops to scurry
Across to Brooklyn. Bellying figures clutch
At wide-brimmed hats and bend to meet the weather,
Alarmed for fresh-worn silks and flurried feather.

Then hissing deluge splashes down to beat
The darkly glistening flatness of the street.
Only the cars nose on through rain-lashed twilight:
Only the Sherman Statue, angel-guided,
Maintains its mock-heroic martial gesture.

A sallow waiter brings me beans and pork . . .
Outside there's fury in the firmament.
Ice-cream, of course, will follow; and I'm content.
O Babylon! O Carthage! O New York!

Falling Asleep

Voices moving about in the quiet house:
Thud of feet and a muffled shutting of doors:
Everyone yawning. Only the clocks are alert.

Out in the night there's autumn-smelling gloom
Crowded with whispering trees; across the park
A hollow cry of hounds like lonely bells:
And I know that the clouds are moving across the moon;
The low, red, rising moon. Now herons call
And wrangle by their pool; and hooting owls
Sail from the wood above pale stooks of oats.

Waiting for sleep, I drift from thoughts like these;
And where to-day was dream-like, build my dreams.
Music . . . there was a bright white room below,
And someone singing a song about a soldier,
One hour, two hours ago: and soon the song
Will be "*last night*"; but now the beauty swings
Across my brain, ghost of remembered chords
Which still can make such radiance in my dream
That I can watch the marching of my soldiers,
And count their faces; faces; sunlit faces.

Falling asleep . . . the herons, and the hounds. . . .
September in the darkness; and the world
I've known; all fading past me into peace.

John Hall Wheelock (*Am. b. 1886*)

Bonac

Du bist Orplid, mein Land, das ferne leuchtet–Mörike

I

This is enchanted country, lies under a spell,
Bird-haunted, ocean-haunted—land of youth,
Land of first love, land of death also, perhaps,
And desired return. Sea-tang and honeysuckle
Perfume the air, where the old house looks out
Across mild lowlands, meadows of scrub and pine,
A shell echoing the sea's monotone
That haunts these shores. And here, all summer through,
From dawn to dusk, there will be other music,
Threading the sea's music: at rise of sun,
With jubilation half-awakened birds
Salute his coming again, the lord of life,
His ambulatory footstep over the earth,
Who draws after him all that tide of song–
Salute the oncoming day, while from the edges
Of darkness, westward, fading voices call,
Night's superseded voices, the whip-poor-will's
Lamentation and farewell. Morning and noon
And afternoon and evening, the singing of birds
Lies on this country like an incantation:
Robin and wren, catbird, phoebe and chat,
Song-sparrow's music-box tune, and from the slender
Arches of inmost shade, the woodland's roof,
Where few winds come, flutelike adagio or
Wild syrinx-cry and high raving of the thrush,
Their clang and piercing pierce the spirit through–
Look off into blue heaven, you shall witness
Angelic motions, the volt and sidewise shift
Of the swallow in mid-air. Enchanted land,
Where time has died; old ocean-haunted land;
Land of first love, where grape and honeysuckle
Tangle their vines, where the beach-plum in spring
Snows all the inland dunes; bird-haunted land,
Where youth still dwells forever, your long day

Draws to its close, bringing for evening-star
Venus, a bud of fire in the pale west,
Bringing dusk and the whip-poor-will again,
And the owl's tremolo and the firefly,
And gradual darkness. Silently the bat,
Over still lawns that listen to the sea,
Weaves the preoccupation of his flight.
The arch of heaven soars upward with all its stars.

II

Summer fades soon here, autumn in this country
Comes early and exalted. Where the wild land,
With its sparse bayberry and huckleberry,
Slopes seaward, where the seaward dunes go down,
Echoing, to the sea; over the beaches,
Over the shore-line stretching east and west,
The ineffable slant light of autumn lingers.
The roof of heaven is higher now, the clouds
That drag, trailing, along the enormous vault
Hang higher, the wide ways are wider now.
Sea-hawks wander the ocean solitudes,
Sea-winds walk there, the waters grow turbulent,
And inland also a new restlessness
Walks the world, remembering something lost,
Seeking something remembered: wheeling wings
And songless woods herald the great departure,
Cattle stray, swallows gather in flocks,
The cloud-travelling moon through gusty cloud
Looks down on the first pilgrims going over,
And hungers in the blood are whispering, "Flee!
Seek otherwhere, here is no lasting home."
Now bird-song fails us, now an older music
Is vibrant in the land–the drowsy cry
Of grasshopper and cricket, earth's low cry
Of sleepy love, her inarticulate cry,
Calling life downward, promising release
From these vague longings, these immortal torments.
The drowsy voice drones on–oh, siren voice:
Aeons of night, millenniums of repose,
Soundless oblivion, divine surcease,

Dark intermingling with the primal darkness,
Oh, not to be, to slough this separate being,
Flow home at last! The alert spirit listens,
Hearing, meanwhile, far off, along the coast,
Rumors of the rhythm of some wakeful thing,
Reverberations, oceanic tremors,
The multitudinous motions of the sea,
With all its waters, all its warring waves.

Afternoon: Amagansett Beach

The broad beach,
Sea-wind and the sea's irregular rhythm,
Great dunes with their pale grass, and on the beach
Driftwood, tangle of bones, an occasional shell,
Now coarse, now carven and delicate–whorls of time
Stranded in space, deaf ears listening
To lost time, old oceanic secrets.
Along the water's edge, in pattern casual
As the pattern of the stars, the pin-point air-holes
Left by the sand-flea under the receding spume,
Wink and blink out again. A gull drifts over,
Wide wings crucified against the sky–
His shadow travels the shore, upon its margins
You will find his signature: one long line,
Two shorter lines curving out from it, a nearly
Perfect graph of the bird himself in flight.
His footprint is his image fallen from heaven.

Night Thoughts in Age

Light, that out of the west looked back once more
Through lids of cloud, has closed a sleepy eye;
The heaven of stars bends over me its silence,
A harp through which the wind of time still whispers
Music some hand has hushed but left there trembling–
Conceits of an aging man who lies awake
Under familiar rafters, in this leafy
Bird-singing, haunted, green, ancestral spot
Where time has made such music! For often now,
In this belovèd country whose coastal shores

Look seaward, without limit, to the south–
Land of flung spume and spray, sea-winds and -voices,
Where the gull rides the gale on equal wing
With motionless body and downward-bending head,
Where, in mid-summer days, offshore, the dolphin
Hurdles the water with arching leap and plunge–
I meditate, lying awake, alone,
On the sea's voice and time's receding music,
Felt ebbing in the heart and shrunken vein–
How time, that takes us all, will at the last,
In taking us, take the whole world we are dreaming:
Sun, wind and sea, whisper of rain at night,
The young, hollow-cheeked moon, the clouds of evening
Drifting in a great solitude–all these
Shall time take away, surely, and the face
From which the eyes of love look out at us
In this brief world, this horror-haunted kingdom
Of beauty and of longing and of terror,
Of phantoms and illusion, of appearance
And disappearance–magic of leger-de-main,
Trick of the prestidigitator's wand–
The huge phantasmagoria we are dreaming:
This shall time take from us, and take forever,
When we are taken by that receding music.
O marvel of things, fabulous dream, too soon,
Too soon will the wild blood cry out and death
Quell, with one blow, the inscrutable fantasy!
Shall prayer change this? Youth is the hour for prayer,
That has so much to pray for; a man's life,
Lived howsoever, is a long reconcilement
To the high, lonely, unforgiving truth,
Which will not change for his or any prayer,
Now or hereafter: in that reconcilement
Lies all of wisdom. Age is the hour for praise,
Praise that is joy, praise that is acquiescence,
Praise that is adoration and gratitude
For all that has been given and not been given.
Night flows on. The wind, that all night through
Quickened the treetops with a breath of ocean,
Veers inland, falls away, and the sea's voice.

Learned in lost childhood, a remembered music,
By day or night, through love, through sleep, through
  dream,
Still breathing its perpetual benediction,
Has dwindled to a sigh. By the west window,
In the soft dark the leaves of the sycamore
Stir gently, rustle, and are still, are listening
To a silence that is music. The old house
Is full of ghosts, dear ghosts on stair and landing,
Ghosts in chamber and hall; garden and walk
Are marvellous with ghosts, where so much love
Dwelt for a little while and made such music,
Before it too was taken by the tide
That takes us all, of time's receding music.
Oh, all is music! All has been turned to music!
All that is vanished has been turned to music!
And these familiar rafters, that have known
The child, the young man and the man, now shelter
The aging man who lies here, listening, listening–
All night, in a half dream, I have lain here listening.

H.D. (*Am. b. 1886*)

Oread

whirl up, sea–
whirl your pointed pines,
splash your great pines
on our rocks,
hurl your green over us,
cover us with your pools of fir.

Helen

All Greece hates
the still eyes in the white face,
the luster as of olives
where she stands,
and the white hands.

All Greece reviles
the wan face when she smiles,
hating it deeper still
when it grows wan and white,
remembering past enchantments
and past ills.

Greece sees unmoved,
God's daughter, born of love,
the beauty of cool feet
and slenderest knees,
could love indeed the maid,
only if she were laid,
white ash amid funereal cypresses.

Robinson Jeffers (*Am. b. 1887*)

Hurt Hawks

I

The broken pillar of the wing jags from the clotted shoulder,
The wing trails like a banner in defeat,
No more to use the sky forever but live with famine
And pain a few days: cat nor coyote
Will shorten the week of waiting for death, there is game without talons.
He stands under the oak-bush and waits
The lame feet of salvation; at night he remembers freedom
And flies in a dream, the dawns ruin it.
He is strong and pain is worse to the strong, incapacity is worse.
The curs of the day come and torment him
At distance, no one but death the redeemer will humble that head,
The intrepid readiness, the terrible eyes.

The wild God of the world is sometimes merciful to those
That ask mercy, not often to the arrogant.
You do not know him, you communal people, or you have forgotten him;
Intemperate and savage, the hawk remembers him;
Beautiful and wild, the hawks, and men that are dying, remember him.

II

I'd sooner, except the penalties, kill a man than a hawk; but the great redtail
Had nothing left but unable misery
From the bone too shattered for mending, the wing that trailed under his talons when he moved.
We had fed him six weeks, I gave him freedom,
He wandered over the foreland hill and returned in the evening, asking for death,
Not like a beggar, still eyed with the old
Implacable arrogance. I gave him the lead gift in the twilight. What fell was relaxed,
Owl-downy, soft feminine feathers; but what
Soared: the fierce rush: the night-herons by the flooded river cried fear at its rising
Before it was quite unsheathed from reality.

Summer Holiday

When the sun shouts and people abound
One thinks there were the ages of stone and the age of bronze
And the iron age; iron the unstable metal;
Steel made of iron, unstable as his mother; the towered-up cities
Will be stains of rust on mounds of plaster.
Roots will not pierce the heaps for a time, kind rains will cure them,
Then nothing will remain of the iron age
And all these people but a thigh-bone or so, a poem
Stuck in the world's thought, splinters of glass
In the rubbish dumps, a concrete dam far off in the mountain . . .

To the Stone-Cutters

Stone-cutters fighting time with marble, you fore-defeated
Challengers of oblivion
Eat cynical earnings, knowing rock splits, records fall down,
The square-limbed Roman letters
Scale in the thaws, wear in the rain. The poet as well
Builds his monument mockingly;
For man will be blotted out, the blithe earth die, the brave sun
Die blind and blacken to the heart:
Yet stones have stood for a thousand years, and pained
thoughts found
The honey of peace in old poems.

Ante Mortem

It is likely enough that lions and scorpions
Guard the end; life never was bonded to be endurable nor the
act of dying
Unpainful; the brain burning too often
Earns, though it held itself detached from the object, often a
burnt age.
No matter, I shall not shorten it by hand.
Incapable of body or unmoved of brain is no evil, one always
went envying
The quietness of stones. But if the striped blossom
Insanity spread lewd splendors and lightning terrors at the end
of the forest;
Or intolerable pain work its known miracle,
Exile the monarch soul, set a sick monkey in the office . . .
remember me
Entire and balanced when I was younger,
And could lift stones, and comprehend in the praises the
cruelties of life.

Original Sin

The man-brained and man-handed ground-ape, physically
The most repulsive of all hot-blooded animals
Up to that time of the world: they had dug a pitfall
And caught a mammoth, but how could their sticks and stones
Reach the life in that hide? They danced around the pit,
shrieking

With ape excitement, flinging sharp flints in vain, and the stench of their bodies
Stained the white air of dawn; but presently one of them
Remembered the yellow dancer, wood-eating fire
That guards the cave-mouth: he ran and fetched him, and others
Gathered sticks at the wood's edge; they made a blaze
And pushed it into the pit, and they fed it high, around the mired sides
Of their huge prey. They watched the long hairy trunk
Waver over the stifle-trumpeting pain,
And they were happy.

Meanwhile the intense color and nobility of sunrise,
Rose and gold and amber, flowed up the sky. Wet rocks were shining, a little wind
Stirred the leaves of the forest and the marsh flag-flowers; the soft valley between the low hills
Became as beautiful as the sky; while in its midst, hour after hour, the happy hunters
Roasted their living meat slowly to death.

These are the people
This is the human dawn. As for me, I would rather
Be a worm in a wild apple than a son of man.
But we are what we are, and we might remember
Not to hate any person, for all are vicious;
And not to be astonished at any evil, all are deserved;
And not fear death; it is the only way to be cleansed.

Ave Caesar

No bitterness: our ancestors did it.
They were only ignorant and hopeful, they wanted freedom but wealth too.
Their children will learn to hope for a Caesar.
Or rather—for we are not aquiline Romans but soft mixed colonists—
Some kindly Sicilian tyrant who'll keep
Poverty and Carthage off until the Romans arrive.
We are easy to manage, a gregarious people,
Full of sentiment, clever at mechanics, and we love our luxuries.

Rock and Hawk

Here is a symbol in which
Many high tragic thoughts
Watch their own eyes.

This gray rock, standing tall
On the headland, where the seawind
Lets no tree grow,

Earthquake-proved, and signatured
By ages of storms: on its peak
A falcon has perched.

I think, here is your emblem
To hang in the future sky;
Not the cross, not the hive,

But this; bright power, dark peace;
Fierce consciousness joined with final
Disinterestedness;

Life with calm death; the falcon's
Realist eyes and act
Married to the massive

Mysticism of stone,
Which failure cannot cast down
Nor success make proud.

Shine, Perishing Republic

While this America settles in the mould of its vulgarity, heavily thickening to empire,
And protest, only a bubble in the molten mass, pops and sighs out, and the mass hardens,

I sadly smiling remember that the flower fades to make fruit, the fruit rots to make earth.
Out of the mother; and through the spring exultances, ripeness and decadence; and home to the mother.

You making haste haste on decay: not blameworthy; life is good, be it stubbornly long or suddenly
A mortal splendor: meteors are not needed less than mountains: shine, perishing republic.

But for my children, I would have them keep their distance from the thickening center; corruption
Never has been compulsory, when the cities lie at the monster's feet there are left the mountains.

And boys, be in nothing so moderate as in love of man, a clever servant, insufferable master.
There is the trap that catches noblest spirits, that caught–they say–God, when he walked on earth.

Edwin Muir (*Br. b. 1887*)

The Journey

First in the North. The black sea-tangle beaches,
Brine-bitter stillness, tablet strewn morass,
Tall women against the sky with heads covered,
The witch's house below the black-toothed mountain,
Wave-echo in the roofless chapel,
The twice-dead castle on the swamp-green mound,
Darkness at noon-day, wheel of fire at midnight,
The level sun and the wild shooting shadows.

How long ago? Then sailing up to summer
Over the edge of the world. Black hill of water,
Rivers of running gold. The sun! The sun!
Then the free summer isles.
But the ship hastened on and brought him to
The towering walls of life and the great kingdom.

Where long he wandered seeking that which sought him
Through all the little hills and shallow valleys
Of the green world. One whose form and features,
Race and speech he knew not, shapeless, tongueless,
Known to him only by the impotent heart,
And whether at all on earth the place of meeting,
Beyond all knowledge. Only the little hills,
Head-high, and the winding valleys,
Winding, returning, until there grew a pattern,
And it was held. And there stood each in his station
With the hills between them. And that was the meaning.

Though sometimes through the wavering light and shadow
He thought he saw it a moment as he watched
The red deer walking by the riverside
At evening, when the bells were ringing,
And the bright stream leapt silent from the mountain
High in the sunset. But as he looked, nothing
Was there but lights and shadows.

And then the vision
Of the conclusion without fulfilment.
The plain like glass, and in the crystal grave
That which he had sought, that which had sought him
Glittering in death. And all the dead scattered
Like fallen stars, clustered like leaves hanging
From the sad boughs of the mountainous tree of Adam
Planted far down in Eden. And on the hills
The gods reclined and conversed with each other
From summit to summit.

Conclusion
Without fulfilment. Thence the dream rose upward,
The living dream sprung from the dying vision,
Overarching all. Beneath its branches
He builds in faith and doubt his shaking house.

The West

We followed them into the west,
And left them there, and said good-bye. For now
We could go no farther, could not step one step
Beyond the little earthen mound that hid
Their traces from us; for this was an end.
It was as if the west had ended there.
And yet we knew another west ran on,
A west beyond the west, and towards it travelled
Those we had followed to this stopping place.
So we returned by the east and north and south
To our own homes, remembering sometimes there,
Sometimes forgetting, thinking yet not thinking,
Bound by the ancient custom of our country.

But from the east newcomers constantly
Pour in among us, mix with us, pass through us,
And travel towards the west; and that migration
Has been from the beginning, it is said,
And long before men's memory it was woven
Into the tranquil pattern of our lives.
And that great movement like a quiet river,
Which always flowing yet is always the same,
Begets a stillness. So that when we look
Out at our life we see a changeless landscape,
And all disposed there in its due proportion,
The young and old, the good and bad, the wise and foolish,
All these are there as if they had been for ever,
And motionless as statues, prototypes
Set beyond time, for whom the sun stands still.
And each day says in its passing, "This is all."–
While the unhurrying progress goes its way,
And we upon it, year by year by year,
Led through the endless stations of the sun.
There are no aborigines in our country,
But all came hither so, and shall leave so,
Even as these friends we followed to their west.

And yet this is a land, and we say "Now",
Say "Now" and "Here", and are in our own house.

Horses

Those lumbering horses in the steady plough,
On the bare field–I wonder why, just now,
They seemed terrible, so wild and strange,
Like magic power on the stony grange.

Perhaps some childish hour has come again,
When I watched fearful, through the blackening rain,
Their hooves like pistons in an ancient mill
Move up and down, yet seem as standing still.

Their conquering hooves which trod the stubble down
Were ritual that turned the field to brown,
And their great hulks were seraphim of gold,
Or mute ecstatic monsters on the mould.

And oh the rapture, when, one furrow done,
They marched broad-breasted to the sinking sun!
The light flowed off their bossy sides in flakes;
The furrows rolled behind like struggling snakes.

But when at dusk with steaming nostrils home
They came, they seemed gigantic in the gloam,
And warm and glowing with mysterious fire
That lit their smouldering bodies in the mire.

Their eyes as brilliant and as wide as night
Gleamed with a cruel apocalyptic light.
Their manes the leaping ire of the wind
Lifted with rage invisible and blind.

Ah, now it fades! it fades! and I must pine
Again for that dread country crystalline,
Where the blank field and the still-standing tree
Were bright and fearful presences to me.

The Wayside Station

Here at the wayside station, as many a morning,
I watch the smoke torn from the fumy engine
Crawling across the field in serpent sorrow.
Flat in the east, held down by stolid clouds,
The struggling day is born and shines already
On its warm hearth far off. Yet something here
Glimmers along the ground to show the seagulls
White on the furrows' black unturning waves.

But now the light has broadened.
I watch the farmstead on the little hill,
That seems to mutter: "Here is day again"
Unwillingly. Now the sad cattle wake
In every byre and stall,
The ploughboy stirs in the loft, the farmer groans
And feels the day like a familiar ache
Deep in his body, though the house is dark.
The lovers part
Now in the bedroom where the pillows gleam
Great and mysterious as deep hills of snow,
An inaccessible land. The wood stands waiting
While the bright snare slips coil by coil around it,

Dark silver on every branch. The lonely stream
That rode through darkness leaps the gap of light,
Its voice grown loud, and starts its winding journey
Through the day and time and war and history.

The Enchanted Knight

Lulled by La Belle Dame Sans Merci he lies
  In the bare wood below the blackening hill.
The plough drives nearer now, the shadow flies
  Past him across the plain, but he lies still.

Long since the rust its gardens here has planned,
  Flowering his armour like an autumn field.
From his sharp breast-plate to his iron hand
  A spider's web is stretched, a phantom shield.

When footsteps pound the turf beside his ear
  Armies pass through his dream in endless line,
And one by one his ancient friends appear;
  They pass all day, but he can make no sign.

When a bird cries within the silent grove
  The long-lost voice goes by, he makes to rise
And follow, but his cold limbs never move,
  And on the turf unstirred his shadow lies.

But if a withered leaf should drift
  Across his face and rest, the dread drops start
Chill on his forehead. Now he tries to lift
  The insulting weight that stays and breaks his heart.

From *Variations on a Time Theme*

At the dead centre of the boundless plain
Does our way end? Our horses pace and pace
Like steeds for ever labouring on a shield,
Keeping their solitary heraldic courses.

Our horses move on such a ground, for them
Perhaps the progress is all ease and pleasure,
But it is heavy work for us, the riders,
Whose hearts have flown so far ahead they are lost
  Long past all finding
While we sit staring at the same horizon.

Time has such curious stretches, we are told,
And generation after generation
May travel them, sad stationary journey,
Of what device, what meaning?
Yet these coursers
Have seen all and will see all. Suppliantly
The rocks will melt, the sealed horizons fall
Before their onset–and the places
Our hearts have hid in will be viewed by strangers
Sitting where we are, breathing the foreign air
Of the new realm they have inherited.
But we shall fall here on the plain.

It may be
These steeds would stumble and the long road
end
(So legend says) if they should lack their riders.
But then a rider
Is always easy to find. Yet we fill a saddle
At least. We sit where others have sat before us
And others will sit after us.

It cannot be
These animals know their riders, mark the change
When one makes way for another. It cannot be
They know this wintry wilderness from spring.
For they have come from regions dreadful past
All knowledge. They have borne upon their saddles
Forms fiercer than the tiger, borne them calmly
As they bear us now.

And so we do not hope
That their great coal-black glossy hides
Should keep a glimmer of the autumn light
We still remember, when our limbs were weightless
As red leaves on a tree, and our silvery breaths
Went on before us like new-risen souls
Leading our empty bodies through the air.
A princely dream. Now all that golden country
Is razed as bare as Troy. We cannot return,
And shall not see the kingdom of our heirs.

These beasts are mortal, and we who fall so lightly,
Fall so heavily, are, it is said, immortal.
Such knowledge should armour us against all change,
And this monotony. Yet these worn saddles
Have powers to charm us to obliviousness.
They were appointed for us, and the scent of the ancient leather
Is strong as a spell. So we must mourn or rejoice
For this our station, our inheritance
As if it were all. This plain all. This journey all.

Rupert Brooke (*Br. 1887–1915*)

Clouds

Down the blue night the unending columns press
In noiseless tumult, break and wave and flow,
Now tread the far South, or lift rounds of snow
Up to the white moon's hidden loveliness.
Some pause in their grave wandering comradeless,
And turn with profound gesture vague and slow,
As who would pray good for the world, but know
Their benediction empty as they bless.

They say that the Dead die not, but remain
Near to the rich heirs of their grief and mirth.
I think they ride the calm mid-heaven, as these,
In wise majestic melancholy train,
And watch the moon, and the still-raging seas,
And men, coming and going on the earth.

The Old Vicarage, Grantchester

(Café des Westens, Berlin, May 1912)

Just now the lilac is in bloom,
All before my little room;
And in my flower-beds, I think,
Smile the carnation and the pink;
And down the borders, well I know,
The poppy and the pansy blow . . .

Oh! there the chestnuts, summer through,
Beside the river make for you
A tunnel of green gloom, and sleep
Deeply above; and green and deep
The stream mysterious glides beneath,
Green as a dream and deep as death.
–Oh, damn! I know it! And I know
How the May fields all golden show,
And when the day is young and sweet,
Gild gloriously the bare feet
That run to bathe . . .
Du lieber Gott!
Here am I, sweating, sick, and hot,
And there the shadowed waters fresh
Lean up to embrace the naked flesh.
Temperamentvoll German Jews
Drink beer around;–and *there* the dews
Are soft beneath a morn of gold.
Here tulips bloom as they are told;
Unkempt about those hedges blows
An English unofficial rose;
And there the unregulated sun
Slopes down to rest when day is done,
And wakes a vague unpunctual star,
A slippered Hesper; and there are
Meads towards Haslingfield and Coton
Where *das Betreten*'s not *verboten*. . . .

εἴθε γενοίμην . . . would I were
In Grantchester, in Grantchester!–
Some, it may be, can get in touch
With Nature there, or Earth, or such.
And clever modern men have seen
A Faun a-peeping through the green,
And felt the Classics were not dead,
To glimpse a Naiad's reedy head,
Or hear the Goat-foot piping low; . . .
But these are things I do not know.
I only know that you may lie
Day-long and watch the Cambridge sky,

And, flower-lulled in sleepy grass,
Hear the cool lapse of hours pass,
Until the centuries blend and blur
In Grantchester, in Grantchester. . . .
Still in the dawnlit waters cool
His ghostly lordship swims his pool,
And tries the strokes, essays the tricks,
Long learnt on Hellespont, or Styx,
Dan Chaucer hears his river still
Chatter beneath a phantom mill.
Tennyson notes, with studious eye,
How Cambridge waters hurry by . . .
And in that garden, black and white,
Creep whispers through the grass all night;
And spectral dance, before the dawn,
A hundred Vicars down the lawn;
Curates, long dust, will come and go
On lissom, clerical, printless toe;
And oft between the boughs is seen
The sly shade of a Rural Dean . . .
Till, at a shiver in the skies,
Vanishing with Satanic cries,
The prim ecclesiastic rout
Leaves but a startled sleeper-out,
Grey heavens, the first bird's drowsy calls,
The falling house that never falls.

God! I will pack, and take a train,
And get me to England once again!
For England's the one land, I know,
Where men with Splendid Hearts may go;
And Cambridgeshire, of all England,
The shire for Men who Understand;
And of *that* district I prefer
The lovely hamlet Grantchester.
For Cambridge people rarely smile,
Being urban, squat, and packed with guile;
And Royston men in the far South
Are black and fierce and strange of mouth;

At Over they fling oaths at one,
And worse than oaths at Trumpington,
And Ditton girls are mean and dirty,
And there's none in Harston under thirty,
And folks in Shelford and those parts
Have twisted lips and twisted hearts,
And Barton men make Cockney rhymes,
And Coton's full of nameless crimes,
And things are done you'd not believe
At Madingley, on Christmas Eve.
Strong men have run for miles and miles,
When one from Cherry Hinton smiles;
Strong men have blanched, and shot their wives,
Rather than send them to St. Ives;
Strong men have cried like babes, bydam,
To hear what happened at Babraham.
But Grantchester! ah, Grantchester!
There's peace and holy quiet there,
Great clouds along pacific skies,
And men and women with straight eyes,
Lithe children lovelier than a dream,
A bosky wood, a slumbrous stream,
And little kindly winds that creep
Round twilight corners, half asleep.
In Grantchester their skins are white;
They bathe by day, they bathe by night;
The women there do all they ought;
The men observe the Rules of Thought.
They love the Good; they worship Truth;
They laugh uproariously in youth;
(And when they get to feeling old,
They up and shoot themselves, I'm told) . . .

Ah God! to see the branches stir
Across the moon at Grantchester!
To smell the thrilling-sweet and rotten
Unforgettable, unforgotten
River-smell, and hear the breeze
Sobbing in the little trees.

Say, do the elm-clumps greatly stand,
Still guardians of that holy land?
The chestnuts shade, in reverend dream,
The yet unacademic stream?
Is dawn a secret shy and cold
Anadyomene, silver-gold?
And sunset still a golden sea
From Haslingfield to Madingley?
And after, ere the night is born,
Do hares come out about the corn?
Oh, is the water sweet and cool,
Gentle and brown, above the pool?
And laughs the immortal river still
Under the mill, under the mill?
Say, is there Beauty yet to find?
And Certainty? and Quiet kind?
Deep meadows yet, for to forget
The lies, and truths, and pain? . . . oh! yet
Stands the Church clock at ten to three?
And is there honey still for tea?

The Soldier

If I should die, think only this of me:
  That there's some corner of a foreign field
That is for ever England. There shall be
  In that rich earth a richer dust concealed;
A dust whom England bore, shaped, made aware,
  Gave, once, her flowers to love, her ways to roam,
A body of England's, breathing English air,
  Washed by the rivers, blest by suns of home.

And think, this heart, all evil shed away,
  A pulse in the eternal mind, no less
  Gives somewhere back the thoughts by England given;
Her sights and sounds; dreams happy as her day;
  And laughter, learnt of friends; and gentleness,
    In hearts at peace, under an English heaven.

Edith Sitwell (*Br. b. 1887*)

From *The Sleeping Beauty*

When we come to that dark house,
Never sound of wave shall rouse
The bird that sings within the blood
Of those who sleep in that deep wood:
For in that house the shadows now
Seem cast by some dark unknown bough.
The gardener plays his old bagpipe
To make the melons' gold seeds ripe;
The music swoons with a sad sound–
"Keep, my lad, to the good safe ground!
For once, long since, there was a felon
With guineas gold as the seeds of a melon,
And he would sail for a far strand
To seek a waking, clearer land–
A land whose name is only heard
In the strange singing of a bird.
The sea was sharper than green grass,
The sailors would not let him pass,
For the sea was wroth and rose at him
Like the turreted walls of Jerusalem,
Or like the towers and gables seen
Within a deep-boughed garden green.
And the sailors bound and threw him down
Among those wrathful towers to drown.
And oh, far best," the gardener said,
"Like fruits to lie in your kind bed–
To sleep as snug as in the grave
In your kind bed, and shun the wave,
Nor ever sigh for a strange land
And songs no heart can understand."

Hornpipe

SAILORS come
To the drum
Out of Babylon;
  Hobby-horses

Foam, the dumb
Sky rhinoceros-glum

Watched the courses of the breakers' rocking-horses and with Glaucis,
Lady Venus on the settee of the horsehair sea!
Where Lord Tennyson in laurels wrote a gloria free,
In a borealic iceberg came Victoria; she
Knew Prince Albert's tall memorial took the colours of the floreal
And the borealic iceberg; floating on they see
New-arisen Madam Venus for whose sake from far
Came the fat and zebra'd emperor from Zanzibar
Where like golden bouquets lay far Asia, Africa, Cathay,
All laid before that shady lady by the fibroid Shah.
Captain Fracasse stout as any water-butt came, stood
With Sir Bacchus both a-drinking the black tarr'd grapes' blood
Plucked among the tartan leafage
By the furry wind whose grief age
Could not wither–like a squirrel with a gold star-nut.
Queen Victoria sitting shocked upon the rocking-horse
Of a wave said to the Laureate, "This minx of course
Is as sharp as any lynx and blacker-deeper than the drinks and quite as
Hot as any hottentot, without remorse!
For the minx,"
Said she,
"And the drinks,
You can see
Are hot as any hottentot and not the goods for me!"

Colonel Fantock

Thus spoke the lady underneath the trees:
I was a member of a family
Whose legend was of hunting–(all the rare
And unattainable brightness of the air)–
A race whose fabled skill in falconry
Was used on the small song-birds and a winged
And blinded Destiny. . . . I think that only
Winged ones know the highest eyrie is so lonely.

There in a land, austere and elegant,
The castle seemed an arabesque in music;
We moved in an hallucination born
Of silence, which like music gave us lotus
To eat, perfuming lips and our long eyelids
As we trailed over the sad summer grass,
Or sat beneath a smooth and mournful tree.

And Time passed, suavely, imperceptibly.

But Dagobert and Peregrine and I
Were children then; we walked like shy gazelles
Among the music of the thin flower-bells.
And life still held some promise,–never ask
Of what,–but life seemed less a stranger, then,
Than ever after in this cold existence.
I always was a little outside life–
And so the things we touch could comfort me;
I loved the shy dreams we could hear and see–
For I was like one dead, like a small ghost,
A little cold air wandering and lost.

All day within the straw-roofed arabesque
Of the towered castle and the sleepy gardens wandered
We; those delicate paladins the waves
Told us fantastic legends that we pondered.

And the soft leaves were breasted like a dove,
Crooning old mournful tales of untrue love.

When night came, sounding like the growth of trees,
My great-grandmother bent to say good-night,
And the enchanted moonlight seemed transformed
Into the silvery tinkling of an old
And gentle music-box that played a tune
Of Circean enchantments and far seas;
Her voice was lulling like the splash of these.
When she had given me her good-night kiss,
There, in her lengthened shadow, I saw this
Old military ghost with mayfly whiskers,–
Poor harmless creature, blown by the cold wind,
Boasting of unseen unreal victories
To a harsh unbelieving world unkind:
For all the battles that this warrior fought

Were with cold poverty and helpless age–
His spoils were shelters from the winter's rage.
And so for ever through his braggart voice,
Through all that martial trumpet's sound, his soul
Wept with a little sound so pitiful,
Knowing that he is outside life for ever
With no one that will warm or comfort him. . . .
He is not even dead, but Death's buffoon
On a bare stage, a shrunken pantaloon.
His military banner never fell,
Nor his account of victories, the stories
Of old apocryphal misfortunes, glories
Which comforted his heart in later life
When he was the Napoleon of the schoolroom
And all the victories he gained were over
Little boys who would not learn to spell.

All day within the sweet and ancient gardens
He had my childish self for audience–
Whose body flat and strange, whose pale straight hair
Made me appear as though I had been drowned–
(We all have the remote air of a legend)–
And Dagobert my brother whose large strength,
Great body and grave beauty still reflect
The Angevin dead kings from whom we spring;
And sweet as the young tender winds that stir
In thickets when the earliest flower-bells sing
Upon the boughs, was his just character;
And Peregrine the youngest with a naïve
Shy grace like a faun's, whose slant eyes seemed
The warm green light beneath eternal boughs.
His hair was like the fronds of feathers, life
In him was changing ever, springing fresh
As the dark songs of birds . . . the furry warmth
And purring sound of fires was in his voice
Which never failed to warm and comfort me.

And there were haunted summers in Troy Park
When all the stillness budded into leaves;
We listened, like Ophelia drowned in blond
And fluid hair, beneath stag-antlered trees;

Then, in the ancient park the country-pleasant
Shadows fell as brown as any pheasant,
And Colonel Fantock seemed like one of these.
Sometimes for comfort in the castle kitchen
He drowsed, where with a sweet and velvet lip
The snapdragons within the fire
Of their red summer never tire.
And Colonel Fantock liked our company;
For us he wandered over each old lie,
Changing the flowering hawthorn, full of bees,
Into the silver helm of Hercules,
For us defended Troy from the top stair
Outside the nursery, when the calm full moon
Was like the sound within the growth of trees.

But then came one cruel day in deepest June,
When pink flowers seemed a sweet Mozartian tune,
And Colonel Fantock pondered o'er a book.
A gay voice like a honeysuckle nook–
So sweet,–said, "It is Colonel Fantock's age
Which makes him babble." . . . Blown by winter's rage
The poor old man then knew his creeping fate,
The darkening shadow that would take his sight
And hearing; and he thought of his saved pence
Which scarce would rent a grave . . . That youthful voice
Was a dark bell which ever clanged "Too late"–
A creeping shadow that would steal from him
Even the little boys who would not spell–
His only prisoners. . . . On that June day
Cold Death had taken his first citadel.

Mademoiselle Richarde

Beside the haunted lake where nereids seem
Court ladies in a dark deserted dream,
Who were perfected in their glacial chill
By Mademoiselle Richarde, I wandered still;
Among the enchanted waters that seem green
Deep mirrors, their cold beauty's shade is seen. . . .
A swan-like waterfall now dies
Singing its cold elegies.

An air sighs without memory and lost . . .
The leaves are cold and seeking like a ghost.

* * * *

There are sad ghosts whose living was not life
But a small complaining, dying without strife,
A little reading by sad candlelight
Of some unowned, uncared-for book, a slight
Rustling then, a settling down to sleep.
And cold unutterable Darkness deep
Has soothed them and has smoothed their eyelids fast,
And they have their own resting-place at last
Who longed for this from hopeless distances . . .
Poor unloved creatures whose existences
Were spent upon the surface of another's
Life; the Darkness seems like their own mother's
Touch; they are so used to fireless life, so old
That they would scarcely know the grave is cold;
But life had so forgotten this poor dead
That death had left them still unburièd.
He had no room for them in all his grace
Though they would only need a little place;
Age shrinks our hearts and makes our bodies wane
Until we seem a little child again–
But not the children that we used to be,
Blind to the heaven childish eyes can see.

* * * *

Yet there are those who do not feel the cold;
And Mademoiselle Richarde was thus,–both old
And sharp, content to be the cold wind's butt;
A tiny spider in a gilded nut,
She lived and rattled in the emptiness
Of other people's splendours; her rich dress
Had muffled her old loneliness of heart.
This was her life; to live another's part,
To come and go unheard, a ghost unseen
Among the courtly mirrors glacial green,
Placed just beyond her reach for fear that she
Forget her loneliness, her image see

Grown concrete, not a ghost by cold airs blown.
So each reflection blooms there but her own;
She sits at other people's tables, raises
Her hands at other people's joys and praises
Their cold amusements, drawing down the blinds
Over her face for other's griefs,–the winds
Her sole friends now, grown grey and grim as she,
They have forgotten how to hear or see.
And her opinions are not her own,
But meaningless half words by cold airs blown
Through keyholes . . . words that were not meant for her.
"Madame la Duchesse said, 'The spring winds stir!' "
(Madame la Duchesse, old and gold japanned,
Whirled like a typhoon over the grey land
In her wide carriage, while a dead wind grieves
Among those seeking ghosts, the small grey leaves.)
So now, like Echo, she is soundless fleet
Save for the little talk she can repeat,–
Small whispers listened for at courtly doors.
She swims across the river-dark vast floors
To fires that seem like rococo gilt carving,
Nor ever knows her shrunken heart is starving,
Till, crumbling into dust, grown blind and dumb
With age, at last she hears her sole friend come,
Consoling Darkness smooths her eyelids fast
And she has her own resting-place at last.

The Swans

In the green light of water, like the day
Under green boughs, the spray
And air-pale petals of the foam seem flowers,–
Dark-leaved arbutus blooms with wax-pale bells
And their faint honey-smells,
The velvety syringa with smooth leaves,
Gloxinia with a green shade in the snow,
Jasmine and moon-clear orange-blossoms and green blooms
Of the wild strawberries from the shade of woods.
Their showers
Pelt the white women under the green trees,

Venusia, Cosmopolita, Pistillarine–
White solar statues, white rose-trees in snow
Flowering for ever, child-women, half stars
Half flowers, waves of the sea, born of a dream.

Their laughter flying through the trees like doves,
These angels come to watch their whiter ghosts
In the air-pale water, archipelagos
Of stars and young thin moons from great wings falling
As ripples widen.
These are their ghosts, their own white angels these!
O great wings spreading–
Your bones are made of amber, smooth and thin
Grown from the amber dust that was a rose
Or nymph in swan-smooth waters.
But Time's winter falls
With snows as soft, as soundless. . . . Then, who knows
Rose-footed swan from snow, or girl from rose?

The Youth with the Red-Gold Hair

The gold-armoured ghost from the Roman road
Sighed over the wheat
"Fear not the sound and the glamour
Of my gold armour–
(The sound of the wind and the wheat)
Fear not its clamour. . . .
Fear only the red-gold sun with the fleece of a fox
Who will steal the fluttering bird you hide in your breast.
Fear only the red-gold rain
That will dim your brightness, O my tall tower of the corn,
You,–my blonde girl. . . ."
But the wind sighed "Rest". . . .
The wind in his grey knight's armour–
The wind in his grey night armour–
Sighed over the fields of the wheat, "He is gone. . . . Forlorn."

You, the Young Rainbow

You, the young Rainbow of my tears, the gentle Halcyon
Over the troubled waters of my heart:
Lead now, as long ago, my grief, your flock, over the hollow
Hills to the far pastures of lost heaven.
But they are withered, the meadows and the horizon
Of the gentle Halcyon, hyacinthine sun;
Cold are the boughs, the constellations falling
From the spring branches; and your heart is far
And cold as Arcturus, the distance of all light-years
From the flowering earth and darkness of my heart.

Street Song

"Love my heart for an hour, but my bone for a day–
At least the skeleton smiles, for it has a morrow:
But the hearts of the young are now the dark treasure of Death,
And summer is lonely.

"Comfort the lonely light and the sun in its sorrow,
Come like the night, for terrible is the sun
As truth, and the dying light shows only the skeleton's hunger
For peace, under the flesh like the summer rose.

"Come through the darkness of death, as once through the
branches
Of youth you came, through the shade like the flowering door
That leads into Paradise, far from the street,–you, the unborn
City seen by the homeless, the night of the poor.

"You walk in the city ways, where Man's threatening shadow
Red-edged by the sun like Cain, has a changing shape–
Elegant like the Skeleton, crouched like the Tiger,
With the age-old wisdom and aptness of the Ape.

"The pulse that beats in the heart is changed to the hammer
That sounds in the Potter's Field where they build a new
world
From our Bone, and the carrion-bird days' foul droppings and
clamour–
But you are my night, and my peace,–

"The holy night of conception, of rest, the consoling
Darkness when all men are equal,–the wrong and the right,
And the rich and the poor are no longer separate nations,–
They are brothers in night."

This was the song I heard; but the Bone is silent!
Who knows if the sound was that of the dead light calling,–
Of Caesar rolling onward his heart, that stone,
Or the burden of Atlas falling?

Marianne Moore (*Am. b. 1887*)

The Fish

wade
through black jade.
  Of the crow-blue mussel-shells, one keeps
  adjusting the ash-heaps;
    opening and shutting itself like
an
injured fan.
  The barnacles which encrust the side
  of the wave, cannot hide
    there for the submerged shafts of the
sun,
split like spun
  glass, move themselves with spotlight swiftness
  into the crevices–
    in and out, illuminating
the
turquoise sea
  of bodies. The water drives a wedge
  of iron through the iron edge
    of the cliff; whereupon the stars,
pink
rice-grains, ink-
  bespattered jelly-fish, crabs like green
  lilies, and submarine
    toadstools, slide each on the other.

All
external
  marks of abuse are present on this
  defiant edifice–
    all the physical features of
ac-
cident–lack
  of cornice, dynamite grooves, burns, and
  hatchet strokes, these things stand
    out on it; the chasm-side is
dead.
Repeated
  evidence has proved that it can live
  on what can not revive
    its youth. The sea grows old in it.

A Grave

Man looking into the sea,
taking the view from those who have as much right to it as you have to it yourself,
it is human nature to stand in the middle of a thing,
but you cannot stand in the middle of this;
the sea has nothing to give but a well excavated grave.
The firs stand in a procession, each with an emerald turkey-foot at the top,
reserved as their contours, saying nothing;
repression, however, is not the most obvious characteristic of the sea;
the sea is a collector, quick to return a rapacious look.
There are others besides you who have worn that look–
whose expression is no longer a protest; the fish no longer investigate them
for their bones have not lasted:
men lower nets, unconscious of the fact that they are desecrating a grave,
and row quickly away–the blades of the oars
moving together like the feet of water-spiders as if there were no such thing as death.
The wrinkles progress among themselves in a phalanx–beautiful under networks of foam,

and fade breathlessly while the sea rustles in and out of the seaweed;
the birds swim through the air at top speed, emitting cat-calls as heretofore–
the tortoise-shell scourges about the feet of the cliffs, in motion beneath them;
and the ocean, under the pulsation of lighthouses and noise of bell-buoys,
advances as usual, looking as if it were not that ocean in which dropped things are bound to sink–
in which if they turn and twist, it is neither with volition nor consciousness.

Virginia Britannia

Pale sand edges England's Old
Dominion. The air is soft, warm, hot
above the cedar-dotted emerald shore
known to the red bird, the red-coated musketeer,
the trumpet-flower, the cavalier,
the parson, and the wild parishioner. A deer-
track in a church-floor
brick, and a fine pavement tomb with engraved top, remain.
The now tremendous vine-encompassed hackberry
starred with the ivy-flower,
shades the church tower;
And a great sinner lyeth here under the sycamore.

A fritillary zigzags
toward the chancel-shaded resting-place
of this unusual man and sinner who
waits for a joyful resurrection. We-re-wo-
co-mo-co's fur crown could be no
odder than we were, with ostrich, Latin motto,
and small gold horse-shoe
as arms for an able sting-ray-hampered pioneer–
painted as a Turk, it seems–continuously
exciting Captain Smith
who, patient with
his inferiors, was a pugnacious equal, and to

Powhatan as unflattering
as grateful. Rare Indian, crowned by
Christopher Newport! The Old Dominion has
all-green box-sculptured grounds.
An almost English green surrounds
them. Care has formed among unEnglish insect
sounds,
the white wall-rose. As
thick as Daniel Boone's grape-vine, the stem has wide-
spaced great
blunt alternating ostrich-skin warts that were thorns.
Care has formed walls of yew
since Indians knew
the Fort Old Field and narrow tongue of land that Jamestown
was.

Observe the terse Virginian,
the mettlesome gray one that drives the
owl from tree to tree and imitates the call
of whippoorwill or lark or katydid–the lead-
grey lead-legged mocking-bird with head
held half away, and meditative eye as dead
as sculptured marble
eye, alighting noiseless, musing in the semi-sun,
standing on tall thin legs as if he did not see,
conspicuous, alone,
on the stone-
topped table with lead cupids grouped to form the pedestal.

Narrow herring-bone-laid bricks,
a dusty pink beside the dwarf box-
bordered pansies, share the ivy-arbor shade
with cemetery lace settees, one at each side,
and with the bird: box-bordered tidewater gigantic jet black pansies–splendour; pride–
not for a decade
dressed, but for a day, in over-powering velvet; and
grey-blue-Andalusian-cock-feather pale ones,
ink-lined on the edge, fur-
eyed, with ochre
on the cheek. The at first slow, saddle-horse quick cavalcade

of buckeye-burnished jumpers
and five-gaited mounts, the work-mule and
show-mule and witch-cross door and 'strong sweet prison'
are a part of what has come about–in the Black
idiom–from 'advancin' back-
wards in a circle'; from taking the Potomac
cowbirdlike, and on
The Chickahominy establishing the Negro,
inadvertent ally and best enemy of tyranny. Rare
unscent-
ed, provident-
ly hot, too sweet, inconsistent flower-bed! Old Dominion

flowers are curious. Some wilt
in daytime and some close at night. Some
have perfume; some have not. The scarlet much-quilled
fruiting pomegranate, the African violet,
fuchsia and camellia, none; yet
the house-high glistening green magnolia's velvet-
textured flower is filled
with anaesthetic scent as inconsiderate as
the gardenia's. Even the gardenia-sprig's
dark vein on greener
leaf when seen
against the light, has not near it more small bees than the
frilled

silk substanceless faint flower of
the crape-myrtle has. Odd Pamunkey
princess, birdclaw-ear-ringed; with a pet racoon
from the Mattaponi (what a bear!) Feminine
odd Indian young lady! Odd thin–
gauze-and-taffeta-dressed English one! Terrapin
meat and crested spoon
feed the mistress of French plum-and-turquoise-piped
chaise-longue;
of brass-knobbed slat front door, and everywhere open
shaded house on Indian-
named Virginian
streams in counties named for English lords. The rattle-snake
soon

said from our once dashingly
undiffident first flag, 'don't tread on
me'–tactless symbol of a new republic.
Priorities were cradled in this region not
noted for humility; spot
that has high-singing frogs, cotton-mouth snake sand cotton-fields; a unique
Lawrence pottery with loping wolf design; and too
unvenomous terrapin in tepid greenness,
idling near the sea-top;
tobacco-crop
records on church walls; a Devil's Woodyard; and the one-
brick-

thick serpentine wall built by
Jefferson. Like strangler figs choking
a banyan, not an explorer, no imperialist,
not one of us, in taking what we
pleased–in colonizing as the
saying is–has been a synonym for mercy.
The redskin with the deer-
fur crown, famous for his cruelty, is not all brawn
and animality. The outdoor tea-table,
the mandolin-shaped big
and little fig,
the silkworm-mulberry, the French mull dress with the
Madeira-

vine-accompanied edge are,
when compared with what the colonists
found here in Tidewater Virginia, stark
luxuries. The mere brown hedge-sparrow, with reckless
ardour, unable to suppress
his satisfaction in man's trustworthy nearness,
even in the dark
flutes his ecstatic burst of joy–the caraway seed-
spotted sparrow perched in the dew-drenched juniper
beside the window-ledge;
this little hedge-
sparrow that wakes up seven minutes sooner than the lark.

The live oak's darkening filagree
of undulating boughs, the etched
solidity of a cypress indivisible
from the now agèd English hackberry,
become with lost identity,
part of the ground, as sunset flames increasingly
against the leaf-chiselled
blackening ridge of green; while clouds, expanding above
the town's assertiveness, dwarf it, dwarf arrogance
that can misunderstand
importance; and
are to the child an intimation of what glory is.

John Crowe Ransom (*Am. b. 1888*)

Bells for John Whiteside's Daughter

There was such speed in her little body,
And such lightness in her footfall,
It is no wonder her brown study
Astonishes us all.

Her wars were bruited in our high window.
We looked among orchard trees and beyond,
Where she took arms against her shadow,
Or harried unto the pond

The lazy geese, like a snow cloud
Dripping their snow on the green grass,
Tricking and stopping, sleepy and proud,
Who cried in goose, Alas,

For the tireless heart within the little
Lady with rod that made them rise
From their noon apple-dreams and scuttle
Goose-fashion under the skies!

But now go the bells, and we are ready,
In one house we are sternly stopped
To say we are vexed at her brown study,
Lying so primly propped.

Piazza Piece

–I am a gentleman in a dustcoat trying
To make you hear. Your ears are soft and small
And listen to an old man not at all,
They want the young men's whispering and sighing.
But see the roses on your trellis dying
And hear the spectral singing of the moon;
For I must have my lovely lady soon,
I am a gentleman in a dustcoat trying.

–I am a lady young in beauty waiting
Until my truelove comes, and then we kiss.
But what grey man among the vines is this
Whose words are dry and faint as in a dream?
Back from my trellis, Sir, before I scream!
I am a lady young in beauty waiting.

Philomela

Procne, Philomela, and Itylus,
Your names are liquid, your improbable tale
Is recited in the classic numbers of the nightingale.
Ah, but our numbers are not felicitous,
It goes not liquidly for us.

Perched on a Roman ilex, and duly apostrophized,
The nightingale descanted unto Ovid;
She has even appeared to the Teutons, the swilled and gravid;
At Fontainebleau it may be the bird was gallicized;
Never was she baptized.

To England came Philomela with her pain,
Fleeing the hawk her husband; querulous ghost,
She wanders when he sits heavy on his roost,
Utters herself in the original again,
The untranslatable refrain.

Not to these shores she came! this other Thrace,
Environ barbarous to the royal Attic;
How could her delicate dirge run democratic,
Delivered in a cloudless boundless public place
To an inordinate race?

I pernoctated with the Oxford students once,
And in the quadrangles, in the cloisters, on the Cher,
Precociously knocked at antique doors ajar,
Fatuously touched the hems of the hierophants,
Sick of my dissonance.

I went out to Bagley Wood, I climbed the hill;
Even the moon had slanted off in a twinkling,
I heard the sepulchral owl and a few bells tinkling,
There was no more villainous day to unfulfil,
The diuturnity was still.

Up from the darkest wood where Philomela sat,
Her fairy numbers issued. What then ailed me?
My ears are called capacious but they failed me,
Her classics registered a little flat!
I rose, and venomously spat.

Philomela, Philomela, lover of song,
I am in despair if we may make us worthy,
A bantering breed sophistical and swarthy;
Unto more beautiful, persistently more young,
Thy fabulous provinces belong.

The Equilibrists

Full of her long white arms and milky skin
He had a thousand times remembered sin.
Alone in the press of people traveled he,
Minding her jacinth, and myrrh, and ivory.

Mouth he remembered: the quaint orifice
From which came heat that flamed upon the kiss,
Till cold words came down spiral from the head,
Gray doves from the officious tower illsped.

Body: it was a white field ready for love,
On her body's field, with the gaunt tower above,
The lilies grew, beseeching him to take,
If he would pluck and wear them, bruise and break.

Eyes talking: Never mind the cruel words,
Embrace my flowers, but not embrace the swords.
But what they said, the doves came straightway flying
And unsaid: Honor, Honor, they came crying.

Importunate her doves. Too pure, too wise,
Clambering on his shoulder, saying, Arise,
Leave me now, and never let us meet,
Eternal distance now command thy feet.

Predicament indeed, which thus discovers
Honor among thieves, Honor between lovers.
O such a little word is Honor, they feel!
But the gray word is between them cold as steel.

At length I saw these lovers fully were come
Into their torture of equilibrium;
Dreadfully had forsworn each other, and yet
They were bound each to each, and they did not forget.

And rigid as two painful stars, and twirled
About the clustered night their prison world,
They burned with fierce love always to come near,
But Honor beat them back and kept them clear.

Ah, the strict lovers, they are ruined now!
I cried in anger. But with puddled brow
Devising for those gibbeted and brave
Came I descanting: Man, what would you have?

For spin your period out, and draw your breath,
A kinder saeculum begins with Death.
Would you ascend to Heaven and bodiless dwell?
Or take your bodies honorless to Hell?

In Heaven you have heard no marriage is,
No white flesh tinder to your lecheries,
Your male and female tissue sweetly shaped
Sublimed away, and furious blood escaped.

Great lovers lie in Hell, the stubborn ones
Infatuate of the flesh upon the bones;
Stuprate, they rend each other when they kiss,
The pieces kiss again—no end to this.

But still I watched them spinning, orbited nice.
Their flames were not more radiant than their ice.
I dug in the quiet earth and wrought the tomb
And made these lines to memorize their doom:

Epitaph

Equilibrists lie here; stranger, tread light;
Close, but untouching in each other's sight;
Mouldered the lips and ashy the tall skull,
Let them lie perilous and beautiful.

Blue Girls

Twirling your blue skirts, travelling the sward
Under the towers of your seminary,
Go listen to your teachers old and contrary
Without believing a word.

Tie the white fillets then about your lustrous hair
And think no more of what will come to pass
Than bluebirds that go walking on the grass
And chattering on the air.

Practice your beauty, blue girls, before it fail;
And I will cry with my loud lips and publish
Beauty which all our power shall never establish,
It is so frail.

For I could tell you a story which is true:
I know a lady with a terrible tongue,
Blear eyes fallen from blue,
All her perfections tarnished–and yet it is not long
Since she was lovelier than any of you.

Parting, Without a Sequel

She has finished and sealed the letter
At last, which he so richly has deserved,
With characters venomous and hatefully curved,
And nothing could be better.

But even as she gave it
Saying to the blue-capped functioner of doom,
"Into his hands," she hoped the leering groom
Might somewhere lose and leave it.

Then all the blood
Forsook the face. She was too pale for tears,
Observing the ruin of her younger years.
She went and stood

Under her father's vaunting oak
Who kept his peace in wind and sun, and glistened
Stoical in the rain; to whom she listened
If he spoke.

And now the agitation of the rain
Rasped his sere leaves, and he talked low and gentle
Reproaching the wan daughter by the lintel;
Ceasing and beginning again.

Away went the messenger's bicycle,
His serpent's track went up the hill forever,
And all the time she stood there hot as fever
And cold as any icicle.

Painted Head

By dark severance the apparition head
Smiles from the air a capital on no
Column or a Platonic perhaps head
On a canvas sky depending from nothing;

Stirs up an old illusion of grandeur
By tickling the instinct of heads to be
Absolute and to try decapitation
And to play truant from the body bush;

But too happy and beautiful for those sorts
Of head (homekeeping heads are happiest)
Discovers maybe thirty unwidowed years
Of not dishonoring the faithful stem;

Is nameless and has authored for the evil
Historian headhunters neither book
Nor state and is therefore distinct from tart
Heads with crowns and guilty gallery heads;

So that the extravagant device of art
Unhousing by abstraction this once head
Was capital irony by a loving hand
That knew the no treason of a head like this;

Makes repentance in an unlovely head
For having vinegarly traduced the flesh
Till, the hurt flesh recusing, the hard egg
Is shrunken to its own deathlike surface;

And an image thus. The body bears the head
(So hardly one they terribly are two)
Feeds and obeys and unto please what end?
Not to the glory of tyrant head but to

The increase of body. Beauty is of body.
The flesh contouring shallowly on a head
Is a rock-garden needing body's love
And best bodiness to colorify

The big blue birds sitting and sea-shell flats
And caves, and on the iron acropolis
To spread the hyacinthine hair and rear
The olive garden for the nightingales.

Prelude to an Evening

Do not enforce the tired wolf
Dragging his infected wound homeward
To sit tonight with the warm children
Naming the pretty kings of France.

The images of the invaded mind
Being as monsters in the dreams
Of your most brief enchanted headful,
Suppose a miracle of confusion:

That dreamed and undreamt become each other
And mix the night and day of your mind;
And it does not matter your twice crying
From mouth unbeautied against the pillow

To avert the gun of the swarthy soldier,
For cry, cock-crow, or the iron bell
Can crack the sleep-sense of outrage,
Annihilate phantoms who were nothing.

But now, by our perverse supposal,
There is a drift of fog on your mornings;
You in your peignoir, dainty at your orange-cup,
Feel poising round the sunny room

Invisible evil, deprived and bold.
All day the clock will metronome
Your gallant fear; the needles clicking,
The heels detonating the stair's cavern.

Freshening the water in the blue bowls
For the buckberries with not all your love,
You shall be listening for the low wind,
The warning sibilance of pines.

You like a waning moon, and I accusing
Our too banded Eumenides,
You shall make Noes but wanderingly,
Smoothing the heads of the hungry children.

Captain Carpenter

Captain Carpenter rose up in his prime
Put on his pistols and went riding out
But had got wellnigh nowhere at that time
Till he fell in with ladies in a rout.

It was a pretty lady and all her train
That played with him so sweetly but before
An hour she'd taken a sword with all her main
And twined him of his nose for evermore.

Captain Carpenter mounted up one day
And rode straightway into a stranger rogue
That looked unchristian but be that as may
The Captain did not wait upon prologue.

But drew upon him out of his great heart
The other swung against him with a club
And cracked his two legs at the shinny part
And let him roll and stick like any tub.

Captain Carpenter rode many a time
From male and female took he sundry harms
He met the wife of Satan crying "I'm
The she-wolf bids you shall bear no more arms."

Their strokes and counters whistled in the wind
I wish he had delivered half his blows
But where she should have made off like a hind
The bitch bit off his arms at the elbows.

And Captain Carpenter parted with his ears
To a black devil that used him in this wise
O Jesus ere his threescore and ten years
Another had plucked out his sweet blue eyes.

Captain Carpenter got up on his roan
And sallied from the gate in hell's despite
I heard him asking in the grimmest tone
If any enemy yet there was to fight?

"To any adversary it is fame
If he risk to be wounded by my tongue
Or burnt in two beneath my red heart's flame
Such are the perils he is cast among.

"But if he can he has a pretty choice
From an anatomy with little to lose
Whether he cut my tongue and take my voice
Or whether it be my round red heart he choose."

It was the neatest knave that ever was seen
Stepping in perfume from his lady's bower
Who at this word put in his merry mien
And fell on Captain Carpenter like a tower.

I would not knock old fellows in the dust
But there lay Captain Carpenter on his back
His weapons were the old heart in his bust
And a blade shook between rotten teeth alack.

The rogue in scarlet and grey soon knew his mind
He wished to get his trophy and depart
With gentle apology and touch refined
He pierced him and produced the Captain's heart.

God's mercy rest on Captain Carpenter now
I thought him Sirs an honest gentleman
Citizen husband soldier and scholar enow
Let jangling kites eat of him if they can.

But God's deep curses follow after those
That shore him of his goodly nose and ears
His legs and strong arms at the two elbows
And eyes that had not watered seventy years.

The curse of hell upon the sleek upstart
That got the Captain finally on his back
And took the red red vitals of his heart
And made the kites to whet their beaks clack clack.

T. S. Eliot (*Br. b. 1888*)

The Love Song of J. Alfred Prufrock

S'io credesse che mia risposta fosse
A persona che mai tornasse al mondo,
Questa fiamma staria senza piu scosse.
Ma perciocche giammai di questo fondo
Non torno vivo alcun, s'i'odo il vero,
Senza tema d'infamia ti rispondo.

Let us go then, you and I,
When the evening is spread out against the sky
Like a patient etherised upon a table;
Let us go, through certain half-deserted streets,
The muttering retreats
Of restless nights in one-night cheap hotels
And sawdust restaurants with oyster-shells:
Streets that follow like a tedious argument
Of insidious intent
To lead you to an overwhelming question . . .
Oh, do not ask, "What is it?"
Let us go and make our visit.

In the room the women come and go
Talking of Michelangelo.

The yellow fog that rubs its back upon the window-panes,
The yellow smoke that rubs its muzzle on the window-panes
Licked its tongue into the corners of the evening,
Lingered upon the pools that stand in drains,
Let fall upon its back the soot that falls from chimneys,
Slipped by the terrace, made a sudden leap,
And seeing that it was a soft October night,
Curled once about the house, and fell asleep.

And indeed there will be time
For the yellow smoke that slides along the street
Rubbing its back upon the window-panes;
There will be time, there will be time
To prepare a face to meet the faces that you meet;
There will be time to murder and create,

And time for all the works and days of hands
That lift and drop a question on your plate;
Time for you and time for me,
And time yet for a hundred indecisions,
And for a hundred visions and revisions,
Before the taking of a toast and tea.

In the room the women come and go
Talking of Michelangelo.

And indeed there will be time
To wonder, "Do I dare?" and, "Do I dare?"
Time to turn back and descend the stair,
With a bald spot in the middle of my hair–
[They will say: "How his hair is growing thin!"]
My morning coat, my collar mounting firmly to the chin,
My necktie rich and modest, but asserted by a simple pin–
[They will say: "But how his arms and legs are thin!"]
Do I dare
Disturb the universe?
In a minute there is time
For decisions and revisions which a minute will reverse.

For I have known them all already, known them all–
Have known the evenings, mornings, afternoons,
I have measured out my life with coffee spoons;
I know the voices dying with a dying fall
Beneath the music from a farther room.
  So how should I presume?

And I have known the eyes already, known them all–
The eyes that fix you in a formulated phrase,
And when I am formulated, sprawling on a pin,
When I am pinned and wriggling on the wall,
Then how should I begin
To spit out all the butt-ends of my days and ways?
  And how should I presume?

And I have known the arms already, known them all–
Arms that are braceleted and white and bare
[But in the lamplight, downed with light brown hair!]
Is it perfume from a dress

That makes me so digress?
Arms that lie along a table, or wrap about a shawl.
  And should I then presume?
  And how should I begin?

Shall I say, I have gone at dusk through narrow streets
And watched the smoke that rises from the pipes
Of lonely men in shirt-sleeves, leaning out of windows? . . .

I should have been a pair of ragged claws
Scuttling across the floors of silent seas.

* * * *

And the afternoon, the evening, sleeps so peacefully!
Smoothed by long fingers,
Asleep . . . tired . . . or it malingers,
Stretched on the floor, here beside you and me.
Should I, after tea and cakes and ices,
Have the strength to force the moment to its crisis?
But though I have wept and fasted, wept and prayed,
Though I have seen my head [grown slightly bald] brought in
    upon a platter,
I am no prophet–and here's no great matter;
I have seen the moment of my greatness flicker,
And I have seen the eternal Footman hold my coat, and snicker,
And in short, I was afraid.

And would it have been worth it, after all,
After the cups, the marmalade, the tea,
Among the porcelain, among some talk of you and me,
Would it have been worth while,
To have bitten off the matter with a smile,
To have squeezed the universe into a ball
To roll it toward some overwhelming question,
To say: "I am Lazarus, come from the dead,
Come back to tell you all, I shall tell you all"
If one, settling a pillow by her head,
  Should say: "That is not what I meant at all.–
  That is not it, at all."

And would it have been worth it, after all,
Would it have been worth while,
After the sunsets and the dooryards and the sprinkled streets,
After the novels, after the teacups, after the skirts that trail along the floor–
And this, and so much more?–
It is impossible to say just what I mean!
But as if a magic lantern threw the nerves in patterns on a screen:
Would it have been worth while
If one, settling a pillow or throwing off a shawl,
And turning toward the window, should say:
"That is not it at all,
That is not what I meant, at all."

* * * *

No! I am not Prince Hamlet, nor was meant to be;
Am an attendant lord, one that will do
To swell a progress, start a scene or two,
Advise the prince; no doubt, an easy tool,
Deferential, glad to be of use,
Politic, cautious, and meticulous;
Full of high sentence, but a bit obtuse;
At times, indeed, almost ridiculous–
Almost, at times, the Fool.

I grow old . . . I grow old . . .
I shall wear the bottoms of my trousers rolled.

Shall I part my hair behind? Do I dare to eat a peach?
I shall wear white flannel trousers, and walk upon the beach.
I have heard the mermaids singing, each to each.

I do not think that they will sing to me.

I have seen them riding seaward on the waves
Combing the white hair of the waves blown back
When the wind blows the water white and black.

We have lingered in the chambers of the sea
By sea-girls wreathed with seaweed red and brown
Till human voices wake us, and we drown.

Preludes

I

The winter evening settles down
With smell of steaks in passageways.
Six o'clock.
The burnt-out ends of smoky days.
And now a gusty shower wraps
The grimy scraps
Of withered leaves about your feet
And newspapers from vacant lots;
The showers beat
On broken blinds and chimney-pots,
And at the corner of the street
A lonely cab-horse steams and stamps.
And then the lighting of the lamps.

II

The morning comes to consciousness
Of faint stale smells of beer
From the sawdust-trampled street
With all its muddy feet that press
To early coffee-stands.
With the other masquerades
That time resumes,
One thinks of all the hands
That are raising dingy shades
In a thousand furnished rooms.

III

You tossed a blanket from the bed,
You lay upon your back, and waited;
You dozed, and watched the night revealing
The thousand sordid images
Of which your soul was constituted;
They flickered against the ceiling.
And when all the world came back
And the light crept up between the shutters
And you heard the sparrows in the gutters,
You had such a vision of the street

As the street hardly understands;
Sitting along the bed's edge, where
You curled the papers from your hair,
Or clasped the yellow soles of feet
In the palms of both soiled hands.

IV

His soul stretched tight across the skies
That fade behind a city block,
Or trampled by insistent feet
At four and five and six o'clock;
And short square fingers stuffing pipes,
And evening newspapers, and eyes
Assured of certain certainties,
The conscience of a blackened street
Impatient to assume the world.

I am moved by fancies that are curled
Around these images, and cling:
The notion of some infinitely gentle
Infinitely suffering thing.

Wipe your hand across your mouth, and laugh;
The worlds revolve like ancient women
Gathering fuel in vacant lots.

Sweeney Among the Nighingales

ὤμοι, πέπληγμαι καιρίαν πληγὴν ἔσω.

Apeneck Sweeney spreads his knees
Letting his arms hang down to laugh,
The zebra stripes along his jaw
Swelling to maculate giraffe.

The circles of the stormy moon
Slide westward toward the River Plate,
Death and the Raven drift above
And Sweeney guards the hornèd gate.

Gloomy Orion and the Dog
Are veiled; and hushed the shrunken seas;
The person in the Spanish cape
Tries to sit on Sweeney's knees

Slips and pulls the table cloth
Overturns a coffee-cup,
Reorganised upon the floor
She yawns and draws a stocking up;

The silent man in mocha brown
Sprawls at the window-sill and gapes;
The waiter brings in oranges
Bananas figs and hothouse grapes;

The silent vertebrate in brown
Contracts and concentrates, withdraws;
Rachel *née* Rabinovitch
Tears at the grapes with murderous paws;

She and the lady in the cape
Are suspect, thought to be in league;
Therefore the man with heavy eyes
Declines the gambit, shows fatigue,

Leaves the room and reappears
Outside the window, leaning in,
Branches of wistaria
Circumscribe a golden grin;

The host with someone indistinct
Converses at the door apart,
The nightingales are singing near
The Convent of the Sacred Heart,

And sang within the bloody wood
When Agamemnon cried aloud,
And let their liquid siftings fall
To stain the stiff dishonoured shroud.

The Waste Land

BURIAL OF THE DEAD

April is the cruellest month, breeding
Lilacs out of the dead land, mixing
Memory and desire, stirring

Dull roots with spring rain.
Winter kept us warm, covering
Earth in forgetful snow, feeding
A little life with dried tubers.
Summer surprised us, coming over the Starnbergersee
With a shower of rain; we stopped in the colonnade,
And went on in sunlight, into the Hofgarten,
And drank coffee, and talked for an hour.
Bin gar keine Russin, stamm' aus Litauen, echt deutsch.
And when we were children, staying at the archduke's,
My cousin's, he took me out on a sled,
And I was frightened. He said, Marie,
Marie, hold on tight. And down we went.
In the mountains, there you feel free.
I read, much of the night, and go south in the winter.

What are the roots that clutch, what branches grow
Out of this stony rubbish? Son of man,
You cannot say, or guess, for you know only
A heap of broken images, where the sun beats,
And the dead tree gives no shelter, the cricket no relief,
And the dry stone no sound of water. Only
There is shadow under this red rock,
(Come in under the shadow of this red rock),
And I will show you something different from either
Your shadow at morning striding behind you
Or your shadow at evening rising to meet you;
I will show you fear in a handful of dust.

Frisch weht der Wind
Der Heimat zu,
Mein Irisch Kind,
Wo weilest du?

"You gave me hyacinths first a year ago;
They called me the hyacinth girl."
–Yet when we came back, late, from the Hyacinth garden,
Your arms full, and your hair wet, I could not
Speak, and my eyes failed, I was neither
Living nor dead, and I knew nothing,
Looking into the heart of light, the silence.
Od' und leer das Meer.

Madame Sosostris, famous clairvoyante,
Had a bad cold, nevertheless
Is known to be the wisest woman in Europe,
With a wicked pack of cards. Here, said she,
Is your card, the drowned Phoenician Sailor,
(Those are pearls that were his eyes. Look!)
Here is Belladonna, the Lady of the Rocks,
The lady of situations.
Here is the man with three staves, and here the Wheel,
And here is the one-eyed merchant, and this card,
Which is blank, is something he carries on his back,
Which I am forbidden to see. I do not find
The Hanged Man. Fear death by water.
I see crowds of people, walking round in a ring.
Thank you. If you see dear Mrs. Equitone,
Tell her I bring the horoscope myself:
One must be so careful these days.

Unreal City,
Under the brown fog of a winter dawn,
A crowd flowed over London Bridge, so many,
I had not thought death had undone so many.
Sighs, short and infrequent, were exhaled,
And each man fixed his eyes before his feet.
Flowed up the hill and down King William Street,
To where Saint Mary Woolnoth kept the hours
With a dead sound on the final stroke of nine.
There I saw one I knew, and stopped him, crying: "Stetson!
You who were with me in the ships at Mylae!
That corpse you planted last year in your garden,
Has it begun to sprout? Will it bloom this year?
Or has the sudden frost disturbed its bed?
Oh keep the Dog far hence, that's friend to men,
Or with his nails he'll dig it up again!
You! hypocrite lecteur!–mon semblable,–mon frère!"

II. A GAME OF CHESS

The Chair she sat in, like a burnished throne,
Glowed on the marble, where the glass
Held up by standards wrought with fruited vines
From which a golden Cupidon peeped out

(Another hid his eyes behind his wing)
Doubled the flames of sevenbranched candelabra
Reflecting light upon the table as
The glitter of her jewels rose to meet it,
From satin cases poured in rich profusion;
In vials of ivory and coloured glass
Unstoppered, lurked her strange synthetic perfumes,
Unguent, powdered, or liquid–troubled, confused
And drowned the sense in odours; stirred by the air
That freshened from the window, these ascended
In fattening the prolonged candle-flames,
Flung their smoke into the laquearia,
Stirring the pattern on the coffered ceiling.
Huge sea-wood fed with copper
Burned green and orange, framed by the coloured stone,
In which sad light a carvèd dolphin swam.
Above the antique mantel was displayed
As though a window gave upon the sylvan scene
The change of Philomel, by the barbarous king
So rudely forced; yet there the nightingale
Filled all the desert with inviolable voice
And still she cried, and still the world pursues,
"Jug Jug" to dirty ears.
And other withered stumps of time
Were told upon the walls; staring forms
Leaned out, leaning, hushing the room enclosed.
Footsteps shuffled on the stair.
Under the firelight, under the brush, her hair
Spread out in fiery points
Glowed into words, then would be savagely still.

"My nerves are bad to-night. Yes, bad. Stay with me.
Speak to me. Why do you never speak. Speak.
  What are you thinking of? What thinking?
    What?
I never know what you are thinking. Think."

I think we are in rats' alley
Where the dead men lost their bones.

"What is that noise?"
                    The wind under the door.

What is that noise now? What is the wind doing?"
Nothing again nothing.
"Do
You know nothing? Do you see nothing? Do
you remember
Nothing?"

I remember
Those are pearls that were his eyes.
"Are you alive, or not? Is there nothing in your head?"
But
O O O O that Shakespeherian Rag–
It's so elegant
So intelligent
"What shall I do now? What shall I do?"
"I shall rush out as I am, and walk the street
With my hair down, so. What shall we do tomorrow?
What shall we ever do?"
The hot water at ten.
And if it rains, a closed car at four.
And we shall play a game of chess,
Pressing lidless eyes and waiting for a knock upon the door.

When Lil's husband got demobbed, I said–
I didn't mince my words, I said to her myself,
HURRY UP PLEASE ITS TIME
Now Albert's coming back, make yourself a bit smart.
He'll want to know what you done with that money he
gave you
To get yourself some teeth. He did, I was there.
You have them all out, Lil, and get a nice set,
He said, I swear, I can't bear to look at you.
And no more can't I, I said, and think of poor Albert,
He's been in the army four years, he wants a good time,
And if you don't give it him, there's others will, I said.
Oh is there, she said. Something o' that, I said.
Then I'll know who to thank, she said, and give me a straight
look.
HURRY UP PLEASE ITS TIME
If you don't like it you can get on with it, I said.
Others can pick and choose if you can't.

But if Albert makes off, it won't be for lack of telling.
You ought to be ashamed, I said, to look so antique.
(And her only thirty-one.)
I can't help it, she said, pulling a long face,
It's them pills I took, to bring it off, she said.
(She's had five already, and nearly died of young George.)
The chemist said it would be all right, but I've never been the
same.
You *are* a proper fool, I said.
Well, if Albert won't leave you alone, there it is, I said,
What you get married for if you don't want children?
HURRY UP PLEASE ITS TIME
Well, that Sunday Albert was home, they had a hot gammon,
And they asked me in to dinner, to get the beauty of it hot–
HURRY UP PLEASE ITS TIME
HURRY UP PLEASE ITS TIME
Goonight Bill. Goonight Lou. Goonight May.
Goonight.
Ta ta. Goonight. Goonight.
Good night, ladies, good night, sweet ladies, good night, good
night.

III. THE FIRE SERMON

The river's tent is broken: the last fingers of leaf
Clutch and sink into the wet bank. The wind
Crosses the brown land, unheard. The nymphs are departed.
Sweet Thames, run softly, till I end my song.
The river bears no empty bottles, sandwich papers,
Silk handkerchiefs, cardboard boxes, cigarette ends
Or other testimony of summer nights. The nymphs are departed.
And their friends, the loitering heirs of city directors;
Departed, have left no addresses.
By the waters of Leman I sat down and wept . . .
Sweet Thames, run softly till I end my song,
Sweet Thames, run softly, for I speak not loud or long.
But at my back in a cold blast I hear
The rattle of the bones, and chuckle spread from ear to ear.
A rat crept softly through the vegetation
Dragging its slimy belly on the bank

While I was fishing in the dull canal
On a winter evening round behind the gashouse
Musing upon the king my brother's wreck
And on the king my father's death before him.
White bodies naked on the low damp ground
And bones cast in a little low dry garret,
Rattled by the rat's foot only, year to year.
But at my back from time to time I hear
The sound of horns and motors, which shall bring
Sweeney to Mrs. Porter in the spring.
O the moon shone bright on Mrs. Porter
And on her daughter
They wash their feet in soda water
Et O ces voix d'enfants, chantant dans la coupole!

Twit twit twit
Jug jug jug jug jug jug
So rudely forc'd.
Tereu

Unreal City
Under the brown fog of a winter noon
Mr. Eugenides, the Smyrna merchant
Unshaven, with a pocket full of currants
C.i.f. London: documents at sight,
Asked me in demotic French
To luncheon at the Cannon Street Hotel
Followed by a weekend at the Metropole.

At the violet hour, when the eyes and back
Turn upward from the desk, when the human engine waits
Like a taxi throbbing waiting,
I Tiresias, though blind, throbbing between two lives,
Old man with wrinkled female breasts, can see
At the violet hour, the evening hour that strives
Homeward, and brings the sailor home from sea,
The typist home at teatime, clears her breakfast, lights
Her stove, and lays out food in tins.
Out of the window perilously spread
Her drying combinations touched by the sun's last rays,
On the divan are piled (at night her bed)

Stockings, slippers, camisoles, and stays.
I Tiresias, old man with wrinkled dugs
Perceived the scene, and foretold the rest–
I too awaited the expected guest.
He, the young man carbuncular, arrives,
A small house agent's clerk, with one bold stare,
One of the low on whom assurance sits
As a silk hat on a Bradford millionaire.
The time is now propitious, as he guesses,
The meal is ended, she is bored and tired,
Endeavours to engage her in caresses
Which still are unreproved, if undesired.
Flushed and decided, he assaults at once;
Exploring hands encounter no defence;
His vanity requires no response,
And makes a welcome of indifference.
(And I Tiresias have foresuffered all
Enacted on this same divan or bed;
I who have sat by Thebes below the wall
And walked among the lowest of the dead.)
Bestows one final patronising kiss,
And gropes his way, finding the stairs unlit . . .

She turns and looks a moment in the glass,
Hardly aware of her departed lover;
Her brain allows one half-formed thought to pass:
"Well now that's done: and I'm glad it's over."
When lovely woman stoops to folly and
Paces about her room again, alone,
She smoothes her hair with automatic hand,
And puts a record on the gramophone.

"This music crept by me upon the waters"
And along the Strand, up Queen Victoria Street.
O City city, I can sometimes hear
Beside a public bar in Lower Thames Street,
The pleasant whining of a mandoline
And a clatter and a chatter from within
Where fishmen lounge at noon: where the walls
Of Magnus Martyr hold
Inexplicable splendour of Ionian white and gold.

The river sweats
Oil and tar
The barges drift
With the turning tide
Red sails
Wide
To leeward, swing on the heavy spar.
The barges wash
Drifting logs
Down Greenwich reach
Past the Isle of Dogs.
          Weialala leia
          Wallala leialala

Elizabeth and Leicester
Beating oars
The stern was formed
A gilded shell
Red and gold
The brisk swell
Rippled both shores
Southwest wind
Carried down stream
The peal of bells
White towers
          Weialala leia
          Wallala leialala

"Trams and dusty trees.
Highbury bore me. Richmond and Kew
Undid me. By Richmond I raised my knees
Supine on the floor of a narrow canoe."

"My feet are at Moorgate, and my heart
Under my feet. After the event
He wept. He promised 'a new start'.
I made no comment. What should I resent?"

"On Margate sands.
I can connect
Nothing with nothing.
The broken fingernails of dirty hands.

My people humble people who expect
Nothing."
La la

To Carthage then I came

Burning burning burning burning
O Lord Thou pluckest me out
O Lord Thou pluckest

burning

IV. DEATH BY WATER

Phlebas the Phoenician, a fortnight dead,
Forgot the cry of gulls, and the deep sea swell
And the profit and loss.
A current under sea
Picked his bones in whispers. As he rose and fell
He passed the stages of his age and youth
Entering the whirlpool.
Gentile or Jew
O you who turn the wheel and look to windward,
Consider Phlebas, who was once handsome and tall as you.

V. WHAT THE THUNDER SAID

After the torchlight red on sweaty faces
After the frosty silence in the gardens
After the agony in stony places
The shouting and the crying
Prison and palace and reverberation
Of thunder of spring over distant mountains
He who was living is now dead
We who were living are now dying
With a little patience

Here is no water but only rock
Rock and no water and the sandy road
The road winding above among the mountains
Which are mountains of rock without water
If there were water we should stop and drink
Amongst the rock one cannot stop or think

Sweat is dry and feet are in the sand
If there were only water amongst the rock
Dead mountain mouth of carious teeth that cannot spit
Here one can neither stand nor lie nor sit
There is not even silence in the mountains
But dry sterile thunder without rain
There is not even solitude in the mountains
But red sullen faces sneer and snarl
From doors of mudcracked houses
If there were water
And no rock
If there were rock
And also water
And water
A spring
A pool among the rock
If there were the sound of water only
Not the cicada
And dry grass singing
But sound of water over a rock
Where the hermit-thrush sings in the pine trees
Drip drop drip drop drop drop drop
But there is no water

Who is the third who walks always beside you?
When I count, there are only you and I together
But when I look ahead up the white road
There is always another one walking beside you
Gliding wrapt in a brown mantle, hooded
I do not know whether a man or a woman
–But who is that on the other side of you?

What is that sound high in the air
Murmur of maternal lamentation
Who are those hooded hordes swarming
Over endless plains, stumbling in cracked earth
Ringed by the flat horizon only
What is the city over the mountains
Cracks and reforms and bursts in the violet air
Falling towers

Jerusalem Athens Alexandria
Vienna London
Unreal
A woman drew her long black hair out tight
And fiddled whisper music on those strings
And bats with baby faces in the violet light
Whistled, and beat their wings
And crawled head downward down a blackened wall
And upside down in air were towers
Tolling reminiscent bells, that kept the hours
And voices singing out of empty cisterns and exhausted
wells.

In this decayed hole among the mountains
In the faint moonlight, the grass is singing
Over the tumbled graves, about the chapel
There is the empty chapel, only the wind's home.
It has no windows, and the door swings,
Dry bones can harm no one.
Only a cock stood on the rooftree
Co co rico co co rico
In a flash of lightning. Then a damp gust
Bringing rain

Ganga was sunken, and the limp leaves
Waited for rain, while the black clouds
Gathered far distant, over Himavant.
The jungle crouched, humped in silence.
Then spoke the thunder
DA
Datta: what have we given?
My friend, blood shaking my heart
The awful daring of a moment's surrender
Which an age of prudence can never retract
By this, and this only, we have existed
Which is not to be found in our obituaries
Or in memories draped by the beneficent spider
Or under seals broken by the lean solicitor
In our empty rooms
DA

Dayadhvam: I have heard the key
Turn in the door once and turn once only
We think of the key, each in his prison
Thinking of the key, each confirms a prison
Only at nightfall, aethereal rumours
Revive for a moment a broken Coriolanus
DA
Damyata: The boat responded
Gaily, to the hand expert with sail and oar
The sea was calm, your heart would have responded
Gaily, when invited, beating obedient
To controlling hands

I sat upon the shore
Fishing, with the arid plain behind me
Shall I at least set my lands in order?
London Bridge is falling down falling down falling down
Poi s'ascose nel foco che gli affina
Quando fiam ceu chelidon–O swallow swallow
Le Prince d'Aquitaine à la tour abolie
These fragments I have shored against my ruins
Why then Ile fit you. Hieronymo's mad againe.
Datta. Dayadhvam. Damyata.
Shantih shantih shantih

Animula

"Issues from the hand of God, the simple soul"
To a flat world of changing lights and noise,
To light, dark, dry or damp, chilly or warm;
Moving between the legs of tables and of chairs,
Rising or falling, grasping at kisses and toys,
Advancing boldly, sudden to take alarm,
Retreating to the corner of arm and knee,
Eager to be reassured, taking pleasure
In the fragrant brilliance of the Christmas tree,
Pleasure in the wind, the sunlight and the sea;
Studies the sunlit pattern on the floor
And running stags around a silver tray;
Confounds the actual and the fanciful,

Content with playing-cards and kings and queens,
What the fairies do and what the servants say.
The heavy burden of the growing soul
Perplexes and offends more, day by day;
Week by week, offends and perplexes more
With the imperatives of 'is and seems'
And may and may not, desire and control.
The pain of living and the drug of dreams
Curl up the small soul in the window seat
Behind the *Encyclopaedia Britannica.*
Issues from the hand of time the simple soul
Irresolute and selfish, misshapen, lame,
Unable to fare forward or retreat,
Fearing the warm reality, the offered good,
Denying the importunity of the blood,
Shadow of its own shadows, spectre in its own gloom,
Leaving disordered papers in a dusty room;
Living first in the silence after the viaticum.

Pray for Guiterriez, avid of speed and power,
For Boudin, blown to pieces,
For this one who made a great fortune,
And that one who went his own way.
Pray for Floret, by the boarhound slain between the
yew trees,
Pray for us now and at the hour of our birth.

East Coker

I

In my beginning is my end. In succession
Houses rise and fall, crumble, are extended,
Are removed, destroyed, restored, or in their place
Is an open field, or a factory, or a by-pass.
Old stone to new building, old timber to new fires,
Old fires to ashes, and ashes to the earth
Which is already flesh, fur and faeces,
Bone of man and beast, cornstalk and leaf.
Houses live and die: there is a time for building
And a time for living and for generation

And a time for the wind to break the loosened pane
And to shake the wainscot where the field-mouse trots
And to shake the tattered arras woven with a silent
  motto.

In my beginning is my end. Now the light falls
Across the open field, leaving the deep lane
Shuttered with branches, dark in the afternoon,
Where you lean against a bank while a van passes,
And the deep lane insists on the direction
Into the village, in the electric heat
Hypnotised. In a warm haze the sultry light
Is absorbed, not refracted, by grey stone.
The dahlias sleep in the empty silence.
Wait for the early owl.

In that open field
If you do not come too close, if you do not come too
  close,
On a summer midnight, you can hear the music
Of the weak pipe and the little drum
And see them dancing around the bonfire
The association of man and woman
In daunsinge, signifying matrimonie–
A dignified and commodious sacrament.
Two and two, necessarye coniunction,
Holding eche other by the hand or the arm
Whiche betokeneth concorde. Round and round the fire
Leaping through the flames, or joined in circles,
Rustically solemn or in rustic laughter
Lifting heavy feet in clumsy shoes,
Earth feet, loam feet, lifted in country mirth
Mirth of those long since under earth
Nourishing the corn. Keeping time,
Keeping the rhythm in their dancing
As in their living in the living seasons
The time of the seasons and the constellations
The time of milking and the time of harvest
The time of the coupling of man and woman
And that of beasts. Feet rising and falling.
Eating and drinking. Dung and death.

Dawn points, and another day
Prepares for heat and silence. Out at sea the dawn wind
Wrinkles and slides. I am here
Or there, or elsewhere. In my beginning.

II

What is the late November doing
With the disturbance of the spring
And creatures of the summer heat,
And snowdrops writhing under feet
And hollyhocks that aim too high
Red into grey and tumble down
Late roses filled with early snow?
Thunder rolled by the rolling stars
Simulates triumphal cars
Deployed in constellated wars
Scorpion fights against the Sun
Until the Sun and Moon go down
Comets weep and Leonids fly
Hunt the heavens and the plains
Whirled in a vortex that shall bring
The world to that destructive fire
Which burns before the ice-cap reigns.

That was a way of putting it – not very satisfactory:
A periphrastic study in a worn-out poetical fashion,
Leaving one still with the intolerable wrestle
With words and meanings. The poetry does not matter.
It was not (to start again) what one had expected.
What was to be the value of the long looked forward to,
Long hoped for calm, the autumnal serenity
And the wisdom of age? Had they deceived us
Or deceived themselves, the quiet-voiced elders,
Bequeathing us merely a receipt for deceit?
The serenity only a deliberate hebetude,
The wisdom only the knowledge of dead secrets
Useless in the darkness into which they peered
Or from which they turned their eyes. There is, it seems
to us,
At best, only a limited value

In the knowledge derived from experience.
The knowledge imposes a pattern, and falsifies,
For the pattern is new in every moment
And every moment is a new and shocking
Valuation of all we have been. We are only undeceived
Of that which, deceiving, could no longer harm.
In the middle, not only in the middle of the way
But all the way, in a dark wood, in a bramble,
On the edge of a grimpen, where is no secure foothold,
And menaced by monsters, fancy lights,
Risking enchantment. Do not let me hear
Of the wisdom of old men, but rather of their folly,
Their fear of fear and frenzy, their fear of possession,
Of belonging to another, or to others, or to God.
The only wisdom we can hope to acquire
Is the wisdom of humility: humility is endless.

The houses are all gone under the sea.

The dancers are all gone under the hill.

III

O dark dark dark. They all go into the dark,
The vacant interstellar spaces, the vacant into the vacant,
The captains, merchant bankers, eminent men of letters,
The generous patrons of art, the statesmen and the rulers,
Distinguished civil servants, chairmen of many committees,
Industrial lords and petty contractors, all go into the dark,
And dark the Sun and Moon, and the Almanach de Gotha
And the Stock Exchange Gazette, the Directory of Directors,
And cold the sense and lost the motive of action.
And we all go with them, into the silent funeral,
Nobody's funeral, for there is no one to bury.
I said to my soul, be still, and let the dark come upon you
Which shall be the darkness of God. As, in a theatre,
The lights are extinguished, for the scene to be changed
With a hollow rumble of wings, with a movement of darkness
on darkness,
And we know that the hills and the trees, the distant panorama
And the bold imposing façade are all being rolled away–

Or as, when an underground train, in the tube, stops too long
  between stations
And the conversation rises and slowly fades into silence
And you see behind every face the mental emptiness deepen
Leaving only the growing terror of nothing to think about;
Or when, under ether, the mind is conscious but conscious of
  nothing–
I said to my soul, be still, and wait without hope
For hope would be hope for the wrong thing; wait without love
For love would be love of the wrong thing; there is yet faith
But the faith and the love and the hope are all in the waiting.
Wait without thought, for you are not ready for thought:
So the darkness shall be the light, and the stillness the dancing.
Whisper of running streams, and winter lightning.
The wild thyme unseen and the wild strawberry,
The laughter in the garden, echoed ecstasy
Not lost, but requiring, pointing to the agony
Of death and birth.

You say I am repeating
Something I have said before. I shall say it again.
Shall I say it again? In order to arrive there,
To arrive where you are, to get from where you are not,
  You must go by a way wherein there is no ecstasy.
In order to arrive at what you do not know
  You must go by a way which is the way of ignorance.
In order to possess what you do not possess
  You must go by the way of dispossession.
In order to arrive at what you are not
  You must go through the way in which you are not.
And what you do not know is the only thing you know
And what you own is what you do not own
And where you are is where you are not.

IV

The wounded surgeon plies the steel
That questions the distempered part;
Beneath the bleeding hands we feel
The sharp compassion of the healer's art
Resolving the enigma of the fever chart.

Our only health is the disease
If we obey the dying nurse
Whose constant care is not to please
But to remind of our, and Adam's curse,
And that, to be restored, our sickness must grow worse.

The whole earth is our hospital
Endowed by the ruined millionaire,
Wherein, if we do well, we shall
Die of the absolute paternal care
That will not leave us, but prevents us everywhere.

The chill ascends from feet to knees,
The fever sings in mental wires.
If to be warmed, then I must freeze
And quake in frigid purgatorial fires
Of which the flame is roses, and the smoke is briars.

The dripping blood our only drink,
The bloody flesh our only food:
In spite of which we like to think
That we are sound, substantial flesh and blood–
Again, in spite of that, we call this Friday good.

V

So here I am, in the middle way, having had twenty years–
Twenty years largely wasted, the years of *l'entre deux guerres*–
Trying to learn to use words, and every attempt
Is a wholly new start, and a different kind of failure
Because one has only learnt to get the better of words
For the thing one no longer has to say, or the way in which
One is no longer disposed to say it. And so each venture
Is a new beginning, a raid on the inarticulate
With shabby equipment always deteriorating
In the general mess of imprecision of feeling,
Undisciplined squads of emotion. And what there is to conquer
By strength and submission, has already been discovered
Once or twice, or several times, by men whom one cannot hope
To emulate–but there is no competition–
There is only the fight to recover what has been lost
And found and lost again and again: and now, under conditions
That seem unpropitious. But perhaps neither gain nor loss.
For us, there is only the trying. The rest is not our business.

Home is where one starts from. As we grow older
The world becomes stranger, the pattern more complicated
Of dead and living. Not the intense moment
Isolated, with no before and after,
But a lifetime burning in every moment
And not the lifetime of one man only
But of old stones that cannot be deciphered.
There is a time for the evening under starlight,
A time for the evening under lamplight
(The evening with the photograph album).
Love is most nearly itself
When here and now cease to matter.
Old men ought to be explorers
Here and there does not matter
We must be still and still moving
Into another intensity
For a further union, a deeper communion
Through the dark cold and the empty desolation,
The wave cry, the wind cry, the vast waters
Of the petrel and the porpoise. In my end is my beginning.

Conrad Aiken (*Am. b. 1889*)

from
Preludes for Memnon,
or
Preludes to Attitude
I

Winter for a moment takes the mind; the snow
Falls past the arclight; icicles guard a wall;
The wind moans through a crack in the window;
A keen sparkle of frost is on the sill.
Only for a moment; as spring too might engage it,
With a single crocus in the loam, or a pair of birds;
Or summer with hot grass; or autumn with a yellow leaf.
Winter is there, outside, is here in me:

Drapes the planets with snow, deepens the ice on the moon,
Darkens the darkness that was already darkness.
The mind too has its snows, its slippery paths,
Walls bayonetted with ice, leaves ice-encased.
Here is the in-drawn room, to which you return
When the wind blows from Arcturus: here is the fire
At which you warm your hands and glaze your eyes;
The piano, on which you touch the cold treble;
Five notes like breaking icicles; and then silence.

The alarm-clock ticks, the pulse keeps time with it,
Night and the mind are full of sounds. I walk
From the fire-place, with its imaginary fire,
To the window, with its imaginary view.
Darkness, and snow ticking the window: silence,
And the knocking of chains on a motor-car, the tolling
Of a bronze bell, dedicated to Christ.
And then the uprush of angelic wings, the beating
Of wings demonic, from the abyss of the mind:
The darkness filled with a feathery whistling, wings
Numberless as the flakes of angelic snow,
The deep void swarming with wings and sound of wings,
The winnowing of chaos, the aliveness
Of depth and depth and depth dedicated to death.

Here are the bickerings of the inconsequential,
The chatterings of the ridiculous, the iterations
Of the meaningless. Memory, like a juggler,
Tosses its colored balls into the light, and again
Receives them into darkness. Here is the absurd,
Grinning like an idiot, and the omnivorous quotidian,
Which will have its day. A handful of coins,
Tickets, items from the news, a soiled handkerchief,
A letter to be answered, notice of a telephone call,
The petal of a flower in a volume of Shakspere,
The program of a concert. The photograph, too,
Propped on the mantel, and beneath it a dry rosebud;
The laundry bill, matches, an ash-tray, Utamaro's
Pearl-fishers. And the rug, on which are still the crumbs
Of yesterday's feast. These are the void, the night,
And the angelic wings that make it sound.

What is the flower? It is not a sigh of color,
Suspiration of purple, sibilation of saffron,
Nor aureate exhalation from the tomb.
Yet it is these because you think of these,
An emanation of emanations, fragile
As light, or glisten, or gleam, or coruscation,
Creature of brightness, and as brightness brief.
What is the frost? It is not the sparkle of death,
The flash of time's wing, seeds of eternity;
Yet it is these because you think of these.
And you, because you think of these, are both
Frost and flower, the bright ambiguous syllable
Of which the meaning is both no and yes.

Here is the tragic, the distorting mirror
In which your gesture becomes grandiose;
Tears form and fall from your magnificent eyes,
The brow is noble, and the mouth is God's.
Here is the God who seeks his mother, Chaos,–
Confusion seeking solution, and life seeking death.
Here is the rose that woos the icicle; the icicle
That woos the rose. Here is the silence of silences
Which dreams of becoming a sound, and the sound
Which will perfect itself in silence. And all
These things are only the uprush from the void,
The wings angelic and demonic, the sound of the abyss
Dedicated to death. And this is you.

from
Preludes to Definition
Time in the Rock
XCIII

Or else, in an afternoon of minor reflection,
the savage sunset tamed, and in your garden
the bright stripes beneath your feet, fool
you think from footstep to footstep how easily
man's genius can compose an ode to death.
The honeysuckle puts down its tendrils from the wall
and seeks to embrace you, the seedlings
break the earth as you watch and seem to approach,
the thrush clings with cold claws of a serpent

to his favourite bough and sings. What can you say
that these have not said, are not saying,
you with your consciousness of time? time
swings with the tendril, sings in the birdsong, clings
with the bird-claw, it is time
which thrusts like the leaf's eye from the cold earth.
These already know death, in the mere adventure
in the mere going forth they know and seek it gladly,
they embrace it tightly, what can you say
that is not known to the cold claws of the thrush?
Your ode to death is not in a phrase,
nor in a hymn to darkness, nor in a knowledge
of timelessness, or the sad iteration
of time. Your ode to death is in the lifting
of a single eyelash. Lift it and see.

South End

The benches are broken, the grassplots brown and bare,
the laurels dejected, in this neglected square.
Dogs couple undisturbed. The roots of trees
heave up the bricks in the sidewalk as they please.

Nobody collects the papers from the grass,
nor the dead matches, nor the broken glass.
The elms are old and shabby; the houses, around,
stare lazily through paintless shutters at forgotten ground.

Out of the dusty fountain, with the dust,
the leaves fly up like birds on a sudden gust.
The leaves fly up like birds, and the papers flap,
or round the legs of benches wrap and unwrap.

Here, for the benefit of some secret sense,
warm-autumn-afternoon finds permanence.
No one will hurry, or wait too long, or die:
all is serenity, under a serene sky.

Dignity shines in old brick and old dirt,
in elms and houses now hurt beyond all hurt.
A broken square, where little lives or moves;
these are the city's earliest and tenderest loves.

Blind Date

No more the swanboat on the artificial lake
its paddled path through neon light shall take;
the stars are turned out on the immortal ferris wheel,
dark and still are the cars of the Virginia Reel.
Baby, it is the last of all blind dates,
and this we keep with the keeper of the golden gates.

For the last time, my darling, the chute-the-chutes,
the Tunnel of Love, the cry "all men are brutes,"
the sweaty dance-hall with the juke-box playing,
pretzels and beer, and our young love a-Maying:
baby, it is the last of all blind dates,
and this we keep with the keeper of the golden gates.

The radios in a thousand taxis die;
at last man's music fades from the inhuman sky;
as, short or long, fades out the impermanent wave
to find in the ether or the earth its grave.
Baby, it is the last of all blind dates,
and this we keep with the keeper of the golden gates.

Hold hands and kiss, it will never come again,
look in your own eyes and remember the deep pain,
how hollow the world is, like a bubble burst,
yes, and all beauty by some wretchedness accursed!
Baby, it is the last of all blind dates,
and this we keep with the keeper of the golden gates.

Love now the footworn grass, the trampled flowers,
and the divided man of crowds, for he is ours–
love him, yes, love him now, this sundered being,
who most himself seeks when himself most fleeing–
baby, it is the last of all blind dates,
and this we keep with the keeper of the golden gates.

But look–the scenic railway is flashed from red to green–
and swiftly beneath our feet as this machine
our old star plunges down the precipitous sky,
down the hurrahs of space! So soon to die!–
But baby, it is the last of all blind dates;
and we shall keep it with the keeper of the golden gates.

from
The Kid
The Awakening
VII

Dark was the forest, dark was the mind:
dark the trail that he stooped to find:
dark, dark, dark, in the midnight lost,
in self's own midnight, the seeking ghost.
Listen to the tree, press leaves apart:
listen to the blood, the evergreen heart:
deep, deep, deep, the water in the soul,
there will I baptize, and there be whole.
Dark, dark, dark, in this knowledge immersed,
by filth, by fire, and by frost aspersed,
in horror, in terror, in the depths of sleep,
I shudder, I grow, and my roots are deep.
The leaf is spoken: the granite is said:
now I am born, for the king is dead:
now I awake, for the father is dead.
Dark is the forest when false dawn looms–
darkest now, when the true day comes.
Now I am waking: now I begin:
writhe like a snake from the outworn skin:
and I open my eyes: and the world looks in!

Fredegond Shove (*Br. 1889–1949*)

The New Ghost

"And he casting away his garment rose and came to Jesus."

And he cast it down, down, on the green grass,
Over the young crocuses, where the dew was–
He cast the garment of his flesh that was full of death,
And like a sword his spirit showed out of the cold sheath.

He went a pace or two, he went to meet his Lord,
And, as I said, his spirit looked like a clean sword,
And seeing him the naked trees began shivering,
And all the birds cried out aloud as it were late spring.

And the Lord came on, He came down, and saw
That a soul was waiting there for Him, one without flaw,
And they embraced in the churchyard where the robins play,
And the daffodils hang down their heads, as they burn away.

The Lord held his head fast, and you could see
That He kissed the unsheathed ghost that was gone free–
As a hot sun, on a March day, kisses the cold ground;
And the spirit answered, for he knew well that his peace was
found.

The spirit trembled, and sprang up at the Lord's word–
As on a wild, April day, springs a small bird–
So the ghost's feet lifting him up, he kissed the Lord's cheek,
And for the greatness of their love neither of them could speak.

But the Lord went then, to show him the way,
Over the young crocuses, under the green may
That was not quite in flower yet–to a far-distant land;
And the ghost followed, like a naked cloud holding the sun's
hand.

A Dream in Early Spring

Now when I sleep the thrush breaks through my dreams
With sharp reminders of the coming day:
After his call, one minute I remain
Unwaked, and on the darkness which is Me
There springs the image of a daffodil,
Growing upon a grassy bank alone,
And seeming with great joy his bell to fill
With drops of golden dew, which on the lawn
He shakes again, where they lie bright and chill.

His head is drooped; the shrouded winds that sing
Bend him which way they will: never on earth
Was there before so beautiful a ghost;
Alas! he had a less than flower-birth,
And like a ghost indeed must shortly glide
From all but the sad cells of memory,
Where he will linger, an imprisoned beam,
Or fallen shadow of the golden world,
Long after this and many another dream.

Katherine Garrison Chapin (*Am. b. 1890*)

The Other Journey

Valley of ancient life, how many visions died,
In this bright sand, how many dreams were born,
The falcon and the angel side by side,
The limbs of love from bleeding body torn.
Who shall discern the fire on the hill
Or rise again obedient to a will?

Summon the princely chariot from the halls,
The hunter and the hunted, in their chase,
Bright spear suspended. For the one who falls,
Another rises who shall take his place,
And on the timeless surface of the walls,
With deeper line mark out a different face.

The broken fragments of Man's searching lie
In cycles from first dark to later dark;
A goddess sucks the udders of the sky,
Goat-headed Fate sits in his moving barque;
Sirius erect, celestial majesty,
Steers his slight boat across a star-divided sea.

Valley of ancient time, here fresh creation
Lies like a dew upon each living shape
Throbs in singing bird throat, in the motion
Of dancing feet, moves in coil of snake.
The Queen's white garment flutters
As she receives the key of life within her long thin fingers.

And life is center of the Temple's plan
Which moves forever forward in design;
In measure of the microcosm, man,
Man living, not destroyed, not sacrificed
(A drooped Head on a Cross)
But man, source of fertile power, linked with the planet's
  source.

Where tall papyrus-budded columns rise
In flowering rows, their peristyle and place
Stand in conjunction with revolving skies,

Earth-season rhythms, axis-turn and base;
Man's heart-beat and its blood;
Its time of ebbing and its mounting flood.

Among these living symbols in charged air
Of December desert, through still night and day,
I look beyond the clear horizon for another star,
Search on the hills for that thin ray
Which severed earth and sky, gather
The ancient legends of a Son and Mother.

Isis or Mary, with her Child asleep,
Dipped in the river to wash His swaddling clothes,
And from the drops which fell and settled deep
In Earth, seed sprang, and a dark tree arose,
A bitter balsam tree. Its wide
Branches cut to make the cross on which He died.

O Poet risen from the tomb! The god,
Dead, lives in his son. Death
Of the Son dying that man may find
Again a living breath.
He shall take power from the dead
Nor ask for bleeding testament, nor thorn-crowned head.

Nor ask for pity. Earth is taken by the strong,
The strong in secret wisdom,
Who know the wrath, the violence that belong
To life, from stir of womb and the first cry,
To the last measure of its ecstasy.

* * * *

Up from this western sea fresh wind blows in.
The Pleiads are about my head and stars drip down
In bronzed and burned out meteors to the sand.

I hear you cry, O birds, I know the light begins,
I stand within the current of your wings
Who followed where you led, around the listening earth
To find its talisman.
For the last time you circle to depart,
Bright ibis and dark raven, and the poet's rook
Who wove a rhythmic spell about my heart.

Clouds rise. I stand
Here under swing of homing gulls,
And watch a wave, crested and beautiful,
Come in to cover and erase
Like a last trace, a final word
Of poem, the delicate cross-bow mark
Of bird, left in the ebbing sand.

Edna St. Vincent Millay (*Am. 1892–1950*)

Euclid alone has looked on Beauty bare

Euclid alone has looked on Beauty bare.
Let all who prate of Beauty hold their peace,
And lay them prone upon the earth and cease
To ponder on themselves, the while they stare
At nothing, intricately drawn nowhere
In shapes of shifting lineage; let geese
Gabble and hiss, but heroes seek release
From dusty bondage into luminous air.
O blinding hour, O holy, terrible day,
When first the shaft into his vision shone
Of light anatomized! Euclid alone
Has looked on Beauty bare. Fortunate they
Who, though once only and then but far away,
Have heard her massive sandal set on stone.

Oh, sleep forever in the Latmian cave

Oh, sleep forever in the Latmian cave,
Mortal Endymion, darling of the Moon!
Her silver garments by the senseless wave
Shouldered and dropped and on the shingle strewn,
Her fluttering hand against her forehead pressed,
Her scattered looks that trouble all the sky,
Her rapid footsteps running down the west–
Of all her altered state, oblivious lie!

Whom earthen you, by deathless lips adored,
Wild-eyed and stammering to the grasses thrust,
And deep into her crystal body poured
The hot and sorrowful sweetness of the dust:
Whereof she wanders mad, being all unfit
For mortal love, that might not die of it.

V. Sackville-West (*Br. b. 1892*)

On the Lake

A candle lit in darkness of black waters,
A candle set in the drifting prow of a boat,
And every tree to itself a separate shape,
Now plumy, now an arch; tossed trees
Still and dishevelled; dishevelled with past growth,
Forgotten storms; left tufted, tortured, sky-rent,
Even now in stillness; stillness on the lake,
Black, reflections pooled, black mirror
Pooling a litten candle, taper of fire;
Pooling the sky, double transparency
Of sky in water, double elements,
Lying like lovers, light above, below;
Taking, from one another, light; a gleaming,
A glow reflected, fathoms deep, leagues high,
Two distances meeting at a film of surface
Thin as a membrane, sheet of surface, fine
Smooth steel; two separates, height and depth,
Able to touch, giving to one another
All their profundity, all their accidents,
–Changeable mood of clouds, permanent stars,–
Like thoughts in the mind hanging a long way off,
Revealed between lovers, friends. Peer in the water
Over the boat's edge; seek the sky's night-heart;
Are they near, are they far, those clouds, those stars
Given, reflected, pooled? are they so close
For a hand to clasp, to lift them, feel their shape,
Explore their reality, take a rough possession?

Oh no! too delicate, too shy for handling,
They tilt at a touch, quiver to other shapes,
Dance away, change, are lost, drowned, scared;
Hands break the mirror, speech's crudity
The surmise, the divining;
Such things so deeply held, so lightly held,
Subtile, imponderable, as stars in water
Or thoughts in another's thoughts.
Are they near, are they far, those stars, that knowledge?
Deep? shallow? solid? rare? The boat drifts on,
And the litten candle single in the prow,
The small, immediate candle in the prow,
Burns brighter in the water than any star.

A Dream

Down the long path beneath the garden wall,
She stooped, setting her plants in the winter dusk.
She knew she must make an end of setting her plants,
Though why she must make an end she nothing knew.
Was it the end of the year that made her urgent?
Was it the end of the day? for night came down,
And the heavy sky grew black above the wall,
And the trees were quiet in a stillness worse than storm
As the great white stealthy flakes began to fall,
But still she stooped with her trowel, setting her plants.

And the ground grew white with the imperceptible drift
Of the silent snow from a black and loaded heaven,
And candles came around her, stuck in silver;
Candelabra of silver, with horns of flame,
Burning the snow to a ruddy glow as she set
The fragile year's-end plants of her dying hopes.

But the candles failed to mount with the mounting snow;
The silver bases and then the silver stems
Were buried under the drift, and the drift invaded
The very candles and stems of tender wax,
So that the flames alone remained above the snow,
But the flames persisted, travelling as she travelled,
And the snow touched them not, nor melted they the snow.

Then came the fallow deer with delicate steps,
Printing their steps around her as she stooped,
And their antlers burned with little flames at the tip,
Little daggers of gold at every point,
Pricket and sorel and buck, and the doe with her fawn.

And she knew that she neared the end of the garden path,
And the deer and the buried candles travelled with her,
But still she knew that she would not make an end
Of setting her plants before the shroud came round her.

John Peale Bishop (*Am. 1892–1944*)

Apparition

I have seen in the Virginia forest
Cool pallid light of an undersea day;
Coral of the isles arose, encrusted spray,
Branches submerged and overhead wild shell.

What was it then I saw? Flashing sea-scale,
Flicker of tail? Sea-bud, sunlight or syren
Smiling, which even in a boy might move
Felicity, or failing scatter foam as hail?

What did I then? Rose, swam or sank.
The end was moss. Around me April chuckled,
The catbird cried upon a dogwood bough,
And day came crashing through pale judas-bud.

Perspectives are Precipices

Sister Anne, Sister Anne,
Do you see anybody coming?

I see a distance of black yews
Long as the history of the Jews.

I see a road sunned with white sand,
Wide plains surrounding silence. And

Far-off, a broken colonnade
That overthrows the sun with shade.

Sister Anne, Sister Anne,
Do you see nobody coming?

A man

Upon that road a man who goes
Dragging a shadow by its toes.

Diminishing he goes, head bare
Of any covering even hair.

A pitcher depending from one hand
Goes mouth down. And dry is sand.

Sister Anne, Sister Anne,
What do you see?

His dwindling stride. And he seems blind
Or worse to the prone man behind.

Sister Anne! Sister Anne!

I see a road. Beyond nowhere
Defined by cirrus and blue air.

I saw a man but he is gone
His shadow gone into the sun.

Ode

Why will they never sleep
Those great women who sit
Peering at me with parrot eyes?
They sit with grave knees; they keep
Perpetual stare; and their hands move
As though hands could be aware–
Forward and back, to begin again–
As though on tumultous shuttles of wind they wove
Shrouds out of air.

The three are sisters. There is one
Who sits divine in weeping stone
On a small chair of skeleton
And is most inescapable.

I have walked through many mirrors
But always unaccompanied.
I have been as many men, as many ghosts,
As there are days. The boy was seen
Always at rainfall, mistily, not lost.
I have tried changing shapes
But always, alone, I have heard
Her shadow coming nearer, and known
The awful grasp of striding hands
Goddess! upon
The screaming metamorphosis.

One has a face burned hard
As the red Cretan clay,
Who wears a white torso scarred
With figures like a calendar.
She sits among broken shafts
Of stone; she is and still will be
Who feeds on cities, gods and men
Weapons of bronze and curious ornaments
Reckoning the evens as the odds.
Her least movement recalls the sea.

The last has idiot teeth
And a brow not made
For any thoughts, but suffering.
Tired, she repeats
In an idiot singing
A song shaped like a ring:
"Now is now and never Then
Dead Virgins will bear no men
And now that we speak of love, of love,
The woman's beneath
That's burdened with love
And the man's above
While the thing is done and done.
One is one and Three is three
Children may come from a spark in the sun
But One is one and never Three
And never a Virgin shall bear a Son
While the shadow lasts of the gray ash-tree!"

Phantasmal marbles!
There was One who might have saved
Me from the grave dissolute stones
And parrot eyes. But He is dead,
Christ is dead. And in a grave
Dark as a sightless skull He lies
And of His bones are charnels made.

The Return

Night and we heard heavy and cadenced hoofbeats
Of troops departing: the last cohorts left
By the North Gate. That night some listened late
Leaning their eyelids toward Septentrion.

Morning flared and the young tore down the trophies
And warring ornaments: arches were strong
And in the sun but stone; no longer conquests
Circled our columns; all our state was down

In fragments. In the dust, old men with tufted
Eyebrows whiter than sunbaked faces gulped
As it fell. But they no more than we remembered
The old sea-fights, the soldiers' names and sculptors'.

We did not know the end was coming: nor why
It came; only that long before the end
Were many wanted to die. Then vultures starved
And sailed more slowly in the sky.

We still had taxes. Salt was high. The soldiers
Gone. Now there was much drinking and lewd
Houses all night loud with riot. But only
For a time. Soon the taverns had no roofs.

Strangely it was the young the almost boys
Who first abandoned hope; the old still lived
A little, at last a little lived in eyes.
It was the young whose child did not survive.

Some slept beneath the simulacra, until
The gods' faces froze. Then was fear.
Some had response in dreams, but morning restored
Interrogation. Then O then, O ruins!

Temples of Neptune invaded by the sea
And dolphins streaked like streams sportive
As sunlight rode and over the rushing floors
The sea unfurled and what was blue raced silver.

The Hours

In the real dark night of the soul it is always three o'clock in the morning.–F. Scott Fitzgerald

I

All day, knowing you dead,
I have sat in this long-windowed room,
Looking upon the sea and, dismayed
By mortal sadness, though without thought to resume
Those hours which you and I have known–
Hours when youth like an insurgent sun
Showered ambition on an aimless air,
Hours foreboding disillusion,
Hours which now there is none to share.
Since you are dead, I leave them all alone.

II

A day like any day. Though any day now
We expect death. The sky is overcast,
And shuddering cold as snow the shoreward blast.
And in the marsh, like a sea astray, now
Waters brim. This is the moment when the sea
Being most full of motion seems motionless.
Land and sea are merged. The marsh is gone.
And my distress
Is at the flood. All but the dunes are drowned.
And brimming with memory I have found
All hours we ever knew, but have not found
The key. I cannot find the lost key
To the silver closet you as a wild child hid.

III

I think of all you did
And all you might have done, before undone
By death, but for the undoing of despair.
No promise such as yours when like the spring

You came, colors of jonquils in your hair,
Inspired as the wind, when the woods are bare
And every silence is about to sing.

None had such promise then, and none
Your scapegrace wit or your disarming grace;
For you were bold as was Danaë's son,
Conceived like Perseus in a dream of gold.
And there was none when you were young, not one,
So prompt in the reflecting shield to trace
The glittering aspect of a Gorgon age.

Despair no love, no fortune could assuage . . .
Was it a fault in your disastrous blood
That beat from no fortunate god,
The failure of all passion in mid-course?
You shrank from nothing as from solitude,
Lacking the still assurance, and pursued
Beyond the sad excitement by remorse.

Was it that having shaped your stare upon
The severed head of time, upheld and blind,
Upheld by the stained hair,
And seen the blood upon that sightless stare,
You looked and were made one
With the strained horror of those sightless eyes?
You looked, and were not turned to stone.

IV

You have outlasted the nocturnal terror,
The head hanging in the hanging mirror,
The hour haunted by a harrowing face.
Now you are drunk at last. And that disgrace
You sought in oblivious dives you have
At last, in the dissolution of the grave.

V

I have lived with you the hour of your humiliation.
I have seen you turn upon the others in the night
And of sad self-loathing
Concealing nothing
Heard you cry: *I am lost. But you are lower!*
And you had that right.
The damned do not so own their damnation.

I have lived with you some hours of the night,
The late hour
When the lights lower,
The late hour
When the lights go out,

When the dissipation of the night is past,
Hour of the outcast and the outworn whore,
That is past three and not yet four–
When the old blackmailer waits beyond the door
And from the gutter with unpitying hands
Demands the same sad guiltiness as before,
The hour of utter destitution
When the soul knows the horror of its loss
And knows the world too poor
For restitution,
Past three o'clock
And not yet four–
When not pity, pride,
Or being brave,
Fortune, friendship, forgetfulness of drudgery
Or of drug avails, for all has been tried,
And nothing avails to save
The soul from recognition of its night.

The hour of death is always four o'clock.
It is always four o'clock in the grave.

VI

Having heard the bare word that you had died,
All day I have lingered in this lofty room,
Locked in the light of sea and cloud,
And thought, at cost of sea-hours, to illume
The hours that you and I have known,
Hours death does not condemn, nor love condone.

And I have seen the sea-light set the tide
In salt succession toward the sullen shore
And while the waves lost on the losing sand
Seen shores receding and the sands succumb.

The waste retreats; glimmering shores retrieve
Unproportioned plunges; the dunes restore
Drowned confines to the disputed kingdom–
Desolate mastery, since the dark has come.

The dark has come. I cannot pluck you bays,
Though here the bay grows wild. For fugitive
As surpassed fame the leaves this sea-wind frays.
Why should I promise what I cannot give?

I cannot animate with breath
Syllables in the open mouth of death.
Dark, dark. The shore here has a habit of light.
O dark! I leave you to oblivious night!

Archibald MacLeish (*Am. b. 1892*)

The Silent Slain

We too, we too, descending once again
The hills of our own land, we too have heard
Far off–Ah, que ce cor a longue haleine–
The horn of Roland in the passages of Spain,
The first, the second blast, the failing third,
And with the third turned back and climbed once more
The steep road southward, and heard faint the sound
Of swords, of horses, the disastrous war,
And crossed the dark defile at last, and found
At Roncevaux upon the darkening plain
The dead against the dead and on the silent ground
The silent slain–

L'an trentiesme de mon eage

And I have come upon this place
By lost ways, by a nod, by words,
By faces, by an old man's face
At Morlaix lifted to the birds,

By hands upon the tablecloth
At Aldebori's, by the thin
Child's hands that opened to the moth
And let the flutter of the moonlight in,

By hands, by voices, by the voice
Of Mrs. Whitman on the stair,
By Margaret's "If we had the choice
To choose or not–" through her thick hair,

By voices, by the creak and fall
Of footsteps on the upper floor,
By silence waiting in the hall
Between the doorbell and the door,

By words, by voices, a lost way–
And here above the chimney stack
The unknown constellations sway–
And by what way shall I go back?

Signature for Tempo

I

Think that this world against the wind of time
Perpetually falls the way a hawk
Falls at the wind's edge but is motionless–

Think that this silver snail the moon will climb
All night upon time's curving stalk
That as she climbs bends, bends beneath her–

Yes

And think that we remember the past time.

II

These live people,
These more
Than three dimensional
By time protracted edgewise into heretofore
People,
How shall we bury all
These time-shaped people,
In graves that have no more
Than three dimensions?
Can we dig

With such sidlings and declensions
As to coffin bodies big
With memory?
And how
Can the earth's contracted Now
Enclose these knuckles and this crooked knee
Sprawled over hours of a sun long set?

Or do these bones forget?

III
Borne
Landward on relinquishing seas,
Worn
By the sliding of water

Whom time goes over wave by wave, do I lie
Drowned in a crumble of surf at the sea's edge?–

And wonder now what ancient bones are these
That flake on sifting flake
Out of deep time have shelved this shallow ledge
Where the waves break–

You, Andrew Marvell

And here face down beneath the sun
And here upon earth's noonward height
To feel the always coming on
The always rising of the night

To feel creep up the curving east
The earthy chill of dusk and slow
Upon those under lands the vast
And ever climbing shadow grow

And strange at Ecbatan the trees
Take leaf by leaf the evening, strange
The flooding dark about their knees
The mountains over Persia change

And now at Kermanshah the gate
Dark empty and the withered grass
And through the twilight now the late
Few travelers in the westward pass

And Baghdad darken and the bridge
Across the silent river gone
And through Arabia the edge
Of evening widen and steal on

And deepen on Palmyra's street
The wheel rut in the ruined stone
And Lebanon fade out and Crete
High through the clouds and overblown

And over Sicily the air
Still flashing with the landward gulls
And loom and slowly disappear
The sails above the shadowy hulls

And Spain go under and the shore
Of Africa the gilded sand
And evening vanish and no more
The low pale light across that land

Nor now the long light on the sea

And here face downward in the sun
To feel how swift how secretly
The shadow of the night comes on . . .

Ezry

Maybe you ranted in the Grove–
Maybe!–but you found the mark
That measures altitude above
Sea-level for a poet's work.

Mad if you were or fool instead
You found the bench-mark in the stone–
Horizon over arrow-head–
Alder and dock had overgrown.

These later and more cautious critics
Think themselves high if they look down
From Rome's or England's steeple–spit
On fools below them in the town:

Not you! Although the absolute sea
Is far down from the Muses' Wood,
You gauged the steep declivity,
Giddy with grandeur where you stood.

Hypocrite Auteur

mon semblable, mon frère

1

Our epoch takes a voluptuous satisfaction
In that perspective of the action
Which pictures us inhabiting the end
Of everything with death for only friend.

Not that we love death,
Not truly, not the fluttering breath,
The obscene shudder of the finished act–
What the doe feels when the ultimate fact
Tears at her bowels with its jaws.

Our taste is for the opulent pause
Before the end comes. If the end is certain
All of us are players at the final curtain:
All of us, silence for a time deferred,
Find time before us for one sad last word.
Victim, rebel, convert, stoic–
Every role but the heroic–
We turn our tragic faces to the stalls
To wince our moment till the curtain falls.

2

A world ends when its metaphor has died.

An age become an age, all else beside,
When sensuous poets in their pride invent
Emblems for the soul's consent
That speak the meanings men will never know
But man-imagined images can show:
It perishes when those images, though seen,
No longer mean.

3

A world was ended when the womb
Where girl held God became the tomb
Where God lies buried in a man:
Botticelli's image neither speaks nor can
To our kind. His star-guided stranger
Teaches no longer, by the child, the manger,
The meaning of the beckoning skies.

Sophocles, when his reverent actors rise
To play the king with bleeding eyes,
No longer shows us on the stage advance
God's purpose in the terrible fatality of chance.

No woman living, when the girl and swan
Embrace in verses, feels upon
Her breast the awful thunder of that breast
Where God, made beast, is by the blood confessed.

Empty as conch shell by the water cast
The metaphor still sounds but cannot tell,
And we, like parasite crabs, put on the shell
And drag it at the sea's edge up and down.

This is the destiny we say we own.

4
But are we sure
The age that dies upon its metaphor
Among these Roman heads, these mediaeval towers,
Is ours?–
Or ours the ending of that story?

The meanings in a man that quarry
Images from blinded eyes
And white birds and the turning skies
To make a world of were not spent with these
Abandoned presences.

The journey of our history has not ceased:
Earth turns us still toward the rising east,
The metaphor still struggles in the stone,
The allegory of the flesh and bone
Still stares into the summer grass
That is its glass,
The ignorant blood
Still knocks at silence to be understood.

Poets, deserted by the world before,
Turn round into the actual air:
Invent the age! Invent the metaphor!

Wilfred Owen (*Br. 1893–1918*)

The Send-off

Down the close, darkening lanes they sang their way
To the siding-shed,
And lined the train with faces grimly gay.

Their breasts were stuck all white with wreath and spray
As men's are, dead.

Dull porters watched them, and a casual tramp
Stood staring hard,
Sorry to miss them from the upland camp.
Then, unmoved, signals nodded, and a lamp
Winked to the guard.

So secretly, like wrongs hushed-up, they went.
They were not ours:
We never heard to which front these were sent.

Nor there if they yet mock what women meant
Who gave them flowers.

Shall they return to beatings of great bells
In wild train-loads?
A few, a few, too few for drums and yells,
May creep back, silent, to village wells
Up half-known roads.

Spring Offensive

Halted against the shade of a last hill,
They fed, and, lying easy, were at ease
And, finding comfortable chests and knees,
Carelessly slept. But many there stood still
To face the stark, blank sky beyond the ridge,
Knowing their feet had come to the end of the world.

Marvelling they stood, and watched the long grass swirled
By the May breeze, murmurous with wasp and midge,
For though the summer oozed into their veins
Like an injected drug for their bodies' pains,
Sharp on their souls hung the imminent line of grass,
Fearfully flashed the sky's mysterious glass.

Hour after hour they ponder the warm field–
And the far valley behind, where the buttercup
Had blessed with gold their slow boots coming up,
Where even the little brambles would not yield,
But clutched and clung to them like sorrowing hands;
They breathe like trees unstirred.

Till like a cold gust thrills the little word
At which each body and its soul begird
And tighten them for battle. No alarms
Of bugles, no high flags, no clamorous haste–
Only a lift and flare of eyes that faced
The sun, like a friend with whom their love is done.
O larger shone that smile against the sun,–
Mightier than his whose bounty these have spurned.

So, soon they topped the hill, and raced together
Over an open stretch of herb and heather
Exposed. And instantly the whole sky burned
With fury against them; earth set sudden cups
In thousands for their blood; and the green slope
Chasmed and steepened sheer to infinite space.

* * * *

Of them who running on that last high place
Leapt to swift unseen bullets, or went up
On the hot blast and fury of hell's upsurge,
Or plunged and fell away past this world's verge,
Some say God caught them even before they fell.

But what say such as from existence' brink
Ventured but drave too swift to sink,
The few who rushed in the body to enter hell,
And there out-fiending all its fiends and flames
With superhuman inhumanities,
Long-famous glories, immemorial shames–
And crawling slowly back, have by degrees
Regained cool peaceful air in wonder–
Why speak not they of comrades that went under?

Anthem for Doomed Youth

What passing-bells for these who die as cattle?
  Only the monstrous anger of the guns.
  Only the stuttering rifles' rapid rattle
Can patter out their hasty orisons.
No mockeries for them from prayers or bells,
  Nor any voice of mourning save the choirs,–
The shrill, demented choirs of wailing shells;
  And bugles calling for them from sad shires.

What candles may be held to speed them all?
  Not in the hands of boys, but in their eyes
Shall shine the holy glimmers of good-byes.
  The pallor of girls' brows shall be their pall;
Their flowers the tenderness of silent minds,
And each slow dusk a drawing-down of blinds.

The End

After the blast of lightning from the East,
The flourish of loud clouds, the Chariot Throne;
After the drums of Time have rolled and ceased,
And by the bronze west long retreat is blown,

Shall life renew these bodies? Of a truth
All death will He annul, all tears assuage?–
Fill the void veins of Life again with youth,
And wash, with an immortal water, Age?

When I do ask white Age he saith not so:
"My head hangs weighed with snow."
And when I hearken to the Earth, she saith:
"My fiery heart shrinks, aching. It is death.
Mine ancient scars shall not be glorified,
Nor my titanic tears, the sea, be dried."

Exposure

Our brains ache, in the merciless iced east winds that knive
  us . . .
Wearied we keep awake because the night is silent . . .
Low, drooping flares confuse our memory of the salient . . .
Worried by silence, sentries whisper, curious, nervous,
    But nothing happens.

Watching, we hear the mad gusts tugging on the wire,
Like twitching agonies of men among its brambles.
Northward, incessantly, the flickering gunnery rumbles,
Far off, like a dull rumour of some other war.
What are we doing here?

The poignant misery of dawn begins to grow . . .
We only know war lasts, rain soaks, and clouds sag stormy.
Dawn massing in the east her melancholy army
Attacks once more in ranks on shivering ranks of gray,
But nothing happens.

Sudden successive flights of bullets streak the silence.
Less deadly than the air that shudders black with snow,
With sidelong flowing flakes that flock, pause, and renew,
We watch them wandering up and down the wind's non-chalance,
But nothing happens.

Pale flakes with fingering stealth come feeling for our faces–
We cringe in holes, back on forgotten dreams, and stare, snow-dazed,
Deep into grassier ditches. So we drowse, sun-dozed,
Littered with blossoms trickling where the blackbird fusses.
Is it that we are dying?

Slowly our ghosts drag home: glimpsing the sunk fires, glozed
With crusted dark-red jewels; crickets jingle there;
For hours the innocent mice rejoice: the house is theirs;
Shutters and doors, all closed: on us the doors are closed,–
We turn back to our dying.

Since we believe not otherwise can kind fires burn;
Nor ever suns smile true on child, or field, or fruit.
For God's invincible spring our love is made afraid;
Therefore, not loath, we lie out here; therefore were born,
For love of God seems dying.

To-night, His frost will fasten on this mud and us,
Shrivelling many hands, puckering foreheads crisp.
The burying-party, picks and shovels in their shaking grasp,
Pause over half-known faces. All their eyes are ice,
But nothing happens.

Strange Meeting

It seemed that out of battle I escaped
Down some profound dull tunnel, long since scooped
Through granites which titanic wars had groined.
Yet also there encumbered sleepers groaned,
Too fast in thought or death to be bestirred.
Then, as I probed them, one sprang up, and stared
With piteous recognition in fixed eyes,
Lifting distressful hands as if to bless.
And by his smile, I knew that sullen hall,
By his dead smile I knew we stood in Hell.
With a thousand pains that vision's face was grained;
Yet no blood reached there from the upper ground,
And no guns thumped, or down the flues made moan.
"Strange friend," I said, "here is no cause to mourn."
"None," said the other, "save the undone years,
The hopelessness. Whatever hope is yours,
Was my life also; I went hunting wild
After the wildest beauty in the world,
Which lies not calm in eyes, or braided hair,
But mocks the steady running of the hour,
And if it grieves, grieves richlier than here.
For by my glee might many men have laughed,
And of my weeping something had been left,
Which must die now. I mean the truth untold,
The pity of war, the pity war distilled.
Now men will go content with what we spoiled.
Or, discontent, boil bloody, and be spilled.
They will be swift with swiftness of the tigress,
None will break ranks, though nations trek from progress.
Courage was mine, and I had mystery,
Wisdom was mine, and I had mastery;
To miss the march of this retreating world
Into vain citadels that are not walled.
Then, when much blood had clogged their chariot-wheels
I would go up and wash them from sweet wells,
Even with truths that lie too deep for taint.
I would have poured my spirit without stint
But not through wounds; not on the cess of war.
Foreheads of men have bled where no wounds were.

I am the enemy you killed, my friend.
I knew you in this dark; for so you frowned
Yesterday through me as you jabbed and killed.
I parried; but my hands were loath and cold.
Let us sleep now. . . ."

Donald Davidson (*Am. b. 1893*)

Lee in the Mountains
1865–1870

Walking into the shadows, walking alone
Where the sun falls through the ruined boughs of locusts
Up to the president's office. . . .
Hearing the voices
Whisper, *Hush, it is General Lee!* And strangely
Hearing my own voice say, *Good morning, boys.*
(Don't get up. You are early. It is long
Before the bell. You will have long to wait
On these cold steps. . . .)
The young have time to wait.
But soldiers' faces under their tossing flags
Lift no more by any road or field,
And I am spent with old wars and new sorrow.
Walking the rocky path, where steps decay
And the paint cracks and grass eats on the stone.
It is not General Lee, young men . . .
It is Robert Lee in a dark civilian suit who walks,
An outlaw fumbling for the latch, a voice
Commanding in a dream where no flag flies.
My father's house is taken and his hearth
Left to the candle-drippings where the ashes
Whirl at a chimney-breath on the cold stone.
I can hardly remember my father's look, I cannot
Answer his voice as he calls farewell in the misty
Mounting where riders gather at gates.
He was old then–I was a child–his hand
Held out for mine, some daybreak snatched away,
And he rode out, a broken man. Now let
His lone grave keep, surer than cypress roots,
The vow I made beside him. God too late

Unseals to certain eyes the drift
Of time and the hopes of men and a sacred cause.
The fortune of the Lees goes with the land
Whose sons will keep it still. My mother
Told me much. She sat among the candles,
Fingering the *Memoirs*, now so long unread.
And as my pen moves on across the page
Her voice comes back, a murmuring distillation
Of old Virginia times now faint and gone,
The hurt of all that was and cannot be.

Why did my father write? I know he saw
History clutched as a wraith out of blowing mist
Where tongues are loud, and a glut of little souls
Laps at the too much blood and the burning house.
He would have his say, but I shall not have mine.
What I do is only a son'sdevoir
To a lost father. Let him only speak.
The rest must pass to men who never knew
(But on a written page) the strike of armies,
And never heard the long Confederate cry
Charge through the muzzling smoke or saw the bright
Eyes of the beardless boys go up to death.
It is Robert Lee who writes with his father's hand-
The rest must go unsaid and the lips be locked.

If all were told, as it cannot be told-
If all the dread opinion of the heart
Now could speak, now in the shame and torment
Lashing the bound and trampled States-

If a word were said, as it cannot be said-

I see clear waters run in Virginia's valley
And in the house the weeping of young women
Rises no more. The waves of grain begin.
The Shenandoah is golden with new grain.
The Blue Ridge, crowned with a haze of light,
Thunders no more. The horse is at plough. The rifle
Returns to the chimney crotch and the hunter's hand.
And nothing else than this? Was it for this
That on an April day we stacked our arms
Obedient to a soldier's trust? To lie

Ground by heels of little men,
Forever maimed, defeated, lost, impugned?
And was I then betrayed? Did I betray?

If it were said, as still it might be said–
If it were said, and a word should run like fire,
Like living fire into the roots of grass,
The sunken flag would kindle on wild hills,
The brooding hearts would waken, and the dream
Stir like a crippled phantom under the pines,
And this torn earth would quicken into shouting
Beneath the feet of ragged bands–
The pen
Turns to the waiting page, the sword
Bows to the rust that cankers and the silence.

Among these boys whose eyes lift up to mine
Within gray walls where droning wasps repeat
A hollow reveillé, I still must face,
Day after day, the courier with his summons
Once more to surrender, now to surrender all.
Without arms or men I stand, but with knowledge only
I face what long I saw, before others knew,
When Pickett's men streamed back, and I heard the tangled
Cry of the Wilderness wounded, bloody with doom.

The mountains, once I said, in the little room
At Richmond, by the huddled fire, but still
The President shook his head. The mountains wait,
I said, in the long beat and rattle of siege
At cratered Petersburg. Too late
We sought the mountains and those people came.
And Lee is in mountains now, beyond Appomattox,
Listening long for voices that never will speak
Again; hearing the hoofbeats come and go and fade
Without a stop, without a brown hand lifting
The tent-flap, or a bugle call at dawn,
Or ever on the long white road the flag
Of Jackson's quick brigades. I am alone,
Trapped, consenting, taken at last in mountains.

It is not the bugle now, or the long roll beating.
The simple stroke of a chapel bell forbids

The hurtling dream, recalls the lonely mind.
Young men, the God of your fathers is a just
And merciful God Who in this blood once shed
On your green altars measures out all days,
And measures out the grace
Whereby alone we live;
And in His might He waits,
Brooding within the certitude of time,
To bring this lost forsaken valor
And the fierce faith undying
And the love quenchless
To flower among the hills to which we cleave,
To fruit upon the mountains whither we flee,
Never forsaking, never denying
His children and His children's children forever
Unto all generations of the faithful heart.

On a Replica of the Parthenon

Why do they come? What do they seek
Who build but never read their Greek?
The classic stillness of a pool
Beleaguered in its certitude
By aimless motors that can make
Only incertainty more sure;
And where the willows crowd the pure
Expanse of clouds and blue that stood
Around the gables Athens wrought,
Shop-girls embrace a plaster thought,
And eye Poseidon's loins ungirt,
And never heed the brandished spear
Or feel the bright-eyed maiden's rage
Whose gaze the sparrows violate;
But the sky drips its spectral dirt,
And gods, like men, to soot revert.
Gone is the mild, the serene air.
The golden years are come too late.
Pursue not wisdom or virtue here,
But what blind motion, what dim last
Regret of men who slew their past
Raised up this bribe against their fate.

Mark Van Doren (*Am. b. 1894*)

Return to Ritual

The mother of life indulges all our wandering
Down the lone paths that narrow into peace.
She knows too well the gradual discovery
And the slow turning round until we cease:
Resolved upon the wide road once again
Whose dust hangs over day and mantles men.

Here is the drumming phalanx, here is the multitude;
Listen, and let us watch them over the stile.
We that remember clean moss ways and the tamaracks,
Let us be timorous now and shudder awhile.
We shall be early enough, no matter when,
Mother of dust, O mother of dust and men.

How times passes, here by the wall of eternity!
Even so soon we summon her; we are prepared.
Already these feet are lifting in a wild sympathy;
Who can remember the cool of a day unshared?
Mother of marches, mother, receive us then.
Listen! The dust is humming a song to the men.

This Amber Sunstream

This amber sunstream, with an hour to live,
Flows carelessly, and does not save itself;
Nor recognizes any entered room–
This room; nor hears the clock upon a shelf,
Declaring the lone hour; for where it goes
All space in a great silence ever flows.

No living man may know it till this hour,
When the clear sunstream, thickening to amber,
Moves like a sea, and the sunk hulls of houses
Let it come slowly through, as divers clamber,
Feeling for gold. So now into this room
Peer the large eyes, unopen to their doom.

Another hour and nothing will be here.
Even upon themselves the eyes will close.
Nor will this bulk, withdrawing, die outdoors
In night, that from another silence flows.
No living man in any western room
But sits at amber sunset round a tomb.

Private Worship

She lay there in the stone folds of his life
Like a blue flower in granite. This he knew;
And knew how now inextricably the petals
Clung to the rock; recessed beyond his hand-thrust;
More deeply in, past more forgotten windings
Than his rude tongue could utter, praising her.

He praised her with his eyes, beholding oddly
Not what another saw, but what she added,
Thinning today and shattering with a slow smile,
To the small flower within, to the saved secret.
She was not his to have; except that something,
Always like petals falling, entered him.

She was not his to keep–except the brightness,
Flowing from her, that lived in him like dew;
And the kind flesh he could remember touching,
And the unconscious lips, and both her eyes:
These lay in him like leaves, beyond the last turn
Breathing the rocky darkness till it bloomed.

It was not large, this chamber of the blue flower,
Nor could the scent escape; nor the least color
Ebb from that place and stain the outer stone.
Nothing upon his grey sides told the fable,
Nothing of love or lightness, nothing of song;
Nothing of her at all. Yet he could fancy–

Oh, he could feel where petals spread their softness,
Gathered from windfalls of her when she smiled;
Growing some days, he thought, as if to burst him–
Oh, he could see the split halves, and the torn flower
Fluttering in sudden sun; and see the great stain–
Oh, he could see what tears had done to stone.

Civil War

The country is no country I have seen,
And no man goes there who is now alive, and no man
Ever is going to leave there. But they try;
Waving a million beards that on pale faces
Blacken with time and spread.
It is a field of bodies of blue boys,
And gray boys, grown half way into the ground.
The wind is dark that sways them;
All of them bending with it, south or north,
All of the straining here; but no one knowing
Of any fellow by who gazes too.
It is a field of legless bearded boys
With bright unnecessary buttons on their breasts,
And skirts of coats that hold them in the sod.
The bodies twist,
The circular, small eyes are mad with being;
A million mouths fly open without sound;
But none can tear his coat up, that must come
With roots and worms or come not up at all.

Away in Carolina, Maine, Wisconsin,
Boys who kept their legs walked long and long.
They set their feet in furrows, or in aisles;
They strolled with girls, were taken, and were fathers;
Had old companionship; and last were covered
Quietly with smooth boards, and grass, and stone.
Stiffly now they hold society;
Forever thus they lie without a want.

In the forbidden country where the sod
Grows down and down, with restless blue roots, gray
  roots,
In the dark windy land no one can leave,
Separate necks yearn homeward;
Separate hungry shoulders pull and pull.
Wind, oh wind, I did not come to stay;
I must be there tomorrow, not to miss–
But the dark wind is earless, and the day
Is endless, and the grasses hiss and hiss.

Young Woman at a Window

Who so valiant to decide?
Who so prompt and proper-active?
Yet each muscle in her brain
Relaxes now; is unrestrictive;
Lets her lean upon this dark
November night wind; lets it work–

Oh, lets it ask her if she thinks,
Oh, lets it whisper if she knows
How much of time is like a stream
Down which her headless body flows;
How many answers, proudly made,
Will be like minnows overlaid

With inch on inch of glossy black,
With depth on depth of sliding water;
Lets it dare her to predict
Those floods of silence coming later;
Till she melts, and leaning long
Is only conscious of wind-song.

Who so valorous of voice?
Who so staunch upon the ground?
But wind-and-water-song at work
Stops both her ears against the sound
Of someone here she used to know;
Of someone saying: It is so.

She leans and loses every word.
Her loudest wisdom well is gone.
But still the current of the night
Comes with its foaming on and on;
Pours round the sill; dissolves the hands;
And still the dreamless body stands.

Phelps Putnam (*Am. 1894–1948*)

Hasbrouck and the Rose

Hasbrouck was there and so were Bill
And Smollet Smith the poet, and Ames was there.
After his thirteenth drink, the burning Smith,
Raising his fourteenth trembling in the air,
Said, "Drink with me, Bill, drink up to the Rose."
But Hasbrouck laughed like old men in a myth,
Inquiring, "Smollet, are you drunk? What rose?"
And Smollet said, "I drunk? It may be so;
Which comes from brooding on the flower, the flower
I mean toward which mad hour by hour
I travel brokenly; and I shall know,
With Hermes and the alchemists–but, hell,
What use is it talking that way to you?
Hard-boiled, unbroken egg, what can you care
For the enfolded passion of the Rose?"
Then Hasbrouck's voice rang like an icy bell:

"Arcane romantic flower, meaning what?
Do you know what it meant? Do I?
We do not know.
Unfolding pungent Rose, the glowing bath
Of ecstasy and clear forgetfulness;
Closing and secret bud one might achieve
By long debauchery–
Except that I have eaten it, and so
There is no call for further lunacy.
In Springfield, Massachusetts, I devoured
The mystic, the improbable, the Rose.
For two nights and a day, rose and rosette
And petal after petal and the heart,
I had my banquet by the beams
Of four electric stars which shone
Weakly into my room, for there,
Drowning their light and gleaming at my side,
Was the incarnate star
Whose body bore the stigma of the Rose.

And that is all I know about the flower;
I have eaten it–it has disappeared.
There is no Rose."

Young Smollet Smith let fall his glass; he said,
"O Jesus, Hasbrouck, am I drunk or dead?"

Ballad of a Strange Thing

His name was Chance, Jack Chance, he said,
And that his family was dead.
He was a lucid fool, his eyes
Were cool and he beyond surprise.
Into the township Pollard Mill
He came in autumn alone one day,
Loafing along those roads which still,
Though dying in the grass, report
That lumber-sledges went that way.
He came idly and in our town
He raised a flight of birds, a brown
And silver flock, and underneath
Their wings were tinged with gold; his breath
Blew and the birds dipped and rose
As if they surely lived which were
But lies of the calm sorcerer.

Autumn came bringing free
Melancholy, but to me
Brought Jack, when I was sitting there
In the open barn doorway where
The sun moved in and I could get,
Drifting by, the sound and smell
Of late bees and of mignonette
From the dying garden by the wall,
And hear the thin defeated bell
Of distant time, and see the tall
Elms beyond the orchard slopes
Rising improbably, like hopes
Swaying above the mind, and I
Was sitting there and he came by.

Under his hat I saw his eyes
Measuring without disguise
The ripeness of my house,
And measuring myself, and he
Turned in and approached and spoke to me.
He had decided undismayed
This was the place for Chance, and I
The boy for him; and so he stayed.

And then the days moved gravely by,
Time drowned in fluent clarity
Flowing between him and me,
Who only lay along the walls
Unshamed of indolence, and heard
The dusty harvesters' harsh calls
To sweating teams, loading the sheaves
On the steep withered fields–their care
Was none of ours; or reasoned there
Where the mill-pond burned with leaves
And rustled at the dam, on those
Stark thoughts that rose
Out of cool spoken words, or we
Loafing in the arbor ate
Slowly the warm grapes, the rusty
Creaking swallows skimmed
The long ridgepoles, the day grew late
Easily, and dimmed.

At night we made a fire to mark
A spot of mirth against the dark,
There in a pasture which lay high
On the nearness of the sky.
Other countrymen would come,
Young farmers, farmers' men and sons,
One after one they learned to come
And laugh with Chance and tap the old
Keg of cider, acrid gold,
Which we had borne carefully
Out of the cellar where it lay,
Drowsing wickedly it lay

Waiting for us to set free
Its vigor and its treachery.
Then Jack would sing his bawdy songs:
That old ballad which belongs
To timelessness, *The Bastard King*,
Or *Doctor Tanner*, or *Mademoiselle*,
Or *Lil* who died of letchering.
She died with her boots on, as they tell,
With a champion lad between her knees.
Or he would sometimes please,
If drinking brought delusion near,
To tell corrosive tales, the mere
Garments of lies, the cunning kind
Which echo somewhat in the mind,
And then they go, and you are more
Dull and baffled than before.

There went by then, in such a way,
Serene October; the last day
Came and the night was newly cold,
But the fire was high and the old
Cider burned within and we,
A dozen foolish farmers, kept
Alive the late hilarity
Of autumn, and the township slept.
Then Chance arose from where he sat
Against the keg and cocked his hat
Sideways and walking slow around
The fire, said—"I have always found
Nothing new among much change,
But this I tell you now is strange:

It was at noon, the hour of sleep
For those who use their nights
In the deluding piracy
Of shadowy delights.

And so I slept, above the bank
Above the River Still,
Under an oak, the least of two
That rose under the hill.

But a sound crept through my nerves
And I woke and I could hear
Feet running fast and close,
Down the hill and near.

Then stop; and heard a noise like sobs
And stood up quietly
And peering saw that a breathless girl
Was clutching the other tree.

And then a man came following,
Loping leisurely,
And when he stood beside her said,
'I knew you would wait for me.'

And then she turned at bay; she was
Astonishingly rare,
A young ascetic fury she
Was something almost strange to me
With her honey fallen hair.

'Yes–and have waited even too long,
Before now, to be glad,
Watching your insolence too long–
Oh, you were the gorgeous lad
With your dark lovely face and all
The women you have had.

I have seen the rabbits follow you
Unasked and eagerly;
O ladies, you should see him now,
Begging a kiss of me.'

She ceased, and we all three were still
While he admired her,
And I kept hidden watching them,
For I have that character.

He did not mock her when he spoke,
'Where do they get these dull
Flash melodramas in their skulls?
And such a dainty skull.

Listen, I keep no list of names
For vanity; and I
Dislike the names and the odors and ways
Of women; I am shy
Of their domestic wills; and I
Am tired of the melting lie.

But there you are–and sometimes love
Is more than remembered skill.'
'Love,' she said, 'is the rust which ate
The clean rancor of my will.'

He raised his quiet hand to touch
Her hair, but she
Turned sharply down the bank and he
Now followed instantly.

And there below the godly stream
Was whispering in its beard,
And she cried, 'Save me, River Still!'
Then stepped and disappeared.

Well–so far nothing strange;
But after that the queer
Began, and I have seen these things,
And I, the bastard son of change,
Would dare to call them queer.

I saw the girl had gone entirely,
And in her place a dry
Shivering graceful sheaf of reeds
Sprang up, suddenly high;

And that he, following so close
That her hair was in his face,
Clutched and had no girl but had
Sharp reeds in his embrace.

He stepped back, looking at his hands
All laced with blood, a spike
Broke short and stood between his ribs
Most murderous like.

This feller was not eager now,
But only dazed,
And pulled the wet spike from his side,
Fumbling and amazed.

He stooped slowly to bathe his hands,
Then from his pocket drew
A folded knife and cut one reed,
Murmuring, 'This will do.

Sometimes there's music in these girls,
Sometimes,' and sitting then
He made a whistle which he tried
And changed and tried again.

He blew five even notes and stopped,
But the sound rippled away
Slowly, as if a sweet clang came
From the leaves and hummed away.

And then there came along the bank
A black majestic goat
With yellow eyes and gilded horns
And a white beard at its throat.

The goat lay down before his feet
Respectfully, dipping its head,
And the man laughed and, 'Can this be
A messenger?' he said.

And played again and now more wild
And cloudily intricate,
And the goat arose and danced like one
Hieratic and sedate.

And that is all," said Chance, and then
He said, "So long," and walked away
Casually, as if the night were day.
And we jumped up calling, and then
Stood silent for over us coldly fell
Five piercing notes, each like a spark

We stood there stiffly and immersed,
Hearing laughter in the dark,
Until I spoke, being the first,
"We had better go home now to bed
We have drunk too much," I said.

Thereafter the rains beat down
The autumn, the drenched leaves came down
From the black trees, choking the ditches,
And over the sea came sons-of-bitches
With a hollow quarrel, the talking rats
Of England and of Europe slithered
Down the hawsers, doffed their hats
And squealed; and the plague spread and came,
Taking the cleanly name
Of honor for its strange device,
Even to our town; the conscript lice
Played soldiers over Pollard Mill
And pitched their camp on the River Still;
But no more Jack, and we were more
Dull and baffled than before.

E. E. Cummings (*Am. b. 1894*)

the Cambridge ladies who live in furnished souls

the Cambridge ladies who live in furnished souls
are unbeautiful and have comfortable minds
(also, with the church's protestant blessings
daughters, unscented shapeless spirited)
they believe in Christ and Longfellow, both dead,
are invariably interested in so many things–
at the present writing one still finds
delighted fingers knitting for the is it Poles?
perhaps. While permanent faces coyly bandy
scandal of Mrs. N and Professor D
. . . . the Cambridge ladies do not care, above
Cambridge if sometimes in its box of
sky lavender and cornerless, the
moon rattles like a fragment of angry candy

POEM, OR BEAUTY HURTS MR. VINAL

take it from me kiddo
believe me
my country, 'tis of

you, land of the Cluett
shirt Boston Garter and Spearmint
Girl With The Wrigley Eyes(of you
land of the Arrow Ide
and Earl &
Wilson
Collars)of you i
sing: land of Abraham Lincoln and Lydia E. Pinkham,
land above all of Just Add Hot Water And Serve–
from every B. V. D.

let freedom ring

amen. i do however protest, anent the un
-spontaneous and otherwise scented merde which
greets one(Everywhere Why)as divine poesy per
that and this radically defunct periodical. i would
suggest that certain ideas gestures
rhymes, like Gillette Razor Blades
having been used and reused
to the mystical moment of dullness emphatically are
Not To Be Resharpened. (Case in point

if we are to believe these gently O sweetly
melancholy trillers amid the thrillers
these crepuscular violinists among my and your
skyscrapers–Helen & Cleopatra were Just Too Lovely,
The Snail's On The Thorn enter Morn and God's
In His andsoforth

do you get me?)according
to such supposedly indigenous
throstles Art is O World O Life
a formula: example, Turn Your Shirttails Into
Drawers and If It Isn't An Eastman It Isn't A
Kodak therefore my friends let
us now sing each and all fortissimo A–
mer
i

ca, I
love,
You. And there're a
hund-red-mil-lion-oth-ers, like
all of you successfully if
delicately gelded (or spaded)
gentlemen(and ladies)–pretty

littleliverpill–
hearted-Nojolneeding-There's-A-Reason
americans(who tensetendoned and with
upward vacant eyes, painfully
perpetually crouched, quivering, upon the
sternly allotted sandpile
–how silently
emit a tiny violetflavoured nuisance: Odor?

ono.
comes out like a ribbon lies flat on the brush

a man who had fallen among thieves

a man who had fallen among thieves
lay by the roadside on his back
dressed in fifteenthrate ideas
wearing a round jeer for a hat

fate per a somewhat more than less
emancipated evening
had in return for consciousness
endowed him with a changeless grin

whereon a dozen staunch and leal
citizens did graze at pause
then fired by hypercivic zeal
sought newer pastures or because

swaddled with a frozen brook
of pinkest vomit out of eyes
which noticed nobody he looked
as if he did not care to rise

one hand did nothing on the vest
its wideflung friend clenched weakly dirt
while the mute trouserfly confessed
a button solemnly inert.

Brushing from whom the stiffened puke
i put him all into my arms
and staggered banged with terror through
and a million billion trillion stars

serene immediate silliest and whose

serene immediate silliest and whose
vast one function being to enter a Toy and
emerging(believably enlarged)make how
many stopped millions of female hard for their
millions of stopped male to look at(now
-fed infantile eyes drooling unmind
grim yessing childflesh perpetually acruise
and her quick way of slowly staring and such hair)
the Californian handpicked thrill mechanically
packed and released for all this very diminishing
vicarious ughhuh world(the pertly papped
muchmouthed)her way of beginningly finishing
(and such hair) the expensively democratic tyrannically
dumb
    Awake, chaos: we have napped.

my specialty is living said

my specialty is living said
a man(who could not earn his bread
because he would not sell his head)

squads right impatiently replied
two billion pubic lice inside
one pair of trousers (which had died)

my father moved through dooms of love

my father moved through dooms of love
through sames of am through haves of give,
singing each morning out of each night
my father moved through depths of height

this motionless forgetful where
turned at his glance to shining here;
that if(so timid air is firm)
under his eyes would stir and squirm

newly as from unburied which
floats the first who,his april touch
drove sleeping selves to swarm their fates
woke dreamers to their ghostly roots

and should some why completely weep
my father's fingers brought her sleep:
vainly no smallest voice might cry
for he could feel the mountains grow.

Lifting the valleys of the sea
my father moved through griefs of joy;
praising a forehead called the moon
singing desire into begin

joy was his song and joy so pure
a heart of star by him could steer
and pure so now and now so yes
the wrists of twilight would rejoice

keen as midsummer's keen beyond
conceiving mind of sun will stand,
so strictly(over utmost him
so hugely)stood my father's dream

his flesh was flesh his blood was blood:
no hungry man but wished him food;
no cripple wouldn't creep one mile
uphill to only see him smile.

Scorning the pomp of must and shall
my father moved through dooms of feel;
his anger was as right as rain
his pity was as green as grain

septembering arms of year extend
less humbly wealth to foe and friend
than he to foolish and to wise
offered immeasurable is

proudly and(by octobering flame
beckoned)as earth will downward climb,
so naked for immortal work
his shoulders marched against the dark

his sorrow was as true as bread:
no liar looked him in the head;
if every friend became his foe
he'd laugh and build a world with snow.

My father moved through theys of we,
singing each new leaf out of each tree
(and every child was sure that spring
danced when she heard my father sing)

then let men kill which cannot share,
let blood and flesh be mud and mire,
scheming imagine,passion willed,
freedom a drug that's bought and sold

giving to steal and cruel kind,
a heart to fear,to doubt a mind,
to differ a disease of same,
conform the pinnacle of am

though dull were all we taste as bright,
bitter all utterly things sweet,
maggoty minus and dumb death
all we inherit,all bequeath

and nothing quite so least as truth
–i say though hate were why men breathe–
because my father lived his soul
love is the whole and more than all

it was a goodly co

it was a goodly co
which paid to make man free
(for man is enslaved by a dread dizziz
and the sooner it's over the sooner to biz
don't ask me what it's pliz)

then up rose bishop budge from kew
a anglican was who
(with a rag and a bone and a hank of hair)'d
he picked up a thousand pounds or two
and he smote the monster merde

then up rose pride and up rose pelf
and ghibelline and guelph
and ladios and laddios
(on radios and raddios)
did save man from himself

ye duskiest despot's goldenest gal
did wring that dragon's tail
(for men must loaf and women must lay)
and she gave him a desdemonial
that took his breath away

all history oped her teeming womb
said demon for to doom
yea(fresh complexions being oke
with him)one william shakespeare broke
the silence of the tomb

then up rose mr lipshits pres
(who always nothing says)
and he kisséd the general menedjerr
and they smokéd a robert burns cigerr
to the god of things like they err

plato told

plato told

him:he couldn't
believe it(jesus

told him;he
wouldn't believe
it)lao

tsze
certainly told
him,and general
(yes

mam)
sherman;
and even
(believe it
or
not)you
told him:i told
him;we told him
(he didn't believe it,no
sir)it took
a nipponized bit of
the old sixth
avenue
el;in the top of his head:to tell
him

pity this busy monster, manunkind

pity this busy monster, manunkind,

not. Progress is a comfortable disease:
your victim(death and life safely beyond)

plays with the bigness of his littleness
–electrons deify one razorblade
into a mountainrange;lenses extend

unwish through curving wherewhen till unwish
returns on its unself.
                                        A world of made
is not a world of born–pity poor flesh

and trees,poor stars and stones,but never this
fine specimen of hypermagical

ultraomnipotence. We doctors know

a hopeless case if–listen:there's a hell
of a good universe next door;let's go

what if a much of a which of a wind

what if a much of a which of a wind
gives the truth to summer's lie;
bloodies with dizzying leaves the sun

and yanks immortal stars awry?
Blow king to beggar and queen to seem
(blow friend to fiend:blow space to time)
–when skies are hanged and oceans drowned,
the single secret will still be man

what if a keen of a lean wind flays
screaming hills with sleet and snow:
strangles valleys by ropes of thing
and stifles forests in white ago?
Blow hope to terror;blow seeing to blind
(blow pity to envy and soul to mind)
–whose hearts are mountains,roots are trees,
it's they shall cry hello to the spring

what if a dawn of a doom of a dream
bites this universe in two,
peels forever out of his grave
and sprinkles nowhere with me and you?
Blow soon to never and never to twice
(blow life to isn't:blow death to was)
– all nothing's only our hugest home;
the most who die,the more we live

Robert Graves (*Br. b. 1895*)

Sirocco at Deyá

(for Will Price)

How most unnatural-seeming, yet how proper:
The sea like a cat with fur rubbed the wrong way,
As the sirocco with its furnace flavour
Dashes at full tilt around the village
["From every-which-a-way, hot as a two-buck pistol"]
Stripping green olives from the blown-back boughs,
Scorching the roses, blinding the eyes with sand;
While slanderous tongues in the small cafés
And in the tightly-shuttered granite houses
Clack defamation, incite and invite
Knives to substantiate their near-murders . . .

But look, a great grey cloud broods nonchalant
On the mountain top nine hundred feet above us,
Motionless and turgid, blotting out the sun,
And from it sneers a supercilious Devil:
"Mere local wind: no messenger of mine!"

The Blue-fly

Five summer days, five summer nights,
The ignorant, loutish, giddy blue-fly
Hung without motion on the cling peach,
Humming occasionally: "O my love, my fair one!"
As in the *Canticles*.

Magnified one thousand times, the insect
Looks farcically human; laugh if you will!
Bald head, stage-fairy wings, blear eyes,
A caved-in chest, hairy black mandibles,
Long spindly thighs.

The crime was detected on the sixth day.
What then could be said or done? By anyone?
It would have been vindictive, mean and what-not
To swat that fly for being a blue-fly,
For debauch of a peach.

Is it fair, either, to bring a microscope
To bear on the case, even in search of truth?
Nature, doubtless, has some compelling cause
To glut the carriers of her epidemics–
Nor did the peach complain.

Cat-goddesses

A perverse habit of cat-goddesses–
Even the blackest of them, black as coals
Save for a new moon blazing on each breast,
With coral tongues and beryl eyes like lamps,
Long-leggèd, pacing three by three in nines–
This obstinate habit is to yield themselves,
In verisimilar love-ecstasies,
To tatter-eared and slinking alley-toms
No less below the common run of cats

Than they above it; which they do for spite,
To provoke jealousy–not the least abashed
By such gross-headed, rabbit-coloured litters
As soon they shall be happy to desert.

A Love Story

The full moon easterly rising, furious,
Against a winter sky ragged with red;
The hedges high in snow, and owls raving–
Solemnities not easy to withstand:
A shiver wakes the spine.

In boyhood, having encountered the scene,
I suffered horror: I fetched the moon home,
With owls and snow, to nurse in my head
Throughout the trials of a new spring,
Famine unassuaged.

But fell in love, and made a lodgement
Of love on those chill ramparts.
Her image was my ensign: snows melted,
Hedges sprouted, the moon tenderly shone,
The owls trilled with tongues of nightingale.

These were all lies, though they matched the time,
And brought me less than luck: her image
Warped in the weather, turned beldamish.
Then back came winter on me at a bound,
The pallid sky heaved with a moon-quake.

Dangerous it had been with love-notes
To serenade Queen Famine.
In tears I recomposed the former scene,
Let the snow lie, watched the moon rise, suffered the owls,
Paid homage to them of unevent.

On Dwelling

Courtesies of good-morning and good-evening
From rustic lips fail as the town encroaches:
Soon nothing passes but the cold quick stare
Of eyes that see ghosts, yet too many for fear.

Here I too walk, silent myself, in wonder
At a town not mine though plainly coextensive
With mine, even in days coincident:
In mine I dwell, in theirs like them I haunt.

And the green country, should I turn again there?
My bumpkin neighbours loom even ghostlier:
Like trees they murmur or like blackbirds sing
Courtesies of good-morning and good-evening.

To Sleep

The mind's eye sees as the heart mirrors:
Loving in part, I did not see you whole,
Grew flesh-enraged that I could not conjure
A whole you to attend my fever-fit
In the doubtful hour between a night and day
And be Sleep that had kept so long away.

Of you sometimes a hand, a brooch, a shoe
Wavered beside me, unarticulated–
As the vexed insomniac dream-forges;
And the words I chose for your voice to speak
Echoed my own voice with its dry creak.

Now that I love you, now that I recall
All scattered elements of will that swooped
By night as jealous dreams through windows
To circle above the beds like bats,
Or as dawn-birds flew blindly at the panes
In curiosity rattling out their brains–

Now that I love you, as not before,
Now you can be and say, as not before:
The mind clears and the heart true-mirrors you
Where at my side an early watch you keep
And all self-bruising heads loll into sleep.

The Straw

Peace, the wild valley streaked with torrents,
A hoopoe perched on his warm rock. Then why
This tremor of the straw between my fingers?

What should I fear? Have I not testimony
In her own hand, signed with her own name
That my love fell as lightning on her heart?

These questions, bird, are not rhetorical.
Watch how the straw twitches and leaps
As though the earth quaked at a distance.

Requited love; but better unrequited
If this chance instrument gives warning
Of cataclysmic anguish far away.

Were she at ease, warmed by the thought of me,
Would not my hand stay steady as this rock?
Have I undone her by my vehemence?

The Survivor

To die with a forlorn hope, but soon to be raised
By hags, the spoilers of the field; to elude their claws
And stand once more on a well-swept parade-ground,
Scarred and bemedalled, sword upright in fist
At head of a new undaunted company:

Is this joy? to be doubtless alive again,
And the others dead? Will your nostrils gladly savour
The fragrance, always new, of a first hedge-rose?
Will your ears be charmed by the thrush's melody
Sung as though he had himself devised it?

And is this joy: after the double suicide
(Heart against heart) to be restored entire,
To smooth your hair and wash away the life-blood,
And presently seek a young and innocent bride,
Whispering in the dark: "for ever and ever"?

Edmund Blunden (*Br. b. 1896*)

The Pike

From shadows of rich oaks outpeer
The moss-green bastions of the weir,
Where the quick dipper forages
In elver-peopled crevices.
And a small runlet trickling down the sluice
Gossamer music tires not to unloose.

Else round the broad pool's hush
Nothing stirs.
Unless sometime a straggling heifer crush
Through the thronged spinny whence the pheasant whirs;
Or martins in a flash
Come with wild mirth to dip their magical wings,
While in the shallow some doomed bulrush swings
At whose hid root the diver vole's teeth gnash.

And nigh this toppling reed, still as the dead
The great pike lies, the murderous patriarch,
Watching the waterpit shelving and dark
Where through the plash his lithe bright vassals thread.

The rose-finned roach and bluish bream
And staring ruffe steal up the stream
Hard by their glutted tyrant, now
Still as a sunken bough.

He on the sandbank lies,
Sunning himself long hours
With stony gorgon eyes:
Westward the hot sun lowers.

Sudden the grey pike changes, and quivering, poises for slaughter;
Intense terror wakens around him, the shoals scud awry, but there chances
A chub unsuspecting; the prowling fins quicken, in fury he lances;
And the miller that opens the hatch stands amazed at the whirl in the water.

Old Homes

O happiest village! how I turned to you
Beyond estranging years that cloaked my view
With all their wintriness of fear and strain;
I turned to you, I never turned in vain.
Through fields yet ringing sad with fancy's dirge,
Landscapes that hunt poor sleep to bedlam's verge,
Green grow your leas, and sweet resound your woods,
And laughing children paddle in your floods.

There the old houses where we lived abide,
And I shall see them, though hot tears should hide
The gaze of "home" from that which now I hold.
What though pulled down?–to me they're as of old.
The garrets creak as I tiptoe the boards
To find the last lone tenant's fabled hoards,
And silver on the dun November sky
Through jarring panes I see the flood race by
Brown hop-hills where the black bines moulder out.
To these same panes, when full moon comes about,
I hastening home lift daring eyes to learn
If ghost eyes through their sullen crystal burn,
And feel what sight cannot report, and fall
A-shuddering even to face the unlit hall.

Passages crooked and slanted, ceilings stooped,
And yews with drowsy arras overdrooped
The windows of that home; the broad hearths wept
With every shower; adry the great vats slept,
Where one time kercher'd maids had toiled with a will:
Such nooks were here, a hundred scarce would fill.
And in the farm beside, the barn's sunk tiles
Enclosed a space like to the church's aisles.

Then all about these vasty walls our play
Would hold the evening's lanterned gloom at bay,
And senses young received each new-found thing
As meadows feel and glow with inbreathed spring:
Thence we have journeyed out to blue hills round,
The pilgrims of a day's enchanted ground,
And where we'd seen the crow or heron fly
Have made our chartless way, passed far inns by,

On edge of lily ponds have heard the jack
From unknown holes leap, and shrunk trembling back,
Have seen strange chimneys smoke, new runnels foam,
Until quite surfeited we turned for home,
Whose white walls rosy with the westering light
Still of our journey seemed the noblest sight.

Thence too when high wind through the black clouds' pouring,
Bowing the strong trees' creaking joints, went roaring,
Adventure was to splash through the sightless lane
When church-bells filled a pause of wind and rain,
And once within the venerable walls
To hear the elms without like waterfalls,
While the cold arches murmured every prayer,
And Advent hymns bade the round world prepare,
Prepare! The next day with pale seas amazed
We scarce had marvelled as we gaped and gazed
If this had been the tempest harbinger
Of the world's end and final Arbiter:
The pollards in the yellow torrent drowning,
The weir's huge jaw a-gnashing, all heaven frowning.

But there at length, beside that thunderous weir,
Our lot was cast, and no less generous here
Came each long day; not even the hours we spent
Under old Grammar's eye unkindly went.
We found his learning dry, in faith, and hit
Disaster in our sleights for leavening it;
But the big desks cut with heroic names,
The gilded panel trumpeting past fames,
Shields, pictures, solemn books of stars and sages,
Kindled our pride in sense of mightier ages,
That school had seen, and cannot see again.
Fair, fair befall her, though no urchin pen
Crawl through the summer hours beneath her beams,
Nor playground haunters' shout bestir her dreams;
Honoured among her aspens may she rise,
And her red walls long soothe the traveller's eyes.

Thence issued we among the scampering crew,
And crossed the green, and from the bridge down threw

Our dinner crumbs to waiting roach; or soft
Marauding climbed the cobwebbed apple-loft,
And the sweet smell of Blenheims lapped in straw
Made stolen pleasure seem a natural law;
Escape and plunder hurried us at last
To the weir-cottage where our lot was cast,
Poor as church mice, yet rich at every turn,
Who never guessed that man was made to mourn.

In this same country as the time fulfilled
When hops like ribbons on the maypole frilled
Their colonnaded props mile after mile,
And tattered armies gathered to the spoil,
We too invaded the green arbours ere
The day had glistened on earth's dewy hair,
And through the heat have picked and picked apace,
To fill our half-bin and not lose the race,
While our bin partner, fierce of eye and tongue,
Disliked our style and gave "when I was young".
And all about the clearing setts revealed
The curious colours of the folk afield,
The raven hair, the flamy silk, the blue
Washed purple with all weathers; crime's dark crew;
Babes at the breast; old sailors chewing quids;
And hyacinth eyes beneath soon-dropt eyelids.
The conquest sped, the bramlings, goldings small,
The heavy fuggles to the bins came all,
Garden past garden heard the measurer's horn
Blow truce–advance! until a chillier morn
Saw the last wain load up with pokes and go,
And an empty saddened field looked out below
On trees where smouldered the quick fever-tinge
Of Autumn, on the river's glaucous fringe,
And our own cottage, its far lattice twinkling
Across tired stubble sown with sheep-bells' tinkling.
On airy wings the warning spirit sighed,
But we, we heard not, thinking of Christmastide.

A love I had, as childhood ever will,
And our first meeting I'll remember still;

When to the farmhouse first we went, the may
With white and red lit hedgerows all the way,
And there I saw her, in a red-may cloak
To church going by; so delicately she spoke,
So gracefully stept, so innocent-gay was her look,
I got a flower; she put it in her book.
And after, many eves, we walked for hours
Like loving flowers among the other flowers,
And blushed for pride when other girls and boys
Laughed at us sweethearts in the playhour's noise–
No more, this was a silly simple thing;
Those two can never now walk so in spring;
But to look back to child with child primrosing
Is all the sweetness of each spring's unclosing.

Vision on vision blooms; long may they bloom,
Through years that bring the philosophic gloom,
Sweetening sleep with its strange agonies racked,
And shedding dew on every parching tract,
In every pleasant place a virtue adding,
A herb of grace to keep the will from madding:
And, happiest village, still I turn to you,
The alabaster box of spikenard, you;
To your knoll trees, your slow canal return
In your kind farms or cottages sojourn;
Enjoy the whim that on your church tower set
The lead cowl like a Turkish minaret;
Beat all your bounds, record each kiln and shed,
And watch the blue mists on each calm close spread.
My day still breaks beyond your poplared East
And in your pastoral still my life has rest.

The Sunlit Vale

I saw the sunlit vale, and the pastoral fairy-tale;
The sweet and bitter scent of the may drifted by;
And never have I seen such a bright bewildering green,
    But it looked like a lie,
    Like a kindly meant lie.

When gods are in dispute, one a Sidney, one a brute,
It would seem that human sense might not know, might not
spy;
But though nature smile and feign where foul play has stabbed
and slain,
There's a witness, an eye,
Nor will charms blind that eye.

Nymph of the upland song and the sparkling leafage young,
For your merciful desire with these charms to beguile,
For ever be adored; muses yield you rich reward;
But you fail, though you smile–
That other does not smile.

Louise Bogan (*Am. b. 1897*)

Medusa

I had come to the house, in a cave of trees,
Facing a sheer sky.
Everything moved,–a bell hung ready to strike,
Sun and reflection wheeled by.

When the bare eyes were before me
And the hissing hair,
Held up at a window, seen through a door.
The stiff bald eyes, the serpents on the forehead
Formed in the air.

This is a dead scene forever now.
Nothing will ever stir.
The end will never brighten it more than this,
Nor the rain blur.

The water will always fall, and will not fall,
And the tipped bell make no sound.
The grass will always be growing for hay
Deep on the ground.

And I shall stand here like a shadow
Under the great balanced day,
My eyes on the yellow dust, that was lifting in the wind,
And does not drift away.

Cassandra

To me, one silly task is like another.
I bare the shambling tricks of lust and pride.
This flesh will never give a child its mother,–
Song, like a wing, tears through my breast, my side,
And madness chooses out my voice again,
Again. I am the chosen no hand saves:
The shrieking heaven lifted over men,
Not the dumb earth, wherein they set their graves.

The Mark

Where should he seek, to go away
That shadow will not point him down?
The spear of dark in the strong day
Beyond the upright body thrown,
Marking no epoch but its own.

Loosed only when, at noon and night,
The body is the shadow's prison.
The pivot swings into the light;
The center left, the shadow risen
To range out into time's long treason.

Stand pinned to sight, while now, unbidden,
The apple loosens, not at call,
Falls to the field, and lies there hidden,–
Another and another fall
And lie there hidden, in spite of all

The diagram of whirling shade,
The visible, that thinks to spin
Forever webs that time has made
Though momently time wears them thin
And all at length are gathered in.

To be Sung on the Water

Beautiful, my delight,
Pass, as we pass the wave.
Pass, as the mottled night
Leaves what it cannot save,
Scattering dark and bright.

Beautiful, pass and be
Less than the guiltless shade
To which our vows were said;
Less than the sound of the oar
To which our vows were made,–
Less than the sound of its blade
Dipping the stream once more.

Fiend's Weather

O embittered joy,
You fiend in fair weather,
Foul winds from secret quarters
Howl here together.

They yell without sleet
And freeze without snow;
Through them the broken Pleiades
And the Brothers show,

And Orion's steel,
And the iron of the Plough.
This is your night, my worthy fiend,
You can triumph now.

In this wind to wrench the eye
And curdle the ear,
The church steeple rises purely to the heavens;
The sky is clear.

And even tomorrow
Stones without disguise
In true-colored fields
Will glitter for your eyes.

Several Voices out of a Cloud

Come, drunks and drug-takers; come, perverts unnerved!
Receive the laurel, given, though late, on merit; to whom
    and wherever deserved.

Parochial punks, trimmers, nice people, joiners true-blue,
Get the hell out of the way of the laurel. It is deathless
    And it isn't for you.

Henceforth, From the Mind

Henceforth, from the mind,
For your whole joy, must spring
Such joy as you may find
In any earthly thing,
And every time and place
Will take your thought for grace.

Henceforth, from the tongue,
From shallow speech alone,
Comes joy you thought, when young,
Would wring you to the bone,
Would pierce you to the heart
And spoil its stop and start.

Henceforward, from the shell,
Wherein you heard, and wondered
At oceans like a bell
So far from ocean sundered–
A smothered sound that sleeps
Long lost within lost deeps,

Will chime you change and hours,
The shadow of increase,
Will sound you flowers
Born under troubled peace–
Henceforth, henceforth
Will echo sea and earth.

Ruth Pitter (*Br. b. 1897*)

The Unicorn

Hate me or love, I care not, as I pass
To those hid citadels
Where in the depth of my enchanted glass
The changeless image dwells;
To where for ever blooms the nameless tree;
For ever, alone and fair,
The lovely Unicorn beside the sea
Is laid, and slumbers there.

Give or withhold, all's nothing, as I go
On to those glimmering grounds
Where falling secretly and quiet as snow
The silent music sounds;
Where earth is withered away before the eyes,
And heaven hangs in the air,
For in the oak the bird of paradise
Alights, and triumphs there.

Slay me or spare, it matters not: I fly
Ever, for ever rest
Alone and with a host: in the void sky
There do I build my nest:
I lay my beams from star to star, and make
My house where all is bare;
Hate, slay, withhold, I rear it for thy sake
And thou art with me there.

Rainy Summer

Remember, though we cannot write it, the delicate dream.
Though the wheat be cankered, the woodbine and wild rose
Drink, and exhale in perfume their pensive being:
The lily's life prolonged plays on to an extreme
And elegiac poignancy; the bee goes
Solitary with subdued hum in the green, beyond our seeing.

We are spirits, though, the dream denied, we are also ghosts.
We repose in our secret place, in the rainy air,
By the small fire, the dim window, in the ancient house;
Kind to the past, and thoughtful of our hosts,
Shadows of those now beyond thought and care,
Phantoms that the silence engenders, the flames arouse.

Those we have never seen, and those we shall see no more,
Haunting the tender gloom and the wan light,
Are there, as the secret bird is there, is betrayed
By the leaf that moved when she slipped from her twig by the
door,
As the mouse unseen is perceived by her gliding shade,
As the silent owl is known by the wind of her flight.

Thus poor, forgotten, in a summer without sun,
In a decaying house, an unvisited place,
We remember the delicate dream, the voice of the clay;
Recalling the body before the life was begun,
Stealing through blood and bone with bodiless grace
In the elfish night and green cool gloom of the day.

Urania

Winter and night, the white frost and the darkness
fall, and the hands of life release the spirit;
gladly she goes hence to her starry pasture.

Frostbound, the plough leans idle on the headland;
now the benighted hind forsakes the furrow;
earth is at peace, no longer vexed with labour.

With still delight the soul receives the omen,
thinks on her travail in the sowing season,
calmly remembers all the heat of harvest:

knows that the end is fairest; sees the heavens
hung with creation: in the woody valley
sees on the earth one star that steals toward her.

It is Urania: through the darkened woodland
now she advances: now she brings her vestal
lamp to the tomb, with nameless consolation.

The Beautiful Negress

Her gait detached her from the moving throng:
Like night, advancing with long pace and slow,
Or like unhurrying fate she seemed to go,
By an eternal Purpose borne along.
An unregretful elegiac Song
Swelled in her wake; she gathered up my woe
Into epitome, and left it so;
Still dark, but made harmonious and strong.
O solemn Beauty, when upon my way
You walked in majesty, did not the tear
Leap up to crown you with more light than day?
Did not the silent voice within the ear
Cry Fly with her to the soul's Africa,
Night, tragedy, the veiled, the end prefer?

Dun-Colour

Subtle almost beyond thought are these dim colours,
The mixed, the all-including, the pervasive,
Earth's own delightful livery, banqueting
The eye with dimness that includes all brightness;
Complexity which the mind sorts out, as the sunlight
Resolves into many purities the mingled
Dun fleeces of the moorland; the quartz sparkles,
The rosy heath glows, the mineral-like mosses
And the heathbells and the myriad lichens
Start each into the eye a separate splendour:
So in the mind's sun bloom the dim dun-colours.

The dry vermilion glow of familiar redbreast
Is not his real glory: that is the greenish,
Light-toned, light-dissembling, eye-deceiving
Dun of his smooth-sloped back, and on his belly
The whitish dun is laid to deceive the shadow:
In the dear linnet the olive-dun is lovely,
And the primrose-duns in the yellowhammer: but most
beguiling,
Perhaps because of the perfect shape, is the ash-dun,
That quietest, most urbane, unprofaneable colour
Reserved as her livery of beauty to the hedge-sparrow.
There is a royal azure in her blood,
As her eggs prove, and in her nature gold,
For her children's throats are kingcups; but she veils
them,
Mingled and blended, in her rare dun-colour.

For the rose-duns, and the blue-duns, look to the finches:
For the clear clear brown-duns, to the fallow deer
(How the sudden tear smarts in the eye wearied of cities)
And for all these and more to the many toadstools,
Which alone have the violet-dun, livid yet lovely:
But the most delicate duns are seen in the gentle
Monkeys from the great forests, the silvan spirits:
Wonderful! that these, almost our brothers,
Should be dressed so rarely, in sulphurous-dun and greenish;
O that a man had grassy hair like these dryads!
O that I too were attired in such dun-colours!

The Military Harpist

Strangely assorted, the shape of song and the bloody man.

Under the harp's gilt shoulder and rainlike strings,
Prawn-eyed, with prawnlike bristle, well-waxed moustache,
With long tight cavalry legs, and the spurred boot
Ready upon the swell, the Old Sweat waits.

Now dies, and dies hard, the stupid, well-relished fortissimo,
Wood-wind alone inviting the liquid tone,
The voice of the holy and uncontending, the harp.

Ceasing to ruminate interracial fornications,
He raises his hands, and his wicked old mug is David's,
Pastoral, rapt, the king and the poet in innocence,
Singing Saul in himself asleep, and the ancient Devil
Clean out of countenance, as with an army of angels.

He is now where his bunion has no existence.
Breathing an atmosphere free of pipeclay and swearing,
He wears the starched nightshirt of the hereafter, his halo
Is plain manly brass with a permanent polish,
Requiring no oily rag and no Soldier's Friend.

His place is with the beloved poet of Israel,
With the wandering minnesinger and the loves of Provence,
With Blondel footsore and heartsore, the voice in the darkness
Crying like beauty bereaved beneath many a donjon,
O Richard! O king! where is the lion of England?
With Howell, Llewellyn, and far in the feral north
With the savage fame of the hero in glen and in ben,
At the morning discourse of saints in the island Eire,
And at nameless doings in the stone-circle, the dreadful grove.

Thus far into the dark do I delve for his likeness:
He harps at the Druid sacrifice, where the golden string
Sings to the golden knife and the victim's shriek.
Strangely assorted, the shape of song and the bloody man.

The Estuary

Light, stillness and peace lie on the broad sands,
On the salt-marshes the sleep of the afternoon.
The sky's immaculate; the horizon stands
Steadfast, level and clear over the dune.

There are voices of children, musical and thin,
Not far, nor near, there in the sandy hills;
As the light begins to wane, so the tide comes in,
The shallow creek at our feet silently fills:

And silently, like sleep to the weary mind,
Silently, like the evening after the day,
The big ship bears inshore with the inshore wind,
Changes her course, and comes on up through the bay,

Rolling along the fair deep channel she knows,
Surging along, right on top of the tide.
I see the flowery wreath of foam at the bows,
The long bright wash streaming away from her side:

I see the flashing gulls that follow her in,
Screaming and tumbling, like children wildly at play,
The sea-born crescent arising, pallid and thin,
The flat safe twilight shore shelving away.

Whether remembered or dreamed, read of or told,
So it has dwelt with me, so it shall dwell with me ever:
The brave ship coming home like a lamb to the fold,
Home with the tide into the mighty river.

Sacheverell Sitwell (*Br. b. 1897*)

From *Landscape with the Giant Orion: Orion Seeks the Goddess Diana*

We will wait by the chestnut and the ilex tree,
There's a fable acting, and the thud of footsteps,
The lightning flickers but there is no thunder.
Listen, ah! listen to the distant wind;
It is cold, snow cold, it blows from bitter rocks
Where the nymphs cry out aloud and weep in sorrow:
They tell the loves of deities and demi-gods,
In a thousand passions from the age of Chaos,
They cry like sea birds on the grey, salt sea
For bitterness of love and never for its sweets;
Hark! how they weep; the wind is bitter cold.

Day is breaking, these are the pains of birth,
This tragic destiny is heralded with sorrow,
With rumour in the leaves and with the nymphs lamenting,
It is near, and nearer, it is in this wood,
The trees are as grass to it, they tread as that,
Not grass by the fountain, but the breast high pampas
That trips the feet and cuts them with its hedge of swords.
Whosoever is coming might be wading in the waves,
Might be climbing a slope, and out of breath for that,
For he sighs and groans, he stumbles and he stops,
And the boughs bend back again, or snap and fall.

Then there was breath, the hottest wind that blew,
And the giant Orion, like a tower above us,
Came out through the trees towards the rising sun;
The nymphs cried loudly from the topmost heights
Of the rape of Merope, and her lover, blinded;
For this was the history, that he snared the girl
On the island, Chios, in the dark blue sea,
And Oenopion, her father, took this dread revenge,
Blinding him with torches while he slept with her;
His strong hair tied to many stems of oaks
That he dreamed to be the knotting of her hands in play.

So Vulcan, the god of fire, to whom he prayed,
Gave him a guide, who stood upon his shoulder
And held his hair for steadiness and chose his march,
Climbing to his shoulders when Orion lay down,
And here he was, who spoke to us and had to shout,
So great his height above us, and so loud the tread of feet,
But Orion never heeded us, he groped his way
As a man blindfolded, or who walks in sleep,
For an oracle had told him how to gain his sight:
He must look into the rising sun and find it there,
At the light's first glitter, in a morning of no mist.

We were to see this miracle more wondrous still,
Night's battlements shivered, and the high walls of day
Heaped into a throne above the sun's white horses,
Where they trembled and chafed for him to take the reins;
This made a pedestal, a throne of clouds,
And high on its forehead, showed the crescent moon

Coloured like the corn, this was the hunter's month:
Below it, emptiness, that took on life,
Till Diana, the huntress, stood above the day,
And the wind blew from out the dawn, and chill it seemed,
For the nymphs ever wept with it, and cried their sorrows.

She was still as a statue, and as cold as that,
Staring with heartless eyes on blind Orion,
Her bow and quiver hung on her, ready for the chase,
In calm indifference of true divinity,
And spake not, nor moved, but stood for eyes to see
While Orion, with day upon his aching lids,
Came out through the trees on to the shores of morning
Clean swept by tides, and sparkling of freshness,
Where he touched the Ocean, and the shiver from its waves
Told him of sunrise, and he looked for that
With sightless gaze above the distant island.

It was crossing the sea and had not reached to him,
On a bridge that glittered, on a bridge of golden boats,
Tethered like horses, for they tossed their heads,
And then the bridge touched him, and with fearful glance
He looked along its timbers to the heart of fire,
And found his sight in that, and plucked it out;
It was like a red flaming, like a world on fire,
For his eyes ran and smarted and he could not see,
But the sight was in them, like a strong light in darkness,
And he looked away, to rest them, to the snow white clouds,
As hills, or white sails, where all the air was blue.

Too late, too late, although he had his eyes,
For the goddess, Diana, faded as he saw her,
The nymphs sang no more, the miracle was done.
Then he lifted his horn, and all the hollow shore
Echoed, and murmured long, and held the sound,
It rang in every cave mouth, it floated on each bay,
Blown from nowhere, for his head was in the clouds
That trailed, like a string of flags, among the trees
Where he turned from the shore into the ilex wood;
He was joined from earth to heaven by this stratagem,
But the goddess had gone, the clouds were but of air.

The vision cracked and fell from us till next white dawn,
When the giant, Orion, came out from the night
In the lifting shades, before the fire of day;
His steps were hammer blows, were drums, or thunder,
In the shadowy forest, in the breath of ferns,
Where he started his quarry and sounded for the dogs,
And we heard them give tongue down a fitful wind
That sighed in the pine trees, brought their baying near to us;
And all the time we heard his footsteps and the winding of his
horn,
But Orion was hidden, though the world caught fire,
And the wind played traitor while we listened for him.

It was always thus: we heard him in the forest boughs
And he passed us, down the coast, along the cliffs,
Hunting the earth for what his eyes had lost,
That day they came back to him out of the light;
But he never found her, she was like the wind
That blows out of nowhere and is never seen,
That has no wings, but they are wet with rain,
And all we know is wetness of her feathers,
As if she slept in dew, or on the calmness of the waters;
Thus was the goddess, she had hidden from him,
And all day he hunted, and he did not find her.

Then, in a morning that was pale with mist,
When the webs of the spider hung like clocks to blow,
Like dandelion clocks, that tell the fates by breath
On their white hairs of wisdom in the groundsel grass,
(But the webs shone with dew, as never dandelion),
By those webs of the spider, spun from branch to branch
Orion went into the heart of mist,
And lost the scent and found no answer to his horn,
For it echoed back, as from a town of stone;
Shuddered, and deafened him, and shook again,
He was lost, all lost, where all the walls were sound.

It was her sacred mountain, in a heart of mist,
A wood of wild rocks where every echo called,
Where words bent back at you as soon as spoken
From rocks like houses, or like sudden islands;
Here the stags wandered, but he did not heed them,

They were her animals to draw her chariot,
Two white stags chosen from this snow white herd,
Pale as the hand, no taller than the shoulder
To their branching horns, all even in the boughs,
With ten points, twice over, to each pair of crowns,
Held by these kings and queens, and proudly carried.

They wandered as they willed, there was no hand to hurt them,
And were white out of the mist, and quickly gone again,
In this wood of white flowers of the snow pale peony,
Like snow, first seen upon a bush of roses,
Sweet cups of snow, or like the snowball melted,
Then turned to roses, to wild open roses,
Wider than known, and sister to the lotus,
With a heart of honey of a honey colour,
Lying like the lotus on an air like water;
The wood all full of them, in all the mist,
And white stags walk among them, pale as all the petals.

Where was her cave? Where was Diana's grotto,
In the side of the hill, within the hanging valley?
Was it masked with ferns, or did the roses hide it?
All the mist echoed, all the rocks were walls,
Orion was lost in it, who'd found his eyes,
But saw no better through the roses' wiles.
All snow was the same to him, its flowers alike,
In this world apart, upon her sacred mountain,
Where the mist never lifted, where the clouds were in the valleys;
Here he would wander and listen for her horn,
But never came the call to him, and all the trees were still.

So this was her enchantment to imprison him,
And Orion broke the circle of that magic forest;
He'll never find that wood again, nor see its flowers,
Though they blow for all who love them on the sacred mountain:
The giant Orion goes a-hunting in the wood,
In all the wide and level land, in all the hills,
We'll hearken in the dawn, when every footfall is gigantic,
To Orion in the ilex wood, or to the dying Actaeon,
We shall hear, but never see them, all their world is dead;
O come, then, to her mountain, for her cups of snow,
And look upon these blossoms of so long ago.

John Wheelwright (*Am. 1897–1940*)

Apocryphal Apocalypse

Wisemen to glossators unknown
when the Assisian or the Galilean
entered to the death which made his life
lustless in hope to find with keener sperm
have said:
"We liked him, but we found him hard to chat with.
His conversation bored us more than talk."
You gluttons for seedless speech and vegex meat
who fondle terms to dull their definitions
and chew in vain each mouthful more and more
of day by day to find water taste sweet;
though sunk in boredom beyond excavations,
dose yourselves with bottled conversation's
pedantic antidote to boredom's poison.
Make of the Dictionary your Book of Truth
to hear the Apocalypse of Wheels with puckered lips:

Beware, beware like dogs with indoor faces
all fops and frumps who think it good, or better
for every man to follow his ideal:
anti William Carlos Williams Oscar Williamses
(less Apollonian than plumbers, laureate)
Waldos, un-Emersonian frank
(imbecile in paradisian beatitude)
who ruminate on something . . . something
which men who lack a more definite term call Holy, Holy
(wholly holy, hale, and wholly wholesome).
Combatting thought with thought's own element
Pied Piper fops flute the Youth towards Baby's Cave.
But above all Bores, the Hegelian Yes-Man Frump
beware who reconciles thought's hostile poles with smiles
(synthetic smiles) to prove his platitude
quite true: "Evil is the shadow side of Good."
God-the-Eternal-Bore-of-Bores subsists
in see-saw half-affirmation
(As A.E. and E.A.

Robinson have said at greater length
who each caught deaths of cold from Cosmic Chill)
but the Truth lives in contradictions of the flesh.
Transfigurated bone can cast no shadow.
Something there is that does not love a Bore.

From Gestures to the Dead

As Tate grows old some child will fondle him
as his mother's children fondled grandpapa.
Be resolute, for there is no solution;
as I grow old, dark slumber fades to gray.
Ulysses Grant fought for the Constitution
and chewed his old cigars while it whirled over
the piazza steps, into an ancient dump-cart
where films of dust so lightly lie upon
Constantine's Declaration of Independence
Habeas corpus, requiescat in pace.
Booth evaded the fame he sought, by speaking
justly of Lincoln, *sic semper tyrannis.*
It was banal enough to be immortal.
You, Judas, sacrificed for our Messiah.
You, Brutus, needful for our Caesar cult.
Yours is the signal deed for all our history
for pure liberty, for freedom, not reform.
Some men fight fate with its own fatal weapons,
and ever believe they kill themselves for the life
of the thing they kill, as Lincoln died for the Union.

Others that fail find that no path lies open
but the bridle-path of remaining dignified.
It took Robert E. Lee three days to become a 'traitor,'
and he rode to his gray end, a college president.
When men of action fail, and failing, ask
sanctuary of thinkers, destiny rests.
There is nothing more to say. Can Tate and I
stand against the black drift of storm

forever changeless, against a changing sky?

Horace Gregory (*Am. b. 1898*)

Stanzas for My Daughter

Tell her I love
she will remember me
always, for she
is of my tissues made;
she will remember
these streets where the moon's shade
falls and my shadow mingles
with shadows sprung
from a midnight tree.

Tell her I love that I
am neither in earth nor sky,
stone nor cloud,
but only this
walled garden she knows well
and which her body is.

Her eyes alone shall make
me blossom for her sake;
contained within her, all
my days shall flower or die,
birthday or funeral
concealed where no man's eye
finds me unless she says:
He is my flesh and I
am what he was.

Live beyond hope,
beyond October trees
spent with fire, these
ministers of false Spring
making our bodies stir
with spurious flowering
under snow that covers
hope and hopeful lovers
and fades in timeless seas.

Live beyond hope, my care

that makes a prison for your eyes (and hair
golden as autumn grass
swept by the morning sun)
for you shall walk with praise
when all my ways are run.

Take all my love, but spend
such love to build your mind
'gainst hope that leaves behind
my winter night and snow
falling at the year's end.

Tell her I know
                    that living is too long
for our love to endure;
the tenuous and strong
web of time (outlasting
girls and men–love's rapid signature
of hand and lip and eye)
gleams as if wires were strung
across a sunset sky.

Tell her that girls and men
are shadows on the grass
where time's four seasons pass;
tell her that I have seen
                              O many a nervous queen
of girls (Madonna, glorious
white-towered goddess) fade
while walking in noon's shade,
separate limbs and foreheads bright,
now dim, anonymous. . . .

Tell her I love
                    to make these words a song
with her careful lips,
                              O bride,
Spring and bridegroom at your side,
save them for the deep and long
silences when northstar light
perishes down quicksilver steep
walls of flesh where love and death
make a counterfeit of sleep.

Take this wreath to celebrate
union of the fire and rain,
bone and tissue.
Sleep, O bride,
for the waking limbs divide
into separate walls again.

Tell her that flesh is spirited
into earth:
this wreath is grown
from black bronze roots to weave a crown
for the death mask and the head
fixed with its metallic smile
upward where generations climb
making garlands of their own
not of iron and of stone.

The Postman's Bell Is Answered Everywhere

God and the devil in these letters,
stored in tin trunks, tossed in wastebaskets,
or ticketed away in office files:
love, hate and business, mimeographed sheets, circulars,
bills of lading, official communiques,
accounts rendered, even the anonymous letter says,
Do not forget.

And in that long list: Dean Swift to Stella,
Walpole to Hannah More, Carlyle to Jane.
And what were Caesar's Gallic Wars other than letters
of credit for future empire?

Do not forget me,
I shall wear laurels to face the world;
you shall remember the head in bronze,
profile on coin.

As the bell rings, here is the morning paper and more letters:
the postdate, 10 P.M.: "It is an effort
for me to write; I have grown older.
I have two daughters and a son and business prospers,
but my hair is white. Why can't we meet for lunch?
It has been a long time since we met;

I doubt if you would know me, if you glanced quickly
at my overcoat and hat and saw them vanish
in a crowded street. . . ."

Or at another door, ". . . O you must not forget
you held me in your arms, while the small room
trembled in darkness; do you recall the slender, violet
dawn between the trees next morning through the park?
Since I'm a woman, how can I unlearn
the arts of love within a single hour;
how can I close my eyes before a mirror,
believe I am not wanted, that hands, lips, breast
are merely deeper shadows behind the door
where all is dark? . . ."

Or, "Forgive me if I intrude, the dream I had
last night was of your face; it was a child's face,
wreathed with the sun's hair, or pale in moonlight,
more of a child than woman, it followed me
wherever I looked, pierced everything I saw,
proved that you could not leave me, that I am always
at your side. . . ."

Or, "I alone am responsible for my own death" or,
"I am White, Christian, Unmarried, 21," or, "I
am happy to accept
Your Invitation," or, "Remember that evening
at the Savoy-Plaza,"
or, "It was I who saw the fall of France."

As letters are put aside, another bell
rings in another day; it is, perhaps, not too late to remember
the words that leave you naked in their sight,
the warning, "You have not forgotten me;
these lines were written by an unseen hand
twelve hours ago, do not reply at this address, these are the last
words I shall write."

Haunted Odysseus: The Last Testament

Do you see them? I mean the Dead:
They have come back again; I feel them walking
About the room, and a face has entered
Through that closed door.

I have seen them rising
In fountains out of rocks, the unwept slain,
The green moon-shadow on white breasts and thighs,
And heard their raining voices in the wind;
I saw pale hair
Floating in golden waves against the dark,
I saw hands reaching toward invisible fruit
That once had dropped through summer's heat
Above them.

This was in their country,
The Palace of the Dead, snow falling as crystals fall
From a dark sky. I heard the sound
Of thick waters moving against rocks, the shore;
Their houses had been burned by fires
Greater than the sun: there were blackened walls,
Each hearth, each portal
Open in ruins to gray sleet.
I saw a ledge, a handrail and no stair,
Only the deeper darkness and the depth
Of another corridor or pit.

Then from the shadows
I saw a wavering light and heard,
"My dear, my hope, my love," the light
Spoke to me, and I said, "Mother,
What dream, what evil sent you among these ruins,
Lost as a child is lost
In the mischances of love and war?"

"Death," she replied,
"I am spirit only: all that was flesh
Is fallen into earth or consumed by fire–
The human fate that waits for all of us
Has little patience for those grown delicate and old.
Then my transparent veins released my spirit
To walk among the unwary, the undone.
I am the vision that speaks to you in sleep;
You cannot hold my shade within your arms,
Even my slightest breath has turned to frost;
It dare not touch you–this is my last
Good night."

Where the light spoke a star
Shone through the portal and was gone.
My brain clouded with tears; I had forgotten
To ask her of the way back to life.
Then I remembered that a shade
Had stepped between us,
The blinded foreigner from Thebes
Who stood as if a tree grew at my side;
I heard the sound of leaves above my head,
And saw a black bough pointed east.

Perhaps my escape
Was almost fortuitous. And now at winter's midnight
The Dead are here whispering through snow;
They crowd upon me
Between walls of a room or in a quiet street:
"*Mea culpa, mea culpa,*" from earth or ceiling,
"The fault is our fault, *mea culpa*, we are to blame,
We are wanderers of Hell in every city,
The faithless, the unloved.
If at the last turn of the wheel in Heaven
The first cause of our fate is in the stars,
We shall wait for you behind an open door
And in your shadow as you walk the stairs."

Stephen Vincent Benét (*Am. 1898–1943*)

A Song of Breath

I heard the song of breath
Go up from city and country,
The even breath of the sleeper,
The tired breath of the sick,
The dry cough in the throat
Of the man with the death-sweat on him,
And the quiet monotone
We breathe but do not hear.

The harsh gasp of the runner,
The long sigh of power
Heaving the weight aloft,
The grey breath of the old.
Men at the end of strength
With their lungs turned lead and fire,
Panting like thirsty dogs;
A child's breath, blowing a flame.

The breath that is the voice,
The silver, the woodwinds speaking,
The dear voice of your lover,
The hard voice of your foe,
And the vast breath of wind,
Mysterious over mountains,
Caught in pines like a bird
Or filling all hammered heaven.

I heard the song of breath,
Like a great strand of music,
Blown between void and void,
Uncorporal as the light.
The breath of nations asleep,
And the piled hills they sleep in,
The word that never was flesh
And yet is nothing but life.

What are you, bodiless sibyl,
Unseen except as the frost-cloud
Puffed from a silver mouth
When the hard winter's cold?
We cannot live without breath,
And yet we breathe without knowledge,
And the vast strand of sound
Goes on, eternally sighing,
Without dimension or space,
Without beginning or end.

I heard the song of breath
And lost it in all sharp voices,
Even my own voice lost
Like a thread in that huge strand,

Lost like a skein of air,
And with it, continents lost
In the great throat of Death.
I trembled, asking in vain,
Whence come you, whither art gone?
The continents flow and melt
Like wax in the naked candle,
Burnt by the wick of time–
Where is the breath of the Chaldees,
The dark, Minoan breath?
I said to myself in hate,
Hearing that mighty rushing,
Though you raise a new Adam up
And blow fresh fire in his visage,
He has only a loan of air,
And gets but a breathing-space.
But then I was quieted.

I heard the song of breath,
The gulf hollow with voices,
Fused into one slow voice
That never paused or was faint.
Man, breathing his life,
And with him all life breathing,
The young horse and the snake,
Beetle, lion and dove,
Solemn harps of the fir,
Trumpets of sea and whirlwind
And the vast, tiny grass
Blown by a breath and speaking.
I heard these things. I heard
The multitudinous river.
When I came back to my life,
My voice was numb in my ears,
I wondered that I still breathed.

Malcolm Cowley (*Am. b. 1898*)

William Wilson

A man there is of fire and straw
consumed with fire, whom first I saw
once at a dance, where nearer and nearer
there swirled a mist, and lights grew dim,
And I came face to face with him
outlined against me in a mirror,
  my own eyes staring from a mirror.

As red as wine, as white as wine,
his face which is not and is mine
and apes my face's pantomime.
  It makes a threatening movement, halts,
and orchestras in perfect time
continue the Blue Danube Waltz,
  heavily dying to a waltz.

He makes a movement and retires,
this man of straw and many fires,
Iago doubled with Othello;
  often I startle up in bed
to find him lying there, my fellow;
  often I wish that he were dead,
and hack him often skin and bone,
and dreaming often, hear my own
life's blood drip on the crumpled pillow,
where once, immortal as a stone,
true love lay strangled by Othello.

The Urn

Wanderers outside the gates, in hollow
landscapes without memory, we carry
each of us an urn of native soil,
of not impalpable dust a double handful

carelessly gathered (was it garden mould,
or wood-soil fresh with hemlock needles, pine
and princess pine, this little earth we bore
in secret, vainly, over the frontier?)

A parcel of the soil not wide enough
or firm enough to build a dwelling on,
or deep enough to dig a grave, but cool
and sweet enough to sink the nostrils in
and find the smell of home, or in the ears
rumors of home like oceans in a shell.

Hart Crane (*Am. 1899–1932*)

Legend

As silent as a mirror is believed
Realities plunge in silence by . . .

I am not ready for repentance;
Nor to match regrets. For the moth
Bends no more than the still
Imploring flame. And tremorous
In the white falling flakes
Kisses are,–
The only worth all granting.

It is to be learned–
This cleaving and this burning,
But only by the one who
Spends out himself again.

Twice and twice
(Again the smoking souvenir,
Bleeding eidolon!) and yet again.
Until the bright logic is won
Unwhispering as a mirror
Is believed.

Then, drop by caustic drop, a perfect cry
Shall string some constant harmony,–
Relentless caper for all those who step
The legend of their youth into the noon.

Praise for an Urn

In Memoriam: Ernest Nelson

It was a kind and northern face
That mingled in such exile guise
The everlasting eyes of Pierrot
And, of Gargantua, the laughter.

His thoughts, delivered to me
From the white coverlet and pillow,
I see now, were inheritances–
Delicate riders of the storm.

The slant moon on the slanting hill
Once moved us toward presentiments
Of what the dead keep, living still,
And such assessments of the soul

As, perched in the crematory lobby,
The insistent clock commented on,
Touching as well upon our praise
Of glories proper to the time.

Still, having in mind gold hair,
I cannot see that broken brow
And miss the dry sound of bees
Stretching across a lucid space.

Scatter these well-meant idioms
Into the smoky spring that fills
The suburbs, where they will be lost.
They are no trophies of the sun.

Paraphrase

Of a steady winking beat between
Systole, diastole spokes-of-a-wheel
One rushing from the bed at night
May find the record wedged in his soul.

Above the feet the clever sheets
Lie guard upon the integers of life:
For what skims in between uncurls the toe,
Involves the hands in purposeless repose.

But from its bracket how can the tongue tell
When systematic morn shall sometime flood
The pillow–how desperate is the light
That shall not rouse, how faint the crow's cavil

As, when stunned in that antarctic blaze,
Your head, unrocking to a pulse, already
Hollowed by air, posts a white paraphrase
Among bruised roses on the papered wall.

Passage

Where the cedar leaf divides the sky
I heard the sea.
In sapphire arenas of the hills
I was promised an improved infancy.

Sulking, sanctioning the sun,
My memory I left in a ravine,–
Casual louse that tissues the buckwheat,
Aprons rocks, congregates pears
In moonlit bushels
And wakens alleys with a hidden cough.

Dangerously the summer burned
(I had joined the entrainments of the wind).
The shadows of boulders lengthened my back:
In the bronze gongs of my cheeks
The rain dried without odour.

"It is not long, it is not long;
See where the red and black
Vine-stanchioned valleys–": but the wind
Died speaking through the ages that you know
And hug, chimney-sooted heart of man!
So was I turned about and back, much as your smoke
Compiles a too well-known biography.

The evening was a spear in the ravine
That throve through very oak. And had I walked
The dozen particular decimals of time?
Touching an opening laurel, I found
A thief beneath, my stolen book in hand.

"Why are you back here–smiling an iron coffin?"
"To argue with the laurel," I replied:
"Am justified in transience, fleeing
Under the constant wonder of your eyes–."

He closed the book. And from the Ptolemies
Sand troughed us in a glittering abyss.
A serpent swam a vertex to the sun
–On unpaced beaches leaned its tongue and drummed.
What fountains did I hear? what icy speeches?
Memory, committed to the page, had broke.

From *Voyages*

II

And yet this great wink of eternity,
Of rimless floods, unfettered leewardings,
Samite sheeted and processioned where
Her undinal vast belly moonward bends,
Laughing the wrapt inflections of our love;

Take this Sea, whose diapason knells
On scrolls of silver snowy sentences,
The sceptred terror of whose sessions rends
As her demeanors motion well or ill,
All but the pieties of lovers' hands.

And onward, as bells off San Salvador
Salute the crocus lustres of the stars,
In these poinsettia meadows of her tides,–
Adagios of islands, O my Prodigal,
Complete the dark confessions her veins spell.

Mark how her turning shoulders wind the hours,
And hasten while her penniless rich palms
Pass superscription of bent foam and wave,–
Hasten, while they are true–sleep, death, desire,
Close round one instant in one floating flower.

Bind us in time, O Seasons clear, and awe.
O minstrel galleons of Carib fire,
Bequeath us to no earthly shore until
Is answered in the vortex of our grave
The seal's wide spindrift gaze toward paradise.

III

Infinite consanguinity it bears–
This tendered theme of you that light
Retrieves from sea plains where the sky
Resigns a breast that every wave enthrones;
While ribboned water lanes I wind
Are laved and scattered with no stroke
Wide from your side, whereto this hour
The sea lifts, also, reliquary hands.

And so, admitted through black swollen gates
That must arrest all distance otherwise,–
Past whirling pillars and lithe pediments,
Light wrestling there incessantly with light,
Star kissing star through wave on wave unto
Your body rocking!
and where death, if shed,
Presumes no carnage, but this single change,–
Upon the steep floor flung from dawn to dawn
The silken skilled transmemberment of song;

Permit me voyage, love, into your hands . . .

V

Meticulous, past midnight in clear rime,
Infrangible and lonely, smooth as though cast
Together in one merciless white blade–
The bay estuaries fleck the hard sky limits.

–As if too brittle or too clear to touch!
The cables of our sleep so swiftly filed,
Already hang, shred ends from remembered stars.
One frozen trackless smile . . . What words
Can strangle this deaf moonlight? For we

Are overtaken. Now no cry, no sword
Can fasten or deflect this tidal wedge,
Slow tyranny of moonlight, moonlight loved
And changed . . . "There's

Nothing like this in the world," you say,
Knowing I cannot touch your hand and look
Too, into that godless cleft of sky
Where nothing turns but dead sands flashing.

"–And never to quite understand!" No,
In all the argosy of your bright hair I dreamed
Nothing so flagless as this piracy.

But now
Draw in your head, alone and too tall here.
Your eyes already in the slant of drifting foam;
Your breath sealed by the ghosts I do not know:
Draw in your head and sleep the long way home.

VI

Where icy and bright dungeons lift
Of swimmers their lost morning eyes,
And ocean rivers, churning, shift
Green borders under stranger skies,

Steadily as a shell secretes
Its beating leagues of monotone,
Or as many waters trough the sun's
Red kelson past the cape's wet stone;

O rivers mingling toward the sky
And harbor of the phoenix' breast–
My eyes pressed black against the prow,
–Thy derelict and blinded guest

Waiting, afire, what name, unspoke,
I cannot claim: let thy waves rear
More savage than the death of kings,
Some splintered garland for the seer.

Beyond siroccos harvesting
The solstice thunders, crept away,
Like a cliff swinging or a sail
Flung into April's inmost day–

Creation's blithe and petalled word
To the lounged goddess when she rose
Conceding dialogue with eyes
That smile unsearchable repose–

Still fervid covenant, Belle Isle,
–Unfolded floating dais before
Which rainbows twine continual hair–
Belle Isle, white echo of the oar!

The imaged Word, it is, that holds
Hushed willows anchored in its glow.
It is the unbetrayable reply
Whose accent no farewell can know.

The Tunnel

To Find the Western path
Right thro' the Gates of Wrath.—Blake

Performances, assortments, résumés–
Up Times Square to Columbus Circle lights
Channel the congresses, nightly sessions,
Refractions of the thousand theatres, faces–
Mysterious kitchens. . . . You shall search them all.
Some day by heart you'll learn each famous sight
And watch the curtain lift in hell's despite;
You'll find the garden in the third act dead,
Finger your knees – and wish yourself in bed
With tabloid crime sheets perched in easy sight.

Then let you reach your hat
and go.
As usual, let you–also
walking down–exclaim
to twelve upward leaving
a subscription praise
for what time slays.

Or can't you quite make up your mind to ride;
A walk is better underneath the L a brisk
Ten blocks or so before? But you find yourself
Preparing penguin flexions of the arms,–
As usual you will meet the scuttle yawn:
The subway yawns the quickest promise home.

Be minimum, then, to swim the hiving swarms
Out of the Square, the Circle burning bright–
Avoid the glass doors gyring at your right,
Where boxed alone a second, eyes take fright
–Quite unprepared rush naked back to light:
And down beside the turnstile press the coin
Into the slot. The gongs already rattle.

And so
of cities you bespeak
subways, rivered under streets
and rivers. . . . In the car
the overtone of motion
underground, the monotone
of motion is the sound
of other faces, also underground–

"Let's have a pencil Jimmy–living now
at Floral Park
Flatbush–on the Fourth of July–
like a pigeon's muddy dream–potatoes
to dig in the field–travlin the town–too–
night after night–the Culver line–the
girls all shaping up–it used to be–"
Our tongues recant like beaten weather vanes.
This answer lives like verdigris, like hair
Beyond extinction, surcease of the bone;
And repetition freezes–"What
"what do you want? getting weak on the links?
fandaddle daddy don't ask for change–IS THIS
FOURTEENTH? it's half past six she said–if
you don't like my gate why did you
swing on it, why *didja*
swing on it
anyhow–"

And somehow anyhow swing–

The phonographs of hades in the brain
Are tunnels that re-wind themselves, and love
A burnt match skating in a urinal–
Somewhere above Fourteenth TAKE THE EXPRESS
To brush some new presentiment of pain–

"But I want service in this office SERVICE
I said–after
the show she cried a little afterwards but–"

Whose head is swinging from the swollen strap?
Whose body smokes along the bitten rails,
Bursts from a smoldering bundle far behind
In back forks of the chasms of the brain,–
Puffs from a riven stump far out behind
In interborough fissures of the mind . . . ?

And why do I often meet your visage here,
Your eyes like agate lanterns–on and on
Below the toothpaste and the dandruff ads?
–And did their riding eyes right through your side,
And did their eyes like unwashed platters ride?
And Death, aloft,–gigantically down
Probing through you–toward me, O evermore!
And when they dragged your retching flesh,
Your trembling hands that night through Baltimore–
That last night on the ballot rounds, did you
Shaking, did you deny the ticket, Poe?

For Gravesend Manor change at Chambers Street.
The platform hurries along to a dead stop.

The intent escalator lifts a serenade
Stilly
Of shoes, umbrellas, each eye attending its shoe, then
Bolting outright somewhere above where streets
Burst suddenly in rain. . . . The gongs recur:
Elbows and levers, guard and hissing door.
Thunder is galvothermic here below. . . . The car
Wheels off. The train rounds, bending to a scream,

Taking the final level for the dive
Under the river–
And somewhat emptier than before,
Demented, for a hitching second, humps; then
Lets go. . . . Toward corners of the floor
Newspapers wing, revolve and wing.
Blank windows gargle signals through the roar.

And does the Daemon take you home, also,
Wop washerwoman, with the bandaged hair?
After the corridors are swept, the cuspidors–
The gaunt sky-barracks cleanly now, and bare,
O Genoese, do you bring mother eyes and hands
Back home to children and to golden hair?

Daemon, demurring and eventful yawn!
Whose hideous laughter is a bellows mirth
–Or the muffled slaughter of a day in birth–
O cruelly to inoculate the brinking dawn
With antennae toward worlds that glow and sink;–
To spoon us out more liquid than the dim
Locution of the eldest star, and pack
The conscience navelled in the plunging wind,
Umbilical to call–and straightway die!

O caught like pennies beneath soot and steam,
Kiss of our agony thou gatherest;
Condensed, thou takest all–shrill ganglia
Impassioned with some song we fail to keep.

And yet, like Lazarus, to feel the slope,
The sod and billow breaking,–lifting ground,
–A sound of waters bending astride the sky
Unceasing with some Word that will not die . . .!

* * * *

A tugboat, wheezing wreaths of steam,
Lunged past, with one galvanic blare stove up the River.
I counted the echoes assembling, one after one,
Searching, thumbing the midnight on the piers.
Lights, coasting, left the oily tympanum of waters;
The blackness somewhere gouged glass on a sky.
And this thy harbor, O my City, I have driven under,
Tossed from the coil of ticking towers. . . . Tomorrow,
And to be. . . . here by the River that is East–
Here at the waters' edge the hands drop memory;
Shadowless in that abyss they unaccounting lie.
How far away the star has pooled the sea–
Or shall the hands be drawn away, to die?

Kiss of our agony Thou gatherest,
O Hand of Fire
gatherest–

The Broken Tower

The bell-rope that gathers God at dawn
Dispatches me as though I dropped down the knell
Of a spent day–to wander the cathedral lawn
From pit to crucifix, feet chill on steps from hell.

Have you not heard, have you not seen that corps
Of shadows in the tower, whose shoulders sway
Antiphonal carillons launched before
The stars are caught and hived in the sun's ray?

The bells, I say, the bells break down their tower;
And swing I know not where. Their tongues engrave
Membrane through marrow, my long-scattered score
Of broken intervals. . . . And I, their sexton slave!

Oval encyclicals in canyons heaping
The impasse high with choir. Banked voices slain!
Pagodas, campaniles with reveilles outleaping–
O terraced echoes prostrate on the plain! . . .

And so it was I entered the broken world
To trace the visionary company of love, its voice
An instant in the wind (I know not whither hurled)
But not for long to hold each desperate choice.

My word I poured. But was it cognate, scored
Of that tribunal monarch of the air
Whose thigh embronzes earth, strikes crystal Word
In wounds pledged once to hope–cleft to despair?

The steep encroachments of my blood left me
No answer (could blood hold such a lofty tower
As flings the question true?)–or is it she
Whose sweet mortality stirs latent power?–

And through whose pulse I hear, counting the strokes
My veins recall and add, revived and sure
The angelus of wars my chest evokes:
What I hold healed, original now, and pure . . .

And builds, within, a tower that is not stone
(Not stone can jacket heaven)–but slip
Of pebbles–visible wings of silence sown
In azure circles, widening as they dip

The matrix of the heart, lift down the eye
That shrines the quiet lake and swells a tower . . .
The commodious, tall decorum of that sky
Unseals her earth, and lifts love in its shower.

Allen Tate (*Am. b. 1899*)

The Mediterranean

Quem das finem, rex magne, dolorum?

Where we went in the boat was a long bay
A slingshot wide, walled by towering stone–
Peaked margin of antiquity's delay,
And we went there out of time's monotone:

Where we went in the black hull no light moved
But a gull white-winged along the feckless wave,
The breeze, unseen but fierce as a body loved,
That boat drove onward like a willing slave:

Where we went in the small ship the seaweed
Parted and gave to us the murmuring shore,
And we made feast and in our secret need
Devoured the very plates Aeneas bore:

Where derelict you see through the low twilight
The green coast that you, thunder-tossed, would win,
Drop sail, and hastening to drink all night
Eat dish and bowl to take that sweet land in!

Where we feasted and caroused on the sandless
Pebbles, affecting our day of piracy,
What prophecy of eaten plates could landless
Wanderers fulfil by the ancient sea?

We for that time might taste the famous age
Eternal here yet hidden from our eyes
When lust of power undid its stuffless rage;
They, in a wineskin, bore earth's paradise.

Let us lie down once more by the breathing side
Of Ocean, where our live forefathers sleep
As if the Known Sea still were a month wide–
Atlantis howls but is no longer steep!

What country shall we conquer, what fair land
Unman our conquest and locate our blood?
We've cracked the hemispheres with careless hand!
Now, from the Gates of Hercules we flood

Westward, westward till the barbarous brine
Whelms us to the tired land where tasseling corn,
Fat beans, grapes sweeter than muscadine
Rot on the vine: in that land were we born.

Aeneas at Washington

I myself saw furious with blood
Neoptolemus, at his side the black Atridae,
Hecuba and the hundred daughters, Priam
Cut down, his filth drenching the holy fires.
In that extremity I bore me well,
A true gentleman, valorous in arms,
Disinterested and honorable. Then fled:
That was a time when civilization
Run by the few fell to the many, and
Crashed to the shout of men, the clang of arms:
Cold victualing I seized, I hoisted up
The old man my father upon my back,
In the smoke made by sea for a new world
Saving little–a mind imperishable
If time is, a love of past things tenuous
As the hesitation of receding love.

(To the reduction of uncitied littorals
We brought chiefly the vigor of prophecy,
Our hunger breeding calculation
And fixed triumphs)

I saw the thirsty dove
In the glowing fields of Troy, hemp ripening
And tawny corn, the thickening Blue Grass
All lying rich forever in the green sun.
I see all things apart, the towers that men
Contrive I too contrived long, long ago.
Now I demand little. The singular passion
Abides its object and consumes desire
In the circling shadow of its appetite.
There was a time when the young eyes were slow,
Their flame steady beyond the firstling fire,
I stood in the rain, far from home at nightfall
By the Potomac, the great Dome lit the water,
The city my blood had built I knew no more
While the screech-owl whistled his new delight
Consecutively dark.

Stuck in the wet mire
Four thousand leagues from the ninth buried city
I thought of Troy, what we had built her for.

Ode to the Confederate Dead

Row after row with strict impunity
The headstones yield their names to the element,
The wind whirrs without recollection;
In the riven troughs the splayed leaves
Pile up, of nature the casual sacrament
To the seasonal eternity of death;
Then driven by the fierce scrutiny
Of heaven to their election in the vast breath,
They sough the rumor of mortality.

Autumn is desolation in the plot
Of a thousand acres where these memories grow
From the inexhaustible bodies that are not
Dead, but feed the grass row after rich row.
Think of the autumns that have come and gone!–
Ambitious November with the humors of the year,
With a particular zeal for every slab,
Staining the uncomfortable angels that rot
On the slabs, a wing chipped here, an arm there:

The brute curiosity of an angel's stare
Turns you, like them, to stone,
Transforms the heaving air
Till plunged to a heavier world below
You shift your sea-space blindly
Heaving, turning like the blind crab.

    Dazed by the wind, only the wind
    The leaves flying, plunge

You know who have waited by the wall
The twilight certainty of an animal,
Those midnight restitutions of the blood
You know–the immitigable pines, the smoky frieze
Of the sky, the sudden call: you know the rage,
The cold pool left by the mounting flood,
Of muted Zeno and Parmenides.
You who have waited for the angry resolution
Of those desires that should be yours tomorrow,
You know the unimportant shrift of death
And praise the vision
And praise the arrogant circumstance
Of those who fall
Rank upon rank, hurried beyond decision–
Here by the sagging gate, stopped by the wall.

    Seeing, seeing only the leaves
    Flying, plunge and expire

Turn your eyes to the immoderate past,
Turn to the inscrutable infantry rising
Demons out of the earth–they will not last.
Stonewall, Stonewall, and the sunken fields of hemp,
Shiloh, Antietam, Malvern Hill, Bull Run.
Lost in that orient of the thick-and-fast
You will curse the setting sun.

    Cursing only the leaves crying
    Like an old man in a storm

You hear the shout, the crazy hemlocks point
With troubled fingers to the silence which
Smothers you, a mummy, in time.

The hound bitch
Toothless and dying, in a musty cellar
Hears the wind only.

Now that the salt of their blood
Stiffens the saltier oblivion of the sea,
Seals the malignant purity of the flood,
What shall we who count our days and bow
Our heads with a commemorial woe
In the ribboned coats of grim felicity,
What shall we say of the bones, unclean,
Whose verdurous anonymity will grow?
The ragged arms, the ragged heads and eyes
Lost in these acres of the ínsane green?
The gray lean spiders come, they come and go;
In a tangle of willows without light
The singular screech-owl's tight
Invisible lyric seeds the mind
With the furious murmur of their chivalry.

We shall say only the leaves
Flying, plunge and expire

We shall say only the leaves whispering
In the improbable mist of nightfall
That flies on multiple wing;
Night is the beginning and the end
And in between the ends of distraction
Waits mute speculation, the patient curse
That stones the eyes, or like the jaguar leaps
For his own image in a jungle pool, his victim.
What shall we say who have knowledge
Carried to the heart? Shall we take the act
To the grave? Shall we, more hopeful, set up the grave
In the house? The ravenous grave?

Leave now
The shut gate and the decomposing wall:
The gentle serpent, green in the mulberry bush,
Riots with his tongue through the hush—
Sentinel of the grave who counts us all!

Mother and Son

Now all day long the man who is not dead
Hastens the dark with inattentive eyes,
The woman with white hand and erect head
Stares at the covers, leans for the son's replies
At last to her importunate womanhood—
Her hand of death, laid on the living bed;
So lives the fierce compositor of blood.

She waits; he lies upon the bed of sin
Where greed, avarice, anger writhed and slept
Till to their silence they were gathered in:
There, fallen with time, his tall and bitter kin
Once fired the passions that were never kept
In the permanent heart, and there his mother lay
To bear him on the impenetrable day.

The falcon mother cannot will her hand
Up to the bed, nor break the manacle
His exile sets upon her harsh command
That he should say the time is beautiful—
Transfigured by her own possessing light:
The sick man craves the impalpable night.

Loosed betwixt eye and lid, the swimming beams
Of memory, blind school of cuttlefish,
Rise to the air, plunge to the cold streams—
Rising and plunging the half-forgotten wish
To tear his heart out in a slow disgrace
And freeze the hue of terror to her face.

Hate, misery, and fear beat off his heart
To the dry fury of the woman's mind;
The son, prone in his autumn, moves apart
A seed blown upon a returning wind.
O child, be vigilant till towards the south
On the flowered wall all the sweet afternoon,
The reaching sun, swift as the cottonmouth,
Strikes at the black crucifix on her breast
Where the cold dusk comes suddenly to rest—
Mortality will speak the victor soon!

The dreary flies, lazy and casual,
Stick to the ceiling, buzz along the wall.
O heart, the spider shuffles from the mould
Weaving, between the pinks and grapes, his pall,
The bright wallpaper, imperishably old,
Uncurls and flutters, it will never fall.

From *Seasons of the Soul*

II Autumn

It had an autumn smell
And that was how I knew
That I was down a well:
I was no longer young;
My lips were numb and blue,
The air was like fine sand
In a butcher's stall
Or pumice to the tongue:
And when I raised my hand
I stood in the empty hall.

The round ceiling was high
And the gray light like shale
Thin, crumbling, and dry:
No rug on the bare floor
Nor any carved detail
To which the eye could glide;
I counted along the wall.
Door after closed door
Through which a shade might slide
To the cold and empty hall.

I will leave this house, I said,
There is the autumn weather–
Here, nor living nor dead;
The lights burn in the town
Where men fear together.
Then on the bare floor,
But tiptoe lest I fall,
I walked years down
Towards the front door
At the end of the empty hall.

The door was false–no key
Or lock, and I was caught
In the house; yet I could see
I had been born to it
For miles of running brought
Me back where I began.
I saw now in the wall
A door open a slit
And a fat grizzled man
Come out into the hall:

As in a moonlit street
Men meeting are too shy
To check their hurried feet
But raise their eyes and squint
As through a needle's eye
Into the faceless gloom,–
My father in a gray shawl
Gave me an unseeing glint
And entered another room!
I stood in the empty hall

And watched them come and go
From one room to another,
Old men, old women–slow,
Familiar; girls, boys;
I saw my downcast mother
Clad in her street-clothes,
Her blue eyes long and small,
Who had no look or voice
For him whose vision froze
Him in the empty hall.

The Cross

There is a place that some men know,
I cannot see the whole of it
Nor how I came there. Long ago
Flame burst out of a secret pit
Crushing the world with such a light
The day-sky fell to moonless black,
The kingly sun to hateful night

For those, once seeing, turning back:
For Love so hates mortality
Which is the providence of life
She will not let it blesséd be
But curses it with mortal strife,
Until beside the blinding rood
Within that world-destroying pit
–Like young wolves that have tasted blood,
Of death, men taste no more of it.
So blind, in so severe a place
(All life before in the black grave)
The last alternatives they face
Of life, without the life to save,
Being from all salvation weaned–
A stag charged both at heel and head:
Who would come back is turned a fiend
Instructed by the fiery dead.

The Swimmers

Kentucky water, clear springs: a boy fleeing
To waters under the dry Kentucky sun;
His little friends of Nomen with him, seeing

Long shadows of grapevine wriggle and run
Over the green swirl; mullein under the ear
Soft as Nausicaä's palm; sullen fun

Brutal as childhood's thin harmonious tear:
O fountain, bosom source undying-dead
Replenish me the spring of love and fear

And give me back the eye that looked and fled
When a thrush idling in the tulip-tree
Unwound the cold dream of the copperhead.

–Along the creek the road was winding; we
Felt the quicksilver sky. I see again
The five companions of that odyssey:

Bill Eaton, Charlie Watson, 'Nigger' Layne
The doctor's son, Harry Duésler who played
The flute; Tate, with the water on his brain.

Dog-days: the dusty leaves where rain delayed
  Hung low on poison-oak and scuppernong,
  For we were following the active shade

Of water, that bells and bickers all night long.
  "No more'n a mile," Layne said. All five stood still.
  Listening, I heard what seemed at first a song;

Peering, I heard the hooves come down the hill.
  The posse passed, twelve horse; the leader's face
  Was worn as limestone on an ancient sill.

Then, as sleepwalkers shift from a hard place
  In bed, and rising to keep a formal pledge
  Descend a ladder into empty space,

We scuttled down the bank below a ledge
  And marched stiff-legged in our common fright
  Along a hog-track by the riffle's edge:

Into a world where sound shaded the sight
  Dropped the dull hooves again; the horsemen came
  Again, all but the leader. It was night

Momently and I feared: eleven same
  Jesus-Christers unmembered and unmade,
  Whose Corpse had died again in dirty shame.

The bank then levelling in a speckled glade
  We stopped to breathe above the swimming-hole;
  I gazed at its reticulated shade

Recoiling in blue fear, and felt it roll
  Over my eyes and ears and lift my hair
  Like seaweed tossing on a sunk atoll.

I rose again. Borne on the copper air
  A distant voice green as a funeral wreath
  Against a grave: "That dead nigger there."

The melancholy sheriff slouched beneath
  A giant sycamore; shaking his head
  He plucked a sassafras twig and picked his teeth:

"We come too late." He spoke to the tired dead
  Whose ragged shirt soaked up the viscous flow
  Of blood in which It lay discomfited.

A butting horse-fly gave one ear a blow
  And glanced off, as the sheriff kicked the rope
  Loose from the neck and hooked it with his toe

Away from the blood.–I looked back down the slope;
  The friends were gone that I had hoped to greet.–
  A single horseman came at a fast lope

And pulled up at the hanged man's horny feet;
  The sheriff noosed the feet, the other end
  The stranger tied to his pommel in a neat

Slip-knot. I saw the Negro's body bend
  And straighten, as a fish-line cast transverse
  Yields to the current that it must subtend.

The sheriff's God-damn was a facile curse
  Not for the dead but for the blinding dust
  That boxed the cortège in a cloudy hearse

And dragged it towards our town. I knew I must
  Not stay till nightfall in that silent road;
  Sliding my bare feet into the warm crust

I hopped the stonecrop like a panting toad
  Mouth open, following the heaving cloud
  That floated to the courthouse square its load

Of limber corpse that took the sun for shroud.
  There were three figures in the dying sun
  Whose light were company where three was crowd.

My breath crackled the dead air like a shotgun
  As sheriff and the stranger disappearing,
  The faceless head lay still. I could not run

Or walk, but stood. Alone in the public clearing
  This private thing was owned by all the town,
  Though never claimed by us within my hearing.

Léonie Adams (*Am. b. 1899*)

Country Summer

Now the rich cherry, whose sleek wood,
And top with silver petals traced
Like a strict box its gems encased,
Has split from out that cunning lid,
All in an innocent green round,
Those melting rubies which it hid;
With moss ripe-strawberry-encrusted,
So birds get half, and minds lapse merry
To taste that deep-red, lark's-bite berry,
And blackcap bloom is yellow-dusted.

The wren that thieved it in the eaves
A trailer of the rose could catch
To her poor droopy sloven thatch,
And side by side with the wren's brood–
O lovely time of beggar's luck–
Opens the quaint and hairy bud;
And full and golden is the yield
Of cows that never have to house,
But all night nibble under boughs,
Or cool their sides in the moist field.

Into the rooms flow meadow airs,
The warm farm baking smell's blown round.
Inside and out, and sky and ground
Are much the same; the wishing star,
Hesperus, kind and early born,
Is risen only finger-far;
All stars stand close in summer air,
And tremble, and look mild as amber;
When wicks are lighted in the chamber,
They are like stars which settled there.

Now straightening from the flowery hay,
Down the still light the mowers look,
Or turn, because their dreaming shook,
And they waked half to other days,
When left alone in the yellow stubble
The rusty-coated mare would graze.

Yet thick the lazy dreams are born,
Another thought can come to mind,
But like the shivering of the wind,
Morning and evening in the corn.

Caryatid

Not at midnight, not at morning, O sweet city,
Shall we come in at your portal, but this girl,
Bearing on her head a broken stone,
In the body shaped to this, the throat and bosom
Poised no less for the burden now the temple is fallen,
Tells the white Athenian wonder overthrown.

There is no clasp which stays beauty forever.
Time has undone her, from porphyry, from bronze.
She is winged every way and will not rest;
But the gesture of the lover shall remain long after,
Where lovely and imponderable there leans
A weight more grave than marble on the breast.

Early Waking

Four hooves rang out and now are still.
In the dark wall the casements hold
Essential day above each sill,
Just light, and colored like thin gold.
Behind those hooves a drowsy course
All night I rode where hearts were clear,
And wishes blessèd at the source,
And for no shape of time stop here.

No more to raise that lively ghost
Which ran quicksilver to the bone:
By a whim's turn the whole was lost
When all its marrow worth was known.
Ghosts can cast shadows in the breast,
And what was present tears to weep,
Not heart nor mind would bid from rest
As fast as sorrow's, ten years deep.

I travel, not for a ghost's sake,
One step from sleep, and not for one
Left sleeping at my side I wake.
Before bricks rosy with the dawn,
The hooves will sound beyond the light:
There are dark roads enough to go
To last us through the end of night,
And I will make my waking slow.

It was for unconcerning light
That has not fallen on earth, to stare
An instant only out of night
And with night's cloudy character,
Before the laden mind shall slip
Past dream and on to brightmost dream
And fetterless high morning dip
Her two cold sandals in the stream.

The Mount

Now I have tempered haste,
The joyous traveller said,
The steed has passed me now
Whose hurrying hooves I fled.
My spectre rides thereon,
I learned what mount he has,
Upon what summers fed;
And wept to know again,
Beneath the saddle swung,
Treasure for whose great theft
This breast was wrung.
His bridle bells sang out,
I could not tell their chime,
So brilliantly he rings,
But called his name as Time.
His bin was morning light,
Those straws which gild his bed
Are of the fallen West.
Although green lands consume
Beneath their burning tread,
In everlasting bright
His hooves have rest.

Those Not Elect

Never, being damned, see paradise.
The heart will sweeten at its look;
Nor hell was known, till paradise
Our senses shook.

Never hear angels at laughter,
For how comports with grief to know
Wisdom in heaven bends to laughter, laughter,
Laughter upon woe?

Never fall dreaming on celestials,
Lest, bound in a ruinous place,
You turn to wander with celestials
Down holy space.

Never taste that fruit with the soul
Whereof the body may not eat,
Lest flesh at length lay waste the soul
In its sick heat.

Grapes Making

Noon sun beats down the leaf; the noon
Of summer burns along the vine
And thins the leaf with burning air,
Till from the underleaf is fanned,
And down the woven vine, the light.
Still the pleached leaves drop layer on layer
To wind the sun on either hand,
And echoes of the light are bound,
And hushed the blazing cheek of light,
The hurry of the breathless noon,
And from the thicket of the vine
The grape has pressed into its round.

The grape has pressed into its round,
And swings, aloof chill green, clean won
Of light, between the sky and ground;
Those hid, soft-flashing lamps yet blind,
Which yield an apprehended sun.
Fresh triumph in a courteous kind,

Having more ways to be, and years,
And easy, countless treasuries,
You whose all-told is still no sum,
Like a rich heart, well-said in sighs,
The careless autumn mornings come,
The grapes drop glimmering to the shears.

Now shady sod at heel piles deep,
An overarching shade, the vine
Across the fall of noon is flung;
And here beneath the leaves is cast
A light to colour noonday sleep,
While cool, bemused the grape is swung
Beneath the eyelids of the vine;
And deepening like a tender thought
Green moves along the leaf, and bright
The leaf above, and leaf has caught,
And emerald pierces day, and last
The faint leaf vanishes to light.

The Reminder

All night there had sought in vain
To coax a sullen eye,
(And pressed to the black pane
The brilliance of their sky)
The winter moon blown high,
And the starred and the clouded train.

They have passed me glittering,
And I heard tone on tone
Of the cold night chime ring,
With will that churned alone
And sight pinned bleak as stone
To what the heart could bring.

Till now the night wears thin,
A roof leans out awry,
And cocks and wheels begin;
And from past morning-cry
A lone, a steadfast eye
Silently looks in.

Alas, Kind Element

Then I was sealed, and like the wintering tree
I stood me locked upon a summer core;
Living, had died a death, and asked no more.
And I lived then, but as enduringly,
And my heart beat, but only as to be.
Ill weathers well, hail, gust and cold I bore,
I held my life as hid, at root, in store:
Thus I lived then, till this air breathed on me.
Till this kind air breathed kindness everywhere,
There where my times had left me I would stay.
Then I was staunch, I knew nor yes nor no;
But now the wishful leaves have thronged the air.
My every leaf leans forth upon the day;
Alas, kind element! which comes to go.

The People in the Park

Under the mock-oranges the children spy,
Where the sod leaves the mould-greened ground,
Underneath the sweet shrub and the mass of June,
Shaping of them soft posture and bird-cry,
Reaving the aimless glances, and have not found
The cause of seeking, or whether the pure cocoon
Of the silk and sheen of being is given to rend.

Liker, and all less like than leaves the eyes,
Unmet, in whose glance the trembled irises
Ward the still anthers of will's secrecy,
As out of the child's vision his ancient wishes pass,
Risen from the devoured garden flesh, and come
In the freshness of flowers, into the daylight womb,
His limbs that bear them with offended grace.

And one is offered elsewhere for his own,
Annunciations, whisperings, to be
More intimately strangered to the bone.
And in the hearts whose many a hope were seen
Stranger than its befallen, than seed more hid,
The plumule's hieroglyph and more hid than these
By petalling days, beneath what has not been,

And in the bodies drying like dried wood,
Nighted, a center and a solitude,
Is an abiding. O not for life young
Alone seek the old looking hearts that have
Green, green to gaze upon forever this scene,
And look as with the longing of the grave,
As on the times they were consumed among.

Then shall it not have been life young alone
Darkness dimensioned, in all things' cradle lain,
But in the hearts of cooling ash intent,
Is its abiding, beneath what has not been,
When all has been foretelling to be spent,
As from its sacred cause of presence then,
Where it is nothing, one with its assent.

Yvor Winters (*Am. b. 1900*)

Quod Tegit Omnia

Earth darkens and is beaded
with a sweat of bushes and
the bear comes forth;
the mind, stored with
magnificence, proceeds into
the mystery of time, now
certain of its choice of
passion, but uncertain of the
passion's end.

When
Plato temporizes on the nature
of the plumage of the soul the
wind hums in the feathers as
across a cord impeccable in
tautness but of no mind:

Time,
the sine-pondere, most
imperturbable of elements,
assumes its own proportions
silently, of its own properties-
an excellence at which one
sighs.

Adventurer in
living fact, the poet
mounts into the spring,
upon his tongue the taste of
air becoming body: is
embedded in this crystalline
precipitate of time.

The Marriage

Incarnate for our marriage you appeared,
Flesh living in the spirit and endeared
By minor graces and slow sensual change.
Through every nerve we made our spirits range.
We fed our minds on every mortal thing:
The lacy fronds of carrots in the spring,
Their flesh sweet on the tongue, the salty wine
From bitter grapes, which gathered through the vine
The mineral drouth of autumn concentrate,
Wild spring in dream escaping, the debate
Of flesh and spirit on those vernal nights,
Its resolution in naïve delights,
The young kids bleating softly in the rain–
All this to pass, not to return again.
And when I found your flesh did not resist,
It was the living spirit that I kissed,
It was the spirit's change in which I lay:
Yea, mind in mind we waited for the day.
When flesh shall fall away, and, falling, stand
Wrinkling with shadow over face and hand,
Still I shall meet you on the verge of dust

And know you as a faithful vestige must.
And in commemoration of our lust,
May our heirs seal us in a single urn,
A single spirit never to return.

The Journey
Snake River Country

I now remembered slowly how I came,
I, sometime living, sometime with a name,
Creeping by iron ways, across the bare
Wastes of Wyoming, turning in despair,
Changing and turning, till the fall of night,
Then throbbing motionless with iron might.
Four days and nights! Small stations by the way,
Sunk far past midnight! Nothing one can say
Names the compassion they stir in the heart.
Obscure men shift and cry, and we depart.

And I remembered with the early sun
That foul-mouthed barber back in Pendleton,
The sprawling streets, the icy station bench,
The Round-up pennants, the latrinal stench.
These towns are cold by day, the flesh of vice
Raw and decisive, and the will precise;
At night the turbulence of drink and mud,
Blue glare of gas, the dances dripping blood,
Fists thudding murder in the shadowy air,
Exhausted whores, sunk to a changeless stare.
Alive in empty fact alone, extreme,
They make each fact a mortuary dream.

Once when the train paused in an empty place,
I met the unmoved landscape face to face;
Smoothing abysses that no stream could slake,
Deep in its black gulch crept the heavy Snake,
The sound diffused, and so intently firm,
It seemed the silence, having change nor term.
Beyond the river, gray volcanic stone
In rolling hills: the river moved alone.
And when we started, charged with mass, and slow,
We hung against it in an awful flow.

Thus I proceeded until early night,
And, when I read the station's name aright,
Descended–at the bidding of a word!
I slept the night out where the thought occurred,
Then rose to view the dwelling where I lay.
Outside, the bare land stretching far away;
The frame house, new, fortuitous, and bright,
Pointing the presence of the morning light;
A train's far screaming, clean as shining steel
Planing the distance for the gliding heel.
Through shrinking frost, autumnal grass uncurled,
In naked sunlight, on a naked world.

A Vision

Years had elapsed; the long room was the same.
At the far end, a log with drooping flame
Cast lengthening shadow. I was there alone,
A presence merely, like a shadow thrown,
Changing and growing dark with what I knew.
Above the roof, as if through a long flue,
The midnight wind poured steadily through pines.
I saw the trees flame thin, in watery lines.

Then, from my station in the empty air,
I saw them enter by the door; that pair
Opened and closed and watched each other move
With murderous eyes and gestures deep with love.
First came the Widow, but she had no face–
Naught but a shadow. At an earth-soaked pace
Her lover followed, weak with fear and lust.
And then I noticed there were years of dust
On floor and table, thought that in my day
No pines had been there. They sat down to play
At cards on a small table, and made tea,
And ate and played in silence. I could see
His lust come on him slowly, and his head
Fall on the table, but uncomforted
He feared to reach across to find her hand.

Deep in her veil I saw the features stand,
A deep jaw open; and a low iron laugh
Came from afar, a furious epigraph
To what I knew not in another place.

What evil was there in that woman's face!
He shrank in fear and told her of his love,
And she smiled coldly on him from above,
Stooped to a bundle lying by her side
And with a sodden tenderness untied
A severed head, gazed, and denied his plea.
He shuddered, heavy with lubricity.

There, steeped in the remote familiar gloom,
What were those demons doing in that room,
Their gestures aging, where the increasing shade
Stalked the dark flame that ever wearier played
As my receding memories left me dull?
My spirit now was but a shadowy hull.
Half-lost, I felt the Lover's shame my own.
I faced the Widow; we two were alone.

I saw the head and grasped it and struck root,
And then I rose, and with a steady foot,
I left her there, retarded in a dream.
Slowly I moved, like a directed beam.
My flesh fused with the cold flesh of the head;
My blood drew from me, from the neck flowed red,
A dark pulse on the darkness. The head stirred
Weakly beneath my fingers, and I heard
A whispered laughter, and the burden grew
In life and fury as my strength withdrew.
As if I labored up a flood of years,
I gathered heavy speed, drenched in arrears,
And limp to drowning, and I drove my flesh
Through the dark rooms adjacent to that mesh.
I was returning by the narrow hall;
Bound in my thought, jaw spread, I could not call.
And yet, with stride suspended in mid air,
I fled more fast, yet more retarded there,
Swung backward by that laughter out of Hell,
Pealing at arm's length like an iron bell.

There in the darkest passage, where my feet
Fled fastest, he laughed loudest, and defeat
Was certain, for he held me in one place,
Fleeing immobile in an empty space,
I looked above me; on the stairway saw
The Widow, like a corpse. Fear drove my jaw
Wide open, and the tremor of that scream
Shattered my being like an empty dream.

The Grave

Great eucalypti, black amid the flame,
Rise from below the slope, above his name.
The light is vibrant at their edges, clings,
Running in all ways through quick whisperings,
Falling in secrecy athwart each stone.
Under a little plaque he waits alone.
There is no faintest tremor in that urn.
Each flake of ash is sure in its return—
Never to alter, a pure quality,
A shadow cast against Eternity.

What has he found there? Life, it seems, is this:
To learn to shorten what has moved amiss;
To temper motion till a mean is hit,
Though the wild meaning would unbalance it;
To stand, precarious, near the utter end;
Betrayed, deserted, and alone descend,
Blackness before, and on the road above
The crowded terror that is human love;
To still the spirit till the flesh may lock
Its final cession in eternal rock.

Then let me pause in this symbolic air,
Each fiery grain immobile as despair,
Fixed at a rigid distance from the earth,
Absorbed each motion that arose from birth.
Here let me contemplate eternal peace,
Eternal station, which annuls release.
Here may I read its meaning, though the eye
Sear with the effort, ere the body die.
For what one is, one sees not; 'tis the lot
Of him at peace to contemplate it not.

Orpheus

In Memory of Hart Crane

Climbing from the Lethal dead,
Past the ruined waters' bed,
In the sleep his music cast
Tree and flesh and stone were fast–
As amid Dodona's wood
Wisdom never understood.

Till the shade his music won
Shuddered, by a pause undone–
Silence would not let her stay.
He could go one only way:
By the river, strong with grief,
Gave his flesh beyond belief.

Yet the fingers on the lyre
Spread like an avenging fire.
Crying loud, the immortal tongue,
From the empty body wrung,
Broken in a bloody dream,
Sang unmeaning down the stream.

John Sutter

I was the patriarch of the shining land,
Of the blond summer and metallic grain;
Men vanished at the motion of my hand,
And when I beckoned they would come again.

The earth grew dense with grain at my desire;
The shade was deepened at the springs and streams;
Moving in dust that clung like pillared fire,
The gathering herds grew heavy in my dreams.

Across the mountains, naked from the heights,
Down to the valley broken settlers came,
And in my houses feasted through the nights,
Rebuilt their sinews and assumed a name.

In my clear rivers my own men discerned
The motive for the ruin and the crime–
Gold heavier than earth, a wealth unearned,
Loot, for two decades, from the heart of Time.

Metal, intrinsic value, deep and dense,
Preanimate, inimitable, still,
Real, but an evil with no human sense,
Dispersed the mind to concentrate the will.

Grained by alchemic change, the human kind
Turned from themselves to rivers and to rocks;
With dynamite broke metal unrefined;
Measured their moods by geologic shocks.

With knives they dug the metal out of stone;
Turned rivers back, for gold through ages piled,
Drove knives to hearts, and faced the gold alone;
Valley and river ruined and reviled;

Reviled and ruined me, my servant slew,
Strangled him from the fig tree by my door.
When they had done what fury bade them do,
I was cursing a beggar, stripped and sore.

What end impersonal, what breathless age,
Incontinent of quiet and of years,
What calm catastrophe will yet assuage
This final drouth of penitential tears?

Sir Gawaine and the Green Knight

Reptilian green the wrinkled throat,
Green as a bough of yew the beard;
He bent his head, and so I smote;
Then for a thought my vision cleared.

The head dropped clean; he rose and walked;
He fixed his fingers in the hair;
The head was unabashed and talked;
I understood what I must dare.

His flesh, cut down, arose and grew.
He bade me wait the season's round,
And then, when he had strength anew,
To meet him on his native ground.

The year declined; and in his keep
I passed in joy a thriving yule;
And whether waking or in sleep,
I lived in riot like a fool.

He beat the woods to bring me meat.
His lady, like a forest vine,
Grew in my arms; the growth was sweet;
And yet what thoughtless force was mine!

By practice and conviction formed,
With ancient stubbornness ingrained,
Although her body clung and swarmed,
My own identity remained.

Her beauty, lithe, unholy, pure,
Took shapes that I had never known;
And had I once been insecure,
Had grafted laurel in my bone.

And then, since I had kept the trust,
Had loved the lady, yet was true,
The knight withheld his giant thrust
And let me go with what I knew.

I left the green bark and the shade,
Where growth was rapid, thick, and still;
I found a road that men had made
And rested on a drying hill.

To the Holy Spirit

from a deserted graveyard
in the Salinas Valley

Immeasurable haze:
The desert valley spreads
Up golden river-beds
As if in other days.
Trees rise and thin away,
And past the trees, the hills,
Pure line and shade of dust,
Bear witness to our wills:
We see them, for we must;
Calm in deceit, they stay.

High noon returns the mind
Upon its local fact:
Dry grass and sand; we find
No vision to distract.
Low in the summer heat,
Naming old graves, are stones
Pushed here and there, the seat
Of nothing, and the bones
Beneath are similar:
Relics of lonely men,
Brutal and aimless, then
As now, irregular.

These are thy fallen sons,
Thou whom I try to reach.
Thou whom the quick eye shuns,
Thou dost elude my speech.
Yet when I go from sense
And trace thee down in thought,
I meet thee, then, intense,
And know thee as I ought.
But thou art mind alone,
And I, alas, am bound
Pure mind to flesh and bone,
And flesh and bone to ground.

These had no thought: at most
Dark faith and blinding earth.
Where is the trammeled ghost?
Was there another birth?
Only one certainty
Beside thine unfleshed eye,
Beside the spectral tree,
Can I discern: these die.
All of this stir of age,
Though it elude my sense
Into what heritage
I know not, seems to fall,
Quiet beyond recall
Into irrelevance.

Roy Campbell (*Br. 1901–1957*)

The Sisters

After hot loveless nights, when cold winds stream
Sprinkling the frost and dew, before the light,
Bored with the foolish things that girls must dream
Because their beds are empty of delight,

Two sisters rise and strip. Out from the night
Their horses run to their low-whistled pleas–
Vast phantom shapes with eyeballs rolling white
That sneeze a fiery steam about their knees:

Through the crisp manes their stealthy prowling hands,
Stronger than curbs, in slow caresses rove,
They gallop down across the milk-white sands
And wade far out into the sleeping cove:

The frost stings sweetly with a burning kiss
As intimate as love, as cold as death:
Their lips, whereon delicious tremors hiss,
Fume with the ghostly pollen of their breath.

Far out on the grey silence of the flood
They watch the dawn in smouldering gyres expand
Beyond them: and the day burns through their blood
Like a white candle through a shuttered hand.

Tristan da Cunha

(to Robert Lyle)

Snore in the foam; the night is vast and blind;
The blanket of the mist about your shoulders,
Sleep your old sleep of rock, snore in the wind,
Snore in the spray! the storm your slumber lulls,
His wings are folded on your nest of boulders
As on their eggs the grey wings of your gulls.

No more as when, so dark an age ago,
You hissed a giant cinder from the ocean,
Around your rocks you furl the shawling snow
Half sunk in your own darkness, vast and grim,
And round you on the deep with surly motion
Pivot your league-long shadow as you swim.

Why should you haunt me thus but that I know
My surly heart is in your own displayed,
Round whom such leagues in endless circuit flow,
Whose hours in such a gloomy compass run–
A dial with its league-long arm of shade
Slowly revolving to the moon and sun.

My pride has sunk, like your grey fissured crags,
By its own strength o'ertoppled and betrayed:
I, too, have burned the wind with fiery flags
Who now am but a roost for empty words,
An island of the sea whose only trade
Is in the voyage of its wandering birds.

Did you not, when your strength became your pyre
Deposed and tumbled from your flaming tower,
Awake in gloom from whence you sank in fire,
To find, Antaeus-like, more vastly grown,
A throne in your own darkness, and a power
Sheathed in the very coldness of your stone?

Your strength is that you have no hope or fear,
You march before the world without a crown,
The nations call you back, you do not hear,
The cities of the earth grow grey behind you,
You will be there when their great flames go down
And still the morning in the van will find you.

You march before the continents, you scout
In front of all the earth; alone you scale
The mast-head of the world, a lorn look-out,
Waving the snowy flutter of your spray
And gazing back in infinite farewell
To suns that sink and shores that fade away.

From your grey tower what long regrets you fling
To where, along the low horizon burning,
The great swan-breasted seraphs soar and sing,
And suns go down, and trailing splendours dwindle,
And sails on lonely errands unreturning
Glow with a gold no sunrise can rekindle.

Turn to the night; these flames are not for you
Whose steeple for the thunder swings its bells;
Grey Memnon, to the tempest only true,
Turn to the night, turn to the shadowing foam,
And let your voice, the saddest of farewells,
With sullen curfew toll the grey wings home.

The wind, your mournful syren, haunts the gloom;
The rocks, spray-clouded, are your signal guns
Whose stony nitre, puffed with flying spume,
Rolls forth in grim salute your broadside hollow
Over the gorgeous burials of suns
To sound the tocsin of the storms that follow.

Plunge forward like a ship to battle hurled,
Slip the long cables of the failing light,
The level rays that moor you to the world:
Sheathed in your armour of eternal frost,
Plunge forward, in the thunder of the fight
To lose yourself as I would fain be lost.

Exiled like you and severed from my race
By the cold ocean of my own disdain,
Do I not freeze in such a wintry space,
Do I not travel through a storm as vast
And rise at times, victorious from the main,
To fly the sunrise at my shattered mast?

Your path is but a desert where you reap
Only the bitter knowledge of your soul:
You fish with nets of seaweed in the deep
As fruitlessly as I with nets of rhyme–
Yet forth you stride, yourself the way, the goal,
The surges are your strides, your path is time.

Hurled by what aim to what tremendous range!
A missile from the great sling of the past,
Your passage leaves its track of death and change
And ruin on the world: you fly beyond
Leaping the current of the ages vast
As lightly as a pebble skims a pond.

The years are undulations in your flight
Whose awful motion we can only guess–
Too swift for sense, too terrible for sight,
We only know how fast behind you darken
Our days like lonely beacons of distress:
We know that you stride on and will not harken.

Now in the eastern sky the fairest planet
Pierces the dying wave with dangled spear,
And in the whirring hollows of your granite
That vaster sea to which you are a shell
Sighs with a ghostly rumour, like the drear
Moan of the nightwind in a hollow cell.

We shall not meet again; over the wave
Our ways divide, and yours is straight and endless,
But mine is short and crooked to the grave:
Yet what of these dark crowds amid whose flow
I battle like a rock, aloof and friendless,
Are not their generations vague and endless
The waves, the strides, the feet on which I go?

The Zulu Girl

(to F. C. Slater)

When in the sun the hot red acres smoulder,
Down where the sweating gang its labour plies,
A girl flings down her hoe, and from her shoulder
Unslings her child tormented by the flies.

She takes him to a ring of shadow pooled
By thorn-trees: purpled with the blood of ticks,
While her sharp nails, in slow caresses ruled,
Prowl through his hair with sharp electric clicks.

His sleepy mouth plugged by the heavy nipple,
Tugs like a puppy, grunting as he feeds:
Through his frail nerves her own deep languors ripple
Like a broad river sighing through its reeds.

Yet in that drowsy stream his flesh imbibes
An old unquenched unsmotherable heat,
The curbed ferocity of beaten tribes,
The sullen dignity of their defeat.

Her body looms above him like a hill
Within whose shade a village lies at rest,
Or the first cloud so terrible and still
That bears the coming harvest in its breast.

On Some South African Novelists

You praise the firm restraint with which they write–
I'm with you there, of course:
They use the snaffle and the curb all right,
But where's the bloody horse?

Brewster Ghiselin (*Am. b. 1903*)

The Known World

With tiger pace and swinging head,
With gentle tread and turning grace
The walking stripes, the walking stripes
Of the mind stride in their too-little place.

But what if it escaped and walked
   In the green city?
There is no city, said the tiger mind.

There is the cage, the absolute bar,
Things as they are, that bind my rage
And wrap my claws, said the turning jaws
And prisoner eyes in their too-little place.

But what if it burst its world and ran
   To the snake-green jungle?
There is no jungle, sighed the striped mind.

New World

I

This is the land our fathers came to find:
They found the old world only, they found the known
Measures of the moods of their own minds:
The blue mountains' dying, the plain's surmise,
The bones and bountiful nakedness and thought
Of barbarous rock, and the green peace of earth;
They found the hostile forests of the heart.
This is the earth that should have had our love,
The loam that deepens by the deepening streams,
The mould that feeds the forest and the flower,
The musk and metal of a stony dust:
Three centuries the foothold of our life,
Never the roothold. How could we love a path?
A place of passage or unwilling rest.
In our blood's need we came from the cold cliffs
Up from the low shores and the smell of spray,
Westward from the duneland and the pines.
We crossed the silent rivers in the plains
And climbed the abrupt west, and fed our need
With dust and sun and the humming juniper,
And came to the broken coast, the barrier sea:
No earth, a pathless glimmering of waves.
No way behind us but the travelled lands,
No way before us but the lemmings' grave.

II

Now meanings bleed like dreams: the past is paling,
Asia, Europe, Africa, the islands.
Unmastered shadows over the known land
Come like the umbra to the mortal city.
Empty and naked, wading the languid grass
Of cactus kingdoms for the snake's possession,
We pace the measures of the heart's release,
We step the prelude of our blood's return.

III

But where is the new world? Only in time,
In moments of the individual mind:

Flashes and fragments: seen in the waste wall
And rock-ridge, heart-defining height and hawkfall
Isolations, and on joshua slopes
Blacked with burnt blocks of rock whose drummings answer
Bourdon and hornvoice, grooves and gold of hills,
Music to name our needs: too briefly seen
Between the many voices of the past:
Brief as the tinsel of the morning star;
Known as the swimmer knows the stumbling wave.
We turn in the bed at dawn, we hear the sunrise,
We hear the silence of the mockingbird:
Over the earth the sudden future comes
Like beauty to the body of one loved.
Then day surrounds us like an empty room.

Crotalus Rex

July's dry emperies have fired a snake
Into his secret crevice: a bulged belly,
One coil of coils on which the dragon walks
Bright and black, under a rock's swelling
Tenses the mirror-slanted light that looks.

It was not this creature you clubbed at twilight
On the naked plain. That one could merely coil,
Mouth wider than talk, tail tingling locustlike.
You remembered there no more than kill, killing
Heard nothing stranger than the last of delight.

He is like those that kept a kingly hoard
Under northern barrows–till shriveling like the griffins
They died of light. Here the inheritor hides.
What call, what footfall, perhaps of stolen Persephone,
Rings in his darkness that we cannot heed?

Of the New Prosody

The lost music returns: a few bring it,
Verse like the straining of pointed waves shoreward:
The stress of the blades, the cradle of the slack between,
Some rising, some falling, the whole
Tumult order and beauty, but above all
The power and the heartbeat and male music of our being.

R. P. Blackmur (*Am. b. 1904*)

From *Sea Island Miscellany*

V

One grey and foaming day
I looked from my lee shore
landwards and across the bay:
my eyes grew small and sore.

Low in the low sea-waves
the coastline sank from sight;
the viewless, full sea-graves
stood open like the night:

(sea waters are most bare
when darkness spreads her trawl,
the sea-night winds her snare
either for ship or soul).

Once along this coast
my fathers made their sail
and were with all hands lost,
outweathered in a gale.

Now from long looking I
have come on second sight,
there where the lost shores lie
the sea is breeding night.

IX

Mirage

The wind was in another country, and
the day had gathered to its heart of noon
the sum of silence, heat, and stricken time.
Not a ripple spread. The sea mirrored
perfectly all the nothing in the sky.
We had to walk about to keep our eyes
from seeing nothing, and our hearts from stopping
at nothing. Then most suddenly we saw
horizon on horizon lifting up
out of the sea's edge a shining mountain
sun-yellow and sea-green; against it surf

flung spray and spume into the miles of sky.
Somebody said mirage, and it was gone,
but there I have been living ever since.

XIV

Where shall I go then
if all I wish is going,
what must I know then
if all I need is knowing?

Sea answer is sea-deep.
Look at the sea and sleep,
ever waves are furling
over and under and back
furling unfurling still furling
over and deeper and black;
look at the sea look down
under the tidal sweep
dark waters are
a still black star
and drown

Views of Boston Common and Nearby

I

Sometimes, as if forewarned, before we die
colon bacilli half-eat us on the sly
and rot the rest. On Chardon Street this night,
between outrageous heart and sober eye,
the breadline slowly inchworms out of sight.

II

These are my enemies, the men who doze
the noontime out along the asphalt path,
pale pupae in the sun. My midnight grows,
as I lie small and naked in my bath,
like theirs, new prey to every wind that blows.

III

O beggar beggar try your art on me.
False insolence will strike on falser pride.
Be sure though that as palm leaves palm you see
that you no more than I can ever hide
our unsuccourable inward beggary.

IV

At every subway port a Sally stands
collecting for the poor a brief thanksgiving.
Observe her feet in newspapers, her hands
in woolen gloves. Such charity demands
even of dead hopes that they go on living.

V

The Burial Ground

Only the dead are faithful, for their trust,
despite the iron fence, the iron doors,
and living grass, like them makes vacant dust.
Lie still, lie quiet, O my ancestors:
you cannot rise, and we the living must.

Richard Eberhart (*Am. b. 1904*)

The Groundhog

In June, amid the golden fields,
I saw a groundhog lying dead.
Dead lay he; my senses shook,
And mind outshot our naked frailty.
There lowly in the vigorous summer
His form began its senseless change,
And made my senses waver dim
Seeing nature ferocious in him.
Inspecting close his maggots' might
And seething cauldron of his being,
Half with loathing, half with a strange love,
I poked him with an angry stick.
The fever arose, became a flame
And Vigour circumscribed the skies,
Immense energy in the sun,
And through my frame a sunless trembling.
My stick had done nor good nor harm.
Then stood I silent in the day
Watching the object, as before;

And kept my reverence for knowledge
Trying for control, to be still,
To quell the passion of the blood;
Until I had bent down on my knees
Praying for joy in the sight of decay.
And so I left; and I returned
In Autumn strict of eye, to see
The sap gone out of the groundhog,
But the bony sodden hulk remained.
But the year had lost its meaning,
And in intellectual chains
I lost both love and loathing,
Mured up in the wall of wisdom.
Another summer took the fields again
Massive and burning, full of life,
But when I chanced upon the spot
There was only a little hair left,
And bones bleaching in the sunlight
Beautiful as architecture;
I watched them like a geometer,
And cut a walking stick from a birch.
It has been three years, now.
There is no sign of the groundhog.
I stood there in the whirling summer,
My hand capped a withered heart,
And thought of China and of Greece,
Of Alexander in his tent;
Of Montaigne in his tower,
Of Saint Theresa in her wild lament.

'In a hard intellectual light'

In a hard intellectual light
I will kill all delight,
And I will build a citadel
Too beautiful to tell

O too austere to tell
And far too beautiful to see,
Whose evident distance
I will call the best of me.

And this light of intellect
Will shine on all my desires,
It will my flesh protect
And flare my bold constant fires,

For the hard intellectual light
Will lay the flesh with nails.
And it will keep the world bright
And closed the body's soft jails.

And from this fair edifice
I shall see, as my eyes blaze,
The moral grandeur of man
Animating all his days.

And peace will marry purpose,
And purity married to grace
Will make the human absolute
As sweet as the human face.

Until my hard vision blears,
And Poverty and Death return
In organ music like the years,
Making the spirit leap, and burn

For the hard intellectual light
That kills all delight
And brings the solemn, inward pain
Of truth into the heart again.

A Legend of Viable Women

I

Maia was one, all gold, fire, and sapphire,
Bedazzling of intelligence that rinsed the senses,
She was of Roman vocables the disburser,
Six couturiers in Paris sat to her hats.

There was Anna, the cool Western evidencer
Who far afield sought surrender in Sicily,
Wept under the rose window of Palma de Mallorca,
For she thought fate had played a child in her hand.

There was Betty, the vigorous; her Packard of Philadelphia
Spurred she; she was at home in Tanganyika,
Who delighted to kill the wild elephant,
Went Eastward on, to the black tigers of Indochine.

There was Margaret of Germany in America, and Jerusalem,
Of mild big eyes, who loved the blood of Englishmen,
Safely to voyage the Eros battlements of Europe,
Protectress to be of young and home, massive the mother.

There was Helen the blond Iowan, actress raddled,
Who dared learning a little, of coyness the teacher,
Laughing subtleties, manipulator of men, a Waldorf
Of elegant fluff, endangering to the serious.

There was Jeannette the cool and long, bright of tooth,
Lady of gay friendship, and of authentic song,
Beyond indifferent to the male seduction
Who to art pledged all her nature's want and call.

There was the sultry Emma of West Virginia,
Calf-eyed, velvet of flesh, mature in youngness,
Gentle the eager learner of nature's dimensions,
Always to her controlling womanhood in thrall.

There was Sue, the quick, the artful, the dashing,
Who broke all the laws; a Villager in her own apartment,
She was baffled by the brains of Plato and Aristotle,
Whose mind contained most modern conceptions.

There was Maxine, a woman of fire and malice
Who knew of revenge and subterfuge the skills,
A dominator, a thin beauty, a woman of arts and letters;
She of many psychological infidelities.

There was savage Catherine, who leaped into the underground,
Her female anger thrown at abstract injustice.
And she could match her wits with international man,
A glory, a wreaker, alas, who now posthumous is.

There was Madge the sinister, who raged through husbands
three.
She was somdel Groddeckian, a spendthrift of morality;
Existentialist that with men was dexterous
And would be in ten years after thirty, thirty-three.

There was a nun of modesty, who with service was heavy
And big with sweet acts all her sweet life long;
Enough wisdom she had for twenty ordinary women
Who percepted love as a breath, and as a song.

II

Where is Kimiko, the alabaster girl of Tokyo,
Living in bamboo among rustling scents and innuendoes,
To whom from Hatteras, the Horn, or Terra del Fuego
Returned as to a starry placement the sea voyager?

Where has time cyclic eventuated Vera
The proud noblewoman of Vienna? Among opera lights
She lived in a gaiety of possessive disasters,
Abandoned to the retaliatory shores of music.

Where is the naked brown girl of the nipa hut,
Under fronds, to Mount Mayon's perfect symmetry,
From the wash of the sea, looking from Legaspi?
Where in nature is this form, so brown, so fair, so free?

Where, who, sold into slavery in white Shanghai,
Walked and breathed in grace on Bubbling Well Road,
Subject to ancient sinuosities and patience,
Whose power was to represent unquestioning obedience?

Where is Hortense, the hermetically sealed?
Where is Hermione, haunted by heavens, who hesitated?
Where is Lucy, of bees and liberty the lover?
Where is Eustacia, of marionettes and Austrian dolls?

III

There were prideful women; women of blood and lust;
Patient women who rouged with scholarship's dust;
There were women who touched the soul of the piano;
Women as cat to mouse with their psychoanalyst.

There were women who did not understand themselves
Locking and unlocking misery's largess yearly;
Fabulous women who could not manumit the world
And babbled in syllables of the past and of money.

There were women committed to sins of treachery
The aborters of privilege and of nature's necessity;
There were the sinners in acedia of frigidity
Who negated even the grossness and grandeur of fear.

There were women without tenderness or pity
There were those more male than feminine men
Who rode the horses of their strident fury,
To whom subtle time made a passing bow.

There were independent women of society
Whose proud wisdom was their father's will.
There were mysterious women, Egyptian as a scarab
To whom scent and sound were a mysterious recall.

IV

Women are like the sea, and wash upon the world
In unalterable tides under the yellowing moon
Whose essential spirit is like nature's own,
To man the shadowy waters, the great room.

They come and go in tides of passion, and show
The melancholy at the heart of fullness,
Time crumples them, these vessels of the generations
Are crushed on the rocks as the green sea urchins.

They are the flesh in its rich, watery symbol,
A summer in July under the tenderest moon,
An island in the sea invincible to touch,
A refuge in man against refulgent ideation.

Women have gone where roll the sea bells
In the long, slow, the wide and the clear waters;
Their flesh which is our love and our loss
Has become the waste waters of the ocean swell.

They are the mothers of man's intelligence
To whom he is held by umbilical time,
And far though he roam, to treat with imagination,
He is brought home to her, as she brings a child.

C. Day Lewis (*Br. b. 1904*)

From *A Time to Dance:*
The Flight

Sing we the two lieutenants, Parer and M'Intosh,
After the War wishing to hie them home to Australia,
Planned they would take a high way, a hazardous crazy air-
way:
Death their foregone conclusion, a flight headlong to failure,
We said. For no silver posh
Plane was their pigeon, no dandy dancer quick-stepping
through heaven,
But a craft of obsolete design, a condemned D.H. nine;
Sold for a song it was, patched up though to write an heroic
Line across the world as it reeled on its obstinate stoic
Course to that southern haven.

On January 8, 1920, their curveting wheels kissed
England goodbye. Over Hounslow huddled in morning
mist
They rose and circled like buzzards while we rubbed our
sleepy eyes:
Like a bird scarce-fledged they flew, whose flying hours are
few–
Still dear is the nest but deeper its desire unto the skies–
And they left us to our sleeping.
They felt earth's warning tug on their wings: vain to advance
Asking a thoroughfare through the angers of the air
On so flimsy a frame: but they pulled up her nose and the
earth went sloping
Away, and they aimed for France.

Fog first, a wet blanket, a kill-joy, the primrose-of-morning's
blight,
Blotting out the dimpled sea, the ample welcome of land,
The gay glance from the bright
Cliff-face behind, snaring the sky with treachery, sneering
At hope's loss of height. But they charged it, flying blind;

They took a compass-bearing against that dealer of doubt,
As a saint when the field of vision is fogged gloriously steels
His spirit against the tainter of air, the elusive taunter:
They climbed to win a way out,
Then downward dared till the moody waves snarled at their wheels.

Landing at last near Conteville, who had skimmed the crest of oblivion,
They could not rest, but rose and flew on to Paris, and there
Trivially were delayed–a defective petrol feed–
Three days: a time hung heavy on
Hand and heart, till they leapt again to the upper air,
Their element, their lover, their angel antagonist.
Would have taken a fall without fame, but the sinewy framework the wrist
Of steel the panting engine wrestled well: and they went
South while the going was good, as a swallow that guide nor goad
Needs on his sunny scent.

At Lyons the petrol pump failed again, and forty-eight hours
They chafed to be off, the haughty champions whose breathing-space
Was an horizon span and the four winds their fan.
Over Italy's shores
A reverse, the oil ran out and cursing they turned about
Losing a hundred miles to find a landing-place.
Not a coast for a castaway this, no even chance of alighting
On sward or wind-smooth sand:
A hundred miles without pressure they flew, the engine fighting
For breath, and its heart nearly burst before they dropped to land.

And now the earth they had spurned rose up against them in anger,
Tier upon tier it towered, the terrible Apennines:
No sanctuary there for wings, not flares nor landing-lines,
No hope of floor and hangar.
Yet those ice-tipped spears that disputed the passage set spurs

To their two hundred and forty horse power; grimly they gained
Altitude, though the hand of heaven was heavy upon them,
The downdraught from the mountains: though desperate eddies spun them
Like a coin, yet unkindly tossed their luck came uppermost
And mastery remained.

Air was all ambushes round them, was avalanche earthquake
Quicksand, a funnel deep as doom, till climbing steep
They crawled like a fly up the face of perpendicular night
And levelled, finding a break
At fourteen thousand feet. Here earth is shorn from sight:
Deadweight a darkness hangs on their eyelids, and they bruise
Their eyes against a void: vindictive the cold airs close
Down like a trap of steel and numb them from head to heel;
Yet they kept an even keel,
For their spirit reached forward and took the controls while their fingers froze.

They had not heard the last of death. When the mountains were passed,
He raised another crest, the long crescendo of pain
Kindled to climax, the plane
Took fire. Alone in the sky with the breath of their enemy
Hot in their face they fought: from three thousand feet they tilted
Over, side-slipped away–a trick for an ace, a race
And running duel with death: flame streamed out behind,
A crimson scarf of, as life-blood out of a wound, but the wind
Of their downfall staunched it; death wilted,
Lagged and died out in smoke–he could not stay their pace.

A lull for a while. The powers of hell rallied their legions.
On Parer now fell the stress of the flight; for the plane had been bumped,
Buffeted, thrashed by the air almost beyond repair:
But he tinkered and coaxed, and they limped
Over the Adriatic on into warmer regions.
Erratic their course to Athens, to Crete: coolly they rode her

Like a tired horse at the water-jumps, they jockeyed her over seas,
Till they came at last to a land whose dynasties of sand
Had seen Alexander, Napoleon, many a straddling invader,
But never none like these.

England to Cairo, a joy-ride, a forty-hour journey at most,
Had cost them forty-four days. What centuried strata of life
Fuelled the fire that haled them to heaven, the power that held
them
Aloft? For their plane was a laugh,
A patch, brittle as matchstick, a bubble, a lift for a ghost:
Bolts always working loose of propeller, cylinder, bearer;
Instruments faulty; filter, magneto, each strut unsound.
Yet after four days, though we swore she never could leave the
ground,
We saw her in headstrong haste diminish towards the east–
That makeshift, mad sky-farer.

Aimed they now for Baghdad, unwritten in air's annals
A voyage. But theirs the fate all flights of logic to refute,
Who obeyed no average law, who buoyed the viewless channels
Of sky with a courage steadfast, luminous. Safe they crossed
Sinai's desert, and daring
The Nejd, the unneighbourly waste of Arabia, yet higher soaring
(Final a fall there for birds of passage, limed and lost
In shifty the sand's embrace) all day they strove to climb
Through stormy rain: but they felt her shorten her stride and
falter,
And they fell at evening time.

Slept that night beside their machine, and the next morning
Raider Arabs appeared reckoning this stranded bird
A gift: like cobras they struck, and their gliding shadows
athwart
The sand were all their warning.
But the aeronauts, knowing iron the coinage here, had brought
Mills bombs and revolvers, and M'Intosh held them off
While Parer fought for life–
A spark, the mechanic's right answer, and finally wrought
A miracle, for the dumb engine spoke and they rose
Convulsively out of the clutch of the desert, the clench of their
foes.

Orchestrate this theme, artificer-poet. Imagine
The roll, crackling percussion, quickening tempo of engine
For a start: the sound as they soar, an octave-upward slur
Scale of sky ascending:
Hours-held note of level flight, a beat unhurried,
Sustaining undertone of movement never-ending:
Wind shrill on the ailerons, flutes and fifes in a flurry
Devilish when they dive, plucking of tense stays.
These hardly heard it, who were the voice, the heavenly air
That sings above always.

We have seen the extremes, the burning, the freezing, the outward face
Of their exploit; heroic peaks, tumbling-to-zero depressions:
Little our graph can show, the line they traced through space,
Of the heart's passionate patience.
How soft drifts of sleep piled on their senses deep
And they dug themselves out often: how the plane was a weight that hung
And swung on their aching nerve; how din drilled through the skull
And sight sickened–so slow earth filtered past below.
Yet nerve failed never, heart clung
To height, and the brain kept its course and the hand its skill.

Baghdad renewed a propeller damaged in desert. Arid
Baluchistan spared them that brought down and spoilt with thirst
Armies of Alexander. To Karachi they were carried
On cloud-back: fragile as tinder their plane, but the winds were tender
Now to their need, and nursed
Them along till teeming India made room for them to alight.
Wilting her wings, the sweltering suns had moulted her bright
Plumage, rotten with rain
The fabric: but they packed her with iron washers and tacked her
Together, good for an hour, and took the air again.

Feats for a hundred flights, they were prodigal of: a fairest
Now to tell–how they foiled death when the engine failed
Above the Irrawaddy, over close-woven forest.
What shoals for a pilot there, what a snarled passage and dark
Shelves down to doom and grip
Of green! But look, balanced superbly, quick off the mark
Swooping like centre three-quarter whose impetus storms a
gap–
Defenders routed, rooted their feet, and their arms are mown
Aside, that high or low aim at his overthrow–
M'Intosh touched her down.

And they picked her up out of it somehow and put her at the
air, a
Sorry hack for such steeplechasing, to leap the sky.
"We'll fly this bloody crate till it falls to bits at our feet,"
Said the mechanic Parer.
And at Moulmein soon they crashed; and the plane by their
spirit's high
Tension long pinned, girded and guarded from dissolution,
Fell to bits at their feet. Wrecked was the undercarriage,
Radiator cracked, in pieces, compasses crocked;
Fallen all to confusion.
Their winged hope was a heap of scrap, but unsplintered their
courage.

Six weeks they worked in sun-glare and jungle damps,
assembling
Fragments to make airworthy what was worth not its weight
in air.
As a surgeon, grafter of skin, as a setter of bones tumbling
Apart, they had power to repair
This good for naught but the grave: they livened her engine
and gave
Fuselage faith to rise rejuvenated from ruin.
Went with them stowaways, not knowing what hazard they
flew in–
Bear-cubs, a baby alligator, lizards and snakes galore;
Mascots maybe, for the plane though twice she was floored
again
Always came up for more.

Till they came to the pitiless mountains of Timor. Yet these, untamed,
Not timorous, against the gradient and Niagara of air they climbed
Scarce-skimming the summits; and over the shark-toothed Timor sea
Lost their bearings, but shirked not the odds, the deaths that lurked
A million to one on their trail:
They reached out to the horizon and plucked their destiny.
On for eight hours they flew blindfold against the unknown,
And the oil began to fail
And their flying spirit waned–one pint of petrol remained
When the land stood up to meet them and they came into their own.

Southward still to Melbourne, the bourn of their flight, they pressed
Till at last near Culcairn, like a last fretted leaf
Falling from brave autumn into earth's breast,
D.H. nine, their friend that had seen them to the end,
Gave up her airy life.
The Southern Cross was splendid above the spot where she fell,
The end of her rainbow curve over our weeping day:
And the flyers, glad to be home, unharmed by that dizzy fall,
Dazed as the dead awoken from death, stepped out of the broken
Body and went away.

What happened then, the roar
and rave of waving crowds
That fêted them, was only
an afterglow of glory
Reflected on the clouds
where they had climbed alone,
Day's golden epilogue:
and them, whose meteor path
Lightened our eyes, whose great
spirit lifted the fog
That sours a doubtful earth,
the stars commemorate.

The Chrysanthemum Show

Here's Abbey Way: here are the rooms
  Where they held the chrysanthemum show–
Leaves like talons of greenfire, blooms
Of a barbarous frenzy, red, flame, bronze–
And a schoolboy walked in the furnace once,
  Thirty years ago.

You might have thought, had you seen him that day
  Mooching from stall to stall,
It was wasted on him–the prize array
Of flowers with their resinous, caustic tang,
Their colours that royally boomed and rang
  Like gongs in the pitchpine hall.

Any tongue could scorch him; even hope tease
  As if it dissembled a leer:
Like smouldering fuse, anxictics
Blindwormed his breast. How should one feel,
Consuming in youth's slow ordeal,
  What flashes from flower to flower?

Yet something did touch him then, at the quick,
  Like a premature memory prising
Through flesh. Those blooms with the bonfire reek
And the flaming of ruby, copper, gold–
There boyhood's sun foretold, retold
  A full gamut of setting and rising.

Something touched him. Always the scene
  Was to haunt his memory–
Not haunt–come alive there, as if what had been
But a flowery idea took flesh in the womb
Of his solitude, rayed out a rare, real bloom.
  I know, for I was he.

And today, when I see chrysanthemums,
  I half envy that boy
For whom they spoke as muffled drums
Darkly messaging, "All decays;
But youth's brief agony can blaze
  Into a posthumous joy."

Peter Quennell (*Br. b. 1905*)

Small Birds

Small birds who sweep into a tree
–A storm of fluttering, stilled as suddenly,
Making the light slip round a shaken berry,
Swinging slim sunlight twigs uncertainly,
Are moved by ripples of light discontent
–Quick waves of anger, breaking through the tree
Into a foam of riot–voices high
And tart as a sloe-berry.

The Divers

Ah, look,
How sucking their last sweetness from the air
These divers run upon the pale sea verge;
An evening air so smooth my hand could round
And grope a circle of the hollow sky
Without a harshness or impediment.

Look now,
How they run cowering and each unknots
A rag, a girdle twisted on his loins,
Stands naked, quivered in the cool of night.

As boldest lovers will tire presently,
When dawn dries up a radiance on the limbs,
And lapse to common sleep,
To the deep tumult of habitual dreams,
Each sighing, with loosened limbs, as if regretfully,
Gives up his body to the foamless surge.

Water combs out his body, and he sinks
Beyond all form and sound.
Only the blood frets on,
Grown fearful, in a shallow dissonance.

Water strains on his hair and drums upon his flank,
Consumes his curious track
And straight or sinuous path
Dissolves as swift, impermanent as light.

Still his strange purpose drives him, like a beam,
Like the suspended shaft of cavern-piercing sun;
And, hardier still,
With wavering hands divides the massive gloom,–
A vast caress through which he penetrates,
Or obscure death withdrawing
Veil upon veil,
Discovering new darkness and profounder terror.

"Consider you your loss,
For now what strength of foot or hand
Can take you by the narrow way you came
Through the clear darkness up again and up.
Watch a procession of the living days,
Where dawn and evening melt so soft together
As wine in water, or milk shed in water,
Filming and clouding into even dullness."

"Who weeps me now with pulse of noisy tears,
Who strikes the breast?
If I regret among the flowing weed,
My regret is
Not vocal, cannot pierce to hidden day,
Momentary, soon quenched, like a strangled flame."

Robert Penn Warren (*Am. b. 1905*)

From Kentucky mountain Farm

III. History Among the Rocks

There are many ways to die
Here among the rocks in any weather:
Wind, down the eastern gap, will lie
Level along the snow, beating the cedar,
And lull the drowsy head that it blows over
To startle a cold and crystalline dream forever.

The hound's black paw will print the grass in May,
And sycamores rise down a dark ravine,
Where a creek in flood, sucking the rock and clay,
Will tumble the laurel, the sycamore away.
Think how a body, naked and lean
And white as the splintered sycamore, would go
Tumbling and turning, hushed in the end,
With hair afloat in waters that gently bend
To ocean where the blind tides flow.

Under the shadow of ripe wheat,
By flat limestone, will coil the copperhead,
Fanged as the sunlight, hearing the reaper's feet.
But there are other ways, the lean men said:
In these autumn orchards once young men lay dead . . .
Grey coats, blue coats. Young men on the mountainside
Clambered, fought. Heels muddied the rocky spring.
Their reason is hard to guess, remembering
Blood on their black moustaches in moonlight.
Their reason is hard to guess and a long time past:
The apple falls, falling in the quiet night.

IV. The Cardinal

Cardinal, lover of shade . . .
Rock and gold is the land in the pulsing noon.
Lover of cedar, lover of shade . . .
Blue is the shadow of cedar on grey limestone,
Where the lizard, devout as an ikon,
Is carved on the stone, throat pulsing on lichen.

At the hour of noon I have seen
The burst of your wings displayed,
Vision of scarlet devised in the slumberous green
. . . Lover of cedar and shade.

What if the lizard, my cardinal,
Depart like a breath from its altar, summer southward fail?
Here is a bough where you can perch, and preen
Your scarlet that from its landscape shall not fade,
Lapped in the cool of the mind's undated shade,
In a whispering tree, like cedar, evergreen.

Bearded Oaks

The oaks, how subtle and marine,
Bearded, and all the layered light
Above them swims; and thus the scene,
Recessed, awaits the positive night.

So, waiting, we in the grass now lie
Beneath the languorous tread of light:
The grasses, kelp-like, satisfy
The nameless motions of the air.

Upon the floor of light, and time,
Unmurmuring, of polyp made,
We rest; we are, as light withdraws,
Twin atolls on a shelf of shade.

Ages to our construction went,
Dim architecture, hour by hour:
And violence, forgot now, lent
The present stillness all its power.

The storm of noon above us rolled,
Of light the fury, furious gold,
The long drag troubling us, the depth:
Dark is unrocking, unrippling, still.

Passion and slaughter, ruth, decay
Descent, minutely whispering down,
Silted down swaying streams, to lay
Foundation for our voicelessness.

All our debate is voiceless here,
As all our rage, the rage of stone;
If hope is hopeless, then fearless fear,
And history is thus undone.

Our feet once wrought the hollow street
With echo when the lamps were dead
At windows, once our headlight glare
Disturbed the doe that, leaping, fled.

I do not love you less that now
The caged heart makes iron stroke,
Or less that all that light once gave
The graduate dark should now revoke.

We live in time so little time
And we learn all so painfully,
That we may spare this hour's term
To practice for eternity.

Original Sin: A Short Story

Nodding, its great head rattling like a gourd,
And locks like seaweed strung on the stinking stone,
The nightmare stumbles past, and you have heard
It fumble your door before it whimpers and is gone:
It acts like the old hound that used to snuffle your door and
moan.

You thought you had lost it when you left Omaha,
For it seemed connected then with your grandpa, who
Had a wen on his forehead and sat on the veranda
To finger the precious protuberance, as was his habit to do,
Which glinted in sun like rough garnet or the rich old brain
bulging through.

But you met it in Harvard Yard as the historic steeple
Was confirming the midnight with its hideous racket,
And you wondered how it had come, for it stood so imbecile,
With empty hands, humble, and surely nothing in pocket:
Riding the rods, perhaps–or grandpa's will paid the ticket.

You were almost kindly then, in your first homesickness,
As it tortured its stiff face to speak, but scarcely mewed;
Since then you have outlived all your homesickness,
But have met it in many another distempered latitude:
Oh, nothing is lost, ever lost! at last you understood.

But it never came in the quantum glare of sun
To shame you before your friends, and had nothing to do
With your public experience or private reformation:
But it thought no bed too narrow–it stood with lips askew
And shook its great head sadly like the abstract Jew.

Never met you in the lyric arsenical meadows
When children call and your heart goes stone in the bosom;
At the orchard anguish never, nor ovoid horror,
Which is furred like a peach or avid like the delicious plum.
It takes no part in your classic prudence or fondled axiom.

Not there when you exclaimed: "Hope is betrayed by
Disastrous glory of sea-capes, sun-torment of whitecaps
–There must be a new innocence for us to be stayed by."
But there it stood, after all the timetables, all the maps,
In the crepuscular clutter of *always*, *always*, or *perhaps*.

You have moved often and rarely left an address,
And hear of the deaths of friends with a sly pleasure,
A sense of cleansing and hope, which blooms from distress;
But it has not died, it comes, its hand childish, unsure,
Clutching the bribe of chocolate or a toy you used to
treasure.

It tries the lock; you hear, but simply drowse:
There is nothing remarkable in that sound at the door.
Later you may hear it wander the dark house
Like a mother who rises at night to seek a childhood
picture;
Or it goes to the backyard and stands like an old horse cold in
the pasture.

From *To a Little Girl, One Year Old, in a Ruined Fortress*

It rained toward day. The morning came sad and white
With silver of sea-sadness and defection of season.
Our joys and convictions are sure, but in that wan light
We moved–your mother and I–in muteness of spirit past
logical reason.

Now sun, afternoon, and again summer-glitter on sea.
As you to a bright toy, the heart leaps. The heart unlocks
Joy, though we know, shamefaced, the heart's weather should
not be
Merely a reflex to solstice, or sport of an aggrieved equinox.

No, the heart should be steadfast: I know that.
And I sit in the late-sunny lee of the watch-house,
At the fortress point, you on my knee now, and the late
White butterflies over gold thistle conduct their ritual carouse.

In whisperless carnival, in vehemence of gossamer,
Pale ghosts of pale passions of air, the white wings weave.
In tingle and tangle of arabesque, they mount light, pair by pair,
As though that tall light were eternal indeed, not merely the summer's reprieve.

You leap on my knee, you exclaim at the sun-stung gyration.
And the upper air stirs, as though the vast stillness of sky
Had stirred in its sunlit sleep and made suspiration,
A luxurious languor of breath, as after love, there is a sigh.

But enough, for the highest sun-scintillant pair are gone
Seaward, past rampart and cliff borne, over blue sea-gleam.
Close to my chair, to a thistle, a butterfly sinks now, flight done.
My gold bloom of thistle, white wings pulse under the sky's dream.

The sky's dream is enormous, I lift up my eyes.
In sunlight a tatter of mist clings high on the mountain-mass.
The mountain is under the sky, and the gray scarps there rise
Past paths where on their appointed occasions men climb and pass.

Past grain-patch, last apron of vineyard, last terrace of olive,
Past chestnut, past cork grove, where the last carts can go,
Past camp of the charcoal maker, where coals glow in the black hive,
The scarps, gray, rise up. Above them is that place I know.

The pines are there, they are large, a deep recess,
Shelf above scarp, enclave of rock, a glade
Benched and withdrawn in the mountain-mass, under the peak's duress.
We came there—your mother and I—and rested in that severe shade.

Pine-blackness mist-tangled, the peak black above: the glade gives
On the empty threshold of air, the hawk-hung delight
Of distance unspooled and bright space spilled—ah, the heart thrives!
We stood in that shade and saw sea and land lift in the far light.

Now the butterflies dance, time-tattered and disarrayed.
I watch them. I think how above that far scarp's sunlit wall
Mist threads in silence the darkness of boughs, and in that shade
Condensed moisture gathers at a needle-tip. It glitters, will fall.

I cannot interpret for you this collocation
Of memories. You will live your own life, and contrive
The language of your own heart, but let that conversation,
In the last analysis, be always of whatever truth you would live.

For fire flames but in the heart of a colder fire.
All voice is but echo caught from a soundless voice.
Height is not deprivation of valley, nor defect of desire,
But defines for the fortunate, that joy in which all joys should rejoice.

Kenneth Rexroth (*Am. b. 1905*)

Lyell's Hypothesis Again

"An attempt to Explain the Former Changes of the Earth's Surface by Causes Now in Operation' – sub-title of Lyell: *Principles of Geology*

I

The mountain road ends here,
Broken away in the chasm where
The bridge washed out years ago.
The first scarlet larkspur glitters
In the first patch of April
Morning sunlight. The engorged creek
Roars and rustles like a military
Ball. Here by the waterfall,
Insuperable life, flushed
With the equinox, sentient
And sentimental, falls away
To the sea and death. The tissue
Of sympathy and agony
That binds the flesh in its Nessus' shirt;

The clotted cobweb of unself
And self; sheds itself and flecks
The sun's bed with darts of blossom
Like flagellant blood above
The water bursting in the vibrant
Air. This ego, bound by personal
Tragedy and the vast
Impersonal vindictiveness
Of the ruined and ruining world,
Pauses in this immortality,
As passionate, as apathetic,
As the lava flow that burned here once;
And stopped here; and said, "This far
And no further." And spoke thereafter
In the simple diction of stone.

II

Naked in the warm April air,
We lie under the redwoods,
In the sunny lee of a cliff.
As you kneel above me I see
Tiny red marks on your flanks
Like bites, where the redwood cones
Have pressed into your flesh.
You can find just the same marks
In the lignite in the cliff
Over our heads. *Sequoia*
Langsdorfii before the ice,
And *sempervirens* afterwards
There is little difference,
Except for all those years.
Here in the sweet, moribund
Fetor of spring flowers, washed,
Flotsam and jetsam together,
Cool and naked together,
Under this tree for a moment,
We have escaped the bitterness
Of love, and love lost, and love
Betrayed. And what might have been,
And what might be, fall equally

Away with what is, and leave
Only these ideograms
Printed on the immortal
Hydrocarbons of flesh and stone.

Vernon Watkins (*Br. b. 1906*)

The Collier

When I was born on Amman hill
A dark bird crossed the sun.
Sharp on the floor the shadow fell;
I was the youngest son.

And when I went to the County School
I worked in a shaft of light.
In the wood of the desk I cut my name:
Dai for Dynamite.

The tall black hills my brothers stood;
Their lessons all were done.
From the door of the school when I ran out
They frowned to watch me run.

The slow grey bells they rung a chime
Surly with grief or age.
Clever or clumsy, lad or lout,
All would look for a wage.

I learnt the valley flowers' names
And the rough bark knew my knees.
I brought home trout from the river
And spotted eggs from the trees.

A coloured coat I was given to wear
Where the lights of the rough land shone.
Still jealous of my favour
The tall black hills looked on.

They dipped my coat in the blood of a kid
And they cast me down a pit,
And although I crossed with strangers
There was no way up from it.

Soon as I went from the County School
I worked in a shaft. Said Jim,
"You will get your chain of gold, my lad,
But not for a likely time."

And one said, "Jack was not raised up
When the wind blew out the light
Though he interpreted their dreams
And guessed their fears by night."

And Tom, he shivered his leper's lamp
For the stain that round him grew;
And I heard mouths pray in the after-damp
When the picks would not break through.

They changed words there in darkness
And still through my head they run,
And white on my limbs is the linen sheet
And gold on my neck the sun.

The Fire in the Snow

White lambs leap. Through miles of snow
Across the muffled fields you go,
Frost-furled and gazing deep,
Lost in a world where white lambs leap.

Into a million eyes of light
You look, beneath that mask of white
Where lambs, wrinkled, without sound,
Bound in the air and print the ground.

You find through crystals white and wet
The buried breath of the violet,
And lost near sunken cairns of stone
Drone-suckled flowers that breed alone.

Your shadow, black on the white snow-field,
Covers the blades your mind revealed.
You linger where grey rocks are still
Covered by a drifted hill.

Your eyes, I know, now read the tract
Beneath snow, where the grain lies packed,
Nor can the Winter sun deceive:
Black shuttles give you their leaves to weave.

Crisp, where you touch the secret loom,
Snow, from the fire-blue sky and from
A black root where all leaves begin,
Flames with a white light on your skin.

Come in. The brilliant, beautiful
Sun has dropped, and the noon-cracked pool
Freezes back. Come, seek from night
Gloom's fire, where the unlit room is white.

I wait, intent, by the firelit stones
Strewn with chopped wood and fallen cones.
Come in, and watch with me in dark
The red spark eating the black bark.

Bright, from fields where the snow lies thick,
From sunk fields to the latch's click
You come; and your eyes, most watchful, glow,
Seeing in the firelight the brightness of snow.

Ophelia

Stunned in the stone light, laid among the lilies,
Still in the green wave, graven in the reed-bed,
Lip-read by clouds in the language of the shallows,
Lie there, reflected.

Soft come the eddies, cold between your fingers.
Rippling through cresses, willow-trunk and reed-root,
Gropes the grey water; there the resting mayfly
Burns like an emerald.

Haunting the path, Laertes falls to Hamlet;
He, the young Dane, the mover of your mountains,
Sees the locked lids, your nunnery of sorrows,
Drowned in oblivion.

Silvered with dawn, the pattern of the bridge-vault
Dancing, a light-skein woven by the stream there,
Travels through shade the story of your dying,
Sweet-named Ophelia.

Dense was your last night, thick with stars unnumbered.
Bruised, the reeds parted. Under them the mud slipped,
Yielding. Scuttling and terrified, the moorhen
Left you to sink there.

Few, faint the petals carried on the surface,
Watched by those bright eyes ambushed under shadow,
Mouse, bird and insect, bore you witness, keeping
Pace ever silent.

Here, then, you lingered, late upon the world's rim,
Matched here the princelike, stopped, and were confounded,
Finding that image altered in the water's
Bitter remembrance.

Passion recalls the tumult of your story,
Midnight revives it, where your name is printed;
Yet from the water, intimate, there echoes:
"Tell this to no man."

Bride-veils of mist fall, brilliant are the sunbeams,
Open the great leaves, all the birds are singing.
Still unawake in purity of darkness
Whiter than daylight

Dream the soft lids, the white, the deathly sleeping;
Closed are the lashes: day is there a legend.
Rise from the fair flesh, from the midnight water,
Child too soon buried.

The Sunbather

Inert he lies on the saltgold sand
And sees through his lids the scarlet sky.
The sea will run back if he breathes a sigh.
He can hide the sun with a roselit hand.

Loitering, he crossed the shingle-shore
Where his eyes looked back at the glint of shells.
With a quoit of stone he startled the bells
That sleep in the rocks' vibrating core.

Thought-blind to the chosen place he passed.
The seagulls rose, and circled, and dropped;
And there, throwing down his coat, he stopped.
He, touching the mould of the world, lies fast.

The noon-sun dodges around his knee.
The sand at his head now trembles pale.
The wind at his temples carries a tale
And before him flies the bewildered sea.

The sun, the sea and the wind are three
But he narrows them down with a dreaming eye.
With his hands at rest and his drawn-up thigh
He can imagine the sacred tree.

For a point of light has seeded all
And the beautiful seed has come to rest
For a sunblown moment in his breast,
A tree where the leaves will never fall.

"Come back. You were with us ages ago.
We have thrown your bones to the carrion gull.
To the dripping cave we have sold your skull,
And the delicate flower which was born to blow

"Is lost in the flow of the marble sea.
We have made seaweeds out of your locks,
And your star-white bones in the vaulted rocks
Lie broken and cold, like shells in the scree."

So Shades converse, and the world's dumb thud
Muffles their argument, Man, more strong,
Gives, to console their frightened song,
The beat that consoles them most, his blood.

The Feather

I stoop to gather a seabird's feather
Fallen on the beach,
Torn from a beautiful drifting wing;
What can I learn or teach,
Running my finger through the comb
And along the horny quill?
The body it was torn from
Gave out a cry so shrill,
Sailors looked from their white road
To see what help was there.
It dragged the winds to a drop of blood
Falling through drowned air,
Dropping from the sea-hawk's beak,
From frenzied talons sharp;
Now if the words they lost I speak
It must be to that harp

Under the strange, light-headed sea
That bears a straw of the nest.
Unless I make that melody,
How can the dead have rest?

Sheer from wide air to the wilderness
The victim fell, and lay;
The starlike bone is fathomless,
Lost among wind and spray.
This lonely, isolated thing
Trembles amid their sound.
I set my finger on the string
That spins the ages round.
But let it sleep, let it sleep
Where shell and stone are cast;
Its ecstasy the Furies keep,
For nothing here is past.
The perfect into night must fly;
On this the winds agree.
How could a blind rock satisfy
The hungers of the sea?

John Betjeman (*Br. b. 1906*)

The Cottage Hospital

At the end of a long-walled garden
  in a red provincial town,
A brick path led to a mulberry
  scanty grass at its feet.
I lay under blackening branches
  where the mulberry leaves hung down
Sheltering ruby fruit globes
  from a Sunday-tea-time heat.
Apple and plum espaliers
  basked upon bricks of brown;
The air was swimming with insects,
  and children played in the street.

Out of this bright intentness
  into the mulberry shade
Musca domestica (housefly)
  swung from the August light
Slap into slithery rigging
  by the waiting spider made
Which spun the lithe elastic
  till the fly was shrouded tight.
Down came the hairy talons
  and horrible poison blade
And none of the garden noticed
  that fizzing, hopeless fight.

Say in what Cottage Hospital
  whose pale green walls resound
With the tap upon polished parquet
  of inflexible nurses' feet
Shall I myself be lying
  when they range the screens around?
And say shall I groan in dying,
  as I twist the sweaty sheet?
Or gasp for breath uncrying,
  as I feel my senses drown'd
While the air is swimming with insects
  and children play in the street?

St. Saviour's, Aberdeen Park, Highbury, London, N.

With oh such peculiar branching and over-reaching of wire
  Trolley-bus standards pick their threads from the London sky
Diminishing up the perspective, Highbury-bound retire
  Threads and buses and standards with plane trees volleying by
And, more peculiar still, that ever-increasing spire
  Bulges over the housetops, polychromatic and high.

Stop the trolley-bus, stop. And here, where the roads unite
  Of weariest worn-out London–no cigarettes, no beer,
No repairs undertaken, nothing in stock–alight;
  For over the waste of willow-herb, look at her, sailing clear,
A great Victorian church, tall, unbroken and bright
  In a sun that's setting in Willesden and saturating us here.

These were the streets my parents knew when they loved and won–
The brougham that crunched the gravel, the laurel-girt paths that wind,
Geranium-beds for the lawn, Venetian blinds for the sun,
A separate tradesman's entrance, straw in the mews behind,
Just in the four-mile radius where hackney carriages run,
Solid Italianate houses for the solid commercial mind.

These were the streets they knew; and I, by descent, belong
To these tall neglected houses divided into flats.
Only the church remains, where carriages used to throng
And my mother stepped out in flounces and my father stepped out in spats
To shadowy stained-glass matins or gas-lit evensong
And back in a country quiet with doffing of chimney hats.

Great red church of my parents, cruciform crossing they knew–
Over these same encaustics they and their parents trod
Bound through a red-brick transept for a once familiar pew
Where the organ set them singing and the sermon let them nod
And up this coloured brickwork the same long shadows grew
As these in the stencilled chancel where I kneel in the Presence of God.

Wonder beyond Time's wonders, that Bread so white and small
Veiled in golden curtains, too mighty for men to see,
Is the Power which sends the shadows up this polychrome wall,
Is God who created the present, the chain-smoking millions and me;
Beyond the throb of the engines is the throbbing heart of all–
Christ, at this Highbury altar, I offer myself to Thee.

Before Invasion, 1940

Still heavy with may, and the sky ready to fall,
Meadows buttercup high, shed and chicken and wire?
And here where the wind leans on a sycamore silver wall,
Are you still taller than sycamores, gallant Victorian spire?

Still fairly intact, and demolishing squads about,
Bracketed station lamp with your oil-light taken away?
Weep, flowering currant, while your bitter cascades are out,
Plant of an age of railways, for flowering into today!

Sunday Afternoon Service in St. Enodoc Church, Cornwall

Come on! come on! This hillock hides the spire,
Now that one and now none. As winds about
The burnished path through lady's-finger, thyme,
And bright varieties of saxifrage,
So grows the tinny tenor faint or loud
And all things draw towards St. Enodoc.

Come on! come on! and it is five to three.

Paths, unfamiliar to golfers' brogues,
Cross the eleventh fairway broadside on
And leave the fourteenth tee for thirteenth green,
Ignoring Royal and Ancient, bound for God.
   Come on! come on! no longer bare of foot,
The sole grows hot in London shoes again.

Jack Lambourne in his Sunday navy-blue
Wears tie and collar, all from Selfridge's.
There's Enid with a silly parasol,
And Graham in gray flannel with a crease
Across the middle of his coat which lay
Pressed 'neath the box of his Meccano set,
Sunday to Sunday.
                                        Still, Come on! come on!
The tinny tenor. Hover-flies remain
More than a moment on a ragwort bunch,
And people's passing shadows don't disturb
Red Admirals basking with their wings apart.
   A mile of sunny, empty sand away,
A mile of shallow pools and lugworm casts,
Safe, faint and surfy, laps the lowest tide.
   Even the villas have a Sunday look.
The Ransome mower's locked into the shed.
"I have a splitting headache from the sun,"
And bedroom windows flutter cheerful chintz
Where, double-aspirined, a mother sleeps;
While father in the loggia reads a book,
Large, desultory, birthday-present size,
Published with coloured plates by *Country Life*,

A Bernard Darwin on *The English Links*
Or Braid and Taylor on *The Mashie Shot.*
  Come on! come on! he thinks of Monday's round–
Come on! come on! that interlocking grip!
Come on! come on! he drops into a doze–
Come on! come on! more far and far away
The children climb a final stile to church;
Electoral Roll still flapping in the porch–
Then the cool silence of St. Enodoc.

My eyes, recovering in the sudden shade,
Discern the long-known little things within–
A map of France in damp above my pew,
Grey-blue of granite in the small arcade
(Late Perp: and not a Parker specimen
But roughly hewn on windy Bodmin Moor),
The modest windows palely glazed with green,
The smooth slate floor, the rounded wooden roof,
The Norman arch, the cable-moulded font–
All have a humble and West Country look.
Oh "drastic restoration" of the guide!
Oh three-light window by a Plymouth firm!
Absurd, truncated screen! oh sticky pews!
Embroidered altar-cloth! untended lamps!
So soaked in worship you are loved too well
For that dispassionate and critic stare
That I would use beyond the parish bounds
Biking in high-banked lanes from tower to tower
On sunny, antiquarian afternoons.
  Come on! come on! a final pull. Tom Blake
Stalks over from the bell-rope to his pew
Just as he slopes about the windy cliffs
Looking for wreckage in a likely tide,
Nor gives the Holy Table glance or nod.
A rattle as red baize is drawn aside,
Miss Rhoda Poulden pulls the tremolo,
The oboe, flute and vox humana stops;
A Village Voluntary fills the air
And ceases suddenly as it began,
Save for one oboe faintly humming on,
As slow the weary clergyman subsides

Tired with his bike-ride from the parish church.
He runs his hands once, twice, across his face
"Dearly beloved . . ." and a bumble-bee
Zooms itself free into the churchyard sun
And so my thoughts this happy Sabbathtide.
Where deep cliffs loom enormous, where cascade
Mesembryanthemum and stone-crop drown,
Where the gull looks no larger than a lark
Hung midway twixt the cliff-top and the sand
Sun-shadowed valleys roll along the sea.
Forced by the backwash, see the nearest wave
Rise to a wall of huge, translucent green
And crumble into spray along the top
Blown seaward by the land-breeze. Now she breaks
And in an arch of thunder plunges down
To burst and tumble, foam on top of foam,
Criss-crossing, baffled, sucked and shot again,
A waterfall of whiteness, down a rock,
Without a source but roller's furthest reach:
And tufts of sea-pink, high and dry for years,
Are flooded out of ledges, boulders seem
No bigger than a pebble washed about
In this tremendous tide. Oh kindly slate!
To give me shelter in this crevice dry.
These shivering stalks of bent-grass, lucky plant,
Have better chance than I to last the storm.
Oh kindly slate of these unaltered cliffs,
Firm, barren substrate of our windy fields!
Oh lichened slate in walls, they knew your worth
Who raised you up to make this House of God!
What faith was his, that dim, that Cornish saint,
Small rushlight of a long-forgotten church,
Who lived with God on this unfriendly shore,
Who knew He made the Atlantic and the stones
And destined seamen here to end their lives
Dashed on a rock, rolled over in the surf,
And not one hair forgotten. Now they lie
In centuries of sand beside the church.
Less pitiable are they than the corpse
Of a large golfer, only four weeks dead,

This sunlit and sea-distant afternoon.
"Praise ye the Lord!" and in another key
The Lord's name by harmonium be praised.
"The Second Evening and the Fourteenth Psalm."

Indoor Games near Newbury

In among the silver birches winding ways of tarmac wander
And the signs to Bussock Bottom, Tussock Wood and Windy Brake,
Gabled lodges, tile-hung churches, catch the lights of our Lagonda
As we drive to Wendy's party, lemon curd and Christmas cake.
Rich the makes of motor whirring, past the pine-plantation purring
Come up, Hupmobile, Delage!
Short the way your chauffeurs travel, crunching over private gravel
Each from out his warm garáge.

Oh but Wendy, when the carpet yielded to my indoor pumps
There you stood, your gold hair streaming, handsome in the hall-light gleaming
There you looked and there you led me off into the game of clumps
Then the new Victrola playing and your funny uncle saying
"Choose your partners for a fox-trot! Dance until its *tea* o'clock!
"Come on, young 'uns, foot it featly!" Was it chance that paired us neatly,
I, who loved you so completely,
You, who pressed me closely to you, hard against your party frock?

"Meet me when you've finished eating!" So we met and no one found us.
Oh that dark and furry cupboard while the rest played hide and seek!
Holding hands our two hearts beating in the bedroom silence round us,

Holding hands and hardly hearing sudden footstep, thud
and shriek.
Love that lay too deep for kissing–"Where *is* Wendy?
Wendy's missing!"
Love so pure it *had* to end,
Love so strong that I was frighten'd when you gripped my
fingers tight and
Hugging, whispered "I'm your friend."

Good-bye Wendy! Send the fairies, pinewood elf and larch
tree gnome,
Spingle-spangled stars are peeping at the lush Lagonda
creeping
Down the winding ways of tarmac to the leaded lights of home.
There, among the silver birches, all the bells of all the
churches
Sounded in the bath-waste running out into the frosty air.
Wendy speeded my undressing, Wendy is the sheet's
caressing
Wendy bending gives a blessing,
Holds me as I drift to dreamland, safe inside my slumberwear.

Ronald Bottrall (*Br. b. 1906*)

Rondeau

(to Edith Sitwell)

Homage to change that scatters the poppy seed
Not for oblivion but like a bright bead
To freshen green corn. Cherish the gillyflower,
Rich topaz or tawny velvet-dropped in shower,
The dewlapped strawberry rolling its sleepy head.

From this graying sphere leap hart-like as flame freed
From inert coal, glow airily with the speed
Of a fritillary circling with its wooer.
Homage to change!

Be thrift, be honesty, be strewn sea-weed,
Look with a glow-worm's eye, grow as a reed
In music; branch, counterpoint, mutate. Tower
As falcon, fall in rose-petals. Honey-hour
It is when hiving brain-cells in us breed
Homage to change.

William Empson (*Br. b. 1906*)

This Last Pain

This last pain for the damned the Fathers found:
"They knew the bliss with which they were not crowned."
Such, but on earth, let me foretell,
Is all, of heaven or of hell.

Man, as the prying housemaid of the soul,
May know her happiness by eye to hole:
He's safe; the key is lost; he knows
Door will not open, nor hole close.

"What is conceivable can happen too,"
Said Wittgenstein, who had not dreamt of you;
But wisely; if we worked it long
We should forget where it was wrong.

Those thorns are crowns which, woven into knots,
Crackle under and soon boil fool's pots;
And no man's watching, wise and long,
Would ever stare them into song.

Thorns burn to a consistent ash, like man;
A splendid cleanser for the frying-pan:
And those who leap from pan to fire
Should this brave opposite admire.

All those large dreams by which men long live well
Are magic-lanterned on the smoke of hell;
This then is real, I have implied,
A painted, small, transparent slide.

These the inventive can hand-paint at leisure,
Or most emporia would stock our measure;
  And feasting in their dappled shade
  We should forget how they were made.

Feign then what's by a decent tact believed
And act that state is only so conceived,
  And build an edifice of form
  For house where phantoms may keep warm.

Imagine, then, by miracle, with me,
(Ambiguous gifts, as what gods give must be)
  What could not possibly be there,
  And learn a style from a despair.

Note on Local Flora

There is a tree native in Turkestan,
Or further east towards the Tree of Heaven,
Whose hard cold cones, not being wards to time,
Will leave their mother only for good cause;
Will ripen only in a forest fire;
Wait, to be fathered as was Bacchus once,
Through men's long lives, that image of time's end.
I knew the Phoenix was a vegetable.
So Semele desired her deity
As this in Kew thirsts for the Red Dawn.

The World's End

"Fly with me then to all's and the world's end
And plumb for safety down the gaps of stars;
Let the last gulf or topless cliff befriend,
What tyrant there our variance debars?"

Alas, how hope for freedom, no bars bind;
Space is like earth, rounded, a padded cell;
Plumb the stars' depth, your lead bumps you behind;
Blind Satan's voice rattled the whole of Hell.

On cushioned air what is such metal worth
To pierce to the gulf that lies so snugly curled?
Each tangent plain touches one top of earth,
Each point in one direction ends the world.

Apple of knowledge and forgetful mere
From Tantalus too differential bend.
The shadow clings. The world's end is here.
This place's curvature precludes its end.

Camping Out

And now she cleans her teeth into the lake:
Gives it (God's grace) for her own bounty's sake
What morning's pale and the crisp mist debars:
Its glass of the divine (that Will could break)
Restores, beyond Nature: or lets Heaven take
(Itself being dimmed) her pattern, who half awake
Milks between rocks a straddled sky of stars.

Soap tension the star pattern magnifies.
Smoothly Madonna through-assumes the skies
Whose vaults are opened to achieve the Lord.
No, it is we soaring explore galaxies,
Our bullet boat light's speed by thousands flies.
Who moves so among stars their frame unties;
See where they blur, and die, and are outsoared.

Arachne

Twixt devil and deep sea, man hacks his caves;
Birth, death; one, many; what is true, and seems;
Earth's vast hot iron, cold space's empty waves:

King spider, walks the velvet roof of streams:
Must bird and fish, must god and beast avoid:
Dance, like nine angels, on pin-point extremes.

His gleaming bubble between void and void,
Tribe-membrane, that by mutual tension stands,
Earth's surface film, is at a breath destroyed.

Bubbles gleam brightest with least depth of lands
But two is least can with full tension strain,
Two molecules; one, and the film disbands.

We two suffice. But oh beware, whose vain
Hydroptic soap my meagre water saves.
Male spiders must not be too early slain.

Legal Fiction

Law makes long spokes of the short stakes of men.
Your well fenced out real estate of mind
No high flat of the nomad citizen
Looks over, or train leaves behind.

Your rights extend under and above your claim
Without bound; you own land in Heaven and Hell;
Your part of earth's surface and mass the same,
Of all cosmos' volume, and all stars as well.

Your rights reach down where all owners meet, in Hell's
Pointed exclusive conclave, at earth's centre
(Your spun farm's root still on that axis dwells);
And up, through galaxies, a growing sector.

You are nomad yet; the lighthouse beam you own
Flashes, like Lucifer, through the firmament.
Earth's axis varies; your dark central cone
Wavers, a candle's shadow, at the end.

The Beautiful Train

(A Japanese one, in Manchuria, from Siberia
southwards, September 1937)

Argentina in one swing of the bell skirt,
Without visible steps, shivering in her power,
Could shunt a call passing from wing to wing.

Laughing the last art to syncopate
Or counterpoint all dances in their turns,
Arbours and balconies and room and shade,
It lopes for home;
And I a twister love what I abhor,

So firm, so burdened, on such light gay feet.

W. H. Auden (*Am. b. 1907*)

Lay Your Sleeping Head, My Love

Lay your sleeping head, my love,
Human on my faithless arm;
Time and fevers burn away
Individual beauty from
Thoughtful children, and the grave
Proves the child ephemeral:
But in my arms till break of day
Let the living creature lie,
Mortal, guilty, but to me
The entirely beautiful.

Soul and body have no bounds:
To lovers as they lie upon
Her tolerant enchanted slope
In their ordinary swoon,
Grave the vision Venus sends
Of supernatural sympathy,
Universal love and hope;
While an abstract insight wakes
Among the glaciers and the rocks
The hermit's sensual ecstasy.

Certainty, fidelity
On the stroke of midnight pass
Like vibrations of a bell,
And fashionable madmen raise
Their pedantic boring cry:
Every farthing of the cost,
All the dreaded cards foretell,
Shall be paid, but from this night
Not a whisper, not a thought,
Not a kiss nor look be lost.

Beauty, midnight, vision dies:
Let the winds of dawn that blow
Softly round your dreaming head
Such a day of sweetness show
Eye and knocking heart may bless,
Find the mortal world enough;

Noons of dryness see you fed
By the involuntary powers,
Nights of insult let you pass
Watched by every human love.

O Where Are You Going?

"O where are you going?" said reader to rider,
"That valley is fatal when furnaces burn,
Yonder's the midden whose odours will madden,
That gap is the grave where the tall return."

"O do you imagine," said fearer to farer,
"That dusk will delay on your path to the pass,
Your diligent looking discover the lacking
Your footsteps feel from granite to grass?"

"O what was that bird," said horror to hearer,
"Did you see that shape in the twisted trees?
Behind you swiftly the figure comes softly,
The spot on your skin is a shocking disease?"

"Out of this house"–said rider to reader,
"Yours never will"–said farer to fearer,
"They're looking for you"–said hearer to horror,
As he left them there, as he left them there.

Canzone

When shall we learn, what should be clear as day,
We cannot choose what we are free to love?
Although the mouse we banished yesterday
Is an enraged rhinoceros today,
Our value is more threatened than we know:
Shabby objections to our present day
Go snooping round its outskirts; night and day
Faces, orations, battles, bait our will
As questionable forms and noises will;
Whole phyla of resentments every day
Give status to the wild men of the world
Who rule the absent-minded and this world.

We are created from and with the world
To suffer with and from it day by day:
Whether we meet in a majestic world
Of solid measurements or a dream world
Of swans and gold, we are required to love
All homeless objects that require a world.
Our claim to own our bodies and our world
Is our catastrophe. What can we know
But panic and caprice until we know
Our dreadful appetite demands a world
Whose order, origin, and purpose will
Be fluent satisfaction of our will?

Drift, Autumn, drift; fall, colours, where you will:
Bald melancholia minces through the world.
Regret, cold oceans, the lymphatic will
Caught in reflection on the right to will:
While violent dogs excite their dying day
To bacchic fury; snarl, though, as they will,
Their teeth are not a triumph for the will
But utter hesitation. What we love
Ourselves for is our power not to love,
To shrink to nothing or explode at will,
To ruin and remember that we know
What ruins and hyaenas cannot know.

If in this dark now I less often know
That spiral staircase where the haunted will
Hunts for its stolen luggage, who should know
Better than you, beloved, how I know
What gives security to any world,
Or in whose mirror I begin to know
The chaos of the heart as merchants know
Their coins and cities, genius its own day?
For through our lively traffic all the day,
In my own person I am forced to know
How much must be forgotten out of love,
How much must be forgiven, even love.

Dear flesh, dear mind, dear spirit, O dear love,
In the depths of myself blind monsters know
Your presence and are angry, dreading Love

That asks its images for more than love;
The hot rampageous horses of my will,
Catching the scent of Heaven, whinny: Love
Gives no excuse to evil done for love,
Neither in you, nor me, nor armies, nor the world
Of words and wheels, nor any other world.
Dear fellow-creature, praise our God of Love
That we are so admonished, that no day
Of conscious trial be a wasted day.
Or else we make a scarecrow of the day,
Loose ends and jumble of our common world,
And stuff and nonsense of our own free will;
Or else our changing flesh may never know
There must be sorrow if there can be love.

In Memory of W. B. Yeats

d. Jan. 1939

I

He disappeared in the dead of winter:
The brooks were frozen, the airports almost deserted,
And snow disfigured the public statues;
The mercury sank in the mouth of the dying day.
O all the instruments agree
The day of his death was a dark cold day.

Far from his illness
The wolves ran on through the evergreen forests,
The peasant river was untempted by the fashionable quays;
By mourning tongues
The death of the poet was kept from his poems.

But for him it was his last afternoon as himself,
An afternoon of nurses and rumours;
The provinces of his body revolted,
The squares of his mind were empty,
Silence invaded the suburbs,
The current of his feeling failed: he became his admirers.

Now he is scattered among a hundred cities
And wholly given over to unfamiliar affections;
To find his happiness in another kind of wood

And be punished under a foreign code of conscience.
The words of a dead man
Are modified in the guts of the living.

But in the importance and noise of tomorrow
When the brokers are roaring like beasts on the floor of the
  Bourse,
And the poor have the sufferings to which they are fairly
  accustomed,
And each in the cell of himself is almost convinced of his
  freedom;
A few thousand will think of this day
As one thinks of a day when one did something slightly unusual.
O all the instruments agree
The day of his death was a dark cold day.

2

You were silly like us: your gift survived it all;
The parish of rich women, physical decay,
Yourself; mad Ireland hurt you into poetry.
Now Ireland has her madness and her weather still,
For poetry makes nothing happen: it survives
In the valley of its saying where executives
Would never want to tamper; it flows south
From ranches of isolation and the busy griefs,
Raw towns that we believe and die in; it survives,
A way of happening, a mouth.

3

Earth, receive an honoured guest;
William Yeats is laid to rest:
Let the Irish vessel lie
Emptied of its poetry.

Time that is intolerant
Of the brave and innocent,
And indifferent in a week
To a beautiful physique,

Worships language and forgives
Everyone by whom it lives;
Pardons cowardice, conceit,
Lays its honours at their feet.

Time that with this strange excuse
Pardoned Kipling and his views,
And will pardon Paul Claudel,
Pardons him for writing well.

In the nightmare of the dark
All the gods of Europe bark,
And the living nations wait,
Each sequestered in its hate;

Intellectual disgrace
Stares from every human face,
And the seas of pity lie
Locked and frozen in each eye.

Follow, poet, follow right
To the bottom of the night,
With your unconstraining voice
Still persuade us to rejoice;

With the farming of a verse
Make a vineyard of the curse,
Sing of human unsuccess
In a rapture of distress;

In the deserts of the heart
Let the healing fountain start,
In the prison of his days
Teach the free man how to praise.

September 1, 1939

I sit in one of the dives
On Fifty-second Street
Uncertain and afraid
As the clever hopes expire
Of a low dishonest decade:
Waves of anger and fear
Circulate over the bright
And darkened lands of the earth,
Obsessing our private lives;
The unmentionable odour of death
Offends the September night.

Accurate scholarship can
Unearth the whole offence
From Luther until now
That has driven a culture mad,
Find what occurred at Linz,
Find what huge imago made
A psychopathic god:
I and the public know
What all schoolchildren learn,
Those to whom evil is done
Do evil in return.

Exiled Thucydides knew
All that a speech can say
About Democracy,
And what dictators do,
The elderly rubbish they talk
To an apathetic grave;
Analysed all in his book,
The enlightenment driven away,
The habit-forming pain,
Mismanagement and grief:
We must suffer them all again.

Into this neutral air
Where blind skyscrapers use
Their full height to proclaim
The strength of Collective Man,
Each language pours its vain
Competitive excuse:
But who can live for long
In an euphoric dream;
Out of the mirror they stare,
Imperialism's face
And the international wrong.

Faces along the bar
Cling to their average day:
The lights must never go out,
The music must always play,
All the conventions conspire
To make this fort assume

The furniture of home;
Lest we should see where we are,
Lost in a haunted wood,
Children afraid of the night
Who have never been happy or good.

The windiest militant trash
Important Persons shout
Is not so crude as our wish:
What mad Nijinsky wrote
About Diaghilev
Is true of the normal heart;
For the error bred in the bone
Of each woman and each man
Craves what it cannot have,
Not universal love
But to be loved alone.

From the conservative dark
Into the ethical life
The dense commuters come,
Repeating their morning vow;
"I *will* be true to the wife,
I'll concentrate more on my work,"
And helpless governors wake
To resume their compulsory game:
Who can release them now,
Who can reach the deaf,
Who can speak for the dumb?

Defenceless under the night
Our world in stupor lies;
Yet, dotted everywhere,
Ironic points of light
Flash out wherever the Just
Exchange their messages:
May I, composed like them
Of Eros and of dust,
Beleaguered by the same
Negation and despair,
Show an affirming flame.

Lady, Weeping at the Crossroads

Lady, weeping at the crossroads
Would you meet your love
In the twilight with his greyhounds,
And the hawk on his glove?

Bribe the birds then on the branches,
Bribe them to be dumb,
Stare the hot sun out of heaven
That the night may come.

Starless are the nights of travel,
Bleak the winter wind;
Run with terror all before you
And regret behind.

Run until you hear the ocean's
Everlasting cry;
Deep though it may be and bitter
You must drink it dry.

Wear out patience in the lowest
Dungeons of the sea,
Searching through the stranded shipwrecks
For the golden key.

Push on to the world's end, pay the
Dread guard with a kiss;
Cross the rotten bridge that totters
Over the abyss.

There stands the deserted castle
Ready to explore;
Enter, climb the marble staircase
Open the locked door.

Cross the silent empty ballroom,
Doubt and danger past;
Blow the cobwebs from the mirror
See yourself at last.

Put your hand behind the wainscot,
You have done your part;
Find the penknife there and plunge it
Into your false heart.

In Praise of Limestone

If it form the one landscape that we the inconstant ones
  Are consistently homesick for, this is chiefly
Because it dissolves in water. Mark these rounded slopes
  With their surface fragrance of thyme and beneath
A secret system of caves and conduits; hear these springs
  That spurt out everywhere with a chuckle
Each filling a private pool for its fish and carving
  Its own little ravine whose cliffs entertain
The butterfly and the lizard; examine this region
  Of short distances and definite places:
What could be more like Mother or a fitter background
  For her son, for the nude young male who lounges
Against a rock displaying his dildo, never doubting
  That for all his faults he is loved, whose works are but
Extensions of his power to charm? From weathered outcrop
  To hill-top temple, from appearing waters to
Conspicuous fountains, from a wild to a formal vineyard,
  Are ingenious but short steps that a child's wish
To receive more attention than his brothers, whether
  By pleasing or teasing, can easily take.

Watch, then, the band of rivals as they climb up and down
  Their steep stone gennels in twos and threes, sometimes
Arm in arm, but never, thank God, in step; or engaged
  On the shady side of a square at midday in
Voluble discourse, knowing each other too well to think
  There are any important secrets, unable
To conceive a god whose temper-tantrums are moral
  And not to be pacified by a clever line
Or a good lay: for, accustomed to a stone that responds,
  They have never had to veil their faces in awe
Of a crater whose blazing fury could not be fixed;
  Adjusted to the local needs of valleys
Where everything can be touched or reached by walking,
  Their eyes have never looked into infinite space
Through the lattice-work of a nomad's comb; born lucky,
  Their legs have never encountered the fungi
And insects of the jungle, the monstrous forms and lives
  With which we have nothing, we like to hope, in common.

So, when one of them goes to the bad, the way his mind works
  Remains comprehensible: to become a pimp
Or deal in fake jewelry or ruin a fine tenor voice
  For effects that bring down the house could happen to all
But the best and the worst of us . . .
                                        That is why, I suppose,
  The best and worst never stayed here long but sought
Immoderate soils where the beauty was not so external,
  The light less public and the meaning of life
Something more than a mad camp. "Come!" cried the granite
    wastes,
  "How evasive is your humor, how accidental
Your kindest kiss, how permanent is death." (Saints-to-be
  Slipped away sighing.) "Come!" purred the clays and
    gravels.
"On our plains there is room for armies to drill; rivers
  Wait to be tamed and slaves to construct you a tomb
In the grand manner: soft as the earth is mankind and both
  Need to be altered." (Intendant Caesars rose and
Left, slamming the door.) But the really reckless were fetched
  By an older colder voice, the oceanic whisper:
"I am the solitude that asks and promises nothing;
  That is how I shall set you free. There is no love;
There are only the various envies, all of them sad."

  They were right, my dear, all those voices were right
And still are; this land is not the sweet home that it looks,
  Nor its peace the historical calm of a site
Where something was settled once and for all: a backward
  And dilapidated province, connected
To the big busy world by a tunnel, with a certain
  Seedy appeal, is that all it is now? Not quite:
It has a worldly duty which in spite of itself
  It does not neglect, but calls into question
All the Great Powers assume; it disturbs our rights. The poet,
  Admired for his earnest habit of calling
The sun the sun, his mind Puzzle, is made uneasy
  By these solid statues which so obviously doubt
His antimythological myth; and these gamins,
  Pursuing the scientist down the tiled colonnade

With such lively offers, rebuke his concern for Nature's
  Remotest aspects: I, too, am reproached, for what
And how much you know. Not to lose time, not to get caught,
Not to be left behind, not, please! to resemble
The beasts who repeat themselves, or a thing like water
  Or stone whose conduct can be predicted, these
Are our Common Prayer, whose greatest comfort is music
  Which can be made anywhere, is invisible,
And does not smell. In so far as we have to look forward
  To death as a fact, no doubt we are right: but if
Sins can be forgiven, if bodies rise from the dead,
  These modifications of matter into
Innocent athletes and gesticulating fountains,
  Made solely for pleasure, make a further point:
The blessed will not care what angle they are regarded from
  Having nothing to hide. Dear, I know nothing of
Either, but when I try to imagine a faultless love
  Or the life to come, what I hear is the murmur
Of underground streams, what I see is a limestone landscape.

E. J. Scovell (*Br. b. 1907*)

Shadows of Chrysanthemums

Where the flowers lean to their shadows on the wall
The shadow flowers outshine them all,
Answering their wild lightness with a deeper tone
And clearer pattern than their own
(For they are like flames in sun, or saints in trance,
Almost invisible, dissolved in radiance).

But space in that shadow world lengthens, its creatures
Fall back and distance takes their features;
The shadows of the flowers that lean away
Are blurred like milky nebulae;
And faint as though a ghost had risen between
The lamplight and the wall, they seem divined, not seen.

The dying, wild chrysanthemums, the white,
Yellow and pink are levelled in light;
But here in their shadows, tones remain, where deep
Is set on deep, and pallors keep
Their far-off stations, and the florets more
Subtly crisp their bright profiles, or are lost in the flower.

A Dark World

Under the pent-house branches the eight swans have come,
Into the black-green water round the roots of the yew;
Like a beam descending the lake, the stairway to their room.

The young swans in their tender smoke-grey feathers, blown
By wind or light to a faint copper smouldering,
Come docile with their parents still, three-quarters grown.

The old swans, built of light like marble, tower and scatter
Light in the dusk; but the young are mate to the yew's shade.
With their dim-green webbed feet like hands they part the
water

And wind among its loops and eyes of mercury,
Less visible than these they have wakened; and beside
The trellised roots they twine their necks as fine and grey.

In groups and in their fugue following one another
They turn to constant music their intercourse; and passing
With neck stretched on, with greyhound brow, brother by
brother,

Or slowlier drawing level, where their mute and furled
Wings touch they loose a feather to float on the night-face
Of water, with white stars to drift as a dark world.

Louis MacNeice (*Br. b. 1907*)

Sunday Morning

Down the road someone is practising scales,
The notes like little fishes vanish with a wink of tails,
Man's heart expands to tinker with his car
For this is Sunday morning, Fate's great bazaar;

Regard these means as ends, concentrate on this Now,
And you may grow to music or drive beyond Hindhead any-
how,
Take corners on two wheels until you go so fast
That you can clutch a fringe or two of the windy past,
That you can abstract this day and make it to the week of time
A small eternity, a sonnet self-contained in rhyme.

But listen, up the road, something gulps, the church spire
Opens its eight bells out, skulls' mouths which will not tire
To tell how there is no music or movement which secures
Escape from the weekday time. Which deadens and endures.

The Individualist Speaks

We with our Fair pitched among the feathery clover
Are always cowardly and never sober,
Drunk with steam-organs, thigh-rub and cream-soda
–We cannot remember enemies in this valley.

As chestnut candles turn to conkers, so we
Knock our brains together extravagantly
Instead of planting them to make more trees
–Who have not as yet sampled God's malice.

But to us urchins playing with paint and filth
A prophet scanning the road on the hither hills
Might utter the old warning of the old sin
–Avenging youth threatening an old war,

Crawling down like lava or termites
Nothing seduces, nothing dissolves, nothing affrights
You who scale off masks and smash the purple lights
-But I will escape, with my dog, on the far side of the Fair.

An Eclogue for Christmas

A. I meet you in an evil time.
B. The evil bells
Put out of our heads, I think, the thought of everything else.
A. The jaded calendar revolves,
Its nuts need oil, carbon chokes the valves,
The excess sugar of a diabetic culture
Rotting the nerve of life and literature;

Therefore when we bring out the old tinsel and frills
To announce that Christ is born among the barbarous hills
I turn to you whom a morose routine
Saves from the mad vertigo of being what has been.

B. Analogue of me, you are wrong to turn to me,
My country will not yield you any sanctuary,
There is no pinpoint in any of the ordnance maps
To save you when your towns and town-bred thoughts collapse,
It is better to die *in situ* as I shall,
One place is as bad as another. Go back where your instincts call
And listen to the crying of the town-cats and the taxis again,
Or wind your gramophone and eavesdrop on great men.

A. Jazz-weary of years of drums and Hawaian guitar,
Pivoting on the parquet I seem to have moved far
From bombs and mud and gas, have stuttered on my feet
Clinched to the streamlined and butter-smooth trulls of the élite,
The lights irritating and gyrating and rotating in gauze–
Pomade-dazzle, a slick beauty of gewgaws–
I who was Harlequin in the childhood of the century,
Posed by Picasso beside an endless opaque sea,
Have seen myself sifted and splintered in broken facets,
Tentative pencillings, endless liabilities, no assets,
Abstractions scalpelled with a palette-knife
Without reference to this particular life.
And so it has gone on; I have not been allowed to be
Myself in flesh or face, but abstracting and dissecting me
They have made of me pure form, a symbol or a pastiche,
Stylised profile, anything but soul and flesh:
And that is why I turn this jaded music on
To forswear thought and become an automaton.

B. There are in the country also of whom I am afraid–
Men who put beer into a belly that is dead,
Women in the forties with terrier and setter who whistle and swank
Over down and plough and Roman road and daisied bank,
Half-conscious that these barriers over which they stride

Are nothing to the barbed wire that has grown round their pride.
A. And two there are, as I drive in the city, who suddenly perturb–
The one sirening me to draw up by the kerb
The other, as I lean back, my right leg stretched creating speed,
Making me catch and stamp, the brakes shrieking, pull up dead:
She wears silk stockings taunting the winter wind,
He carries a white stick to mark that he is blind.
B. In the country they are still hunting, in the heavy shires
Greyness is on the fields and sunset like a line of pyres
Of barbarous heroes smoulders through the ancient air
Hazed with factory dust and, orange opposite, the moon's glare,
Goggling yokel-stubborn through the iron trees,
Jeers at the end of us, our bland ancestral ease;
We shall go down like palaeolithic man
Before some new Ice Age or Genghiz Khan.
A. It is time for some new coinage, people have got so old,
Hacked and handled and shiny from pocketing they have made bold
To think that each is himself through these accidents, being blind
To the fact that they are merely the counters of an unknown Mind.
B. A Mind that does not think, if such a thing can be,
Mechanical Reason, capricious Identity.
That I could be able to face this domination nor flinch–
A. The tin toys of the hawker move on the pavement inch by inch
Not knowing that they are w ound up; it is better to be so
Than to be, like us, wound up and while running down to know–
B. But everywhere the pretence of individuality recurs–
A. Old faces frosted with powder and choked in furs.
B. The jutlipped farmer gazing over the humpbacked wall.
A. The commercial traveller joking in the urinal.
B. I think things draw to an end, the soil is stale.

A. And over-elaboration will nothing now avail,
The street is up again, gas, electricity or drains,
Ever-changing conveniences, nothing comfortable remains
Un-improved, as flagging Rome improved villa and sewer
(A sound-proof library and a stable temperature).
Our street is up, red lights sullenly mark
The long trench of pipes, iron guts in the dark,
And not till the Goths again come swarming down the hill
Will cease the clangour of the pneumatic drill.
But yet there is beauty narcotic and deciduous
In this vast organism grown out of us:
On all the traffic-islands stand white globes like moons,
The city's haze is clouded amber that purrs and croons,
And tilting by the noble curve bus after tall bus comes
With an osculation of yellow light, with a glory like
chrysanthemums.

B. The country gentry cannot change, they will die in their shoes
From angry circumstance and moral self-abuse,
Dying with a paltry fizzle they will prove their lives to be
An ever-diluted drug, a spiritual tautology.
They cannot live once their idols are turned out,
None of them can endure, for how could they, possibly,
without
The flotsam of private property, pekinese and polyanthus,
The good things which in the end turn to poison and pus,
Without the bandy chairs and the sugar in the silver tongs
And the inter-ripple and resonance of years of dinner-gongs?
Or if they could find no more that cumulative proof
In the rain dripping off the conservatory roof?
What will happen when the only sanction the country-
dweller has–

A. What will happen to us, planked and panelled with jazz?
Who go to the theatre where a black man dances like an eel,
Where pink thighs flash like the spokes of a wheel, where we
feel
That we know in advance all the jogtrot and the cake-walk
jokes,
All the bumfun and the gags of the comedians in boaters and
toques,
All the tricks of the virtuosos who invert the usual–

B. What will happen to us when the State takes down the manor wall,
When there is no more private shooting or fishing, when the trees are all cut down,
When faces are all dials and cannot smile or frown–
A. What will happen when the sniggering machine-guns in the hands of the young men
Are trained on every flat and club and beauty parlour and Father's den?
What will happen when our civilisation like a long pent balloon–
B. What will happen will happen; the whore and the buffoon
Will come off best; no dreamers, they cannot lose their dream
And are at least likely to be reinstated in the new régime.
But one thing is not likely–
A. Do not gloat over yourself
Do not be your own vulture, high on some mountain shelf
Huddle the pitiless abstractions bald about the neck
Who will descend when you crumple in the plains a wreck.
Over the randy of the theatre and cinema I hear songs
Unlike anything–
B. The lady of the house poises the silver tongs
And picks a lump of sugar, "ne plus ultra" she says
"I cannot do otherwise, even to prolong my days"–
A. I cannot do otherwise either, tonight I will book my seat–
B. I will walk about the farm-yard which is replete
As with the smell of dung so with memories–
A. I will gorge myself to satiety with the oddities
Of every artiste, official or amateur,
Who has pleased me in my rôle of hero-worshipper
Who has pleased me in my rôle of individual man–
B. Let us lie once more, say "What we think, we can"
The old idealist lie–
A. And for me before I die
Let me go the round of the garish glare–
B. And on the bare and high
Places of England, the Wiltshire Downs and the Long Mynd
Let the balls of my feet bounce on the turf, my face burn in the wind

My eyelashes stinging in the wind, and the sheep like grey stones
Humble my human pretensions–
A. Let the saxophones and the xylophones
And the cult of every technical excellence, the miles of canvas in the galleries
And the canvas of the rich man's yacht snapping and tacking on the seas
And the perfection of a grilled steak–
B. Let all these so ephemeral things
Be somehow permanent like the swallow's tangent wings:
Goodbye to you, this day remember is Christmas, this morn
They say, interpret it your own way, Christ is born.

Valediction

Their verdure dare not show . . . their verdure dare not show . . .
Cant and randy–the seals' heads bobbing in the tide-flow
Between the islands, sleek and black and irrelevant
They cannot depose logically what they want:
Died by gunshot under borrowed pennons,
Sniped from the wet gorse and taken by the limp fins
And slung like a dead seal in a boghole, beaten up
By peasants with long lips and the whisky-drinker's cough.
Park your car in the city of Dublin, see Sackville Street
Without the sandbags in the old photos, meet
The statues of the patriots, history never dies,
At any rate in Ireland, arson and murder are legacies
Like old rings hollow-eyed without their stones
Dumb talismans.
See Belfast, devout and profane and hard,
Built on reclaimed mud, hammers playing in the shipyard,
Time punched with holes like a steel sheet, time
Hardening the faces, veneering with a grey and speckled rime
The faces under the shawls and caps:
This was my mother-city, these my paps.
Country of callous lava cooled to stone,
Of minute sodden haycocks, of ship-sirens' moan,
Of falling intonations–I would call you to book
I would say to you, Look;

I would say, This is what you have given me
Indifference and sentimentality
A metallic giggle, a fumbling hand,
A heart that leaps to a fife band:
Set these against your water-shafted air
Of amethyst and moonstone, the horses' feet like bells of
  hair
Shambling beneath the orange cart, the beer-brown spring
Guzzling between the heather, the green gush of Irish spring.
Cursèd be he that curses his mother. I cannot be
Anyone else than what this land engendered me:
In the back of my mind are snips of white, the sails
Of the Lough's fishing-boats, the bellropes lash their tails
When I would peal my thoughts, the bells pull free–
Memory in apostasy.
I would tot up my factors
But who can stand in the way of his soul's steam-tractors?
I can say Ireland is hooey, Ireland is
A gallery of fake tapestries,
But I cannot deny my past to which my self is wed,
The woven figure cannot undo its thread.
On a cardboard lid I saw when I was four
Was the trade-mark of a hound and a round tower,
And that was Irish glamour, and in the cemetery
Sham Celtic crosses claimed our individuality,
And my father talked about the West where years back
He played hurley on the sands with a stick of wrack.
Park your car in Killarney, buy a souvenir
Of green marble or black bog-oak, run up to Clare,
Climb the cliff in the postcard, visit Galway city,
Romanticise on our Spanish blood, leave ten per cent of pity
Under your plate for the emigrant,
Take credit for our sanctity, our heroism and our sterile want
Columba Kevin and briny Brandan the accepted names,
Wolfe Tone and Grattan and Michael Collins the accepted
  names,
Admire the suavity with which the architect
Is rebuilding the burnt mansion, recollect
The palmy days of the Horse Show, swank your fill,
But take the Holyhead boat before you pay the bill;

Before you face the consequence
Of inbred soul and climatic maleficence
And pay for the trick beauty of a prism
In drug-dull fatalism.
I will exorcise my blood
And not to have my baby-clothes my shroud
I will acquire an attitude not yours
And become as one of your holiday visitors,
And however often I may come
Farewell, my country, and in perpetuum;
Whatever desire I catch when your wind scours my face
I will take home and put in a glass case
And merely look on
At each new fantasy of badge and gun.
Frost will not touch the hedge of fuchsias,
The land will remain as it was,
But no abiding content can grow out of these minds
Fuddled with blood, always caught by blinds;
The eels go up the Shannon over the great dam;
You cannot change a response by giving it a new name.
Fountain of green and blue curling in the wind
I must go east and stay, not looking behind,
Not knowing on which day the mist is blanket-thick
Nor when sun quilts the valley and quick
Winging shadows of white clouds pass
Over the long hills like a fiddle's phrase.
If I were a dog of sunlight I would bound
From Phoenix Park to Achill Sound,
Picking up the scent of a hundred fugitives
That have broken the mesh of ordinary lives,
But being ordinary too I must in course discuss
What we mean to Ireland or Ireland to us;
I have to observe milestone and curio
The beaten buried gold of an old king's bravado,
Falsetto antiquities, I have to gesture,
Take part in, or renounce, each imposture;
Therefore I resign, good-bye the chequered and the quiet hills
The gaudily-striped Atlantic, the linen-mills
That swallow the shawled file, the black moor where half
A turf-stack stands like a ruined cenotaph;

Good-bye your hens running in and out of the white house
Your absent-minded goats along the road, your black cows
Your greyhounds and your hunters beautifully bred
Your drums and your dolled-up Virgins and your ignorant
dead.

Corner Seat

Suspended in a moving night
The face in the reflected train
Looks at first sight as self-assured
As your own face–But look again:

Windows between you and the world
Keep out the cold, keep out the fright;
Then why does your reflection seem
So lonely in the moving night?

Theodore Roethke (*Am. b. 1908*)

Dolor

I have known the inexorable sadness of pencils,
Neat in their boxes, dolor of pad and paper-weight,
All the misery of manila folders and mucilage,
Desolation in immaculate public places,
Lonely reception room, lavatory, switchboard,
The unalterable pathos of basin and pitcher,
Ritual of multigraph, paper-clip, comma,
Endless duplication of lives and objects.
And I have seen dust from the walls of institutions,
Finer than flour, alive, more dangerous than silica,
Sift, almost invisible, through long afternoons of tedium,
Dripping a fine film on nails and delicate eyebrows,
Glazing the pale hair, the duplicate gray standard faces.

Night Crow

When I saw that clumsy crow
Flap from a wasted tree,
A shape in the mind rose up:
Over the gulfs of dream
Flew a tremendous bird
Further and further away
Into a moonless black,
Deep in the brain, far back.

I Cry, Love! Love!

1

Went weeping little bones. But where?
Wasps come when I ask for pigeons.
The sister sands, they slipper soft away.
What else can befall?

Delight me otherly, white spirit,–
Some errand, obscure as the wind's circuit,
A secret to jerk from the lips of a fish.
Is circularity such a shame?
A cat goes wider.

What's a thick? Two-by-two's a shape.
This toad could waltz on a drum:
I hear a most lovely huzza:
I'm king of the boops!

2

Reason? That dreary shed, that hutch for grubby schoolboys!
The hedgewren's song says something else.
I care for a cat's cry and the hugs, live as water.
I've traced these words in sand with a vestigial tail;
Now the gills are beginning to cry.
Such a sweet noise: I can't sleep for it.
Bless me and the maze I'm in!
Hello, thingy spirit.

Mouse, mouse, come out of the ferns,
And small mouths, stay your aimless cheeping:
A lapful of apples sleeps in this grass.
That anguish of concreteness!
The sun playing on loam,
And the first dust of spring listing over backlots,–
I proclaim once more a condition of joy.
Walk into the wind, willie!

In a sodden place, all raps and knocks approve.
A dry cry comes from my own desert;
The bones are lonely.
Beginnings start without shade,
Thinner than minnows.
The live grass whirls with the sun,
Feet run over the simple stones,
There's time enough.
Behold, in the lout's eye,
Love.

3

I hear the owls, the soft callers, coming down from the hemlocks.
The bats weave in and out of the willows,
Wing-crooked and sure,
Downward and upward,
Dipping and veering close to the motionless water.

A fish jumps, shaking out flakes of moonlight.
A single wave starts lightly and easily shoreward,
Wrinkling between reeds in shallower water,
Lifting a few twigs and floating leaves,
Then washing up over small stones.

The shine on the face of the lake
Tilts, backward and forward.
The water recedes slowly,
Gently rocking.

Who untied the tree? I remember now.
We met in a nest. Before I lived.
The dark hair sighed.
We never enter
Alone.

The Dream

I

I met her as a blossom on a stem
Before she ever breathed, and in that dream
The mind remembers from a deeper sleep:
Eye learned from eye, cold lip from sensual lip.
My dream divided on a point of fire;
Light hardened on the water where we were;
A bird sang low; the moonlight sifted in;
The water rippled, and she rippled on.

II

She came toward me in the flowing air,
A shape of change, encircled by its fire.
I watched her there, between me and the moon;
The bushes and the stones danced on and on;
I touched her shadow when the light delayed;
I turned my face away, and yet she stayed.
A bird sang from the center of a tree;
She loved the wind because the wind loved me.

III

Love is not love until love's vulnerable.
She slowed to sigh, in that long interval.
A small bird flew in circles where we stood;
The deer came down, out of the dappled wood.
All who remember, doubt. Who calls that strange?
I tossed a stone, and listened to its plunge.
She knew the grammar of least motion, she
Lent me one virtue, and I live thereby.

IV

She held her body steady in the wind;
Our shadows met, and slowly swung around;
She turned the field into a glittering sea;
I played in flame and water like a boy
And I swayed out beyond the white sea foam;
Like a wet log, I sang within a flame.
In that last while, eternity's confine,
I came to love, I came into my own.

Stephen Spender (*Br. b. 1909*)

The Express

After the first powerful, plain manifesto
The black statement of pistons, without more fuss
But gliding like a queen, she leaves the station.
Without bowing and with restrained unconcern
She passes the houses which humbly crowd outside,
The gasworks, and at last the heavy page
Of death, printed by gravestones in the cemetery.
Beyond the town, there lies the open country
Where, gathering speed, she acquires mystery,
The luminous self-possession of ships on ocean.
It is now she begins to sing–at first quite low
Then loud, and at last with a jazzy madness–
The song of her whistle screaming at curves,
Of deafening tunnels, brakes, innumerable bolts.
And always light, aerial, underneath,
Retreats the elate metre of her wheels.
Steaming through metal landscape on her lines,
She plunges new eras of wild happiness,
Where speed throws up strange shapes, broad curves
And parallels clean like trajectories from guns.
At last, further than Edinburgh or Rome,
Beyond the crest of the world, she reaches night
Where only a low stream-line brightness
Of phosphorus on the tossing hills is light.
Ah, like a comet through flame, she moves entranced,
Wrapt in her music no bird song, no, nor bough
Breaking with honey buds, shall ever equal.

The Landscape near an Aerodrome

More beautiful and soft than any moth
With burring furred antennae feeling its huge path
Through dusk, the air liner with shut-off engines
Glides over suburbs and the sleeves set trailing tall
To point the wind. Gently, broadly, she falls,
Scarcely disturbing charted currents of air.

Lulled by descent, the travellers across sea
And across feminine land indulging its easy limbs
In miles of softness, now let their eyes trained by watching
Penetrate through dusk the outskirts of this town
Here where industry shows a fraying edge.
Here they may see what is being done.

Beyond the winking masthead light
And the landing ground, they observe the outposts
Of work: chimneys like lank black fingers
Or figures, frightening and mad: and squat buildings
With their strange air behind trees, like women's faces
Shattered by grief. Here where few houses
Moan with faint light behind their blinds,
They remark the unhomely sense of complaint, like a dog
Shut out, and shivering at the foreign moon.

In the last sweep of love, they pass over fields
Behind the aerodrome, where boys play all day
Hacking dead grass: whose cries, like wild birds,
Settle upon the nearest roofs
But soon are hid under the loud city.

Then, as they land, they hear the tolling bell
Reaching across the landscape of hysteria,
To where, louder than all those batteries
And charcoaled towers against that dying sky,
Religion stands, the Church blocking the sun.

W. R. Rodgers (*Br. b. 1909*)

Express

As the through-train of words with white-hot whistle
Shrills past the heart's mean halts, the mind's full stops,
With all the signals down; past the small town
Contentment, and the citizens all leaning
And loitering parenthetically
In waiting-rooms, or interrogative on platforms;

Its screaming mouth crammed tight with urgent meaning,
–I, by it borne on, look out and wonder
To what happy or calamitous terminus
I am bound, what anonymity or what renown.

O if at length into Age, the last of all stations,
It slides and slows, and its smoky mane of thunder
Thins out, and I detrain; when I stand in that place
On whose piers and wharves, from all sources and seas,
Men wearily arrive–I pray that still
I may have with me my pities and indignations.

The Fountains

Suddenly all the fountains in the park
Opened smoothly their umbrellas of water,
Yet there was none but me to miss or mark
Their peacock show, and so I moved away
Uneasily, like one who at a play
Finds himself all alone, and will not stay.

Robert Fitzgerald (*Am. b. 1910*)

The Painter

On bluish inlets bristling
Black in the tall north,
Like violet ghosts risen
The great fish swam forth,
And hoary blooms and submarine
Lightning in the cradling west
Lent summer her virid sheen
For the deep eye's interest.

A fleece on furry nothing,
A web of nightfall gray,
And a leaf tangled, mothing
In a well of yellow day,
Gave him a mile of corner
For a picture like a sea–
The sail and the dream sojourner
Outlined in ivory.

A lank hand had his master
To shear through light like tin
And bitter taste of plaster
When jackboots shook Berlin;
And wine clusters, Venetian,
And Burgundy and France,
Coral and carnelian
Bled white under his glance.

Now shall the man of dust live
And the green man of mould?
The whetted winter rustling
Snows on the Baltic cold,
Where ma'amselle and the trooper
Embraced against the fire
Aflame in the icy pupil;
And art unfleshed desire.

Celestine

I. The mother fragrant in her dust and grace,
With leaflike generations burning,
Was not that mother but a grander kind;
And they would know her bloomed, luxurious
turning
Through the deep ballroom's flawless glass:
A queen of iron port and accurate pace,
Who led, as with gigantic mind,
The partner facing her through night and noon,
Enthralled by power of pure mass,
Her sister, the naked moon.

II. Whose intensive rondure filling the spring
Night with radiance, or low
Each evening after reaping in the north,
Beautiful vessel of the afterglow,
All being quiet and all free,
In sexual love or restful lingering

At her most certain coming forth,
They smiled to name their goddess, like a swan
That in the nightstream silently
Took her perfection on.

III. The silver flame in the washed western air
Clear, shivering and bright,
Love's bridal star, would not come punctual there
For she was of those lamps that moved alone;
And they were sunlit worlds, to man's frail eyes
Reflecting the cyclonic furnace light
That still so distant shone,
The golden focus of their paradise;
Round whom in harmony of measured haste
They tended, and receded slower-paced.

IV. The spheres' artificer dreamed out his hour,
Yet this was not revealed;
Not to the watcher in the starlit tower,
Blinded with noting transits on his rim–
Though he had seen the wandering planet run,
Stay and return upon the heavenly field,
And had recorded him;
But to that intellect which is itself a sun,
Of pitiful light the source, and source of flame:
In Prague to Kepler the great vision came.

V. And radiance ruled the firmament.
The massy centers were outflown.
Out of that void of ghostly gossamers
The stars that shone upon the innocent
For chemic flares were known.
The icy constellations came and went,
But fastened upon alpha's height
The driving-clock astronomers
Brought nearer from the sprinkled vast
The blazing body of the night;
And still the whorls beyond, and still and still

In points of cepheids and laggard light
Beyond mindsight or lens, the last
Marches of that giant Past
Faint upon the intense invisible.

History

It is leviathan, mountain and world,
Yet in its grandeur we perceive
This flutter of the impalpable arriving
Like moths and heartbeats, flakes of snow
Falling on wool, or clouds of thought
Trailing rain in the mind: some old one's dream
Of hauling canvas, or the joy of swording
Hard rascals with a smack–for lordly blood
Circulates tenderly and will seep away;
And the winds blowing across the day
From quarters numberless, going where words go
And songs go, even the holy songs, or where
Leaves, showering, go with the spindling grasses.
Into this mountain shade everything passes.
The slave lays down his bones here, and the hero,
Thrown, goes reeling with blinded face;
The long desirèd opens her scorched armpits.
A mountain, so a gloom and air of ghosts,
But charged with utter light if this is light,
A feathery mass, where this beholding
Shines among lustrous fiddles and codices,
Or dusky angels painted against gold
With lutes across their knees. Magical grain
Bound up in splay sheaves on an evening field,
And a bawling calf butchered–these feed
The curious coil of man. A man, this man,
Bred among lakes and railway cars and smoke,
The salt of childhood on his wintry lips,
His full heart ebbing toward the new tide
Arriving, arriving, in laughter and cries,
Down the chaotic dawn and eastern drift,
Would hail the unforeseen, and celebrate
On the great mountain side those sprites,
Tongues of delight, that may remember him–

The yet unborn, trembling in the same rooms,
Breakfasting before the same gray windows,
Lying, grieving again; yet all beyond him,
Who knew he lived in rough Jehovah's breath,
And burned, a quiet wick in a wild night,
Loving what he beheld and will behold.

Solstitium Saeculare

Winter blows on my eaves,
And dry stalks nod in the snow
Pitted by dripping trees.

The strong sun, brought low,
Gives but an evening glare
Through black twigs' to-and-fro

At noon in the cold air.
A rusty windmill grates.
I sit in a Roman chair,

Musing upon Roman fates,
And make peace with Rome
While the solar Fury waits.

I hold my peace at home
And call to my wondering mind
The chaos I came from—

Waste sea and ancient wind
That sailing long I fought,
Unshriven and thin-skinned.

God knows why I perished not,
But made it here by grace
To harbor beyond my thought,

To the stillness of this place.
Here while I live I hold
Young hope in one embrace

With all the ruin of old,
And bless God's will in each;
And bless His word of gold

As far as heart can reach,
Turning the Apostle's page
Or Thomas, who would teach

Peace to the heart's rage.

Charles Henri Ford (*Am. b. 1910*)

(*Before a mob of 10,000 at Owensboro, Ky.*) *Plaint*

I, Rainey Betha, 22,
From the top branch of race-hatred look at you.
My limbs are bound, though boundless the bright sun
Like my bright blood which had to run
Into the orchard that excluded me.
Now I climb death's tree.

The pruninghooks of many mouths
Cut the black-leaved boughs.
The robins of my eyes hover where
Sixteen leaves feel that were a prayer:
Sixteen mouths are open wide,
The minutes, like black cherries,
Drop from my shady side.

Oh who is the forester must tend such a tree, Lord?
Do angels pick the cherry-blood of folk like me, Lord?

"*Baby's in jail; the animal day plays alone*"

Baby's in jail; the animal day plays alone,
tame as the animal baby behind the bars of the crib:
the cub whose nose has not yet dipped
in the reek of excitation,
whose claws have not unbound the hide of habit,
nor scratched at pride, the skin,
and tasted sensation's blood.
Baby will come to grief and love.
Visitors to the family zoo
do not go to see a vegetarian tiger.

If the clover's leaves are four,
good luck's just behind the door.
If your hand goes through a mirror,
the glass is dear, but bad luck's dearer.
Swipe a horsehair from his tail, drown it in a water pail:
it takes thirty days to make
horsehair turn into a snake.
You want a new dress, I do too.
You bite a butterfly, I'll chew a leaf.

Baby will come to love and grief.

Elizabeth Bishop (*Am. b. 1911*)

The Imaginary Iceberg

We'd rather have the iceberg than the ship,
although it meant the end of travel.
Although it stood stock-still like cloudy rock
and all the sea were moving marble.
We'd rather have the iceberg than the ship;
we'd rather own this breathing plain of snow
though the ships' sails were laid upon the sea
as the snow lies undissolved upon the water.
O solemn, floating field,
are you aware an iceberg takes repose
with you, and when it wakes may pasture on your
snows?

This is a scene a sailor'd give his eyes for.
The ship's ignored. The iceberg rises
and sinks again; its glassy pinnacles
correct elliptics in the sky.
This is a scene where he who treads the boards
is artlessly rhetorical. The curtain
is light enough to rise on finest ropes
that airy twists of snow provide.
The wits of these white peaks
spar with the sun. Its weight the iceberg dares
upon a shifting stage and stands and stares.

This iceberg cuts its facets from within.
Like jewelry from a grave
it saves itself perpetually and adorns
only itself, perhaps the snows
which so surprise us lying on the sea.
Good-bye, we say, good-bye, the ship steers off
where waves give in to one another's waves
and clouds run in a warmer sky.
Icebergs behoove the soul
(Both being self-made from elements least visible)
to see them so: fleshed, fair, erected indivisible.

Invitation to Miss Marianne Moore

From Brooklyn, over the Brooklyn Bridge, on this fine
morning,
please come flying.
In a cloud of fiery pale chemicals,
please come flying,
to the rapid rolling of thousands of small blue drums
descending out of the mackerel sky
over the glittering grandstand of harbor-water,
please come flying.

Whistles, pennants and smoke are blowing. The ships
are signaling cordially with multitudes of flags
rising and falling like birds all over the harbor.
Enter: two rivers, gracefully bearing
countless little pellucid jellies
in cut-glass epergnes dragging with silver chains.
The flight is safe; the weather is all arranged.
The waves are running in verses this fine morning.
Please come flying.

Come with the pointed toe of each black shoe
trailing a sapphire highlight,
with a black capeful of butterfly wings and bon-mots,
with heaven knows how many angels all riding
on the broad black brim of your hat,
please come flying.

Bearing a musical inaudible abacus,
a slight censorious frown, and blue ribbons,
   please come flying.
Facts and skyscrapers glint in the tide; Manhattan
is all awash with morals this fine morning,
   so please come flying.

Mounting the sky with natural heroism,
above the accidents, above the malignant movies,
the taxicabs and injustices at large,
while horns are resounding in your beautiful ears
that simultaneously listen to
a soft uninvented music, fit for the musk deer,
   please come flying.

For whom the grim museums will behave
like courteous male bower-birds,
for whom the agreeable lions lie in wait
on the steps of the Public Library,
eager to rise and follow through the doors
up into the reading rooms,
   please come flying.

We can sit down and weep; we can go shopping,
or play at a game of constantly being wrong
with a priceless set of vocabularies,
or we can bravely deplore, but please,
   please come flying.

With dynasties of negative constructions
darkening and dying around you,
with grammar that suddenly turns and shines
like flocks of sandpipers flying,
   please come flying.

Come like a light in the white mackerel sky,
come like a daytime comet
with a long unnebulous train of words,
from Brooklyn, over the Brooklyn Bridge, on this fine
      morning,
   please come flying.

At the Fishhouses

Although it is a cold evening,
down by one of the fishhouses
an old man sits netting,
his net, in the gloaming almost invisible,
a dark purple-brown,
and his shuttle worn and polished.
The air smells so strong of codfish
it makes one's nose run and one's eyes water.
The five fishhouses have steeply peaked roofs
and narrow, cleated gangplanks slant up
to storerooms in the gables
for the wheelbarrows to be pushed up and down
  on.
All is silver: the heavy surface of the sea,
swelling slowly as if considering spilling over,
is opaque, but the silver of the benches,
the lobster pots, and masts, scattered
among the wild jagged rocks,
is of an apparent translucence
like the small old buildings with an emerald
  moss
growing on their shoreward walls.
The big fish tubs are completely lined
with layers of beautiful herring scales
and the wheelbarrows are similarly plastered
with creamy iridescent coats of mail,
with small iridescent flies crawling on them.
Up on the little slope behind the houses,
set in the sparse bright sprinkle of grass,
is an ancient wooden capstan,
cracked, with two long bleached handles
and some melancholy stains, like dried blood,
where the ironwork has rusted.

The old man accepts a Lucky Strike.
He was a friend of my grandfather.
We talk of the decline in the population
and of codfish and herring
while he waits for a herring boat to come in.

There are sequins on his vest and on his thumb.
He has scraped the scales, the principal beauty,
from unnumbered fish with that black old knife,
the blade of which is almost worn away.

Down at the water's edge, at the place
where they haul up the boats, up the long ramp
descending into the water, thin silver
tree trunks are laid horizontally
across the gray stones, down and down
at intervals of four or five feet.

Cold dark deep and absolutely clear,
element bearable to no mortal,
to fish and to seals . . . One seal particularly
I have seen here evening after evening.
He was curious about me. He was interested in music;
like me a believer in total immersion,
so I used to sing him Baptist hymns.
I also sang "A mighty fortress is our God."
He stood up in the water and regarded me
steadily, moving his head a little.
Then he would disappear, then suddenly emerge
almost in the same spot, with a sort of shrug
as if it were against his better judgment.
Cold dark deep and absolutely clear,
the clear gray icy water . . . Back, behind us,
the dignified tall firs begin.
Bluish, associating with their shadows,
a million Christmas trees stand
waiting for Christmas. The water seems suspended
above the rounded gray and blue-gray stones.
I have seen it over and over, the same sea, the same,
slightly, indifferently swinging above the stones,
icily free above the stones,
above the stones and then the world.
If you should dip your hand in,
your wrist would ache immediately,
your bones would begin to ache and your hand would burn
as if the water were a transmutation of fire
that feeds on stones and burns with a dark-gray flame.

If you tasted it, it would first taste bitter,
then briny, then surely burn your tongue.
It is like what we imagine knowledge to be:
dark, salt, clear, moving, utterly free,
drawn from the cold hard mouth
of the world, derived from the rocky breasts
forever, flowing and drawn, and since
our knowledge is historical, flowing, and flown.

J. V. Cunningham (*Am. b. 1911*)

The Helmsman: An Ode

The voyage of the soul is simply
Through age to wisdom;
But wisdom, if it comes,
Comes like the ripening gleam of wheat,

Nourished by comfort, care, rain, sunlight,
And briefly shining
On windy and hot days,
Flashing like snakes underneath the haze.

But this, a memory of childhood,
Of loves forgotten,
And they who gave are still,
Gone now, irrevocable, undone.

O Penury, steadied to thy will,
I tread my own path,
Though Self-Respect, discreet,
Plucks at my arm as I pass down street:–

Querulous and pert! They tell in story
That for proud Ajax,
Vaingloriously self-slain,
Teucer set forth from his friends and kin;

He on the western shore of parting
  Pausèd to address them:
    "Comrades who have with me
Countless misfortunes endured, O mine!

"Brave friends, banish tonight dark sorrow!
  Set the white tables
    With garlands, lamps, with wine!
Drink! and, tomorrow, untravelled seas!"

So sailed guileful Odysseus, so sailed
  Pious Aeneas,
    And cloudless skies brought sleep,
Stilling th' unmasterable, surging deep –

The helmsman stilled, his sea-craft guiding.
  O too confiding
    In star and wind and wave,
Naked thou liest in an unknown grave!

Laurence Whistler (*Br. b. 1912*)

No Answer

In the slow lapse of unrecorded afternoon,
When nothing seems to change but history itself
Unfolding at the pace of clouds or even weeds,
The window murmurs lightly to the vacant room,
And seems as if it commented with mild surprise
On some arrival, timely or unique;
Slow by the rapid stream, perhaps, or quick in the slow skies.

Why does the window murmur – and to whom?
What notable event does it report
That's far above the heads of furniture,
Nor heeded by the absent-minded room?

Is it first cuckoo-fall? – the double word
Dropping like seed into the wood, instant with Spring?

Or is it rose-fall? – end of the first rose,
Spilled from the hand of Summer, pensively?

Perhaps first apple-fall? – scatter and thud,
And Autumn here that moment, cornucopia slanted?

Or is it only the first snow-fall? – one,
One, and then one, slid furtive down, as if
Winter himself had thought the moment haunted?

Windows look out of rooms at poetry,
That pours back through them, lyrical in birds,
Epic in weather, narrative in streams.
But they look only out, half-conscious of a being
Shadowed behind them, borrowing their eyes.

O window, when you murmur, "Do but look!",
Don't ask who listens now. Never inquire
Why soundlessness should grow into a habit,
Helpless and final as the dust.
Suppose
She may be resting yet in the great bed,
Tuned always to your accent, though her heart
Is listening miles away to mine. – Might she
Not lie so still? Never so long, so still?
Should there, long since, have come to you at least,
The flicking over of a page – at least
Her busy pencil, whispering word by word
The letter she would send – at very least
A sigh?
So would she sigh,
In the dark ages of the afternoon,
When you would draw her to some poetry
(Fall of the word, the rose, the fruit, the fleeting crystal),
So would she sigh a war away – since tears,
If tears were let, would rain away the world:
Sigh in the great bed for its emptiness,
The waste of poetry, the waste of years.

The Shape of a Bird

"Break off your argument,
Dearest of patient friends, with whom
I have turned this muted wood
To a long, carpeted room,
Hearing you always invent
New cures for a sickly mood.
Drop your eyes to the floor:
We have strolled, you see, by accident
To a corner we missed before.–
What do you see with your
Imaginative eye?"

"Feathers – a circle of grey:
Little arena empty of strife:
Some murdered ring-dove. Why?–
Very well! I see the way
Death is haunted by life:
A circle of feathers keeping
Vaguely the shape of a bird;
Though, at mere thought of a wind's creeping,
Each could be separately stirred,
The whole image blurred. –
What would you have me see?"

"A man and his children keeping
Vaguely the shape of a family still,
When the meaning is lost that she
Alone could give to that word.
Or again, that man alone,
Keeping by effort of will
The shape of the self she freed,
Like the shape of a lost, migratory bird.
With all coherence gone.
With moods that one by one
To the wind's humour succeed."

Lawrence Durrell (*Br. b. 1912*)

Alexandria

To the lucky now who have lovers or friends,
Who move to their sweet undiscovered ends,
Or whom the great conspiracy deceives,
I wish these whirling autumn leaves:
Promontories splashed by the salty sea,
Groaned on in darkness by the tram
To horizons of love or good luck or more love –
As for me I now move
Through many negatives to what I am.

Here at the last cold Pharos between Greece
And all I love, the lights confide
A deeper darkness to the rubbing tide;
Doors shut, and we the living are locked inside
Between the shadows and the thoughts of peace:
And so in furnished rooms revise
The index of our lovers and our friends
From gestures possibly forgotten, but the ends
Of longings like unconnected nerves,
And in this quiet rehearsal of their acts
We dream of them and cherish them as Facts.

Now when the sea grows restless as a conscript,
Excited by fresh wind, climbs the sea-wall,
I walk by it and think about you all:
B. with his respect for the object, and D.
Searching in sex like a great pantry for jars
Marked "Plum and apple"; and the small, fell
Figure of Dorian ringing like a muffin-bell –
All indeed whom war or time threw up
On this littoral and tides could not move
Were objects for my study and my love.

And then turning where the last pale
Lighthouse, like a Samson blinded, stands
And turns its huge charred orbit on the sands
I think of you – indeed mostly of you,
In whom a writer would only name and lose

The dented boy's lip and the close
Archer's shoulders; but here to rediscover
By tides and faults of weather, by the rain
Which washes everything, the critic and the lover.

At the doors of Africa so many towns founded
Upon a parting could become Alexandria, like
The wife of Lot – a metaphor for tears;
And the queer student in his poky hot
Tenth floor room above the harbour hears
The sirens shaking the tree of his heart,
And shuts his books, while the most
Inexpressible longings like wounds unstitched
Stir in him some girl's unquiet ghost.

So we, learning to suffer and not condemn
Can only wish you this great pure wind
Condemned by Greece, and turning like a helm
Inland where it smokes the fires of men,
Spins weathercocks on farms or catches
The lovers at their quarrel in the sheets;
Or like a walker in the darkness might,
Knocks and disturbs the artist at his papers
Up there alone, upon the alps of night.

Anne Ridler (*Br. b. 1912*)

Zennor

(for J. L. and L. B. Hammond)

Seen from these cliffs the sea circles slowly.
Ponderous and blue today, with waves furled,
Slowly it crosses the curved world.
We wind in its waters with the tide,
But the pendent ships afar
Where the lightest blue and low clouds are
We lose as they hover and over the horizon slide.

When it was a dark blue heaven with foam like stars
 We saw it lean above us from the shore,
 And over the rocks the waves rear
Immense, and coming in with crests on fire;
 We could not understand,
 Watching the sea descend upon the land,
What kept it from flooding the world, being so much higher.

Today it lies in place, and the dun houses,
 The apple-green cloudy oats, the cows that seem
 Compact of the yellow crust of their cream,
Shrink on Amalveor's grey and tawny sides,
 Sucking the last shreds of sun.
 But all life here is carried on
Against the crash and cry of the moving tides.

For a Child Expected

Lovers whose lifted hands are candles in winter,
Whose gentle ways like streams in the easy summer,
Lying together
For secret setting of a child, love what they do,
Thinking they make that candle immortal, those streams
 forever flow,
And yet do better than they know.

So the first flutter of a baby felt in the womb,
Its little signal and promise of riches to come,
Is taken in its father's name;
Its life is the body of his love, like his caress,
First delicate and strange, that daily use
Makes dearer and priceless.

Our baby was to be the living sign of our joy,
Restore to each the other's lost infancy;
To a painter's pillaging eye
Poet's coiled hearing, add the heart we might earn
By the help of love; all that our passion would yield
We put to planning our child.

The world flowed in; whatever we liked we took:
For its hair, the gold curls of the November oak
We saw on our walk;
Snowberries that make a Milky Way in the wood
For its tender hands; calm screen of the frozen flood
For our care of its childhood.

But the birth of a child is an uncontrollable glory;
Cat's cradle of hopes will hold no living baby,
Long though it lay quietly.
And when our baby stirs and struggles to be born
It compels humility: what we began
Is now its own.

For *as the sun that shines through glass*
So Jesus in His Mother was.
Therefore every human creature
Since it shares in His nature,
In candle-gold passion or white
Sharp star should show its own way of light.
May no parental dread or dream
Darken our darling's early beam:
May she grow to her right powers
Unperturbed by passion of ours.

F. T. Prince (*Br. b. 1912*)

Soldiers Bathing

The sea at evening moves across the sand.
Under a reddening sky I watch the freedom of a band
Of soldiers who belong to me. Stripped bare
For bathing in the sea, they shout and run in the warm air;
Their flesh, worn by the trade of war, revives
And my mind towards the meaning of it strives.

All's pathos now. The body that was gross,
Rank, ravenous, disgusting in the act or in repose,
All fever, filth and sweat, its bestial strength
And bestial decay, by pain and labour grows at length
Fragile and luminous. "Poor bare forked animal,"
Conscious of his desires and needs and flesh that rise and fall,
Stands in the soft air, tasting after toil
The sweetness of his nakedness: letting the sea-waves coil
Their frothy tongues about his feet, forgets
His hatred of the war, its terrible pressure that begets
A machinery of death and slavery,
Each being a slave and making slaves of others: finds that he
Remembers lovely freedom in a game,
Mocking himself, and comically mimics fear and shame.

He plays with death and animality.
And reading in the shadows of his pallid flesh, I see
The idea of Michelangelo's cartoon
Of soldiers bathing, breaking off before they were half done
At some sortie of the enemy, an episode
Of the Pisan wars with Florence. I remember how he showed
Their muscular limbs that clamber from the water,
And heads that turn across the shoulder, eager for the slaughter,
Forgetful of their bodies that are bare,
And hot to buckle on and use the weapons lying there.
–And I think too of the theme another found
When, shadowing men's bodies on a sinister red ground,
Another Florentine, Pollaiuolo,
Painted a naked battle: warriors, straddled, hacked the foe,
Dug their bare toes into the ground and slew
The brother-naked man who lay between their feet and drew
His lips back from his teeth in a grimace.
They were Italians who knew war's sorrow and disgrace
And showed, the thing suspended, stripped: a theme
Born out of the experience of war's horrible extreme
Beneath a sky where even the air flows
With *Lacrimae Christi*. For that rage, that bitterness, those
blows,
That hatred of the slain, what could it be
But indirectly or directly a commentary

On the Crucifixion? And the picture burns
With indignation and pity and despair by turns,
Because it is the obverse of the scene
Where Christ hangs murdered, stripped, upon the Cross. I mean,
That is the explanation of its rage.

And we too have our bitterness and pity that engage
Blood, spirit in this war. But night begins,
Night of the mind: who nowadays is conscious of our sins?
Though every human deed concerns our blood,
And even we must know, what nobody has understood,
That some great love is over all we do,
And that is what has driven us to this fury, for so few
Can suffer all the terror of that love:
The terror of that love has set us spinning in this groove
Greased with our blood.
These dry themselves and dress,
Combing their hair, forget the fear and shame of nakedness.
Because to love is frightening we prefer
The freedom of our crimes. Yet, as I drink the dusky air,
I feel a strange delight that fills me full,
Strange gratitude, as if evil itself were beautiful,
And kiss the wound in thought, while in the west
I watch a streak of red that might have issued from Christ's
breast.

In a Province

Because of the memory of one we held dear
Call to mind where she lived and the ruins there
Among the silken shrubs. I have dismounted where
Her children played and watch the pale sky grow clear.

And as for me, standing between the silken shrub and the
broom
And tasting the breath of the blue sage, I must stay
Though my friends are setting out with the first of the day
And they murmur to me, "Do not linger in that gloom,
Remember that tears make whole the heart." But I say
"Is there nowhere I may rest among the shells
Of the ruins and the droppings of white gazelles?
However brief my hours are, I would delay."

The tears that fall from my eyes have wet my hands
Holding the reins of my horse. How many hours
Were sweet to me because of women! These showers
Bring to my mind that day among pale sands,
Call to mind how one came with me unwillingly
On an evening warm as another country's noons
And all seemed of long ago among those dunes
And under a clear sky, under a clear green sky.

John Frederick Nims (*Am. b. 1913*)

Non-Euclidean Elegy

In the foil-and-pastel tea room
Proper as aunty's kiss,
I think of Lobachevski,
Of Riemann who smashed all this.

Tables seem decently skirted,
Their rumps steady and square.
"Seem . . . square," but they aren't; they
Aren't even there.

Once forks and crystal
Were stars on a cloud-lace top,
Till Einstein, the white face heifer,
Got in Kepler's china shop.

Now what looks straight isn't.
What looks solid is loose as balloons.
Eat your soup, watching Cancer
And Scorpio hooked to the spoons.

Walking tight-wires over Niagara?
Simple to what we do
On the crookback highway at noon,
Juggling our ego too,

Juggling tissues and glands
Like a twenty-foot stack of dishes;
On top, our Psyche rides
Pink in a pantie of wishes.

But, in notch of disaster,
Thank you latter-day luck:
If a truck runs (HONK!) over you
It's just an illusory truck.

They'll wax your pallor, load you
With roses and coal-dust rites,
Earth yawns like a bubbling ocean;
Tea rooms teeter like kites.

Midwest

Indiana: no blustering summit or coarse gorge;
No flora lurid as disaster-flares;
No great vacuities where tourists gape
Nor mountains hoarding their height like millionaires.
More delicate: the ten-foot knolls
Give flavor of hill to Indiana souls.

Topography is perfect, curio-size;
Deft as landscape in museum cases.
What is beautiful is friendly and underfoot,
Not flaunted like theater curtains in our faces.
No peak or jungle obscures the blue sky;
Our land rides smoothly in the softest eye.

Man is the prominent fauna of our state.
Elsewhere circus creatures stomp and leer
With heads like crags or clumps. But delirious nature
Once in a lucid interval sobering here
Left (repenting her extravagant plan)
Conspicuous on our fields the shadow of man.

Delmore Schwartz (*Am. b. 1913*)

From *The Repetitive Heart, IV, IX*

IV

For Rhoda

Calmly we walk through this April's day,
Metropolitan poetry here and there,
In the park sit pauper and *rentier*,
The screaming children, the motor car
Fugitive about us, running away,
Between the worker and the millionaire
Number provides all distances,
It is Nineteen Thirty-Seven now,
Many great dears are taken away,
What will become of you and me
(This is the school in which we learn . . .)
Besides the photo and the memory?
(. . . that time is the fire in which we burn.)

(This is the school in which we learn . . .)
What is the self amid this blaze?
What am I now that I was then
Which I shall suffer and act again,
The theodicy I wrote in my high school days
Restored all life from infancy,
The children shouting are bright as they run
(This is the school in which they learn . . .)
Ravished entirely in their passing play!
(. . . that time is the fire in which they burn.)

Avid its rush, that reeling blaze!
Where is my father and Eleanor?
Not where are they now, dead seven years,
But what they were then?
No more? No more?
From Nineteen-Fourteen to the present day,
Bert Spira and Rhoda consume, consume
Not where they are now (where are they now?)
But what they were then, both beautiful;
Each minute bursts in the burning room,

The great globe reels in the solar fire,
Spinning the trivial and unique away.
(How all things flash! How all things flare!)
What am I now that I was then?
May memory restore again and again
The smallest color of the smallest day:
Time is the school in which we learn,
Time is the fire in which we burn.

IX

"*the withness of the body*"
–Whitehead

The heavy bear who goes with me,
A manifold honey to smear his face,
Clumsy and lumbering here and there,
The central ton of every place,
The hungry beating brutish one
In love with candy, anger, and sleep,
Crazy factotum, dishevelling all,
Climbs the building, kicks the football,
Boxes his brother in the hate-ridden city.

Breathing at my side, that heavy animal,
That heavy bear who sleeps with me,
Howls in his sleep for a world of sugar,
A sweetness intimate as the water's clasp,
Trembles and shows the darkness beneath.
–The strutting show-off is terrified,
Dressed in his dress-suit, bulging his pants,
Trembles to think that his quivering meat
Must finally wince to nothing at all.

That inescapable animal walks with me,
Has followed me since the black womb held,
Moves where I move, distorting my gesture,
A caricature, a swollen shadow,
A stupid clown of the spirit's motive,
Perplexes and affronts with his own darkness,
The secret life of belly and bone,
Opaque, too near, my private, yet unknown,
Stretches to embrace the very dear

With whom I would walk without him near,
Touches her grossly, although a word
Would bare my heart and make me clear,
Stumbles, flounders, and strives to be fed
Dragging me with him in his mouthing care,
Amid the hundred million of his kind,
The scrimmage of appetite everywhere.

For the One Who Would Take Man's Life in His Hands

Tiger Christ unsheathed his sword,
Threw it down, became a lamb.
Swift spat upon the species, but
Took two women to his heart.
Samson who was strong as death
Paid his strength to kiss a slut.
Othello that stiff warrior
Was broken by a woman's heart.
Troy burned for a sea-tax, also for
Possession of a charming whore.
What do all examples show?
What must the finished murderer know?

You cannot sit on bayonets,
Nor can you eat among the dead.
When all are killed, you are alone,
A vacuum comes where hate has fed.
Murder's fruit is silent stone,
The gun increases poverty.
With what do these examples shine?
The soldier turned to girls and wine.
Love is the tact of every good,
The only warmth, the only peace.

"What have I said?" asked Socrates,
"Affirmed extremes, cried yes and no,
Taken all parts, denied myself,
Praised the caress, extolled the blow,
Soldier and lover quite deranged
Until their motions are exchanged.

–What do all examples show?
What can any actor know?
The contradiction in every act,
The infinite task of the human heart."

In the Naked Bed, in Plato's Cave

In the naked bed, in Plato's cave,
Reflected headlights slowly slid the wall,
Carpenters hammered under the shaded window,
Wind troubled the window curtains all night long,
A fleet of trucks strained uphill, grinding,
Their freights covered, as usual.
The ceiling lightened again, the slanting diagram
Slid slowly forth.
                    Hearing the milkman's chop,
His striving up the stair, the bottle's chink,
I rose from bed, lit a cigarette,
And walked to the window. The stony street
Displayed the stillness in which buildings stand,
The street-lamp's vigil and the horse's patience.
The winter sky's pure capital
Turned me back to bed with exhausted eyes.

Strangeness grew in the motionless air. The loose
Film grayed. Shaking wagons, hooves' waterfalls,
Sounded far off, increasing, louder and nearer.
A car coughed, starting. Morning, softly
Melting the air, lifted the half-covered chair
From underseas, kindled the looking-glass,
Distinguished the dresser and the white wall.
The bird called tentatively, whistled, called,
Bubbled and whistled, so! Perplexed, still wet
With sleep, affectionate, hungry and cold. So, so,
O son of man, the ignorant night, the travail
Of early morning, the mystery of beginning
Again and again,
                    while Time is unforgiven.

Karl Shapiro (*Am. b. 1913*)

Drug Store

I do remember an apothecary,
And hereabouts 'a dwells

It baffles the foreigner like an idiom,
And he is right to adopt it as a form
Less serious than the living-room or bar;
  For it disestablishes the café,
Is a collective, and on basic country.

Not that it praises hygiene and corrupts
The ice-cream parlor and the tobacconist's
Is it a center; but that the attractive symbols
  Watch over puberty and leer
Like rubber bottles waiting for sick-use.

Youth comes to jingle nickels and crack wise;
The baseball scores are his, the magazines
Devoted to lust, the jazz, the Coca-Cola,
  The lending-library of love's latest.
He is the customer; he is heroized.

And every nook and cranny of the flesh
Is spoken to by packages with wiles.
"Buy me, buy me," they whimper and cajole;
  The hectic range of lipstick pouts,
Revealing the wicked and the simple mouth.

With scarcely any evasion in their eye
They smoke, undress their girls, exact a stance;
But only for a moment. The clock goes round;
  Crude fellowships are made and lost;
They slump in booths like rags, not even drunk.

The Interlude

I

Much of transfiguration that we hear,
The ballet of the atoms, the second law
Of thermo-dynamics, Isis, and the queer

Fertilization of fish, the Catholic's awe
For the life-cycle of the Nazarene,
His wife whom sleeping Milton thought he saw;

Much of the resurrection that we've seen
And taken part in, like the Passion Play,
All of autumnal red and April green,

To those who walk in work from day to day,
To economic and responsible man,
All, all is substance. Life that lets him stay

Uses his substance kindly while she can
But drops him lifeless after his one span.

II

What lives? the proper creatures in their homes?
A weed? the white and giddy butterfly?
Bacteria? necklaces of chromosomes?

What lives? the breathing bell of the clear sky?
The crazed bull of the sea? Andean crags?
Armies that plunge into themselves to die?

People? A sacred relic wrapped in rags,
The ham-bone of a saint, the winter rose,
Do these?–And is there not a hand that drags

The bottom of the universe for those
Who still perhaps are breathing? Listen well,
There lives a quiet like a cathedral close

At the soul's center where substance cannot dwell
And life flowers like music from a bell.

III

Writing, I crushed an insect with my nail
And thought nothing at all. A bit of wing
Caught my eye then, a gossamer so frail

And exquisite, I saw in it a thing
That scorned the grossness of the thing I wrote.
It hung upon my finger like a sting.

A leg I noticed next, fine as a mote,
"And on this frail eyelash he walked," I said,
"And climbed and walked like any mountain-goat."

And in this mood I sought the little head,
But it was lost; then in my heart a fear
Cried out, "A life–why beautiful, why dead!"

It was a mite that held itself most dear,
So small I could have drowned it with a tear.

The Fly

O hideous little bat, the size of snot,
With polyhedral eye and shabby clothes,
To populate the stinking cat you walk
The promontory of the dead man's nose,
Climb with the fine leg of a Duncan-Phyfe
  The smoking mountains of my food
    And in a comic mood
  In mid-air take to bed a wife.

Riding and riding with your filth of hair
On gluey foot or wing, forever coy,
Hot from the compost and green sweet decay,
Sounding your buzzer like an urchin toy–
You dot all whiteness with diminutive stool,
  In the tight belly of the dead
    Burrow with hungry head
  And inlay maggots like a jewel.

At your approach the great horse stomps and paws
Bringing the hurricane of his heavy tail;
Shod in disease you dare to kiss my hand
Which sweeps against you like an angry flail;
Still you return, return, trusting your wing
  To draw you from the hunter's reach
    That learns to kill to teach
  Disorder to the tinier thing.

My peace is your disaster. For your death
Children like spiders cup their pretty hands
And wives resort to chemistry of war.
In fens of sticky paper and quicksands

You glue yourself to death. Where you are stuck
  You struggle hideously and beg,
    You amputate your leg
  Imbedded in the amber muck.

But I, a man, must swat you with my hate,
Slap you across the air and crush your flight,
Must mangle with my shoe and smear your
  blood,
Expose your little guts pasty and white,
Knock you head sidewise like a drunkard's hat,
  Pin your wings under like a crow's,
    Tear off your flimsy clothes
  And beat you as one beats a rat.

Then like Gargantua I stride among
The corpses strewn like raisins in the dust,
The broken bodies of the narrow dead
That catch the throat with fingers of disgust.
I sweep. One gyrates like a top and falls
  And stunned, stone blind, and deaf
    Buzzes its frightful F
  And dies between three cannibals.

Scyros

snuffle and sniff and handkerchief

The doctor punched my vein
  The captain called me Cain
Upon my belly sat the sow of fear
  With coins on either eye
  The President came by
And whispered to the braid what none could hear

  High over where the storm
  Stood steadfast cruciform
The golden eagle sank in wounded wheels
  White Negroes laughing still
  Crept fiercely on Brazil
Turning the navies upward on their keels

Now one by one the trees
Stripped to their naked knees
To dance upon the heaps of shrunken dead
The roof of England fell
Great Paris tolled her bell
And China staunched her milk and wept for bread

No island singly lay
But lost its name that day
The Ainu dived across the plunging sands
From dawn to dawn to dawn
King George's birds came on
Strafing the tulips from his children's hands

Thus in the classic sea
South-east from Thessaly
The dynamited mermen washed ashore
And tritons dressed in steel
Trolled heads with rod and reel
And dredged potatoes from the Aegean floor

Hot is the sky and green
Where Germans have been seen
The moon leaks metal on the Atlantic fields
Pink boys in birthday shrouds
Loop lightly through the clouds
Or coast the peaks of Finland on their shields

That prophet year by year
Lay still but could not hear
Where scholars tapped to find his new remains
Gog and Magog ate pork
In vertical New York
And war began next Wednesday on the Danes

Haircut

O wonderful nonsense of lotions of Lucky Tiger,
Of savory soaps and oils of bottle-bright green,
The gold of liqueurs, the unguents of Newark and Niger,
Powders and balms and waters washing me clean;

In mirrors of marble and silver I see us forever
Increasing, decreasing the puzzles of luminous spaces
As I turn, am revolved and am pumped in the air on a lever,
With the backs of my heads in chorus with all of my faces.

Scissors and comb are mowing my hair into neatness,
Now pruning my ears, now smoothing my neck like a plain;
In the harvest of hair and the chaff of powdery sweetness
My snow-covered slopes grow dark with the woolly rain.

And the little boy cries, for it hurts to sever the curl,
And we too are quietly bleating to part with our coat.
Does the barber want blood in a dish? I am weak as a girl,
I desire my pendants, the fatherly chin of a goat.

I desire the pants of a bear, the nap of a monkey
Which trousers of friction have blighted down to my skin.
I am bare as a tusk, as jacketed up as a flunkey,
With the chest of a moth-eaten camel growing within.

But in death we shall flourish, you summer-dark leaves of my head,
While the flesh of the jaw ebbs away from the shores of my teeth;
You shall cover my sockets and soften the boards of my bed
And lie on the flat of my temples as proud as a wreath.

Auto Wreck

Its quick soft silver bell beating, beating,
And down the dark one ruby flare
Pulsing out red light like an artery,
The ambulance at top speed floating down
Past beacons and illuminated clocks
Wings in a heavy curve, dips down,
And brakes speed, entering the crowd.
The doors leap open, emptying light;
Stretchers are laid out, the mangled lifted
And stowed into the little hospital.
Then the bell, breaking the hush, tolls once,
And the ambulance with its terrible cargo
Rocking, slightly rocking, moves away,
As the doors, an afterthought, are closed.

We are deranged, walking among the cops
Who sweep glass and are large and composed.
One is still making notes under the light.
One with a bucket douches ponds of blood
Into the street and gutter.
One hangs lanterns on the wrecks that cling,
Empty husks of locusts, to iron poles.

Our throats were tight as tourniquets,
Our feet were bound with splints, but now,
Like convalescents intimate and gauche,
We speak through sickly smiles and warn
With the stubborn saw of common sense,
The grim joke and the banal resolution.
The traffic moves around with care,
But we remain, touching a wound
That opens to our richest horror.
Already old, the question Who shall die?
Becomes unspoken Who is innocent?
For death in war is done by hands;
Suicide has cause and stillbirth, logic;
And cancer, simple as a flower, blooms.
But this invites the occult mind,
Cancels our physics with a sneer,
And spatters all we knew of denouement
Across the expedient and wicked stones.

The Minute

The office building treads the marble dark,
The mother-clock with wide and golden dial
Suffers and glows. Now is the hour of birth
Of the tremulous egg. Now is the time of correction.
O midnight, zero of eternity,
Soon on a million bureaus of the city
Will lie the new-born minute.

The new-born minute on the bureau lies,
Scratching the glass with infant kick, cutting
With diamond cry the crystal and expanse

Of timelessness. This pretty tick of death
Etches its name upon the air. I turn
Titanically in distant sleep, expelling
From my lungs the bitter gas of life.

The loathsome minute grows in length and strength,
Bending its spring to forge an iron hour
That rusts from link to link, the last one bright,
The late one dead. Between the shining works
Range the clean angels, studying that tick
Like a strange dirt, but will not pick it up
Nor move it gingerly out of harm's way.

An angel is stabbed and is carried aloft howling,
For devils have gathered on a ruby jewel
Like red mites on a berry; others arrive
To tend the points with oil and smooth the heat.
See how their vicious faces, lit with sweat,
Worship the train of wheels; see how they pull
The tape-worm Time from nothing into thing.

I with my distant heart lie wide awake
Smiling at that Swiss-perfect engine room
Driven by tiny evils. Knowing no harm
Even of gongs that loom and move in towers
And hands as high as iron masts, I sleep,
At which sad sign the angels in a flock
Rise and sweep past me, spinning threads of fear.

Clifford Dyment (*Br. b. 1914*)

The Snow

In no way that I chose to go
Could I escape the falling snow.

I shut my eyes, wet with my fears:
The snow still whispered at my ears.

I stopped my ears in deaf disguise:
The snow still fell before my eyes.

Snow was my comrade, snow my fate,
In a country huge and desolate.

My footsteps made a shallow space,
And then the snow filled up the place,

And all the walking I had done
Was on a journey not begun.

I did not know the distance gone,
But resolutely travelled on

While silently on every hand
Fell the sorrow of the land,

And no way that I chose to go
Could lead me from the grief of snow.

Pastoral

(To the Memory of W. C. Dyment, 1889–1918)

In the old days the white gates swung
Open upon sunned meadows,
And rude streams ran winding
Among the clay banks and the pristine reeds,
And the still cows gazed
With eyes deeper than pools
In the deep shadows of leaves.

The grey gates are blistered with the sun:
The grey gates are closed,
For my child eyes saw the noon
Pass into evening and a cold wind
Saunter among the rushes,
The tall grass, the lanes, and the woods:
Feet scattering the gold of flowers,
Hands plucking and twisting the stems,
Came the sauntering sorrowful stranger.

The Swans

Midstream they met. Challenger and champion,
They fought a war for honour
Fierce, sharp, but with no honour:
Each had a simple aim and sought it quickly.
The combat over the victor sailed away
Broken, but placid as is the gift of swans,
Leaving his rival to his shame alone.
I listened for a song, according to story,
But this swan's death was out of character–
No giving up of the grace of life
In a sad lingering music.
I saw the beaten swan rise on the water
As though to outreach pain, its webbed feet
Banging the river helplessly, its wings
Loose in a last hysteria. Then the neck
Was floating like a rope and the swan was dead.
It drifted away and all around it swan's-down
Bobbed on the river like children's little boats.

A Switch Cut in April

This thin elastic stick was plucked
From gradual growing in a hedge,
Where early mist awakened leaf,
And late damp hands with spiral stroke
Smoothed slumber from the weighted day,
While flowers drooped with colours furled.

I cut quick circles with the stick:
It whistles in the April air
An eager song, a bugle call,
A signal for the running feet,
For rising flyer flashing sun,
And windy tree with surging crest.

This pliant wood like expert whip
Snaps action in its voice, commands
A quiver from the sloth, achieves
A jerk in buds; with stinging lash
A spring of movement in the stiff
And sleeping limbs of winter land.

Stick plucked and peeled, companions lost,
Torn from its rooted stock: I hold
Elate and lithe within my hand
Winged answer to the wings' impulse,
The calyx breaking into flame,
The crystal cast into the light.

Henry Reed (*Br. b. 1914*)

Lessons of the War: Naming of Parts

(to Alan Michell)

Vixi duellis nuper idoneus
Et militavi non sine gloria

Today we have naming of parts. Yesterday,
We had daily cleaning. And tomorrow morning,
We shall have what to do after firing. But today,
Today we have naming of parts. Japonica
Glistens like coral in all of the neighbouring gardens,
And today we have naming of parts.

This is the lower sling swivel. And this
Is the upper sling swivel, whose use you will see,
When you are given your slings. And this is the piling swivel,
Which in your case you have not got. The branches
Hold in the gardens their silent, eloquent gestures,
Which in our case we have not got.

This is the safety-catch, which is always released
With an easy flick of the thumb. And please do not let me
See anyone using his finger. You can do it quite easy
If you have any strength in your thumb. The blossoms
Are fragile and motionless, never letting anyone see
Any of them using their finger.

And this you can see is the bolt. The purpose of this
Is to open the breech, as you see. We can slide it
Rapidly backwards and forwards: we call this

Easing the spring. And rapidly backwards and forwards
The early bees are assaulting and fumbling the flowers:
  They call it easing the Spring.

They call it easing the Spring: it is perfectly easy
If you have any strength in your thumb: like the bolt,
And the breech, and the cocking-piece, and the point of
    balance,
Which in our case we have not got; and the almond-blossom
Silent in all of the gardens and the bees going backwards and
    forwards,
  For today we have naming of parts.

Chrysothemis

I cannot follow them into their world of death,
Or their hunted world of life, though through the house,
Death and the hunted bird sing at every nightfall.
I am Chrysothemis: I sailed with dipping sails,
Suffered the winds I would not strive against,
Entered the whirlpools and was flung outside them,
Survived the murders, triumphs and revenges.
Survived; and remain in a falling, decaying mansion,
A house detested and dark in the setting sun,
The furniture covered with sheets, the gardens empty,
A brother and sister long departed,
A railing mother gone.
It is my house now. I have set myself to protect,
Against the demons that linger inside our walls,
Their saddened, quiet children of darkness and shame:
They lie on inherited beds in their heavy slumbers,
Their faces relaxed to nocturnal innocence.
I will protect them in the decaying palace.

In the dying sun, through slots in the shuttered windows,
I can see the hanging gardens carved on our mountain
Above and below us, terraces, groves and arbours,
The careful rise of the trees to meet the heavens,
The deliberate riot of the wilderness,
The silent arch through which my brother returned,
And again returned.

In the long broad days of summer,
On the great hill the house lay, lost and absorbed and
dreaming,
The gardens glittered under the sweeping sun,
The inmates kept to their rooms, and hope
Rose in the silence.

And indeed
It seemed the agony must die. But then
The house would seem to sigh, and then again,
A sigh and another silence. Through the slotted shutters
I would see them there, my mother and my sister
Wandering and meeting in the garden's quiet
(And I moved from room to room to see them better).
There seemed a truce between them, as if they had
Called off their troops in order to bury their dead.
I could not hear my sister speak; but clearly
She spoke with calm and patience, and my mother gave
The answer designed to please, wistful and eager;
And her words would be quietly taken, twisted and turned,
Ropes, that would loose the rivers to flood again;
The fragile dams would burst, indeed constructed
Only for breaking down.

This was the yawn of time while a murder
Awaited another murder. I did not see
My father's murder, but I see it now always around me,
And I see it shapeless: as when we are sometimes told
Of the heroes who walk out into the snow and blizzard
To spare their comrades' care, we always see
A white direction in which the figure goes,
And a vague ravine in which he stumbles and falls.
My father rises thus from a bath of blood,
Groping from table to chair in a dusky room
Through doorways into darkening corridors,
Falling at last in the howling vestibule.

In the years that followed, the winds of time swept round
The anniversaries of the act; and they
Were shouted down: my mother prepared for them
Music and dance, and called them celebrations.

They did not, fever-laden, creep on her unaware.
But did the nights not turn on her? Did she not
Dream music in the false-dawn faltering, phrases
Repeating endlessly, a figure of the dance
Halting and beckoning?

It is my house now, decaying but never dying,
The soul's museum, preserving and embalming
The shuttered rooms, the amulets, the pictures,
The doorways waiting for perennial surprises,
The children sleeping under the heat of summer,
And lastly the great bronze doors of the bridal chamber,
Huge and unspeaking, not to be pressed and opened,
Not to be lingered near, then or thereafter,
Not to be pounded upon by desolate fists,
Mine least of all.

I sailed with dipping sails.
I was not guilty of anybody's blood.
I will protect them in the decaying house.

With this resolve, concluded like a prayer,
From the eyes of the window gently stealing away,
As in a ritual I wipe the dust from the mirror
And look through the dark at the dim reflection before me.
The lips draw back from the mouth,
The night draws back from the years,
And there is the family smile in the quivering room.

The sun has gone, and the hunted bird demands:
"*Can the liar guard the truth, the deceiver seek it,*
The murderer preserve, the harlot chasten, or the guilty
Shelter the innocent? And shall you protect?"

Morning

Look, my love, on the wall, and here, at this Eastern picture.
How still its scene, and neither of sleep nor waking:
No shadow falls from the tree or the golden mountain,
The boats on the glassy lake have no reflection,
No echo would come if you blew a horn in those valleys.

And look away, and move. Or speak, or sing:
And voices of the past murmur among your words,
Under your glance my dead selves quicken and stir,
And a thousand shadows attend you where you go.

That is your movement. There is a golden stillness,
Soundless and fathomless, and far beyond it;
When brow on brow, or mouth to mouth assembled,
We lie in the calm of morning. And there, outside us,
The sun moves on, the boat jogs on the lake,
The huntsman calls.
And we lie here, our orient peace awaking
No echo, and no shadow, and no reflection.

Randall Jarrell (*Am. b. 1914*)

90 North

At home, in my flannel gown, like a bear to its floe,
I clambered to bed; up the globe's impossible sides
I sailed all night–till at last, with my black beard,
My furs and my dogs, I stood at the northern pole.

There in the childish night my companions lay frozen,
The stiff furs knocked at my starveling throat,
And I gave my great sigh–the flakes came huddling;
Were they really my end? In the darkness I turned to my rest.

Here, the flag snaps in the glare and silence
Of the unbroken ice. And I stand here,
The dogs bark, my beard is black, and I stare
At the North Pole. And now what? Why, go back.

Turn as I please, my step is to the south.
The world–my world spins on this final point
Of cold and wretchedness: all lines, all winds
End in this whirlpool I at last discover.

And it is meaningless. In the child's bed
After the night's voyage, in that warm world
Where people work and suffer till the death
That crowns the pain–in that Cloud-Cuckoo-Land

I reached my North and it had meaning.
Here at the actual pole of my existence,
Where all that I have done is meaningless,
Where I die or live by accident alone–

Where, living or dying, I am still alone;
Here where North, the night, the berg of death
Crowd to me out of the ignorant darkness
I see at last that all the knowledge

I wrung from the darkness–that the darkness flung me–
Is worthless as ignorance: nothing comes from nothing,
The darkness from the darkness. Pain comes from the darkness,
And we call it wisdom. It is pain.

The Cow Wandering in the Bare Field

The cow wandering in the bare field,
Her chain dangling, aimless,–
The Negro sitting in the ashes,
Staring, humming to the cat,–

Their greyed figures, muffled in snow,
Perhaps, outside the starred window,
At that hour when the sun has rusted away,
Range themselves in the only order they know–

These are the inhabitants of the country of the mind,
Or only the marching motion of the mind,
But still, this is what the mind gives the mind.
Standing there, familiar, brutal, and resigned,

A few trees, gelatinous, evergreen,
Powdered and leaden, creaking in one's age's snow–
That is, the mind aging, the sky's covering snow–
Speak, bend, so vacantly as to seem

The thirsty images of a dream.
I summon them, then, from the old darkness
Into this wooden room, dripping and warm,
To chorus for you their bad charm

Because I knew their true living forms.
And how shall I make you, mossy, bearded, mournful,
A stuffed father on a Christmas night,
Cry out in pride and blessedness: O children!

Losses

It was not dying: everybody died.
It was not dying: we had died before
In the routine crashes–and our fields
Called up the papers, wrote home to our folks,
And the rates rose, all because of us.
We died on the wrong page of the almanac,
Scattered on mountains fifty miles away;
Diving on haystacks, fighting with a friend,
We blazed up on the lines we never saw.
We died like ants or pets or foreigners.
(When we left high school nothing else had died
For us to figure we had died like.)

In our new planes, with our new crews, we bombed
The ranges by the desert or the shore,
Fired at towed targets, waited for our scores–
And turned into replacements and woke up
One morning, over England, operational.
It wasn't different: but if we died
It was not an accident but a mistake
(But an easy one for anyone to make).
We read our mail and counted up our missions–
In bombers named for girls, we burned
The cities we had learned about in school–
Till our lives wore out; our bodies lay among
The people we had killed and never seen.
When we lasted long enough they gave us medals;
When we died they said, "Our casualties were low."
They said, "Here are the maps"; we burned the cities.

It was not dying–no, not ever dying;
But the night I died I dreamed that I was dead,
And the cities said to me: "Why are you dying?
We are satisfied, if you are; but why did I die?"

Eighth Air Force

If, in an odd angle of the hutment,
A puppy laps the water from a can
Of flowers, and the drunk sergeant shaving
Whistles *O Paradiso!*–shall I say that man
Is not as men have said: a wolf to man?

The other murderers troop in yawning;
Three of them play Pitch, one sleeps, and one
Lies counting missions, lies there sweating
Till even his heart beats: One; One; One.
O murderers! . . . Still, this is how it's done:

This is a war. . . . But since these play, before they die,
Like puppies with their puppy; since, a man,
I did as these have done, but did not die–
I will content the people as I can
And give up these to them: Behold the man!

I have suffered, in a dream, because of him,
Many things; for this last saviour, man,
I have lied as I lie now. But what is lying?
Men wash their hands, in blood, as best they can:
I find no fault in this just man.

Laurie Lee (*Br. b. 1914*)

Summer Rain

Where in the valley the summer rain
Moves crazed and chill through the crooked trees
The briars bleed green, and the far fox-banks
Their sharp cries tangle in sobbing shades.

I hear the sad rinsing of reeded meadows
The small lakes rise in the wild white rose
The shudder of wings in the streaming cedars
And tears of lime running down the hills.

All day in the tomb of my brain I hear
The cold wheat whisper, the veiled trees mourn,
And behold through windows of weighted ivy
The wet walls blossom with silver snails.

The heron flies up from the stinging waters,
The white swan droops by the dripping reed,
And summer lies swathed in its ripeness, exuding
Damp odours of lilies and alabaster.

In a fever of June she is wrapped and anointed
With deathly sweating of cold jasmine,
And her petals weep wax to the thick green sky
Like churchyard wreaths under domes of glass.

Too long hangs the light in the valley lamenting,
The slow rain sucking the sun's green eye;
And too long do you hide in your vault of clay
While I search for your passion's obliterated stone.

Let the dark night come, let its crack of doom
The sky's heart shatter and empty of grief,
The storm fetch its thunder of hammers and axes,
The green hills break as our graves embrace.

Day of These Days

Such a morning it is when love
leans through geranium windows
and calls with a cockerel's tongue.

When red-haired girls scamper like roses
over the rain-green grass,
and the sun drips honey.

When hedgerows grow venerable,
berries dry black as blood,
and holes suck in their bees.

Such a morning it is when mice
run whispering from the church,
dragging dropped ears of harvest.

When the partridge draws back his spring
and shoots like a buzzing arrow
over grained and mahogany fields.

When no table is bare
and no breast dry,
and the tramp feeds off ribs of rabbit.

Such a day it is when time
piles up the hills like pumpkins,
and the streams run golden.

When all men smell good,
and the cheeks of girls
are as baked bread to the mouth.

As bread and bean flowers
the touch of their lips,
and their white teeth sweeter than cucumbers.

John Berryman (*Am. b. 1914*)

Canto Amor

Dream in a dream the heavy soul somewhere
struck suddenly & dark down to its knees.
A griffin sighs off in the orphic air.

If (Unknown Majesty) I not confess
praise for the rack the rock the live sailor
under the blue sea,–yet I may You bless

always for hér, in fear & joy for hér
whose gesture summons ever when I grieve
me back and is my mage and minister.

–Muses: whose worship I may never leave
but for this pensive woman, now I dare,
teach me her praise! with her my praise receive.–

Three years already of the round world's war
had rolled by stoned & disappointed eyes
when she and I came where we were made for.

Pale as a star lost in returning skies,
more beautiful than midnight stars more frail
she moved towards me like chords, a sacrifice;

entombed in body trembling through the veil
arm upon arm, learning our ancient wound,
we see our one soul heal, recovering pale.

Then priestly sanction, then the drop of sound.
Quickly part to the cavern ever warm
deep from the march, body to body bound,

descend (my soul) out of dismantling storm
into the darkness where the world is made.
. . Come back to the bright air. Love is multiform.

Heartmating hesitating unafraid
although incredulous, she seemed to fill
the lilac shadow with light wherein she played,

whom sorry childhood had made sit quite still,
an orphan silence, unregarded sheen,
listening for any small soft note, not hopeful:

caricature: as once a maiden Queen,
flowering power comeliness kindness grace,
shattered her mirror, wept, would not be seen.

These pities moved. Also above her face
serious or flushed, swayed her fire-gold
not earthly hair, now moonless to unlace,

resistless flame, now in a sun more cold
great shells to whorl about each secret ear,
mysterious histories, strange shore, unfold.

New musics! One the music that we hear,
this is the music which the masters make
out of their minds, profound solemn & clear.

And then the other music, in whose sake
all men perceive a gladness but we are drawn
less for that joy than utterly to take

our trial, naked in the music's vision,
the flowing ceremony of trouble and light,
all Loves becoming, none to flag upon.

Such Mozart made,–an ear so delicate
he fainted at a trumpet-call, a child
so delicate. So merciful that sight,

so stern, we follow rapt who ran a-wild.
Marriage is the second music, and thereof
we hear what we can hear, faithful & mild.

Therefore the streaming torches in the grove
through dark or bright, swiftly and now more near
cherish a festival of anxious love.

Dance for this music, Mistress to music dear,
more, that storm worrics the disordered wood
grieving the midnight of my thirtieth year

and only the trial of our music should
still this irresolute air, only your voice
spelling the tempest may compel our good:

Sing then beyond my song: whirl & rejoice!

From *Homage to Mistress Bradstreet*

(Born 1612 Anne Dudley, married at sixteen Simon Bradstreet, a Cambridge man, steward to the Countess of Warwick and protégé of her father Thomas Dudley secretary to the Earl of Lincoln. Crossed in the *Arbella*, 1630, under Governor Winthrop.)

I

The Governor your husband lived so long
moved you not, restless, waiting for him? Still,
You were a patient woman.–
I seem to see you pausc here still:
Sylvester, Quarles, in moments odd you pored
before a fire at, bright eyes on the Lord,
all the children still.
Simon, . . Simon will listen while you read a Song.

2

Outside the New World winters in grand dark
white air lashing high thro' the virgin stands
foxes down foxholes sigh,
surely the English heart quails, stunned.
I doubt if Simon than this blast, that sea,
spares from his rigour for your poetry
more. We are on each other's hands
who care. Both of our worlds unhanded us. Lie stark,

3

thy eyes look to me mild. Out of maize & air
your body's made, and moves. I summon, see,
from the centuries it.
I think you won't stay. How do we
linger, diminished, in our lovers' air,
implausibly visible, to whom, a year,
years, over interims; or not;
to a long stranger; or not; shimmer & disappear.

4

Jaw-ript, rot with its wisdom, rending then;
then not. When the mouth dies, who misses you?
Your master never died,
Simon ah thirty years past you–
Pockmarkt & westward staring on a haggard deck
it seems I find you, young. I come to check,
I come to stay with you,
and the Governor, & Father, & Simon, and the huddled
men.

5

By the week we landed we were, most, used up.
Strange ships across us, after a fortnight's winds
unfavouring, frightened us;
bone-sad cold, sleet, scurvy; so were ill
many as one day we could have no sermons;
broils, quelled; a fatherless child unkennelled; vermin
crowding & waiting; waiting.
And the day itself he leapt ashore young Henry Winthrop

6

(delivered from the waves; because he found
off their wigwams, sharp-eyed, a lone canoe
across a tidal river,
that water glittered fair & blue
& narrow, none of the other men could swim
and the plantation's prime theft up to him,
shouldered on a glad day
hard on the sumptuous feasting of thanksgiving) drowned.

7

How long with nothing in the ruinous heat,
clams & acorns stomaching, distinction perishing,
at which my heart rose,
with brackish water, we would sing.
When whispers knew the Governor's last bread
was browning in his oven, we were discourag'd.
The Lady Arbella dying–
dyings–at which my heart rose, but I did submit.

8

That beyond the Atlantic wound our woes enlarge
is hard, hard that starvation burnishes our fear,
but I do gloss for You.
Strangers & pilgrims fare we here,
declaring we seek a City. Shall we be deceived?
I know whom I have trusted, & whom I have believed,
and that he is able to
keep   that I have committed to his charge.

9

Winter than summer worse, that first, like a file
on a quick, or the poison suck of a thrilled tooth;
and still we may unpack.
Wolves & storms among, uncouth
board-pieces, boxes, barrels vanish, grow
houses, rise. Motes that hop in sunlight slow
indoors, and I am Ruth
away: open my mouth, my eyes wet: I wóuld smile:

10

vellum I palm, and dream. Their forest dies
to greensward, privets, elms & towers, whence
a nightingale is throbbing.
Women sleep sound. I was happy once . .
(Something keeps on not happening; I shrink?)
These minutes all their passions & powers sink
and I am not one chance
for an unknown cry or a flicker of unknown eyes.

11

Chapped souls ours, by the day Spring's strong winds
swelled,
Jack's pulpits arched, more glad. The shawl I pinned
flaps like a shooting soul
might in such weather Heaven send.
Succumbing half, in spirit, to a salmon sash
I prod the nerveless novel succotash–
I must be disciplined,
in arms, against that one, and our dissidents, and myself.

12

Versing, I shroud among the dynasties;
quaternion on quaternion, tireless I phrase
anything past, dead, far,
sacred, for a barbarous place.
–To please your wintry father? all this bald
abstract didactic rime I read appalled
harassed for your fame
mistress neither of fiery nor velvet verse, on your knees

13

hopeful & shamefast, chaste, laborious, odd,
whom the sea tore.–The damned roar with loss,
so they hug & are mean
with themselves, and I cannot be thus.
Why then do I repine, sick, bad, to long
after what must not be? I lie wrong
once more. For at fourteen
I found my heart more carnal and sitting loose from God.

14

vanity & the follies of youth took hold of me;
then the pox blasted, when the Lord returned.
That year for my sorry face
so-much-older Simon burned,
so Father smiled, with love. Their will be done.
He to me ill lingeringly, learning to shun
a bliss, a lightning blood
vouchsafed, what did seem life. I kissed his Mystery.

15

Drydust in God's eye the aquavivid skin
of Simon snoring lit with fountaining dawn
when my eyes unlid, sad.
John Cotton shines on Boston's sin–
I ám drawn, in pieties that seem
the weary drizzle of an unremembered dream.
Women have gone mad
at twenty-one. Ambition mines, atrocious, in.

16

Food endless, people few, all to be done.
As pippins roast, the question of the wolves
turns & turns.
Fangs of a wolf will keep, the neck
round of a child, that child brave. I remember who
in meeting smiled & was punisht, and I know who
whispered & was stockt.
We lead a thoughtful life. But Boston's cage we shun.

17

The winters close, Springs open, no child stirs
under my withering heart, O seasoned heart
God grudged his aid.
All things else soil like a shirt.
Simon is much away. My executive stales.
The town came through for the cartway by the pales,
but my patience is short.
I revolt from, I am like, these savage foresters

18

whose passionless dicker in the shade, whose glance
impassive & scant, belie their murderous cries
when quarry seems to show.
Again I must have been wrong, twice.
Unwell in a new way. Can that begin?
God brandishes. O love, O I love. Kin,
gather. My world is strange
and merciful, ingrown months, blessing a swelling trance.

19

So squeezed, wince you I scream? I love you & hate
off with you. Ages! *Useless*. Below my waist
he has me in Hell's vise.
Stalling. He let go. Come back: brace
me somewhere. No. No. Yes! everything down
hardens I press with horrible joy down
my back cracks like a wrist
shame I am voiding oh behind it is too late

20

hide me forever I work thrust I must free
now I all muscles & bones concentrate
what is living from dying?
Simon I must leave you so untidy
Monster you are killing me Be sure
I'll have you later Women do endure
I can *can* no longer
and it passes the wretched trap whelming and I am me

21

drencht & powerful, I did it with my body!
One proud tug greens Heaven. Marvellous,
unforbidding Majesty.
Swell, imperious bells. I fly.
Mountainous, woman not breaks and will bend:
sways God nearby: anguish comes to an end.
Blossomed Sarah, and I
blossom. Is that thing alive? I hear a famisht howl.

Dylan Thomas (*Br. 1914–1953*)

The force that through the green fuse drives the flower

The force that through the green fuse drives the flower
Drives my green age; that blasts the roots of trees
Is my destroyer.
And I am dumb to tell the crooked rose
My youth is bent by the same wintry fever.

The force that drives the water through the rocks
Drives my red blood; that dries the mouthing streams
Turns mine to wax.
And I am dumb to mouth unto my veins
How at the mountain spring the same mouth sucks.

The hand that whirls the water in the pool
Stirs the quicksand; that ropes the blowing wind
Hauls my shroud sail.
And I am dumb to tell the hanging man
How of my clay is made the hangman's lime.

The lips of time leech to the fountain head;
Love drips and gathers, but the fallen blood
Shall calm her sores.
And I am dumb to tell a weather's wind
How time has ticked a heaven round the stars.

And I am dumb to tell the lover's tomb
How at my sheet goes the same crooked worm.

Do not go gentle into that good night

Do not go gentle into that good night,
Old age should burn and rave at close of day;
Rage, rage against the dying of the light.

Though wise men at their end know dark is right,
Because their words had forked no lightning they
Do not go gentle into that good night.

Good men, the last wave by, crying how bright
Their frail deeds might have danced in a green bay,
Rage, rage against the dying of the light.

Wild men who caught and sang the sun in flight,
And learn, too late, they grieved it on its way,
Do not go gentle into that good night.

Grave men, near death, who see with blinding sight
Blind eyes could blaze like meteors and be gay,
Rage, rage against the dying of the light.

And you, my father, there on the sad height,
Curse, bless, me now with your fierce tears, I pray.
Do not go gentle into that good night.
Rage, rage against the dying of the light.

After the Funeral

(In Memory of Ann Jones)

After the funeral, mule praises, brays,
Windshake of sailshaped ears, muffle-toed tap
Tap happily of one peg in the thick
Grave's foot, blinds down the lids, the teeth in black,
The spittled eyes, the salt ponds in the sleeves,
Morning smack of the spade that wakes up sleep,
Shakes a desolate boy who slits his throat
In the dark of the coffin and sheds dry leaves,
That breaks one bone to light with a judgment clout,
After the feast of tear-stuffed time and thistles
In a room with a stuffed fox and a stale fern,
I stand, for this memorial's sake, alone
In the snivelling hours with dead, humped Ann
Whose hooded, fountain heart once fell in puddles
Round the parched worlds of Wales and drowned each sun
(Though this for her is a monstrous image blindly
Magnified out of praise; her death was a still drop;
She would not have me sinking in the holy
Flood of her heart's fame; she would lie dumb and deep
And need no druid of her broken body).
But I, Ann's bard on a raised hearth, call all
The seas to service that her wood-tongued virtue
Babble like a bellbuoy over the hymning heads,
Bow down the walls of the ferned and foxy woods
That her love sing and swing through a brown chapel,
Bless her bent spirit with four, crossing birds.

Her flesh was meek as milk, but this skyward statue
With the wild breast and blessed and giant skull
Is carved from her in a room with a wet window
In a fiercely mourning house in a crooked year.
I know her scrubbed and sour humble hands
Lie with religion in their cramp, her threadbare
Whisper in a damp word, her wits drilled hollow,
Her fist of a face died clenched on a round pain;
And sculptured Ann is seventy years of stone.
These cloud-sopped, marble hands, this monumental
Argument of the hewn voice, gesture and psalm,
Storm me forever over her grave until
The stuffed lung of the fox twitch and cry Love
And the strutting fern lay seeds on the black sill.

Poem in October

It was my thirtieth year to heaven
Woke to my hearing from harbour and neighbour wood
And the mussel pooled and the heron
Priested shore
The morning beckon
With water praying and call of seagull and rook
And the knock of sailing boats on the net webbed wall
Myself to set foot
That second
In the still sleeping town and set forth.

My birthday began with the water–
Birds and the birds of the winged trees flying my name
Above the farms and the white horses
And I rose
In rainy autumn
And walked abroad in a shower of all my days.
High tide and the heron dived when I took the road
Over the border
And the gates
Of the town closed as the town awoke.

A springful of larks in a rolling
Cloud and the roadside bushes brimming with whistling
Blackbirds and the sun of October
Summery
On the hill's shoulder,
Here were fond climates and sweet singers suddenly
Come in the morning where I wandered and listened
To the rain wringing
Wind blow cold
In the wood faraway under me.

Pale rain over the dwindling harbour
And over the sea wet church the size of a snail
With its horns through mist and the castle
Brown as owls
But all the gardens
Of spring and summer were blooming in the tall tales
Beyond the border and under the lark full cloud.
There could I marvel
My birthday
Away but the weather turned around.

It turned away from the blithe country
And down the other air and the blue altered sky
Streamed again a wonder of summer
With apples
Pears and red currants
And I saw in the turning so clearly a child's
Forgotten mornings when he walked with his mother
Through the parables
Of sun light
And the legends of the green chapels

And the twice told fields of infancy
That his tears burned my cheeks and his heart moved in mine.
These were the woods the river and sea
Where a boy
In the listening

Summertime of the dead whispered the truth of his joy
To the trees and the stones and the fish in the tide.
　　And the mystery
　　　Sang alive
　Still in the water and singingbirds.

　And there could I marvel my birthday
Away but the weather turned around. And the true
　Joy of the long dead child sang burning
　　　In the sun.
　　It was my thirtieth
Year to heaven stood there then in the summer noon
Though the town below lay leaved with October blood.
　　O may my heart's truth
　　　Still be sung
　On this high hill in a year's turning.

A Refusal to Mourn the Death, by Fire, of a Child in London

Never until the mankind making
Bird beast and flower
Fathering and all humbling darkness
Tells with silence the last light breaking
And the still hour
Is come of the sea tumbling in harness.

And I must enter again the round
Zion of the water bead
And the synagogue of the ear of corn
Shall I let pray the shadow of a sound
Or sow my salt seed
In the least valley of sackcloth to mourn

The majesty and burning of the child's death.
I shall not murder
The mankind of her going with a grave truth
Nor blaspheme down the stations of the breath
With any further
Elegy of innocence and youth.

Deep with the first dead lies London's daughter,
Robed in the long friends,
The grains beyond age, the dark veins of her mother,
Secret by the unmourning water
Of the riding Thames.
After the first death, there is no other.

Fern Hill

Now as I was young and easy under the apple boughs
About the lilting house and happy as the grass was green,
  The night above the dingle starry,
    Time let me hail and climb
  Golden in the heydays of his eyes,
And honoured among wagons I was prince of the apple towns
And once below a time I lordly had the trees and leaves
    Trail with daisies and barley
  Down the rivers of the windfall light.

And as I was green and carefree, famous among the barns
About the happy yard and singing as the farm was home,
  In the sun that is young once only,
    Time let me play and be
  Golden in the mercy of his means,
And green and golden I was huntsman and herdsman, the calves
Sang to my horn, the foxes on the hills barked clear and cold,
    And the sabbath rang slowly
  In the pebbles of the holy streams.

All the sun long it was running, it was lovely, the hay
Fields high as the house, the tunes from the chimneys, it was air
  And playing, lovely and watery
    And fire green as grass.
  And nightly under the simple stars
As I rode to sleep the owls were bearing the farm away,
All the moon long I heard, blessed among stables, the nightjars
  Flying with the ricks, and the horses
    Flashing into the dark.

And then to awake, and the farm, like a wanderer white
With the dew, come back, the cock on his shoulder: it was all
  Shining, it was Adam and maiden,
    The sky gathered again
  And the sun grew round that very day.
So it must have been after the birth of the simple light
In the first, spinning place, the spellbound horses walking warm
  Out of the whinnying green stable
    On to the fields of praise.

And honoured among foxes and pheasants by the gay house
Under the new made clouds and happy as the heart was long,
  In the sun born over and over,
    I ran my heedless ways,
  My wishes raced through the house high hay
And nothing I cared, at my sky blue trades, that time allows
In all his tuneful turning so few and such morning songs
  Before the children green and golden
    Follow him out of grace,

Nothing I cared, in the lamb white days, that time would take me
Up to the swallow thronged loft by the shadow of my hand,
  In the moon that is always rising,
    Nor that riding to sleep
  I should hear him fly with the high fields
And wake to the farm forever fled from the childless land.
Oh as I was young and easy in the mercy of his means,
    Time held me green and dying
  Though I sang in my chains like the sea.

And death shall have no dominion

And death shall have no dominion.
Dead men naked they shall be one
With the man in the wind and the west moon;
When their bones are picked clean and the clean bones gone,
They shall have stars at elbow and foot;
Though they go mad they shall be sane,
Though they sink through the sea they shall rise again;
Though lovers be lost love shall not;
And death shall have no dominion.

And death shall have no dominion.
Under the windings of the sea
They lying long shall not die windily;
Twisting on racks when sinews give way,
Strapped to a wheel, yet they shall not break;
Faith in their hands shall snap in two,
And the unicorn evils run them through;
Split all ends up they shan't crack;
And death shall have no dominion.

And death shall have no dominion.
No more may gulls cry at their ears
Or waves break loud on the seashores;
Where blew a flower may a flower no more
Lift its head to the blows of the rain;
Though they be mad and dead as nails,
Heads of the characters hammer through daisies;
Break in the sun till the sun breaks down,
And death shall have no dominion.

Jean Garrigue (*Am. b. 1914*)

Primer of Plato

All endeavor to be beautiful:
The loved and the loveless as well:
All women rob from duty's time
To pitch adornment to its prime.
The lion in his golden coat
Begets his joy by that; his mate
Beneath that fiery mane repeats
The fury of each sudden sense.
The swan reflecting on the stream
The opposite feathers of the swan-
Webbed dream is like the fox at night
Who glows as in original delight.
Not least, the sun in tedious round
Bestows on rock and land
Principles that all creation
Imitates in adoration.

I never knew this till I
Chanced to see how your bright cheek
Brightened from the gaze of one
Who swam a spirit's Hellespont.
I saw then that beauty was
Both for lover and beloved a feast,
The lover mirroring by his joy
That flush beauty brings, in
His eye her actual face globed small,
And beauty flattered by that glass
Pitched to its highest comeliness,
Doubled and increased until
All would seem
Derived back into first essence.
Both animals and men dwell
In such a mirror of the real
Until in sudden ecstasy
They break the boundaries of that
glass
To be the image each first was.

Lightly Like Music Running

Lightly like music running, our blood
In the darling dogdays of early youth,
We nimbled with vines, ferns were cast over
The limpid lip of the sky, moistness we clambered.
This was the sun come dandling down
Green Babylon in the thronged sheaves–
Shelled such dingles, tan such bloom
By the roved brooksides, all the day long.
Lightly like music running, our blood
In and out of the cloud's woven pastures,
It was all in the shade of the vines and meadows
Where Adam delves, in the green fables
Of the dogdays, in early youth.

Barbara Howes (*Am. b. 1914*)

Light and Dark

Lady, take care; for in the diamond eyes
Of old old men is figured your undoing;
Love is turned in behind the wrinkled lids
To nurse their fear and scorn at their near going.
Flesh hangs like the curtains in a house
Long unused, damp as cellars without wine;
They are the future of us all, when we
Will be dried-leaf-thin, the sour whine
Of a siren's diminuendo. They have no past
But egg-husks shattered to a rubbish heap
By memory's looting. Do not follow them
To their camp pitched in a cranny, do not keep
To the road for them, a weary weary yard
Will bring you in; that beckoning host ahead,
Inn-keeper Death, has but to lift his hat
To topple the oldster in the dust. Read,
Poor old man, the sensual moral; sleep
Narrow in your bed, wear no
More so bright a rose in your lapel;
The spell of the world is loosed, it is time to go.

David Gascoyne (*Br. b. 1916*)

A Wartime Dawn

Dulled by the slow glare of the yellow bulb;
As far from sleep still as at any hour
Since distant midnight; with a hollow skull
In which white vapours seem to reel
Among limp muddles of old thought; till eyes
Collapse into themselves like clams in mud . . .
Hand paws the wall to reach the chilly switch;
Then nerve-shot darkness gradually shakes
Throughout the room. *Lie still.* . . . Limbs twitch;
Relapse to immobility's faint ache. And time
A while relaxes; space turns wholly black.

But deep in the velvet crater of the ear
A chirp of sound abruptly irritates.
A second, a third chirp; and then another far
Emphatic trill and chirrup shrills in answer; notes
From all directions round pluck at the strings
Of hearing with frail finely-sharpened claws.
And in an instant, every wakened bird
Across surrounding miles of air
Outside, is sowing like a scintillating sand
Its throat's incessantly replenished store
Of tuneless singsong, timeless, aimless, blind.

Draw now with prickling hand the curtains back;
Unpin the blackout-cloth; let in
Grim crack-of-dawn's first glimmer through the glass.
All's yet half sunk in Yesterday's stale death,
Obscurely still beneath a moist-tinged blank
Sky like the inside of a deaf mute's mouth. . . .
Nearest within the window's sight, ash-pale
Against a cinder coloured wall, the white
Pearblossom hovers like a stare; rain-wet
The further housetops weakly shine; and there,
Beyond, hangs flaccidly a lone barrage-balloon.

An incommunicable desolation weighs
Like depths of stagnant water on this break of day.–
Long meditation without thought.–Until a breeze
From some pure Nowhere straying, stirs
A pang of poignant odour from the earth, an unheard sigh
Pregnant with sap's sweet tang and raw soil's fine
Aroma, smell of stone, and acrid breath
Of gravel puddles. While the brooding green
Of nearby gardens' grass and trees, and quiet flat
Blue leaves, the distant lilac mirages, are made
Clear by increasing daylight, and intensified.

Now head sinks into pillows in retreat
Before this morning's hovering advance;
(Behind loose lids, in sleep's warm porch, half hears
White hollow clink of bottles,–dragging crunch
Of milk-cart wheels,–and presently a snatch
Of windy whistling as the newsboy's bike winds near,

Distributing to neighbour's peaceful steps
Reports of last-night's battles); at last sleeps.
While early guns on Norway's bitter coast
Where faceless troops are landing, renew fire:
And one more day of War starts everywhere.

Spring MCMXL

London Bridge is falling down, Rome's burnt, and Babylon
The Great is now but dust; and still Spring must
Swing back through Time's continual arc to earth.
Though every land become as a black field
Dunged with the dead, drenched by the dying's blood,
Still must a punctual goddess waken and ascend
The rocky stairs, up into earth's chilled air,
And pass upon her mission through those carrion ranks,
Picking her way among a maze of broken brick
To quicken with her footsteps the short sooty grass between;
While now once more their futile matchwood empires flare and
blaze
And through the smoke men gaze with bloodshot eyes
At the translucent apparition, clad in trembling nascent green,
Of one they can still recognise, though scarcely understand.

Robert Lowell (*Am. b. 1917*)

The Drunken Fisherman

Wallowing in this bloody sty,
I cast for fish that pleased my eye
(Truly Jehovah's bow suspends
No pots of gold to weight its ends);
Only the blood-mouthed rainbow trout
Rose to my bait. They flopped about
My canvas creel until the moth
Corrupted its unstable cloth.

A calendar to tell the day;
A handkerchief to wave away
The gnats; a couch unstuffed with storm
Pouching a bottle in one arm;
A whisky bottle full of worms;
And bedroom slacks: are these fit terms
To mete the worm whose molten rage
Boils in the belly of old age?

Once fishing was a rabbit's foot–
O wind blow cold, O wind blow hot,
Let suns stay in or suns step out:
Life danced a jig on the sperm-whale's spout–
The fisher's fluent and obscene
Catches kept his conscience clean.
Children, the raging memory drools
Over the glory of past pools.

Now the hot river, ebbing, hauls
Its bloody waters into holes;
A grain of sand inside my shoe
Mimics the moon that might undo
Man and Creation too; remorse,
Stinking, has puddled up its source;
Here tantrums thrash to a whale's rage.
This is the pot-hole of old age.

Is there no way to cast my hook
Out of this dynamited brook?
The Fisher's sons must cast about
When shallow waters peter out.
I will catch Christ with a greased worm,
And when the Prince of Darkness stalks
My bloodstream to its Stygian term . . .
On water the Man-Fisher walks.

Mr. Edwards and the Spider

I saw the spiders marching through the air,
Swimming from tree to tree that mildewed day
  In latter August when the hay
  Came creaking to the barn. But where

The wind is westerly,
Where gnarled November makes the spiders fly
Into the apparitions of the sky,
They purpose nothing but their ease and die
Urgently beating east to sunrise and the sea;

What are we in the hands of the great God?
It was in vain you set up thorn and briar
In battle array against the fire
And treason crackling in your blood;
For the wild thorns grow tame
And will do nothing to oppose the flame;
Your lacerations tell the losing game
You play against a sickness past your cure.
How will the hands be strong? How will the heart endure?

A very little thing, a little worm,
Or hourglass-blazoned spider, it is said,
Can kill a tiger. Will the dead
Hold up his mirror and affirm
To the four winds the smell
And flash of his authority? It's well
If God who holds you to the pit of hell,
Much as one holds a spider, will destroy,
Baffle and dissipate your soul. As a small boy

On Windsor Marsh, I saw the spider die
When thrown into the bowels of fierce fire:
There's no long struggle, no desire
To get up on its feet and fly–
It stretches out its feet
And dies. This is the sinner's last retreat;
Yes, and no strength exerted on the heat
Then sinews the abolished will, when sick
And full of burning, it will whistle on a brick.

But who can plumb the sinking of that soul?
Josiah Hawley, picture yourself cast
Into a brick-kiln where the blast
Fans your quick vitals to a coal–
If measured by a glass,

How long would it seem burning! Let there pass
A minute, ten, ten trillion, but the blaze
Is infinite, eternal: this is death,
To die and know it. This is the Black Widow, death.

The Quaker Graveyard in Nantucket

(for Warren Winslow, Dead at Sea)

Let man have dominion over the fishes of the sea and the fowls of the air and the beasts and the whole earth, and every creeping creature that moveth upon the earth.

I

A brackish reach of shoal off Madaket,–
The sea was still breaking violently and night
Had steamed into our North Atlantic Fleet,
When the drowned sailor clutched the drag-net. Light
Flashed from his matted head and marble feet,
He grappled at the net
With the coiled, hurdling muscles of his thighs:
The corpse was bloodless, a botch of reds and whites,
Its open, staring eyes
Were lustreless dead-lights
Or cabin-windows on a stranded hulk
Heavy with sand. We weight the body, close
Its eyes and heave it seaward whence it came,
Where the heel-headed dogfish barks its nose
On Ahab's void and forehead; and the name
Is blocked in yellow chalk.
Sailors, who pitch this portent at the sea
Where dreadnaughts shall confess
Its hell-bent deity,
When you are powerless
To sand-bag this Atlantic bulwark, faced
By the earth-shaker, green, unwearied, chaste
In his steel scales: ask for no Orphean lute
To pluck life back. The guns of the steeled fleet
Recoil and then repeat
The hoarse salute.

II

Whenever winds are moving and their breath
Heaves at the roped-in bulwarks of this pier,
The terns and sea-gulls tremble at your death
In these home waters. Sailor, can you hear
The Pequod's sea wings, beating landward, fall
Headlong and break on our Atlantic wall
Off, Sconset, where the yawing S-boats splash
The bellbuoy, with ballooning spinnakers,
As the entangled, screeching mainsheet clears
The blocks: off Madaket, where lubbers lash
The heavy surf and throw their long lead squids
For blue-fish? Sea-gulls blink their heavy lids
Seaward. The winds' wings beat upon the stones,
Cousin, and scream for you and the claws rush
At the sea's throat and wring it in the slush
Of this old Quaker graveyard where the bones
Cry out in the long night for the hurt beast
Bobbing by Ahab's whaleboats in the East.

III

All you recovered from Poseidon died
With you, my cousin, and the harrowed brine
Is fruitless on the blue beard of the god,
Stretching beyond us to the castles in Spain,
Nantucket's westward haven. To Cape Cod
Guns, cradled on the tide,
Blast the eelgrass about a waterclock
Of bilge and backwash, roil the salt and sand
Lashing earth's scaffold, rock
Our warships in the hand
Of the great God, where time's contrition blues
Whatever it was these Quaker sailors lost
In the mad scramble of their lives. They died
When time was open-eyed,
Wooden and childish; only bones abide
There, in the nowhere, where their boats were tossed
Sky-high, where mariners had fabled news
Of IS, the whited monster. What it cost
Them is their secret. In the sperm-whale's slick

I see the Quakers drown and hear their cry:
"If God himself had not been on our side,
If God himself had not been on our side,
When the Atlantic rose against us, why,
Then it had swallowed us up quick."

IV

This is the end of the whaleroad and the whale
Who spewed Nantucket bones on the thrashed swell
And stirred the troubled waters to whirlpools
To send the Pequod packing off to hell:
This is the end of them, three-quarters fools,
Snatching at straws to sail
Seaward and seaward on the turntail whale,
Spouting out blood and water as it rolls,
Sick as a dog to these Atlantic shoals:
Clamavimus, O depths. Let the sea-gulls wail

For water, for the deep where the high tide
Mutters to its hurt self, mutters and ebbs.
Waves wallow in their wash, go out and out,
Leave only the death-rattle of the crabs,
The beach increasing, its enormous snout
Sucking the ocean's side.
This is the end of running on the waves;
We are poured out like water. Who will dance
The mast-lashed master of the Leviathans
Up from this field of Quakers in their unstoned graves?

V

When the whale's viscera go and the roll
Of its corruption overruns this world
Beyond tree-swept Nantucket and Wood's Hole
And Martha's Vineyard, Sailor, will your sword
Whistle and fall and sink into the fat?
In the great ash-pit of Jehoshaphat
The bones cry for the blood of the white whale,
The fat flukes arch and whack about its ears,
The death-lance churns into the sanctuary, tears
The gun-blue swingle, heaving like a flail,
And hacks the coiling life out: it works and drags

And rips the sperm-whale's midriff into rags,
Gobbets of blubber spill to wind and weather,
Sailor, and gulls go round the stoven timbers
Where the morning stars sing out together
And thunder shakes the white surf and dismembers
The red flag hammered in the mast-head. Hide,
Our steel, Jonas Messias, in Thy side.

VI

Our Lady of Walsingham

There once the penitents took off their shoes
And then walked barefoot the remaining mile;
And the small trees, a stream and hedgerows file
Slowly along the munching English lane,
Like cows to the old shrine, until you lose
Track of your dragging pain.
The stream flows down under the druid tree,
Shiloah's whirlpools gurgle and make glad
The castle of God. Sailor, you were glad
And whistled Sion by that stream. But see:

Our Lady, too small for her canopy,
Sits near the altar. There's no comeliness
At all or charm in that expressionless
Face with its heavy eyelids. As before,
This face, for centuries a memory,
Non est species, neque decor,
Expressionless, expresses God: it goes
Past castled Sion. She knows what God knows,
Not Calvary's Cross nor crib at Bethlehem
Now, and the world shall come to Walsingham.

VII

The empty winds are creaking and the oak
Splatters and splatters on the cenotaph,
The boughs are trembling and a gaff
Bobs on the untimely stroke
Of the greased wash exploding on a shoal-bell
In the old mouth of the Atlantic. It's well;
Atlantic, you are fouled with the blue sailors,
Sea-monsters, upward angel, downward fish:

Unmarried and corroding, spare of flesh
Mart once of supercilious, wing'd clippers,
Atlantic, where your bell-trap guts its spoil
You could cut the brackish winds with a knife
Here in Nantucket, and cast up the time
When the Lord God formed man from the sea's slime
And breathed into his face the breath of life,
And blue-lung'd combers lumbered to the kill.
The Lord survives the rainbow of His will.

The Ghost

(after Sextus Propertius)

A ghost is someone: death has left a hole
For the lead-colored soul to beat the fire:
  Cynthia leaves her dirty pyre
  And seems to coil herself and roll
    Under my canopy,
Love's stale and public playground, where I lie
And fill the run-down empire of my bed.
I see the street, her potter's field, is red
And lively with the ashes of the dead;

But she no longer sparkles off in smoke:
It is the body carted to the gate
  Last Friday, when the sizzling grate
  Left its charred furrows on her smock
    And ate into her hip.
A black nail dangles from a finger-tip
And Lethe oozes from her nether lip.
Her thumb-bones rattle on her brittle hands,
As Cynthia stamps and hisses and demands:

"Sextus, has sleep already washed away
Your manhood? You forget the window-sill
  My sliding wore to slivers? Day
  Would break before the Seven Hills
    Saw Cynthia retreat
And climb your shoulders to the knotted sheet.
You shouldered me and galloped on bare feet
To lay me by the crossroads. Have no fear:
Notus, who snatched your promise, has no ear.

"But why did no one call in my deaf ear?
Your calling would have gained me one more day.
  Sextus, although you ran away
  You might have called and stopped my bier
    A second by your door.
No tears drenched a black toga for your whore
When broken tilestones bruised her face before
The Capitol. Would it have strained your purse
To scatter ten cheap roses on my hearse?

"The State will make Pompilia's Chloris burn:
I knew her secret when I kissed the skull
  Of Pluto in the tainted bowl.
  Let Nomas burn her books and turn
    Her poisons into gold;
The finger-prints upon the potsherd told
Her love. You let a slut, whose body sold
To Thracians, liquefy my golden bust
In the coarse flame that crinkled me to dust.

"If Chloris' bed has left you with your head,
Lover, I think you'll answer my arrears:
  My nurse is getting on in years,
  See that she gets a little bread–
    She never clutched your purse;
See that my little humpback hears no curse
From her close-fisted friend. But burn the verse
You bellowed half a lifetime in my name:
Why should you feed me to the fires of fame?

"I will not hound you, much as you have earned
It, Sextus: I shall reign in your four books–
  I swear this by the Hag who looks
  Into my heart where it was burned:
    Propertius, I kept faith;
If not, may serpents suck my ghost to death
And spit it with their forked and killing breath
Into the Styx where Agamemnon's wife
Founders in the green circles of her life.

"Beat the sycophant ivy from my urn,
That twists its binding shoots about my bones
  Where apple-sweetened Anio drones
  Through orchards that will never burn
    While honest Herakles,
My patron, watches. Anio, you will please
Me if you whisper upon sliding knees:
'Propertius, Cynthia is here:
She shakes her blossoms when my waters clear.'

"You cannot turn your back upon a dream,
For phantoms have their reasons when they come:
  We wander midnights: then the numb
  Ghost wades from the Lethean stream;
    Even the foolish dog
Stops its hell-raising mouths and casts its clog;
At cock-crow Charon checks us in his log.
Others can have you, Sextus; I alone
Hold: and I grind your manhood bone on bone.

Mary Winslow

Her Irish maids could never spoon out mush
Or orange-juice enough; the body cools
And smiles as a sick child
Who adds up figures, and a hush
Grips at the poised relations sipping sherry
And tracking up the carpets of her four
Room kingdom. On the rigid Charles, in snow,
Charon, the Lubber, clambers from his wherry,
And stops her hideous baby-squawks and yells,
Wit's clownish afterthought. Nothing will go
Again. Even the gelded picador
Baiting the twinned runt bulls
With walrus horns before the Spanish Belles
Is veiled with all the childish bibelots.

Mary Winslow is dead. Out on the Charles
The shells hold water and their oarblades drag,
Littered with captivated ducks, and now
The bell-rope in King's Chapel Tower unsnarls
And bells the bestial cow

From Boston Common; she is dead. But stop,
Neighbor, these pillows prop
Her that her terrified and child's cold eyes
Glass what they're not: our Copley ancestress,
Grandiloquent, square-jowled and worldly-wise,
A Cleopatra in her housewife's dress;
Nothing will go again. The bells cry: "Come,
Come home," the babbling Chapel belfry cries:
"Come, Mary Winslow, come; I bell thee home."

Louis O. Coxe (*Am. b. 1918*)

The Veteran

Alive where I lie and hide,
Ghosts and desires by night
With war and its vessels ride
On dream and my heart, in spite
Of miles inland from tide
And memory bled white.

The ships a man has served
Claim like a rousing touch
Delicate on the nerve
And bursting sleep for a watch:
A vessel yearns to curve
Forever an arc too much,

And gives to a man no trust
In sleep rocked under the past:
War and watchtime thrust
Below the dark and cast
The civil man to his lust
And the lookout to his mast.

The Lake

The light that labored to an early fall
Fell in the woods like rain, secret and spare,
And where the autumn road ran to a sprawl
At the lake's edge, four geese blundered into air,

And seemed to pluck my breath in foil of wings
That scooped the gathering dark, and in their ache
For height to take a rhythm from those springs
The heart feeds for the feeding of a lake–

That lake where autumn calls in brant and blue,
The whistler swan, all game and under gun,
Doomed and in wild beauty dear, those few
In pride that preen before the death of sun.

Upward with unseen purchase still they foil
The fallen heart with height as still they quest
For other feeding, one dark more to coil
Around them, perfect still until the last.

Red Right Returning

This red nun on my left hand leans away
From land's last fingerings, and with the tide
Strains gauntly for the hundred-fathom curve:
From here on, navigator, let the sea decide.

Behind lie promises that in our wash
Leap for fulfilment like this fairway nun,
Yet both are naked in dependency,
Brides to horizons when the ship has gone.

Yet this was known before. I come from coasts
Whose days are seaward looking, where the hills
Grew round with watching for the China barks
And mackerel seiners hustling to their sails.

And I have need of all sea-silent men
Whose reticence was loosened in their sons:
Very and Hawthorne held their loneliness
By right of heritage and trampling winds.

Be with me now, you travellers into hearts,
And bring me lucky through each threatened night,
That I may keep my promises and find
Known channels with a red nun on my right.

William Jay Smith (*Am. b. 1918*)

Persian Miniature

Ah, all the sands of the earth lead unto heaven.
I have seen them rise on the wind, a golden thread,
The sands of the earth which enter the eye of heaven,
Over the graves, the poor, white bones of the dead.
Over the buckling ice, the swollen rivers,
Over the ravened plains, and the dry creek-beds,
The sands are moving. I have seen them move,
And where the pines are bent, the orient
Grain awaits the passage of the wind.
Higher still the laden camels thread
Their way beyond the mountains, and the clouds
Are whiter than the ivory they bear
For Death's black eunuchs. Gold, silk, furs
Cut the blood-red morning. All is vain.
I have watched the caravans through the needle's eye
As they turn, on the threshing floor, the bones of the dead,
And green as a grasshopper's leg is the evening sky.

Dream

One day in a dream as I lay at the edge of a cliff,
The black water rose, and the children bobbed in the street.
Death with her bonfires signalled the planes to land
Where glass-beaked birds had pecked at my bound feet.

The water's bare hands reached round the base of the cliff,
And my heart cried, Hope, and my brain, There is nothing unknown.
I looked at my charts, and my kingdoms lay buried in sand,
My desiccate body picked clean as a bird's breast-bone.

The ships for the west weighed anchor; I watched them depart,
And on what impossible port were their prows then set
That they moved with a grace defying the mind and the heart,
With tackle of cloud, with decks encumbered and wet?

The air was like chalk; I was nothing. I thought I had
Reached the end of my dream; and I might have if
The waves had not risen and roared, the winds gone mad,
And when I awoke I lay at the edge of a cliff.

William Meredith (*Am. b. 1919*)

A View of the Brooklyn Bridge

The growing need to be moving around it to see it,
To prevent its freezing, as with sculpture and
metaphor,
Finds now skeins, now strokes of the sun in a dark
Crucifixion etching, until you end by caring
What the man's name was who made it,
The way old people care about names and are
Forever seeing resemblances to people now dead.

Of stone and two metals drawn out so
That at every time of day
They speak out of strong resemblances, as:
Wings whirring so that you see only where
Their strokes finish, or: spokes of dissynchronous
wheels

Whose pictures and poems should accurately be
signed
With the engineer's name, whatever he meant;
These are called: *Tines inflicting a river, justly,*
Or, thinking how its cables owe each something
To the horizontal and something to the vertical:
A graph of the odds against
Any one man's producing a masterpiece

Yet far from his, the engineer's, at sunrise
And again at sunset when,
Like the likenesses the old see,
Loveliness besets it as haphazard as genes:
Fortunate accidents take the form of cities
At either end, the cities give their poor edges

To the river, the buildings there
The fair color that things have to be.
Oh, the paper reeds by a brook
Or the lakes that lie on bayous like a leopard
Are not at more seeming random, or more certain
In their sheen how to stand than these towns are.

And of the rivering vessels so and so
Where the shadow of the bridge rakes them once.
The best you can think is that, come there,
A pilot will know what he's done
When his ship is fingered

Like that greek boy whose name I now forget
Whose youth was a long study to cut stone;
One day his mallet slipped, a goddess willing
Who only meant to take his afternoon,
So that the marble opened on a girl
Seated at music and wonderfully fleshed
And sinewed under linen, riffling a harp;
At which he knew not that delight alone
The impatient muse intended, but coupled with it, grief–
The strings in particular were so light–
And put his chisel down for marvelling on that stone.

Reed Whittemore (*Am. b. 1919*)

An American Takes a Walk

In the middle of this life's journey
He came, like Dante, on a wood
The notes said stood for error
But in his case stood for good,
Where his art and prowess left him
And left him become a child
To whom the wild seemed milder
Than his old neighborhood.

Had he, with those abandoned
Sons of fatal decrees,
Then been found by a shepherd
And bred up to shepherdese,
Or retrieved, like Dante, by Virgil
And led through circles and seas
To some brighter country beyond
His annotated trees,

He could not have been more cared for.
Nature was awfully kind.
Hell in that motherly habit
Put hell quite out of mind.

How in that Arden could human
Frailty be but glossed?
How in that Eden could Adam
Be really, wholly lost?

The Line of an American Poet

That American Poet's future
Was bright because he began
With the know-how of Ford and Chrysler
And the faith of American Can.

He fathomed success's secret
And stuck to his P's and Q's
And urged himself, over and over,
To produce and produce and produce.

His very first models were cleverly
Built; the market boomed.
Some of the world's most critical
Consumers looked, and consumed.

Lines off his line came smoother
And smoother as more and more
Know-how came in the window
And verses rolled out the door,

Until everyone in the market
Knew that his new works were sure
To be just what the country had need of:
Poems uniform, safe and pure.

Shakespeare, Possibly, in California

The weather in London and Stratford-on-Avon was so
Sticky the great man took it as long as he could,
Called up his bank, hired a coach, and with "Oh
For a draught of Keats' vintage," left for good.

In his patio by the sea he lounges now,
Aged and weathered, wrinkled and worn, and saddled
With one of those Ardens that younger and wiser he knew
To be best left to his lovers lost and addled.

His shiny old head heaven's sun, like a patron, caresses.
His sightless old eyes heaven's ocean swells to in praise.
But none of the grace of that landscape his darkness blesses.
He is beyond that, and back in his salad days.

There where a few old players saw the air,
And the rest is a summer silence of sun and sand,
He has come in his dotage to live a life free from care
In a fool's pastoral setting getting tanned.

Howard Nemerov (*Am. b. 1920*)

The Winter Lightning
for Paul

Over the snow at night,
And while the snow still fell,
A sky torn to the bone
Shattered the ghostly world with light;
As though this were the moon's hell,
A world hard as a stone,
  Cold, and blue-white.

As if the storming sea
Should sunder to its floor,
And all things hidden there
Gleam in the moment silently,
So does the meadow at the door
To split and sudden air
  Show stone and tree.

From the drowned world of dark
The sleeping innocence
Surrenders all its seeming;
Under the high, charged carbon arc
Light of the world, a guilty sense
Stiffens the secret dreaming
  Animal park.

So in the camera's glare
The fortunate and famed,
For all their crooked smiles,
Reveal through their regarded stare
How all that's publicly acclaimed
One brutal flash reviles
  For cold despair.

So is the murderer caught
When his lost victim rises
Glaring through dream and light
With icy eyes. That which was thought
In secret, and after wore disguises,
Silts up the drowning sight
  Mind inwrought.

So may the poem dispart
The mirror from the light
Where none can see a seam;
The poet, from his wintry heart
And in the lightning second's sight,
Illuminate this dream
  With a cold art.

Truth

Around, above my bed, the pitch-dark fly
Buzzed in the darkness till in my mind's eye
His blue sound made the image of my thought
An image that his resonance had brought
Out of a common midden of the sun–
A garbage pit, and pile where glittering tin
Cans turned the ragged edges of their eyes
In a mean blindness on mine, where the loud flies

Would blur the summer afternoons out back
Beyond the house. Sleepy, insomniac, black
Remainder of a dream, what house? and when?
Listening now, I knew never again
That winged image as in amber kept
Might come, summoned from darkness where it slept
The common sleep of all such sunken things
By the fly's loud buzzing and his dreaming wings.

I listened in an angry wakefulness;
The fly was bitter. Between dream and guess
About a foundered world, about a wrong
The mind refused, I waited long, long,
And then that humming of the garbage heap
I drew beneath the surface of my sleep
Until I saw the helmet of the king
Of Nineveh, pale gold and glittering
On the king's brow, yet sleeping knew that I
But thought the deepening blue thought of the fly.

Richard Wilbur (*Am. b. 1921*)

The Death of a Toad

A toad the power mower caught,
Chewed and clipped of a leg, with a hobbling hop has got
To the garden verge, and sanctuaried him
Under the cineraria leaves, in the shade
Of the ashen heart-shaped leaves, in a dim,
Low, and a final glade.

The rare original heartsblood goes,
Spends on the earthen hide, in the folds and wizenings, flows
In the gutters of the banked and staring eyes. He lies
As still as if he would return to stone,
And soundlessly attending, dies
Toward some deep monotone,

Toward misted and ebullient seas
And cooling shores, toward lost Amphibia's emperies
Day dwindles, drowning, and at length is gone
In the wide and antique eyes, which still appear
To watch, across the castrate lawn,
The haggard daylight steer.

Bell Speech

The selfsame toothless voice for death or bridal:
It has been long since men would give the time
To tell each someone's-change with a special chime,
And a toll for every year the dead walked through.
And mostly now, above this urgent idle
Town, the bells mark time, as they can do.

This bavardage of early and of late
Is what is wanted, and yet the bells beseech
By some excess that's in their stricken speech
Less meanly to be heard. Were this not so,
Why should Great Paul shake every window plate
To warn me that my pocket watch is slow?

Whether or not attended, bells will chant
With a clear dumb sound, and wide of any word
Expound our hours, clear as the waves are heard
Crashing at Mount Desert, from far at sea,
And dumbly joining, as the night's descent
Makes deltas into dark of every tree.

Great Paul, great pail of sound, still dip and draw
Dark speech from the deep and quiet steeple well,
Bring dark for doctrine, do but dim and quell
All voice in yours, while earth will give you breath.
Still gather to a language without flaw
Our loves, and all the hours of our death.

NOTES

As will be seen, the purpose of these notes is primarily to give biographical information about the various authors in the anthology. The sentences of appreciation which follow are intended *not* as critical estimates but only to call attention to those characteristics in each author's work which make it, in the editors' view, interesting and enjoyable.

D. C.
A. T.

NOTES ON THE BRITISH POETS

HILAIRE BELLOC (1870–1953). Educated at the Oratory School, Edgbaston, and Balliol College, Oxford. From 1906 to 1910 he was a Member of Parliament. Celebrated as a Roman Catholic apologist. Published many historical, biographical, and critical works, and various volumes of essays, poems, and humorous verses. *Collected Verse* (1954).

His poems are a small part of his output; and not all of them are equally good. But he wrote light verse, both satirical and nonsensical, of a classical force and finish, and he is the most accomplished English master of the verse epigram, whether grave or gay, since Landor.

JOHN BETJEMAN (*b.* 1906). Educated at Marlborough and Oxford. He has earned his living as a schoolmaster and journalist, and has made himself eminent not only as a poet but as an authority on English architecture, notably that of the nineteenth century. His poetic works are: *Continual Dew* (1937); *Old Lights for New Chancels* (1940); *New Bats in Old Belfries* (1944); *Selected Poems* (1948); and *A Few Late Chrysanthemums* (1954).

Mr. Betjeman is one of the most widely enjoyed of living poets; and also one of the most original. Not that he is a 'modernist'; on the contrary, he derives his style from poets of the last century, notably Tennyson and Hardy: but he employs it to convey a vision of reality at once individual and contemporary. In his verses, the heterogeneous confusion of present-day England, with its mixture of antique villages and Victorian suburbs and modern mechanized roads and petrol stations, are portrayed in a mingled mood of horror, affection, and amusement, so as to create a new country of the imagination, living and unique as Trollope's Barset. Nor is Mr. Betjeman's poetry without deeper overtones. It is given intensity and pathos by his poignant sense of the precariousness of things human, and by his Anglo-Catholic faith.

LAURENCE BINYON (1869–1943). Born at Lancaster; educated at St. Paul's School and Trinity College, Oxford. A great authority on Oriental art and in later life became Keeper of Prints and Drawings in the British Museum. Was made a C.H. in 1932 for his services to literature. Was Charles Eliot Norton Professor of Poetry, Harvard University, 1933–34. Published books on art, critical studies, plays, poems, and a distinguished translation of the *Divine Comedy* of Dante.

Poetic publications include: *Collected Poems* (1931); *The North Star and other poems* (1941); *The Burning of the Leaves* (1944).

Binyon is among the most eminent of those poets of the twentieth century who carefully pursued a traditional path. The poems included here reveal his accomplished art, his observation of nature, and his sensibility to the beautiful. *The Little Dancers* shows the same sort of aesthetic refinement as a nocturne of Whistler.

EDMUND BLUNDEN (*b.* 1896). Born in London; educated at Christ's Hospital and Queen's College, Oxford. Served in 1914 war; won an M.C. In 1922 was awarded the Hawthornden Prize for *The Shepherd*; Professor of English Literature at Tokyo University, 1924–27; Fellow and Tutor in English Literature at Merton College, Oxford, 1931–43; Professor of English Literature at the University of Hong Kong since 1953. Author of various prose works (including *Undertones of War*) and many volumes of poetry. Was awarded a C.B.E. in 1951.

Mr. Blunden is one of the most distinguished of the 'Georgian' poets. He is both countryman and scholar; the two strains appear in his poetry. His acquaintance with the English countryside is intimate, and he has a fresh eye for its details. But he expresses his vision in a highly literary style, studied, elaborate, and resonant with echoes of the voices of past ages and dead poets. Mr. Blunden's muse does not give up her secret very readily, but once we are in her confidence her company is a source of enduring pleasure.

GORDON BOTTOMLEY (1874–1948). Born at Keighley; educated at Keighley Grammar School. Author of many volumes of verse and plays. In 1923 was awarded the Femina Prize, Paris, and in 1925 the Benson Medal of the Royal Society of Literature. Publications include: *Poems of Thirty Years* (1925); *Poems and Plays* (1953).

A latter-day Pre-Raphaelite; Bottomley's best-known works are drama and verse set in ancient times. In *The End of the World* he writes of the future but manages to make it seem primitive. It is a poem conceived with a strong eerie imagination; a conception curiously enhanced by the slow, muted rhythms and deliberately understated language in which he has chosen to express it.

RONALD BOTTRALL (*b.* 1906). Born in Cornwall; educated at Redruth County School and Pembroke College, Cambridge. Fellowship Princeton University, U.S.A.; taught English in Helsinki, Singapore, and Florence; British Council Representative in Sweden, Italy, and Brazil. Recent works include: *The Palisades of Fear* (1949); *Adam Unparadised* (1954). Awarded O.B.E., 1949. Awarded Syracuse International Poetry Prize, 1954. F.R.S.L.

Mr. Bottrall's clever, ingenious, colloquial poetry is interesting both in itself and because he was one of the first English writers whose work was directly influenced by the school of critics who arose in Cambridge after the first war, under the leadership of I. A. Richards.

ROBERT BRIDGES (1844–1930). Born at Walmer; educated at Eton and Corpus Christi College, Oxford. After qualifying and practising as a doctor he finally gave up medicine for literature in 1882, by which time he had already published three volumes of poems. Numerous further volumes of poetry and plays and literary criticism followed and in 1913 Bridges was appointed Poet Laureate. After 1900 he published several volumes of poetry and *The Testament of Beauty* (1929).

The lyrics which are this great writer's most famous work were most of them written before 1900, but the work he did afterwards has its own beauty and interest. Bridges, who had always been deeply concerned with the technical aspect of his art, sought to develop a freer and more flexible mode of expression, sometimes in lyric, sometimes in a new metre–"rhymeless, loose Alexandrines" as he called them–that should easily accommodate itself to the clear expression of ideas. It was in this metre he wrote his most ambitious work, the long philosophical poem called *The Testament of Beauty*, from which four extracts are given here. Poetry and philosophy are seldom happy companions to each other, nor does Bridges often manage to make them so. But the poem includes some pieces of wonderful natural description; for Bridges was one of the most perceptive landscape painters that England ever produced.

There are poets in this volume who are more imaginative and more passionate than Bridges, but none give a finer or more enduring satisfaction. He has an exquisite quality of feeling at once subtle and serene; and he is a master of his craft, with a just sense of the quality and flavour of every word he employs, and a delicate ear to adjust the movement of his verse to the movement of his thought and sentiment.

RUPERT BROOKE (1887–1915). Born at Rugby, the son of a Rugby master. Educated at Rugby and King's College, Cambridge. He took part in the unsuccessful defence of Antwerp in 1914. He died on his way to take part in the Dardanelles expedition in 1915. His first book of verses was published in 1911 and his *Collected Poems* in 1918.

Rupert Brooke is a notable illustration of the unimportance of being 'contemporary'. Young, beautiful, and brilliant, he expressed admirably the mood of intelligent aspiring youth in the period 1910–14: so that in his lifetime, and for some years after, his poetic reputation was very high. Since then it has declined with the passing of the age of which it was so exact an expression. However, Brooke's exuberant, accomplished rhetoric, strengthened as it is by a sharp eye for visual appearances, can still give pleasure: while connoisseurs of 'period' will always delight in *Grantchester*, so vividly does it convey the flavour of the Georgian Age, just before the 1914 war.

IGNATIUS ROY DUNNACHIE CAMPBELL (1901–57). Born at Durban; educated at Durban High School. By religion Roman Catholic; served during the war of 1939–45 till disabled in 1944. His first volume of poems, *The Flaming Terrapin*, was published in 1924; *Collected Poems* (1955); and *Collected Poems Vol. II* (1957). Has also written autobiographical works and translations.

Campbell was a South African and did not belong to any school of English poets. His work is vividly coloured, exotic, and informed by a conscious and aggressive virility. He has something of D. H. Lawrence in his intense sensual apprehension of the physical world;

and within his limits he is a master of versification. The rhythm of his lines drives onward, with a pulsing controlled energy.

GILBERT KEITH CHESTERTON (1874–1936). Born in London; educated at St. Paul's School. Published his first book, *The Wild Knight and other poems*, in 1900. A prolific professional writer and journalist who produced stories, essays, critical studies, biographies, and an autobiography. Became a Roman Catholic in 1922 and devoted much of his writing to defending the Roman Catholic position.

Chesterton was a great friend of Belloc's, whose political and religious views he shared; he was less of a poet, in the strict sense of the word, but rather a skilful versifier, who used verse as he used prose as a means to expound his opinions as entertainingly and as forcibly as possible, illustrating them with gay coloured decorations in the Pre-Raphaelite manner. His most considerable poetic work, *The Ballad of the White Horse*, shows him doing this in the form of a ballad about King Alfred's war with the Danes. In the extract given here the representatives of various forms of paganism announce their philosophies of life and are answered by Alfred as the representative of Christianity. It is not poetry as we use the word of Hopkins's or Bridges's work; but it is a dazzling performance. And once or twice, as in the speech of Elf the Minstrel, the tone softens to touch something higher and deeper.

MARY ELIZABETH COLERIDGE (1861–1907). Daughter of a lawyer and great-great-niece of Samuel Taylor Coleridge. She was a considerable figure in a distinguished literary circle which included Bridges and Henry Newbolt. A classical scholar and a woman of firm though undogmatic religious faith, Mary Coleridge was the author of novels, essays, and a number of lyrics published after her death, of which a few were written in this century. Her *Collected Poems* were published in 1954. The lyrics are short but varied, including direct outbursts of emotion, ironical epigrams, and mysterious snatches of ballad that recall her great relative, the author of *Christabel*. In all these veins she was successful. She was a woman of remarkable imagination who, were it not that she lacked the finer sense of style, would be one of the greatest of English poetesses. As it is, she has been unjustly neglected.

FRANCES CORNFORD (*b.* 1886). Born at Cambridge; daughter of Francis Darwin and granddaughter of Charles Darwin. She married Prof. F. M. Cornford. Her first *Poems* were published in 1910 and her *Collected Poems* in 1954.

Mrs. Cornford is a woman, a humorist, and a lifelong observer of Cambridgeshire. These aspects appear delightfully in her accomplished, clear-coloured, unpretentious verse.

WILLIAM HENRY DAVIES (1871–1940). Born at Newport, Mon., of Welsh parents. Spent his life as a vagabond and tramp in England and America. His first volume of poems, *The Soul's Destroyer*, was published in 1907, and his famous *Autobiography of a Super-Tramp* in

1908, and *Collected Poems* in 1928. He was also the author of much other work, both prose and poetry.

W. H. Davies appeared in the Georgian books. But he does not belong to the Georgian school or any other. He is an example of that individual phenomenon, the pure lyric poet, who sings spontaneously to please himself: and his songs, though superficially influenced by past writers like Wordsworth or Herrick, sound his own unmistakable note of naïve, fresh sweetness, saved from insipidity by a strain of rough peasant realism.

CECIL DAY LEWIS (*b.* 1904). Born in Ireland; educated at Sherborne School and Wadham College, Oxford. Schoolmaster from 1927 to 1935; editor of books and pamphlets, Ministry of Information, 1941–6; gave the Clark Lectures at Cambridge on 'The Poetic Image', 1947; awarded C.B.E. in 1950; Professor of Poetry at Oxford University, 1951–56. His first work was *Beechen Vigil and other poems* (1925); *Collected Poems* (1954); *Pegasus and other Poems* (1957). Has written poems, critical works, and translations from the classics, and detective novels under the pseudonym of Nicholas Blake.

Mr. Day Lewis's work has gone through various phases. Starting as a 'pure' poet in the Yeats tradition, he was affected, like his friend Auden, by the left-wing idealism of the 'thirties. In his later work he turned to more personal and reflective poetry, partly inspired by that of Hardy. Mr. Day Lewis is a dignified, sincere, tender-hearted writer, who expresses himself in a manner which keeps a steady balance between ancient and modern. The quotation from *A Time to Dance* is specially interesting as a rare instance of the 'modern' style applied to narrative of action. It is illuminating to compare it with the piece of similar narrative, but in a more traditional manner, quoted from Masefield's *Reynard the Fox*.

WALTER DE LA MARE (1873–1956). Born in Kent, educated at St. Paul's Cathedral Choir School. Spent eighteen years in the service of the Standard Oil Company (Anglo-American Branch) before devoting himself to literature. Published his first book, *Songs of Childhood*, in 1902, under the name of Walter Ramal. Since then he has equally distinguished himself as a poet and as the author of short stories and novels, notably *The Memoirs of a Midget* and the collection called *The Riddle*, which explore the same vein of imagination as do his poems. He was made a C.H. in 1948 for his services to literature, and received the O.M., the highest distinction which England has to give, in 1953. Publications include various poems which were collected in two volumes: *Collected Poems* (1942) and *Collected Rhymes and Verses* (1944); since then *The Traveller* (1946), *Inward Companion* (1949), *Winged Chariot* (1951), and *O Lovely England* (1952).

De la Mare's poetical works consist mainly of lyrics, though in recent years he has written two long poems, *The Traveller*, a symbolical narrative, and *Winged Chariot*, a meditation on time. He is an inheritor of the romantic tradition, notably influenced by Coleridge, Blake, and Christina Rossetti. This does not prevent him from being an extremely original author, who has created a world all his own, compounded of childhood memories, minute natural observation, whimsical fantasy and ghostly terror, and which is the image of his own odd profound vision of reality. This vision exhibits itself more fully in his prose than in his poems, for the best of these are brief lyrics played on an instrument which, though capable of exquisite subtleties of phrase and rhythm, is yet too light-weight and limited in range to sustain an extended work. Yet, if de la Mare's poems reveal his vision only in fragmentary glimpses, these are conveyed with an extraordinary intensity. No writer of this age has explored so far into the mysterious hinterland of man's consciousness as this beautiful, elusive, disquieting genius.

LAWRENCE DURRELL (*b.* 1912). Educated at Canterbury. Has lived in the Mediterranean and the Argentine. Was made a F.R.S.L. in 1954. Books of verse: *Ten Poems* (1932); *Transition* (1934); *A Private Country* (1943); *Cities, Plains and People* (1946); *On Seeming to Presume* (1948); *Sappho* (1950); *The Tree of Idleness* (1955); *Selected Poems* (1956).

Mr. Durrell intelligently, vividly, detachedly evokes scenes, generally exotic scenes, and also the personal moods in which he surveyed them, and recollects them.

CLIFFORD HENRY DYMENT (*b.* 1914). Born in Derbyshire of Welsh parents; educated at Loughborough Grammar School. Free-lance journalist and critic 1934–40; writer and director of documentary films for Ministry of Information, British Council and War Office, 1942–8. Atlantic Award for Literature 1950. Publications include: *First Day* (1935); *Selected Poems* (1943); *The Axe in the Wood* (1944); *Poems 1935–48* (1949); *Experiences and Places* (1955); *C. Day Lewis*, in British Council's *Writers and their Work* series (1955).

As has been said in the Introduction, the "modern" and elliptical mode of expression does not usually lend itself to descriptive purposes. But Mr. Dyment has adapted it to illustrate the rural scene with concentrated vividness and a fresh witty fancy. He is one of the most agreeable of recent poets.

THOMAS STEARNS ELIOT (*b.* 1888). Born in St. Louis, Missouri, U.S.A.; educated at Harvard University, the Sorbonne, and Merton College, Oxford. Clark Lecturer, Trinity College, Cambridge, 1926; after a brief period as a schoolmaster, was employed in the Colonial and Foreign department of Lloyds Bank; Director of Faber and Faber; Charles Eliot Norton Professor of Poetry, Harvard University, 1932–33; late editor *The Criterion*; Nobel Prize for Literature 1948. Awarded O.M. 1948. Publications include: *Collected Poems 1909-35* (1936); *Old Possum's Book of Practical Cats* (1939); *Four Quartets* (1944). Plays: *Murder in the Cathedral* (1935); *The Family Reunion* (1939); *The Cocktail Party* (1949); *The Confidential Clerk* (1954). Has also written a number of critical essays.

Mr. Eliot has been, with the possible exception of Yeats, the most influential figure in English poetry during the century. The nature of the revolution he has effected has already been spoken of in the

Introduction. His output has been small, but his range is large, extending as it does from the ironical, dandyish verse of his first volume to the intellectual panorama of *The Waste Land*, the poignant devotional lyrics of *Ash Wednesday*, and the profound meditative poetry of the *Four Quartets*. His method makes him inevitably obscure, and anyone who wishes to get all they can out of him must be prepared to study him as though he were a Greek classic. However, he will find assistance if he chooses, notably in the book on *Four Quartets* written by Miss Helen Gardner. The task is well worth it. Mr. Eliot's complexity is a necessary complexity, for it expresses an extremely complex nature and mind, that of an American deeply soaked in the literature ancient and modern of Europe, who has in the end elected to live as an Englishman in England. The New World and the Old, the past and the present, the Latin and the Saxon, all meet in him. Any mode simpler than his would not have expressed their author fully. Moreover, his poems can also communicate an intense and immediate pleasure. He has a unique power of conveying the atmosphere of the modern city, an impeccable and most original ear for the music of verse and a wonderful gift for the condensed evocative phrase.

> "The pain of living and the drug of dreams
> Inexplicable splendour of Ionian white and gold."

WILLIAM EMPSON (*b.* 1906). Born in Yorkshire; educated at Winchester and Magdalene College, Cambridge. He has occupied Chairs of English Literature in China and Japan; has been Professor of English Literature, Sheffield University, since 1953. He has written three books of literary criticism: *Seven Types of Ambiguity* (1930), *Some Versions of Pastoral* (1935), and *The Structure of Complex Words* (1951), and has also published two collections of verse: *Poems* (1935) and *The Gathering Storm* (1940); *Collected Poems* (1955).

Mr. Empson is an influential and original critic concerned in particular to explore the meanings and implications of individual words. His poems are of a piece with his prose. In them he likes to crystallize an intellectual situation in a metaphysical image which is, most characteristically, a witty concentration of modern scientific thought. At his best, as in *This Last Pain*, he achieves a remarkable and impressive intensity from the very strictness of the formal and intellectual conditions, within which he forces himself to work. Though he has written little, he has exercised a considerable influence, and Mr. Empson has been a model and example to an interesting neo-metaphysical group of young poets who are too young for inclusion in this anthology.

JAMES ELROY FLECKER (1884–1915). Born at Lewisham; educated at Uppingham and Trinity College, Oxford. Entered Consular Service and became Vice-Consul at Beirut in 1911. His first work, *The Bridge of Fire*, appeared in 1907; his collected prose and the plays *Hassan* and *Don Juan* were published posthumously, and *Collected Poems* (1946).

Flecker is a late flower of the aesthetic movement of the 'nineties, and influenced by the example of the Parnassian School in France, who aspired to achieve effects of exotic beauty in picked, jewelled phrases. Of the two poems included here, *The Old Ships* represents him in his typical vein, while in *November Eves* he has for once made a happy try at something simpler and more native.

DAVID GASCOYNE (*b.* 1916). Educated at Salisbury Cathedral Choir School and Regent Street Polytechnic. First book of poems published in 1932. Spent some time in France. Publications include: *Man's Life is This Meat* (1936); *Holderlin's Madness* (1938); *Poems 1937-42* (1943); *A Vagrant and other poems* (1950); *Night Thoughts* (1956); also translations; essay: *Thomas Carlyle* (1951). F R.S.L.

Mr. Gascoyne is one of the most interesting of the poets who made their reputation after the political phase of the 'thirties. At his best he reveals great descriptive power–especially well can he suggest the lurid, livid quality in the modern scene–and a capacity for expressing the sombre visions of a troubled spirit in impassioned rhetorical verse.

WILFRID GIBSON (*b.* 1878). Born at Hexham, Northumberland. Served in the 1914–18 war. Has published a number of volumes of poetry, including: *Collected Poems* (1926); *Solway Ford and other poems* (1945); *Coldknuckles* (1947).

Mr. Gibson is one of the best and most representative of the Georgian poets. He has their characteristic merits, describes the English scene well, and in an apt and unpretentious colloquial diction can convey a nuance of feeling. In poems like *Flannan Isle* he succeeds in achieving Wordsworth's aim of investing what might seem an ordinary and insignificant incident with the "light that never was on sea or land".

ROBERT RANKE GRAVES (*b.* 1895). Born in London; educated at Charterhouse and St. John's College, Oxford. Infantry captain in 1914–18 war; Professor of English Literature, Egyptian University, Cairo, 1926. Has been domiciled in Majorca since 1929. Clark Lecturer at Cambridge University 1954–55. Well known as novelist, critic, and historian as well as poet. Since his *Collected Poems 1914–47* appeared, he has published *Poems and Satires* (1951), *Poems* (1953), and included sixteen pieces more in his *Crowning Privilege* (1955).

Mr. Graves made his name as a poet during the war of 1914; he then wrote straightforward lyric, adorned with a touch of homely, folk-tale fantasy. In his later books Mr. Graves has gradually developed an intellectual strain in his work and 'stripped' his style to evolve a new sort of manner, more difficult than his earlier but weightier and subtler in its effect, concentrated, ironical, idiosyncratic. He is one of the strongest and most individual poets now writing; and, like Yeats, manages, while remaining true to his own inspiration, to bridge the gulf between the old poetry and the new.

THOMAS HARDY (1840–1928). Born at Upper Bockhampton near Dorchester, son of a builder. Started his career as an architect, but turned to literature and first made a name by his magnificent novels. His first volume of poems, *Wessex Poems*, was published in 1898. This was followed by *The Dynasts*, a long epic drama also in verse, in 1903, 1906, and 1908. Awarded O.M. in 1910. His last volume of verse, *Winter Words*, was published in 1928, and *Collected Poems* in 1954.

Hardy's poetry, though it shows the influence of William Barnes, his predecessor as a Dorset poet, and of Browning, from whom he borrowed the idea of the dramatic monologue, is from the first unmistakably personal in style. It is a strange style, blending as it often does, a lilting, lyrical movement, with a diction sometimes ponderous and often prosaic. All the same, it is the only style that could appropriately express Hardy's naïve, intense, and sublime vision of life. Even its apparent clumsiness gives authenticity and pathos to his grimness, his gaiety, his tender, ironical compassion. His very lapses are the lapses of a great and lovable genius: and now and again–*Shut Out that Moon* and *The Voice* are examples–he is stirred by some unusual intensity of feeling to soar upwards in a strain of poignant, throbbing, irresistible song, unparalleled by any other poet in this collection.

RALPH HODGSON (*b.* 1871). Born in Co. Durham, but has passed later part of his life in the U.S.A. Lecturer in English Literature at Sendai University, Japan, 1924–38. Publications: *The Last Blackbird and other lines* (1907); *The Bull* (1913); *Eve and other poems* (1913); *The Mystery and other poems* (1913); *The Song of Honour* (1913); *Poems* (1917). Awarded Queen's Gold Medal, 1954.

Hodgson's work appeared in the Georgian books, and he is typically Georgian in his liking for a simple and unpretentious diction and his gentle, humanitarian sentiment. But his work is given an individuality by the vivid un-English colours in which he paints his pictures and the energy of his lyrical movement. *The Bull* has a graphic concentrated pathos not to be found in the work of most of his fellow Georgians.

GERARD MANLEY HOPKINS (1844–89). Educated at Highgate School and Balliol College, Oxford. Converted to Roman Catholicism in 1866; entered Jesuit novitiate in 1868; Professor of Greek at Dublin University 1884. His poems were first collected and published by his friend Robert Bridges in 1930.

Hopkins is included in this anthology because none of his work appeared till 1930 when his poems were published by his friend Bridges: in fact Hopkins's work was all written in the last century and, as both Yeats and Mr. Eliot have been at pains to point out, it is of its age; a characteristic though original offshoot of nineteenth-century romanticism, and not the expression of a modern born before his time. Ancient or modern, however, Hopkins is a great poet, combining an extraordinary intensity of passion, ecstatic or despairing, with a sensibility to beauty that has a Keatsian delicacy and richness. Added to this, Hopkins was an untiring experimentalist, alike in diction and metre. Sometimes his experiments are so bold as to make his work unintelligible; but at his best he achieves an astonishing and Shakespearean felicity of phrase.

ALFRED EDWARD HOUSMAN (1859–1936). Educated at Bromsgrove School and St. John's College, Oxford. Became one of the most distinguished classical scholars of his time and Professor of Latin, first at the University of London and subsequently at Cambridge. His poetic reputation, however, rests on three books of verses–*A Shropshire Lad* (1896), *Last Poems* (1922), and *More Poems* (1936); *Collected Poems* (1953).

A scholar by profession, Housman was also a scholar poet, a highly conscious artist deliberately blending in his style strains from Greek Anthology, from the songs of Shakespeare, and from the poems of Heine. His form was lucid, polished, and classical, but he employed it to express a feeling for nature and an ironical, pessimistic, agnosticism typical of the romantic age. Though his output was small, he crystallized a prevailing mood of his time with an extraordinary intensity and accomplishment. No poet of his time achieved the same kind of popularity.

RUDYARD KIPLING (1865–1936). Born in Bombay and educated at United Services College, Devon. Worked as a journalist in India from 1882 to 1889. Made his name with the publication of *Departmental Ditties* and a number of short stories from 1886 to 1888. Quickly accepted as one of the leading English writers. For the next forty-odd years or so continued to publish stories for grown-up people and children, poems and novels. Awarded Nobel Prize for Literature in 1907. *Collected Works in Prose and Verse* (1937).

Kipling's verse is only a small part of his achievement. It is as technically virtuosic as his prose. His most individual poems are the colloquial realistic ballads of military life which appeared in the nineteenth century. Mr. Eliot has praised them and Mr. Auden has learnt from them; indeed, any author who wishes to make modern mass society utter itself in verse, can hardly fail to be influenced directly or indirectly by Kipling. His best later poems, like those included in this anthology, are in a more traditional manner. The three included here express his sense of the past and of the romance of history.

DAVID HERBERT LAWRENCE (1885–1930). Born at Eastwood, Nottinghamshire, son of a coal-miner. Educated at the High School and University College, Nottingham. Became a clerk and a schoolmaster; travelled in Italy, New Mexico, and Australia; died of consumption near Nice. Distinguished as novelist, short-story writer as well as poet. *Collected Poems* (1928); *Last Poems* (1933); *Complete Poems* (1957).

Lawrence's poetry is a less important part of his achievement than is his prose; but it is of a piece with it. Like Hardy and Emily Brontë, he is that typical English phenomenon, the poet story-teller whose inspiration seems to express itself equally well in both modes, so that his novels have a poetic intensity and his poems a prose-like realism. Lawrence, moreover, wrote many of his poems in a free verse form which he learnt from Whitman, and which brings them still nearer to prose. Even when he writes in a conventional verse form he is careless of 'style' in the more restricted sense of the term, and is always liable to grow slack and summary in his use of language. But he has an unusual ability to communicate a moment of emotion in all its raw immediacy, and a unique power of apprehending and conveying sensual experience. The reader feels as if he could almost smell and touch the snake and the kangaroo in Lawrence's poems about them.

LAURIE LEE (*b.* 1914). Educated at Slad Village School and Stroud Central School. Publications–poems: *The Sun My Monument* (1944); *The Bloom of Candles* (1947); *My Many-Coated Man* (1955); two verse dramas: *Peasants' Priest* and *The Voyage of Magellan*; travel: *A Rose in Winter* (1955).

Mr. Lee has published little, but enough to show his pleasing individual talent, which unites a fresh sensuousness of temper with a gay, decorative sense and a crisp up-to-date elegance of form.

LOUIS MACNEICE (*b.* 1907). Born in Belfast; educated at Marlborough and Merton College, Oxford. Has been Lecturer in Classics at Birmingham University and Bedford College, and has written and produced for the B.B.C.; also Lecturer of Poetry at Cornell University, 1940; Director of British Institute, Athens, 1950. Has written plays, translations, critical works, and a number of volumes of poetry, including: *Poems* (1935); *Autumn Journal* (1939); *Collected Poems* (1949); *Ten Burnt Offerings* (1952); *Autumn Sequel* (1954) and *Visitations* (1957).

During the early 'thirties when he made his reputation, Mr. MacNeice was associated with the poetic movement led by Auden, Spender, and Day Lewis, and he shared their preoccupation with the contemporary scene and, in some degree, their political bias. But his style was more visual and coloured than theirs–how vividly he describes the Irish landscape, for instance–and his spirit more ironical and light-hearted. At his best he writes with economy, vitality, and a sort of glittering, stream-lined stylishness like that of an up-to-date racing motor-car.

JOHN MASEFIELD (*b.* 1878). Son of a solicitor of Ledbury, Herefordshire; educated at King's School, Warwick; sent at the age of thirteen to the training ship *Conway*. At fifteen and a half was apprenticed to a windjammer, but soon abandoned the sea as a profession. He later decided to become a man of letters and has written books of many kinds, including poetry, plays, and novels. His first book of poems, *Salt-Water Ballads*, appeared in 1902. In the next ten years his reputation steadily rose till, with the publication of *The Everlasting Mercy* in 1911, he was recognized as one of the leading English poets. Has received honorary degrees at Universities of Oxford, Cambridge, Harvard, and Yale; Poet Laureate, 1930; awarded O.M., 1935. Among his most important poetic works are: *The Widow in the Bye-Street*; *Dauber*; *Reynard the Fox*; *Right Royal*; and a number of lyrics.

Mr. Masefield has written a great number of poems of all kinds, but he made his greatest mark by his long narratives of contemporary life. The first was *The Everlasting Mercy* and the most popular

Reynard the Fox, of which an excerpt is given in this anthology. These narratives are best described as an attempt to adapt the manner of Chaucer to the present day. Vigorous and realistic, they shocked some readers at first, but delighted a great many more. Indeed they are the last English narrative poems to be easily read and enjoyed by a wide public. Mr. Masefield has a lively, accurate sense of the English scene and, what is rare among poets, he does know how to tell a story.

Alice Christiana Meynell (1847–1922). Born at Barnes, daughter of Thomas James Thompson. Educated by her father; spent much of her youth in Italy; became a Roman Catholic in 1872; married Wilfrid Meynell in 1877. While still young she made a considerable reputation as a poetess and won the admiration of Rossetti, Meredith, and Patmore. Lectured in U.S.A. on Dickens, Brontës, and seventeenth-century poetry, 1901–2. Her first volume of poems, *Preludes*, appeared in 1875; other publications include: *Poems* (1893); *Other Poems* (1896); *Later Poems* (1902); *A Father of Women and other poems* (1917); *Last Poems* (1923). Also wrote critical essays.

She was a careful artificer, of delicate elaborate verses that express a civilized feminine sensibility, a metaphysical wit, and a firm, clear, Roman Catholic faith.

Edwin Muir (*b.* 1887). Born in the Orkneys; educated at Kirkwall Burgh School, Orkney. Assistant editor of *The New Age*, 1919–20; author, translator; after the war, Director of the British Institute in Prague and in Rome; became Warden of Newbattle Abbey College in 1950; Charles Eliot Norton Lecturer, Harvard University, 1955. Has written criticism, poetry, and autobiography. His volumes of poetry include: *First Poems* (1925); *The Labyrinth* (1949); *Collected Poems 1921–51* (1952) and *One Foot in Eden* (1957).

Mr. Muir is one of the most penetrating literary critics now alive, and his poems have the intellectual acuteness and subtlety to be expected from such a critic. Though their grey colouring and the keen chill wind that blows through them betray their northern origin, they are not specifically Scottish in character, but suggest some nameless saga-like region. Mr. Muir, while not a member of the Symbolist School, is a symbolist in the sense we use the word of Kafka, whose work he has translated. The pictures, at once clear-cut and enigmatic, which he conjures before our mental eye, image his meditations on the nature of spiritual reality.

Wilfred Owen (1893–1918). Born at Oswestry; educated at the Birkenhead Institute and the University of London. Enlisted in the Artists' Rifles in 1915; was awarded the M.C. and killed in action 1918. His poems were first collected in 1920 by Siegfried Sassoon, and a fuller edition with a memoir by Edmund Blunden was published in 1933.

With Mr. Sassoon, Wilfred Owen is the most famous of those poets of the 1914–18 war who wrote to express the horror and indignation which modern warfare produced in them. His aim is best expressed in his own words:

"My subject is War, and the pity of War.
The Poetry is in the pity.
Yet these elegies are to this generation in no sense consolatory. They may be to the next. All a poet can do to-day is warn."

Owen succeeded in his aim. He experimented a little with assonances and half lines but wrote for the most part in a traditional and romantic manner, derived from Keats. It is the passion and pity that fill his heart that make his poems so deeply memorable.

Ruth Pitter (*b.* 1897). Born in Essex; educated at Coborn School, Bow. Has published a number of volumes of poems, including: *First Poems* (1920); *A Trophy of Arms* (1936), for which she was awarded Hawthornden Prize; *Urania* (1950); and *The Ermine* (1953). Queen's Medal for Poetry, 1955.

This beautiful writer, by steadily following her bent without regard to trends and movements, has achieved a distinguished place among living poets. She combines a delicately sharp eye for the natural scene with a visionary still intensity of feeling which glorifies her observation without blurring it. The firm, fastidious nobility of her style is the true mirror of her mind and imagination.

Frank Templeton Prince (*b.* 1912). Born at Kimberley, South Africa; educated in South Africa and at Balliol College, Oxford. During the war was a captain in the Intelligence Corps. He is now a lecturer in English Literature at the University of Southampton. Publications include: *Poems* (1938); *Soldiers Bathing and other poems* (1954).

Mr. Prince is one of the most interesting poets who have made their name in the last twenty years. His poetry is such as might be expected from the distinguished scholar that he is. Though influenced by Yeats and Mr. Eliot and the metaphysical poets, his dignified and thoughtful verse reveals an individual mind and sensibility, enriched and refined by an informed sense of history and a long acquaintance with the European tradition of culture.

Peter Quennell (*b.* 1905). Educated at Berkhamsted Grammar School and Balliol College, Oxford. Professor of English Literature, Tokyo Bunrika Daigaku, 1930. Critic, biographer, and editor. His *Collected Poems* were published in 1926.

Mr. Quennell is now celebrated as a critic and biographer; his poetry is a product of his youth. But there is nothing immature about it. It recalls the poetry of late nineteenth-century France rather than that of twentieth-century England; aesthetic poetry which aims at and achieves an effect of concentrated, ornate and impersonal beauty.

Henry Reed (*b.* 1914). Born and educated in Birmingham; graduated M.A. at Birmingham University. Journalist and broadcaster. Poetic publication: *A Map of Verona* (1946).

Mr. Reed is a modern poet of the educated, careful, aesthetic type and shows the influence of Yeats and Mr. Eliot. His poems are made personal and delightful by his sense of decorative elegance and the play of his neat and graceful wit.

Anne Ridler (*née* Brady) (*b.* 1912). Born at Rugby. In 1938 married Vivian Ridler. She has published two main collections of poems, *The Nine Bright Shiners* (1943) and *The Golden Bird* (1951)–these were preceded by smaller collections: *Poems* and *A Dream Observed*–and three books of verse plays: *Cain* (1944), *The Shadow Factory* (1946), and *Henry Bly* (1950).

Mrs. Ridler's poems are mainly inspired by religion and by the domestic affections, though she has also a vivid sense of place. Her style shows the influence of Mr. Eliot, but the spirit that informs them, warm and feminine and now and again lit up by playful humour, is her own.

William Robert Rodgers (*b.* 1909). Born in Ulster and educated at Queen's University, Belfast. Twelve years a clergyman in County Armagh; joined the B.B.C., 1946–52. His collection of verse, *Awake! and other poems*, was published in 1941.

Mr. Rodgers is one of the most spontaneous and exuberant of modern poets: vividly observant of the sensuous world and delighting in the glittering display of verbal fireworks and metrical virtuosity.

Victoria Sackville-West (*b.* 1892). Born at Knole, Sevenoaks, daughter of Lord Sackville. Educated at home. Married Sir Harold Nicolson. Distinguished as poet, novelist, and biographer. *The Land* received the Hawthornden Prize in 1927. Publications include: *Collected Poems* (1933); *The Eagle and the Dove* (1943); *The Garden* (1946). Was made a C.H. in 1948.

Miss Sackville-West is one of the most accomplished exponents of the traditional style now writing. It is hard to do justice to her in an anthology, for she works most effectively on a big scale. Her two most important works, *The Land* and *The Garden*, are long descriptive pieces in a manner suggested by the Georgics of Virgil. But the shorter pieces here included do something to suggest her sensitive, accurate, descriptive powers and her skill as a craftsman. In *A Dream* she reveals a rarer vein of stately, picturesque fantasy.

Siegfried Sassoon (*b.* 1886). Educated at Marlborough and Clare College, Cambridge. Served in the 1914–18 war and was awarded the M.C. He made his reputation by his war poems. After the war he increased it by his prose work *The Complete Memoirs of George Sherston*: the first part of this, *Memoirs of a Fox-hunting Man*, was awarded the Hawthornden Prize and the James Tait Black Memorial Prize in 1929. He has also published three volumes of autobiography, a biography of Meredith, and a number of volumes of poems, including *Collected Poems* (1947) and *Sequences* (1956). Was awarded a C.B.E. in 1951 and Queen's Medal for Poetry, 1957.

Mr. Sassoon's poems are short but varied in mood. He began as a lyrical and elegiac poet of country life and solitary musing. The war of 1914 affected him violently and he became, with Wilfred Owen, the leader of the writers whose aim was to expose the horror of war. In the post-war years he returned to his earlier vein, varied at times by excursions into the whimsical and the satiric. His work is the expression of a blended disposition. The quality of his sentiment, sometimes tender and nostalgic, sometimes on fire with romantic, defiant bitterness, belongs to his generation. But his art, easy, graceful, sharpened by wit, and with an eye for realistic detail, recalls the eighteenth century. He is a poet of the Cowper type who has grown up under the shadow of Hardy and Housman.

E. J. SCOVELL (*b.* 1907). Educated at Somerville College, Oxford. Married to Charles Elton. Publications: *Shadows of Chrysanthemums and other poems* (1944); *The Midsummer Meadow and other poems* (1946); *The River Steamer and other poems* (1956).

Miss Scovell's output is small but extremely distinguished. She expresses her fine sensibility, especially to natural beauty, with an economical felicity that recalls the best Chinese paintings.

FREDEGOND SHOVE (1889–1949). Born at Downing College, Cambridge, daughter of F. W. Maitland, the eminent historian. Publications: *Dreams and Journeys* (1918); *Daybreak* (1922); *Christina Rossetti* (1931); *Poems* (1956).

Mrs. Shove is a late flower of the Pre-Raphaelite school, a poetess of the school of Christina Rossetti. But her work is unmistakably her own, marked with a characteristic, fresh, wistfulness of sentiment, a characteristic, flute-like music.

EDITH SITWELL (*b.* 1887). Born at Scarborough, daughter of Sir George Sitwell; educated privately. Is an Hon. D.Litt. of Leeds, Durham, and Oxford. Was made a Dame in 1954. Among the volumes of poems are: *Sleeping Beauty* (1918); *Collected Poems* (1930); *Street Songs* (1942); *The Song of the Cold* (1945); *Gardeners and Astronomers* (1953); *Collected Poems* (1957).

Dame Edith Sitwell is one of the most famous of living poets, and one of the most enjoyable. Her work has passed through various phases; the impish, modish, light verses of *Façade*; the romantic evocations of fairy-tale and childhood of the *Sleeping Beauty* and *Troy Park*; the macabre satire of *Gold Coast Customs*, and the poignant lamentations of *The Song of the Cold*. Every phase is marked by the same strong, original personality. Though technically a pioneer, and responsive to the age she lives in, Dame Edith is a child of the aesthetic movement, ultimately inspired by her sensibility to the beautiful. In strains of music, varied but always melodious, she transports us to a world of her own creation, in which fantasy and flippancy, elegance and wistfulness, rapture and horror combine to form an exquisite whole.

SACHEVERELL SITWELL (*b.* 1897). Son of Sir George Sitwell; educated at Eton. Has published poems and a number of prose books which are mainly imaginative studies of art and music. His poems include: *Canons of Giant Art* (1933); *Collected Poems* (1936); *Selected Poems* (1948).

Like his sister, Mr. Sacheverell Sitwell is an aesthetic poet. His sensibility to the beautiful is most frequently stimulated by works of art and antiquity. The rich, musical, entranced verses included in this anthology are an excerpt from one of his *Canons of Giant Art* in which he seeks to convey the imaginative impression made on him by a picture, rather as Walter Pater sought to convey the imaginative impression made on him by the Mona Lisa of Leonardo da Vinci.

STEPHEN SPENDER (*b.* 1909). Educated at University College School, London, and University College, Oxford. A friend of Auden, Day Lewis, and MacNeice, he made his poetic reputation in the 'thirties. Was a member of the Fire Service during the war. Has written poems, dramas, criticism, essays, and an autobiography. *Collected Poems* (1955).

Like Mr. Auden and Mr. Day Lewis Mr. Spender was inspired by left-wing political sympathies. Like them too, his subsequent work has been personal rather than political. His work, however, has always been more introverted than theirs; it has seemed more an expression of his immediate and private reactions to experience. But he has a great gift for description, as is shown by the poems here quoted.

JAMES STEPHENS (1882–1950). Born in Dublin. A fantasist in poetry and prose whose most famous work was *The Crock of Gold* published in 1912. *Collected Poems* (1954).

Mr. Stephens's whimsical, Celtic fancy finds most sustained expression in his prose works. But he is most completely satisfying in his lyrics. The instrument he plays on is a simple one – a pipe perhaps or a penny whistle; but his bird-like tunes are his own and he plays them with an effortless and economical art.

DYLAN MARLAIS THOMAS (1914–53). Born at Swansea; educated at Swansea Grammar School. Distinguished himself as a broadcaster; wrote poems, stories, essays, and fragments of autobiography, *Portrait of the Artist as a Young Dog*. His poetic works include: *Eighteen Poems* (1934); *Collected Poems* (1952); and *Under Milk Wood* (1954), a drama for broadcasting.

Dylan Thomas was the most sensational figure to appear in English poetry during the last twenty years. His concentrated symbolism and the bold tricks he played with language make him a poet of the new school. But his sensuous richness, his pulsing dithyrambic rhythms, and the unselfconscious emotional ardour which informed his lines, recall an earlier romanticism. He is a spellbinder whose spells do not always work; the reader is sometimes dazed and stunned by the confused shower of words Dylan Thomas pours over him. But he has some glittering successes. "I wrote my poems to the glory of God and the love of man," he proclaimed. A poem like *Fern Hill* where childhood's joy, all glowing with the mists of dawn, is conveyed with a wonderful immediacy, bears witness to the truth of this proclamation.

EDWARD THOMAS (1878–1917). Educated at St. Paul's School and Lincoln College, Oxford. Made his living as a free-lance author

writing reviews and topographical and biographical works. Served in
His *Collected Poems* appeared with a preface by Walter de la Mare
the Artists' Rifles in the 1914–18 war and was killed in action at Arras.
in 1920.

Though an author all his life, Edward Thomas only began writing poetry in his thirties, when Robert Frost suggested to him that he should do so. The two men shared a feeling for nature and a common ideal of poetic style, plain, colloquial and understated. Thomas's poetry lacks Frost's shrewd strength, his racy tang of the solid earth; it is dreamier, more contemplative, and coloured by the associations of a picturesque, historical past. The horns of elfland, though muted, sound in his lines as they never do in Frost's. Of all the Georgian school he has survived the most successfully. Indeed his delicately hued water-colours with their meticulous eye for detail, their power to evoke a complex mood in a few simple lines, are as satisfying as anything in twentieth-century English poetry.

VERNON WATKINS (*b.* 1906). Born in Wales and educated at Repton and Magdalene College, Cambridge. Entered Lloyds Bank, 1925; served in R.A.F., 1941–46. His first volume, *The Ballad of the Mari Lwyd*, was published in 1941; this was followed by *The Lamp and the Veil* (1945); *The Lady with the Unicorn* (1948); *The Death-Bell: Poems and Ballads* (1954); and *The North Sea* (poems translated from Heine) (1955).

Like Dylan Thomas, Mr. Watkins is a Welshman, and he too, though using the symbolist mode, is in spirit the child of an earlier romanticism. But he is less forceful, less sensual, less of an experimentalist with words. His musical opalescent verse expresses the impressions of a fastidious, aesthetic sensibility, and the dreams of an imagination soaked in myth and legend, and warmed by Christian sentiment.

LAURENCE WHISTLER (*b.* 1912). Educated at Stowe and Balliol College, Oxford. Awarded King's Gold Medal for Poetry, 1935; served during war of 1939–45; is a poet, engraver on glass, designer, and writer on art and architecture. Awarded O.B.E. in 1955. Publications include: *The World's Room* (collected poems) (1949); *The View from this Window* (1956).

Mr. Whistler when not writing poetry engraves on glass; and his work in both modes is of a piece; revealing a delicate sensibility to the beautiful in art and nature, and an elaborate, carefully controlled craft.

WILLIAM BUTLER YEATS (1865–1939). Born at Sandymount in Ireland; son of John Butler Yeats, a painter; educated partly in Ireland, partly in England. Made his name as a poet with *Poems* (1895); subsequently played a large part in the organization of the Abbey Theatre; divided his time between England and Ireland, but settled in Ireland as a Senator in 1922–28; Nobel Prize for Literature, 1923. All his life published poems, plays, critical works, spiritual meditations. *Collected Poems* (1955).

The career of this wonderful writer is a record at once of consistency and development. From the first, Yeats was a dedicated poet, whose first motive for writing was not so much to express his feelings or ideas as to create objects of beauty by means of a studied and accomplished art. His mode of doing this, however, is varied. He started as a sort of Irish Pre-Raphaelite singing in soft, dreamy words of mists and moonlight and Celtic legend. But during this century he deliberately adopted a new mode at once terse, colloquial and rhetorical, and occasionally distinguished by a highly individual use of symbols drawn from history, art, and his own experience. In this new manner – of which most poems here are examples – Yeats has written love poetry, political poetry, epigrams grave or ironical, elegiac verses, and impassioned philosophical meditations. Yeats's philosophy, a mysterious hotch-potch of aestheticism, Oriental spiritualism, and pagan sensuality, is extremely hard to understand; nor have the critics, who have devoted their time to expounding it, succeeded in making it explicable. But unlike that of Bridges, for instance, Yeats's philosophy did inspire his muse. Indeed he adorned every mode he attempted. If he never profoundly touches the heart, as Hardy does – his work is too coldly and consciously beautiful for that – yet the variety of his achievement, his sustained mastery of his medium, and his glittering, tameless force of temperament combine to make him the only modern poet in the grand style.

ANDREW YOUNG (*b.* 1885). Born in Elgin; educated in Edinburgh at the Royal School and the University. Took Holy Orders and is now Vicar of Stonegate, Sussex, and a Canon of Chichester Cathedral. An authority on wild flowers. His *Collected Poems* appeared in 1950. In 1951 received the degree of LL.D. at Edinburgh University; in 1952 was awarded the Queen's Medal for Poetry.

Mr. Young, like Miss Pitter, by steadily pursuing his own course over a long period of years, has achieved an honourable and independent position among poets writing today. Though, like the Georgians, he is a nature poet writing in a traditional style, he differs from them. For he is not a 'romantic'. His work consists mainly of terse pieces of objective description to which the play of an odd metaphysical wit adds an individual flavour, like that of some pungent country herb.

NOTES ON THE AMERICAN POETS

LÉONIE ADAMS, born in Brooklyn, New York, 9 December 1899, of Southern ancestry, was educated at Barnard College (B.A., 1922). As an undergraduate she began to write poetry. Her first published poem, *April Mortality*, appeared in *The New Republic*; her first book, *Those Not Elect* (1925), introduced a lyric poet of great distinction. In the twenty-five years between her second and her third volume, *Poems: A Selection* (1954), new poetic fashions somewhat obscured her reputation, with all but a handful of admirers who elected her to the Chair of Poetry at the Library of Congress and to membership in the National Institute of Arts and Letters. In 1955 she shared with Louise

Bogan the award of the Bollingen Prize of Yale University. Works: *Those Not Elect* (1925); *High Falcon* (1929); *Poems : A Selection* (1954). Miss Adams's poetry is in the tradition of the great English Romantics, with influences from the seventeenth-century Metaphysicals and, latterly, from the later French Symbolists. She has a powerful intellect which appears in her verse not as 'intellectuality' but as the order of an acute sensibility. She has taught at various colleges and universities, and is now on the creative writing staff of Columbia University.

CONRAD (POTTER) AIKEN was born of New England ancestry in Savannah, Georgia, in 1889. He was educated in New England, entering Harvard with the famous class of 1911, which included T. S. Eliot, John Hall Wheelock, and Van Wyck Brooks. His first book of verse, *Earth Triumphant and Other Tales in Verse*, appeared in 1914. For some years he was contributing editor to *The Dial*; in the early 1920's he moved to England, where he lived for many years. Although Aiken won distinguished awards, including the Pulitzer Prize for Poetry (1929) and the Shelley Memorial Award, his brilliant gifts were not publicly recognized until 1956, when he was given the Bollingen Prize. Principal works: *Scepticisms* (1919); *Selected Poems* (1929); *John Deth and Other Poems* (1930); *Ushant : An Essay* (autobiography, 1952); *Collected Poems* (1953); *A Letter from Li Po* (1955); play: *Mr. Arcularis* (1957). Of the literary generation of Eliot, Pound, Stevens, and Marianne Moore, his less spectacular qualities have not inspired fashions and cults. His style is musical and evocative, even in the long psychological narratives like *John Deth* and *Tetelestai*–two of the finest poems in English of this century; these, along with *Preludes for Memnon* (1931), have won a permanent place in the poetry of our time.

W(YSTAN) H(UGH) AUDEN was born in 1907 in York, England, and attended Gresham's School, Holt, and Christ Church College, Oxford. For five years (1930–35) he taught school at Malvern, England. During the 'thirties he was a leader of the leftist 'Oxford poets,' including Stephen Spender, Louis MacNeice, and C. Day Lewis. In 1937 he drove an ambulance for the Spanish Loyalists. He received the King's Poetry Medal in 1937. He came to the United States in 1939, and shortly afterwards became an American citizen. By 1940 he had written four volumes of poetry, a collection of prose fiction, two anthologies, three plays, and two travel books. Auden has taught at the University of Michigan, Haverford College and the New School in New York City, and has lectured at many other colleges and universities. He was given an award from the American Academy of Arts and Letters in 1945, and he won the Pulitzer Prize in 1948 for *The Age of Anxiety*. A member of the American Academy of Arts and Letters, he lives in New York City. Principal works: *Poems* (1930); *On This Island* (1937); *Selected Poems* (1938); *The Double Man* (1941); *For the Time Being* (1944); *Collected Poetry of W. H. Auden* (1954); *The Age of Anxiety* (1947); criticism: *The Enchafed Flood* (1950); *Nones* (1951); *The Shield of Achilles* (1955).

STEPHEN VINCENT BENÉT (1898–1943) was born in Bethlehem, Pennsylvania. He began early to write poems and continued writing and publishing while a student at Yale University, from which he received a B.A. in 1919 and an M.A. in 1920. A fellowship took him to the Sorbonne for further study. Returning to the United States with his wife Rosemary, he devoted himself primarily to short-story writing. The years 1926 and 1927 saw him again in France, on a Guggenheim Fellowship. There he wrote a long poem about the Civil War, *John Brown's Body*, a popular work which won the Pulitzer Prize in 1928. He was given the Shelley Memorial Award in 1932 and the O. Henry Award for his prose narrative *The Devil and Daniel Webster*, and was made a member of the National Institute of Arts and Letters. During the early years of the 1939–45 war, Benét wrote a number of poems and radio documentaries on behalf of the Allied cause. Principal works: *Five Men and Pompey* (dramatic portraits, 1915); *John Brown's Body* (1928); stories: *Thirteen O'Clock* (1927); *Selected Works of Stephen Vincent Benét* (1942); *Western Star* (unfinished, 1943).

Benét must be described as an accomplished poet of the second order. *John Brown's Body* and some of the shorter poems of American places and heroes will have a permanent place in American literature.

JOHN BERRYMAN was born in McAlester, Oklahoma, in 1914. He studied at the South Kent School, Connecticut, at Columbia University (A.B., 1936), and at Clare College, Cambridge (B.A., 1938). He has taught at a number of universities, including Wayne, Harvard, Princeton, the University of Cincinnati, and the University of Minnesota. He has published short stories, criticism, and reviews, as well as poetry, and has been given numerous awards, among them: *The Kenyon Review*–Doubleday First Prize in 1945 for a short story; *Poetry* magazine's Guarantors and Levinson Awards; the Shelley Memorial Award, 1949; a National Institute of Arts and Letters grant, 1950. He was given a Guggenheim Fellowship in 1953. Berryman is the author of three volumes of verse: *Poems* (1942), *The Dispossessed* (1948), and *Homage to Mistress Bradstreet* (1956). He has also written a critical biography of Stephen Crane in the American Men of Letters Series (1950).

The most accomplished scholar of his generation of American poets, Berryman in *Homage to Mistress Bradstreet* has written one of the half-dozen first-rate long poems by an American of this century. The diction is concentrated and powerful and the rhythms, though somewhat influenced by Hopkins, are distinctly original.

ELIZABETH BISHOP was born in Worcester, Massachusetts, in 1911, and was graduated from Vassar College in 1934. She has been the recipient of several fellowships for poetry, including the Houghton Mifflin (1945), Guggenheim (1947), and Lucy Martin Donnelly (1951) fellowships. A Fellow in American Letters of the Library of Congress, Miss Bishop was a Consultant in Poetry for the Library during 1949–50. She is a member of the American Institute of Arts and Letters from which she won an award in 1951. In 1952 she was given the Shelley Memorial Award, and in 1956 the Pulitzer Prize. Miss Bishop now lives in Rio de Janeiro, Brazil. She is the author of two books of verse: *North and South* (1946) and *Poems: North and South–A Cold Spring* (1955).

Miss Bishop's earlier poems showed the influence of Marianne Moore in their precise denotation of objects and in the use of the direct prose statement. It is the poetry of wit and ironic fantasy.

John Peale Bishop (1892–1944) was born in Charles Town, West Virginia, in the Shenandoah Valley. He was educated at the Mercersburg Academy in Pennsylvania, and was graduated in 1917 from Princeton University where his close friends included Edmund Wilson and F. Scott Fitzgerald. A First Lieutenant of Infantry in the war of 1914–18, he remained in Europe until 1919 in command of a detachment guarding German prisoners. Back in New York, he joined the staff of *Vanity Fair*, later succeeding Edmund Wilson as managing editor. After spending several years in Paris and Sorrento, he returned to New York to work on the staff of Paramount Pictures. In 1926 he went back to France to write poetry and short stories. He came back to America in 1933, settling finally on Cape Cod where he lived a relatively isolated life and wrote little poetry but some of his best critical essays. In 1941 he came to New York City as Publications Director of the Office of the Co-ordinator of Inter-American Affairs, whose assignment it was to plan and supervise South American anthologies. He died of heart failure in 1944. Principal works: fiction: *Many Thousands Gone* (1931); fiction: *Act of Darkness* (1935); *Selected Poems* (1941); *Collected Poems* (ed. with preface and memoir by Allen Tate, 1948); *Collected Essays* (ed. with introduction by Edmund Wilson, 1948).

Bishop's poetry reflects the influence of Yeats, Eliot, and Pound, but he added to this influence aspects distinctively his own: a rich sensuous imagination, unique in his generation. A dozen of his shorter poems, including the brilliantly original *Perspectives Are Precipices*, are a lasting contribution to American poetry.

R(ichard) P(almer) Blackmur was born in 1904 in Springfield, Massachusetts, and attended public schools in Boston. He worked in a bookshop in Cambridge, Mass., and was associated with Lincoln Kirstein in editing *The Hound and Horn*, 1928–29. A free-lance poet and critic for many years, Blackmur held a Guggenheim Fellowship from 1936 to 1938. In 1940 he was appointed Assistant in the Creative Arts Program at Princeton University. He has remained there since that date, except for the years 1943–46, when he was a member of the Institute for Advanced Study at Princeton. A Fellow in American Letters of the Library of Congress, Blackmur is best known for his critical writing. He is now Professor of English at Princeton. Principal works: criticism: *The Double Agent: Essays in Craft and Elucidation* (1935); *From Jordan's Delight* (1937); criticism: *The Expense of Greatness* (1940); *The Second World* (1942); *The Good European and Other Poems* (1947); criticism: *Language as Gesture* (1952); essays: *The Lion and the Honeycomb* (1955).

Blackmur is probably the best living American critic, and his critical essays in the past fifteen years have overshadowed his early poetry.

His first volume, *From Jordan's Delight*, remains one of the best books of verse of his generation.

LOUISE BOGAN was born in 1897 at Livermore Falls, Maine, and attended Mount St. Mary's Academy, Manchester, N.H., the Boston Girls' Latin School, and for one year, Boston University. Her first book of poems, *Body of This Death*, appeared in 1923. Miss Bogan won *Poetry* magazine's John Reed Memorial Prize in 1930 and its Helen Haire Levinson Prize in 1937. She was elected a Fellow in American Letters, Library of Congress, in 1944, and held the Library's Chair of Poetry in 1945–6. She has been a Guggenheim Fellow, and a visiting lecturer at the University of Washington, University of Chicago, and University of Arkansas; in addition to poetry and some fiction she has written since 1929 reviews of poetry for *The New Yorker*. A member of the National Institute of Arts and Letters, she won an Institute award in 1951 and shared with Léonie Adams the Bollingen Prize in 1955. Principal works: *Dark Summer* (1929); *The Sleeping Fury* (1937); *Poems and New Poems* (1941); *Collected Poems 1923–53* (1954).

Miss Bogan has been able to maintain in an age of intellectualism a highly original fusion of the metaphysical tradition and romantic lyricism. One feels that Miss Bogan's lyrics will survive the fashions of the first half of this century that have given notoriety to poets less enduring.

KATHERINE GARRISON CHAPIN was born in Waterford, Connecticut, in 1890, and was privately educated. In 1918 she was married to Francis Biddle, Attorney-General of the United States under Franklin D. Roosevelt. She was a Fellow in American Letters of the Library of Congress, 1944–51. She has published critical essays and reviews in *Poetry* (Chicago), *U.S. Quarterly Book Review*, *The Sewanee Review*, and other leading journals. Her principal works are *Outside the World* (1930), *Bright Mariner* (1933), *Time Has No Shadow* (1936), *Lament for the Stolen* (1938), *Plain Chant for America* (1942). She is the author of two plays, produced in New York in 1929 and 1948. She resides in Washington, D.C.

MALCOLM COWLEY was born in 1898 in Belsano, Pennsylvania. He was graduated from Harvard University in 1920 and spent the following two years studying French history and literature at the University of Montpellier, on an American Field Service Fellowship. After two years of free-lance writing in New York City, Cowley returned to Paris, where he was associated with the Dadaists and helped edit the experimental magazines *Secession* and *Broom*. He was literary editor of *The New Republic* from 1929 to 1944. Cowley continues to contribute to literary magazines and to give lectures. He is a member of the National Institute of Arts and Letters. Principal works: *Blue Juniata* (1929); prose: *Exile's Return: A Narrative of Ideas* (1934; rev. ed., 1951); editor: *After the Genteel Tradition* (1937); *The Dry Season* (1941); prose: *The Literary Situation* (1954).

LOUIS O. COXE was born in Manchester, New Hampshire, in 1918. He was graduated from Princeton University, B.A., in 1940. After teaching for two years at the Brooks School, North Andover, Mass., he spent four years in the Navy, principally as commanding officer aboard two P.C. escort vessels. He has taught English at Princeton University, at the Lawrenceville School, and, as a Briggs-Copeland Fellow, at Harvard University. He was Associate Professor of English at the University of Minnesota, 1949–55; he is now Professor of English at Bowdoin College. Coxe is the author of two books of poems: *The Sea Faring and Other Poems* (1947) and *The Second Man and Other Poems* (1955). He is the co-author with Robert H. Chapman of *Billy Budd*, a play, published in 1952.

Coxe's influences, where they are visible at all, are outside the orbit of modernism: he is regional New England and Robinsonian; introspective and lyrical.

(HAROLD) HART CRANE (1899–1932) was born in Garrettsville, Ohio, the son of a well-to-do manufacturer. He attended public schools in Cleveland and Warren, Ohio. At thirteen Crane began writing verse of promise. Before he had finished high school, he came to New York, where he became acquainted with some leading literary figures, particularly the Imagist group and those associated with *Seven Arts* magazine. For several years he alternated between writing advertising copy in New York and working at such diverse jobs as candy-packer, riveter, and munitions plant laborer in Ohio. He published *White Buildings* in 1926, and continued to work on *The Bridge*, a long mythopoeic poem about American history. *The Bridge* appeared in 1930 and won *Poetry*'s Helen Haire Levinson Prize. Upon receiving a Guggenheim Fellowship in 1931, Crane went to Mexico to write a poem on the history of Montezuma and the Spanish conquest. The following spring, without having begun this work, and in despair over what he considered his failing literary powers, he committed suicide by jumping into the Gulf of Mexico from the steamer that was taking him back to New York. The best biography of Crane is Philip Horton's *Hart Crane : The Life of an American Poet* (1937). *The Letters of Hart Crane*, ably edited by Brom Weber, appeared in 1952. Principal works: *White Buildings* (1926); *The Bridge* (1930); *The Collected Poems of Hart Crane* (edited by Waldo Frank) (1933).

Crane was the most original and powerful imagination that appeared in America in the 1920's.

E(DWARD) E(STLIN) CUMMINGS was born in Cambridge, Massachusetts, in 1894. From Harvard University Cummings received the B.A. in 1915 and the M.A. in 1916. Before America entered the war of 1914–18, he went to France as a driver with the Norton Harjes Ambulance Corps. Because of a mistake of a military official, Cummings was sent to a detention camp for three months; his experiences and observations there formed the basis of his first prose work. *The Ernormous Room*.

After serving as a private in the American Army at Camp Devens, Mass., he spent two years in New York and in 1920 went to Paris, where he studied art and received recognition both as a writer and a painter, Continuing to travel between Europe and New York City, he contributed during the 'twenties to *Vanity Fair*, *The Dial* (whose award for service to American literature he won in 1925), and to numbers of experimental magazines.

In 1931 he travelled on a special visa in the Soviet Union, and he has reported his journey in *Eimi* (1933). Cummings was given in 1950 an award from the Academy of American Poets for "great achievement" over a period of years. He is a member of the American Academy of Arts and Letters. Principal works: novel: *The Enormous Room* (1922); *Tulips and Chimneys* (1923); *XLI Poems* (1925); *Is 5* (1926); play: *Him* (1927); travel journal: *Eimi* (1933); autobiography and criticism: *i: six non-lectures* (1954); *Poems 1923–1954* (1954).

J. V. CUNNINGHAM was born on August 23, 1911, at Cumberland, Maryland. He grew up in Billings, Montana, and Denver, Colorado, and attended Stanford University (A.B. 1934; Ph.D. 1945). He has taught at Stanford University, University of Hawaii, University of Chicago, and University of Virginia. He is now chairman of the department of English at Brandeis University. He has published two volumes of poetry, *The Helmsman* (1942) and *The Judge is Fury* (1947), and a pamphlet, *Doctor Drink* (1950). His other publications include *The Quest of the Opal* (1950), *Woe or Wonder: the Emotional Effect of Shakespearian Tragedy* (1951), and a number of articles in critical and scholarly journals. He is married, and has a daughter, born in 1937. He lives in South Sudbury, Massachusetts.

DONALD (GRADY) DAVIDSON was born in 1893 in Campbellsville, Tennessee, and was educated in Tennessee private schools and at Vanderbilt University, from which he received the B.A. in 1917 and the M.A. in 1922. He is now Professor of English at Vanderbilt University. A member of *The Fugitive* Group, he was a founder and an editor of *The Fugitive* from 1922 to 1925. He was the leader of the Southern 'Agrarians', and was one of twelve contributors to the volume, *I'll Take My Stand*, published in 1930. He has written essays and reviews as well as poetry. Principal works: *An Outland Piper* (1924); *Lee in the Mountains and Other Poems, including The Tall Men* (1938); *The Attack on Leviathan; Regionalism and Nationalism in the United States* (1938); essays: *Still Rebels, Still Yankees* (1957).

EMILY (ELIZABETH) DICKINSON (1830–86) was born, lived, and died in Amherst, Massachusetts, the daughter of a forceful and prominent lawyer. She attended Amherst Academy and, for one year, Mount Holyoke Female Seminary. Her life was outwardly almost eventless: she left Amherst only twice–in 1854 for a trip to Washington and Philadelphia, while her father was serving in Congress; in 1864–65 to Boston, where she was treated for eye trouble. By the mid-'sixties she was withdrawing more completely from the world, and after this time she never went beyond the garden gate (dressed in white), saw only the family and a few intimate friends, and wrote in secret some 1,700 poems –her "letter to the world". Only two of her mature poems were published–and these without her consent–during her lifetime. Since the themes of love and renunciation figure importantly in her verse biographers have speculated ceaselessly upon the "subject" of these poems. Among the names suggested are Benjamin F. Newton, a law student in Miss Dickinson's father's office; the Rev. Charles Wadsworth, the minister whom Emily met in Philadelphia in 1854 and did not see again until 1880; and (according to the most recent "disclosure") Judge Otis Lord, a friend of the family. Miss Dickinson's health began to fail in 1883, and three years later, at the age of fifty-five, she died of Bright's disease. Biographies and critical works about Emily Dickinson include: Genevieve Taggard: *The Life and Mind of Emily Dickinson* (1934); George F. Whicher: *This Was a Poet* (1938); Millicent Todd Bingham: *Ancestors' Brocades* (1945) and *Emily Dickinson: A Revelation* (1954); and Richard Chase: *Emily Dickinson* (1951). Principal works: *Poems* (ed. by Mabel Loomis Todd and T. W. Higginson, 1890); *Poems: Second Series* (ed. by Todd and Higginson, 1891); *Poems: Third Series* (ed. by Todd, 1896); *The Single Hound* (ed. by Martha Dickinson Bianchi, 1914); *Selected Poems* (Preface by Conrad Aiken, 1924); *Further Poems* (ed. by Bianchi and Hampson, 1929); *Unpublished Poems* (ed. by Bianchi and Hampson, 1935); *Complete Letters of Emily Dickinson* (ed. by Mabel L. Todd,, 1931); *Collected Poems* (1937); *Bolts of Melody* (ed. by Mabel L. Todd and Millicent Todd Bingham, 1945); *Letters of Emily Dickinson* (ed. by M. L. Todd, 1951).

No brief critical comment on the greatest American poet of the nineteenth century could do her, or her commentator, justice. What seems to be the definitive edition of her *Poems* (1955), from the scholarly hand of Thomas Johnson, puts to rest most of the problems of an authoritative text; so that criticism and scholarship may henceforth set about its proper tasks.

H(ILDA) D(OOLITTLE) was born in Bethlehem, Pennsylvania, in 1886 and was educated in private schools in Pennsylvania. She entered Bryn Mawr College in 1904, but was obliged by ill health to leave after two years. On a trip abroad in 1911 she met Ezra Pound in London and was drawn into the Imagist movement, becoming one of its leaders. In 1913 H.D. married Richard Aldington, English poet and novelist, who was one of the original Imagist group. She made a short visit to the United States in 1920, but since then has lived in London and in a small town in Switzerland, with a number of trips to Greece to pursue her study of Greek art and history. *Poetry* magazine has awarded H.D. its Guarantors Prize and its Helen Haire Levinson Prize. Principal works: *Collected Poems of H.D.* (1925); *The Usual Star* (1928); *Red Roses for Bronze* (1929); *By Avon River* (1940); *The Walls Do Not Fall* (1944); *Selected Poems* (1957).

H.D. was the only one of the Imagist group for whom "imagism" was more than a slogan: she was born an Imagist poet. Her imagination centres upon ancient Greece and Greek mythology, which seem to liberate her strong command of sense-perception and of the evocative power of ancient names and places. Her verse is based upon the cadence of the phrase, rather than metre, and her "free verse" is highly disciplined.

RICHARD EBERHART was born in Austin, Minnesota, in 1904. He received the B.A. degree from Dartmouth College and from Cambridge University, where he also earned an M.A. in 1933. For nine years he was master of English at St. Mark's School, Southborough, Mass. After four years in the United States Navy, he joined the Butcher Polish Co., Boston, in 1946, and has been vice-president of the firm since 1952. Eberhart has given extensive readings from his poetry. His awards include: the Guarantors Prize from *Poetry* magazine, 1946; the Harriet Monroe Memorial Prize, 1950; and the Shelley Memorial Prize, 1951. Principal works: *Reading the Spirit* (1936); *Poems New and Selected* (1944); *Selected Poems* (1951); *Undercliff* (1953); *Greek Praises* (1957).

Eberhart is a natural poet, unstudied, spontaneous, given to the unintentional grotesque, but, at his best, a poet of originality.

ROBERT FITZGERALD was born in Geneva, New York, in 1910 and spent his first eighteen years in Springfield, Illinois. He attended the Choate School, was graduated from Harvard, and studied Classics and Philosophy at Trinity College, Cambridge. *Poetry* awarded him the Midland Authors Prize in 1932. From 1933 to 1935 he was a reporter for the *New York Herald Tribune*, and for seven years thereafter he was a staff writer on *Time* magazine. After three years in the Navy, he taught at Sarah Lawrence College until 1953, except for 1950–1, when he was Resident Fellow in Creative Writing at Princeton University. A Fellow of the School of Letters in Indiana University in 1951, he received a Guggenheim Fellowship in 1952. Fitzgerald is the author of two early volumes of verse: *Poems* (1935) and *A Wreath for the Sea* (1943); in collaboration with Dudley Fitts he has published translations of Euripides' *Alcestis* and Sophocles' *Antigone* and *Oedipus Rex*. His own translation of *Oedipus at Colonus* appeared in 1941.

Fitzgerald has matured slowly as a poet (he has long been one of our few distinguished translators from the Greek), and his best poems, some of which appear in this anthology, are included in *The Rose of Time* (1956). His diction is marked by classical severity and precision.

JOHN GOULD FLETCHER (1886–1950) was born in Little Rock, Arkansas. At seven he began studying Greek and Latin with private tutors, and he started his formal schooling three years later. At sixteen he left the south for one year at Phillips Academy, and in 1903 he entered Harvard University, where he continued to write verse as an undergraduate. He quit Harvard four months before graduation, his father having died and left him with sufficient means to write and travel. From 1908 until 1933 he lived in England, where he became affiliated with the Imagists. Five of his books were privately printed in 1913. He returned to his family home in Little Rock in 1933. Fletcher committed suicide by drowning in 1950. Principal works: *Irradiations–Sand and Spray* (1915); *Goblins and Pagodas* (1916); *The Black Rock* (1928); prose: *The Two Frontiers: A Study in Historical Psychology* (1930); autobiography: *Life Is My Song* (1937); *Selected Poems* (1938).

Fletcher's early work, influenced by Imagist and post-symbolist theories of the relation of poetry, painting, and music, remains his best. His later phase, in which the influence of Hardy and Lindsay is evident, will probably not survive.

CHARLES HENRI FORD was born in Mississippi in 1913. He founded and edited two avant-garde magazines: *Blues* (Mississippi, 1929–30) and *View* (New York City, 1941–47). He edited *The Mirror of Baudelaire* for New Directions in 1942, and in 1945 he published *A Night with Jupiter and Other Fantastic Stories*. He has published one novel: *The Young and Evil* (Paris, 1933). His poetry has appeared in numerous magazines and anthologies, including several of the New Directions annuals, *Transition Workshop* (1949) and Edith Sitwell's anthology of American poetry (1951). Published editions of his poetry, besides smaller collections, include three full-length books: *The Garden of Disorder and Other Poems* (1939), with introduction by William Carlos Williams, *The Overturned Lake* (1941), and *Sleep in a Nest of Flames* (1949), with introduction by Edith Sitwell. In recent years he has resided in Paris and Rome.

ROBERT (LEE) FROST was born in 1875 in San Francisco, California. His father, a New Englander, died when Frost was ten, and the boy was taken by his school-teacher mother to his grandfather's home in Lawrence, Mass. There he attended grammar and high schools and developed a love for Latin poetry, especially that of Virgil. After a few months at Dartmouth College he went to work as a bobbin-boy in a Lawrence mill. He continued to write verse, and at twenty-two, having been married for two years, he entered Harvard University in 1897, but left two years later without a degree. Frost then worked as country school teacher, cobbler, and editor of a weekly newspaper. In 1900 he was given a farm in Derry, N.H., which he worked for some years, and from 1905 to 1912 he taught school near Derry. After the farm failed, Frost and his family went to England in 1912. He remained there for three years, meeting Wilfrid Gibson, Lascelles Abercrombie, Ezra Pound, and other poets. By 1915 his first two books–*A Boy's Will* and *North of Boston*–had been published, and he returned to the United States to find himself famous. In growing demand as a lecturer, he was made Professor of English at Amherst College in 1916 and taught there until 1938. His career at Amherst was interrupted by two periods at the University of Michigan (1921–23 as poet in residence; 1925–26 as fellow in letters). Recipient of many honorary degrees, Frost has received the Pulitzer Prize four times: in 1924 for *New Hampshire*, in 1931 for *Collected Poems*, in 1937 for *A Further Range*, and in 1943 for *A Witness Tree*. He was awarded the Loines Prize in 1931, the Mark Twain Medal in 1937, and the gold medal of the National Institute of Arts and Letters (of which he is a member) in 1939. That year found him the first incumbent of the Ralph Waldo Emerson Fellowship in poetry at Harvard University. Remaining at Harvard until 1943, he has since that date been George Ticknor Fellow in Humanities at Dartmouth College. Principal works: *North of Boston* (1914); *New Hampshire* (1923); *West-Running Brook* (1928); *Selected*

Poems (1936); *Collected Poems of Robert Frost* (1939); *A Masque of Reason* (1945); *A Masque of Mercy* (1947); *Steeple Bush* (1947); *Complete Poems of Robert Frost* (1949).

JEAN GARRIGUE was born in Evansville, Indiana, in 1914. In 1937 she graduated from the University of Chicago, and she received an M.A. from the University of Iowa in 1943. She has taught at Iowa, Bard College and Queens College, and in 1954–55 she held a Rockefeller grant. *The Kenyon Review* awarded her first prize for a short story in 1944, and she has published critical reviews in *New Republic, The Saturday Review of Literature, The Kenyon Review, Tomorrow,* and other periodicals. A group of her poems appeared in New Directions' *Five Young American Poets* (1944), and she has published two books of poetry: *The Ego and the Centaur* (1947) and *The Monument Rose* (1953). Individual poems have appeared in *The Kenyon Review, Botteghe Oscure, Nation, Poetry, Poetry* (*New York*), *The Quarterly Review of Literature, Wake,* and *The New Yorker.* Since 1940, she has resided mainly in New York City.

BREWSTER GHISELIN was born in Webster Groves, Missouri, in 1903. He grew up in Missouri and California and attended the University of California at Los Angeles and at Berkeley, and Oxford University, England. His poems, stories, and essays have appeared in such magazines and anthologies as *The Hudson Review, The Kenyon Review, Partisan Review, Poetry, The Sewanee Review, Story,* and *A Southern Vanguard.* He is a Professor of English at the University of Utah and director of its annual Writers' Conference.

He has published two volumes of poems–*Against the Circle* (1946) and *The Nets* (1955), and an anthology, *The Creative Process,* which has been reprinted as a Mentor book.

HORACE (VICTOR) GREGORY was born in Milwaukee, Wisconsin, in 1898. He was educated at the Milwaukee School of Fine Arts and the German-English Academy. In 1923 he received his B.A. from the University of Wisconsin, where he began to write poetry, and where his chief interests were Catullus and Lucretius. For the next several years he free-lanced in New York City, living in a poor neighborhood in the Chelsea section and writing poetry and book reviews. He married the poet Marya Zaturenska in 1925. Gregory won the *Poetry*'s Lyric Prize in 1928 and its Helen Haire Levinson Prize in 1934. Since that date he has taught writing and literature at Sarah Lawrence College, Bronxville, N.Y. He was awarded a Guggenheim Fellowship in 1951. Principal works: *Chelsea Rooming House* (1930); *Poems, 1930–1940* (1941); prose: *The Shield of Achilles: Essays on Poetry and Beliefs* (1944); *Selected Poems* (1951).

BARBARA HOWES, a native Bostonian, was born in 1914. She attended Bennington College and for four years afterwards in New York edited the literary quarterly, *Chimera.* Winner of *Poetry* magazine's Bess Hokin Prize, Miss Howes has published poetry and several short stories in numerous literary magazines. The wife of poet William Jay Smith, she divides her residence between New York City and North Pownal, Vermont.

Miss Howes is the author of two books of poems: *The Undersea Farmer* (1948) and *In a Cold Country* (1954).

RANDALL JARRELL was born in Nashville, Tennessee, in 1914. He received from Vanderbilt University both his B.S. (1936) and M A. (1939). After teaching at the University of Texas he spent the years 1942–6 in the Army Air Force. In 1946–47 he was on the faculty of Sarah Lawrence College and acting literary editor of *The Nation*. He has taught at the Salzburg Seminar in American Civilization, Princeton University, and the University of Illinois, and is now Associate Professor of English at the Woman's College of the University of North Carolina. In 1956 he was appointed Consultant in Poetry to the Library of Congress. Principal works: *Blood for a Stranger* (1942); *Little Friend, Little Friend* (1945); *Losses* (1948); criticism: *Poetry and the Age* (1953); *Selected Poems* (1955); novel: *Pictures from an Institution* (1954).

ROBINSON JEFFERS was born in Pittsburgh, Pennsylvania, in 1887. He studied at private schools in the U.S., Switzerland, and Germany, and received his A.B. from Occidental College in 1905 at the age of eighteen. Graduate study took him to the University of Southern California Medical School, the University of Zurich, and the University of Washington School of Forestry. But despite these varied pursuits, it was the writing of poetry that most interested him after his first youthful poems were published in 1904. *Flagons and Apples*, his first volume of verse, appeared in 1912, and Jeffers's desire to pursue a literary career was realized when a cousin died and left him a legacy. In 1914 he and his wife moved to Carmel, Calif., and there, on a bluff overlooking Carmel Bay, Jeffers built himself the stone house and tower in which he has worked for more than forty years. In these rugged surroundings Jeffers has lived with his family in almost complete isolation, making only rare extended trips. A member of the National Institute of Arts and Letters, he was awarded in 1937 a Book-of-the-Month Club Fellowship for distinguished work. Jeffers inaugurated a series of poetry readings at the Library of Congress in 1941. Principal works: *Tamar, and Other Poems* (1924); *Roan Stallion, Tamar, and Other Poems* (1925); *Cawdor, and Other Poems* (1928); *Give Your Heart to the Hawks* (1933); *Selected Poetry of Robinson Jeffers* (1938); *Be Angry at the Sun* (1941); *Medea* (1946, verse rendering of the Euripides play); *The Double Axe* (1948); *Hungerfield* (1954).

(NICHOLAS) VACHEL LINDSAY (1879–1931) was born in Springfield, Illinois. He graduated from Springfield High School and attended Hiram College in Ohio for three years (1897–1900). After study at the Chicago Art Institute and the New York School of Art, Lindsay started in 1906 on the first of his long walking-tours, aimed at spreading his "gospel of beauty' He walked from Florida to Tennessee distributing poems and receiving in exchange food and lodging. After a trip to Europe with his family, he made another walking-tour in 1908 through New Jersey and Pennsylvania. He spent the next several years lecturing for the YMCA in Springfield and for the Anti-Saloon League in central Illinois. With the appearance of *General William Booth*

Enters into Heaven in *Poetry* in 1913 and with the publication of *The Congo* in 1914, Lindsay's popularity was established, and soon he was in great demand as a reader of his own verse. He toured England in 1920. Although now respected, Lindsay felt his powers declining and, depressed by poverty and ill health, he committed suicide in 1931. He was a member of the National Institute of Arts and Letters and had won several awards from *Poetry* magazine: the first Guarantors Prize, the Helen Haire Levinson Prize (1927), and a special Award of Honor (1928). Principal works: *General William Booth Enters Into Heaven* (1913); *The Congo* (1914); *Collected Poems* (1923); *Selected Poems* (1931); *Letters of Nicholas Vachel Lindsay to A. Joseph Armstrong* (ed. by A. J. Armstrong, 1940).

AMY LOWELL (1874–1925) was born in Brookline, Massachusetts, of a distinguished New England family. In 1902 she decided that poetry was her *métier* and turned from participation in civic affairs to a serious study of the craft of poetry. Her first book of verse (*A Dome of Many-Coloured Glass*) appeared in 1912. A year later in England she met Ezra Pound and others in the Imagist movement, of which she later became the leader in this country. In the decade following the publication of her first free-verse poems in 1914, volumes of her verse appeared regularly, and she gave frequent public lectures. She was awarded *Poetry* magazine's Levinson Prize in 1924. She spent her last years at work on a large biography of Keats. She was exhausted by the strain of this undertaking and died of a cerebral haemorrhage in 1925. *What's O'Clock*, which appeared that year, was awarded the Pulitzer Prize in 1926. Principal works: criticism: *Tendencies in Modern American Poetry* (1917); *Can Grande's Castle* (1918); biography: *John Keats* (2 vols., 1925); *Selected Poems* (1928).

ROBERT (TRAILL SPENCE) LOWELL is a native of Boston, Massachusetts, where he was born in 1917. He attended St. Mark's School, Harvard University, and Kenyon College, from which he received the B.A. in 1940. He worked for a year as editorial assistant in a New York publishing house, and later, as a conscientious objector during the latter part of the war of 1939–45, spent five months in a Federal prison. His first book of poems, *Land of Unlikeness*, appeared in a limited edition in 1944. His second, *Lord Weary's Castle*, won the Pulitzer Prize in 1947, and during 1947–8 he was Consultant in Poetry, Library of Congress. A member of the National Institute of Arts and Letters, Lowell has been awarded a Guggenheim Fellowship and a prize from the American Academy of Arts and Letters. He has taught at Iowa and Cincinnati, and lives presently in Boston.

Lowell is the author of three books of verse: *Land of Unlikeness* (1944); *Lord Weary's Castle* (1946); and *Mills of the Kavanaughs* (1951).

ARCHIBALD MACLEISH was born in 1892 in Glencoe, Illinois. Educated at the Hotchkiss School, he received his B.A. from Yale University in 1915 and his LL.B., from Harvard University in 1919. He served in the Army from 1917 to 1919, attaining the rank of captain. After teaching briefly at Harvard, MacLeish practised law in Boston for three years, but decided in 1923 to give up his law career and devote himself to writing full-time. After following the Mexican route of Cortez in preparation for *Conquistador*, he spent several years travelling and writing for *Fortune* magazine. MacLeish was appointed Librarian of Congress in 1939, a position he held until 1944. He continued to experiment with a kind of "social" poetry which he frequently combined with such other forms as ballet, drama, radio documentary, and photography. An influential adviser in the Roosevelt administration, he was appointed Director of the Office of Facts and Figures in 1941 and Assistant Director of the Office of War Information the following year. In 1944–5, as Assistant Secretary of State, he helped draft the constitution for UNESCO. At Harvard since 1949 as Boylston Professor of Rhetoric, he has received international honours for his public career, and in 1953 he won the Bollingen Prize and the Pulitzer Prize. He is a member of the American Academy of Arts and Letters. Principal works: *The Hamlet of A. MacLeish* (1928); *New Found Land* (1930); *Conquistador* (1932); *Poems, 1924–1933* (1933); verse play: *Panic* (1935); verse play: *The Fall of the City* (1937); verse play: *Air Raid* (1938); *Land of the Free* (1938); *A Time to Speak: Selected Prose* (1941); *Actfive* (1948); prose: *Poetry and Opinion* (1950); *Collected Poems 1917–1952* (1952); *Songs for Eve* (1954).

EDGAR LEE MASTERS (1869–1950) was born in Garnett, Kansas, the son of a lawyer. He was brought up in Petersburg and Lewistown, Illinois, the Spoon River country he later made famous. He attended public schools, wrote verse, worked in a printer's office, and read widely. He left Knox College, Galesburg, after one year, and was admitted to the bar in 1891. For more than twenty-five years he was a successful lawyer in Chicago, where he became associated with the Midwestern group which included Carl Sandburg and Vachel Lindsay. His best-known work, *Spoon River Anthology*, was published in 1915. Modeled on *The Greek Anthology*, this collection of free-verse epitaphs, revealing the secret lives of those buried in a Midwestern cemetery, ran through seventy editions by 1940. He gave up his law practice in 1920 and moved to New York City, where he lived for most of his life writing quantities of verse, fiction, boys' stories, and biographies. He died in a suburb of Philadelphia in 1950. Principal works: *Spoon River Anthology* (1915; reissued with introduction by the author, 1942); *Domesday Book* (1920); *The New Spoon River* (1924); *Selected Poems* (1925); autobiography: *Across Spoon River* (1936).

WILLIAM MEREDITH was born in New York City in 1919, attended schools in Connecticut and Massachusetts, and was graduated from Princeton University in 1940. From 1946 to 1952 he taught English and creative writing at Princeton and the University of Hawaii.

Meredith is the author of *Love Letter from an Impossible Land* (1944), a volume in the Yale Series of Younger Poets; his second book of verse, *Ships and Other Figures*, was published in 1948.

EDNA ST. VINCENT MILLAY (1892–1950) was born in Rockland, Maine. From childhood she wrote verse, some of which was published in *St. Nicholas* magazine. She attended Barnard College and received her B.A. from Vassar College in 1917, the year in which her first volume of verse, *Renascence and Other Poems*, appeared. After graduation, Miss Millay moved to Greenwich Village. There she wrote short stories pseudonymously, joined the Provincetown Players, and published three plays in verse. In 1923 she was awarded the Pulitzer Prize for *The Harp-Weaver*, and in 1925 the Metropolitan Opera Association commissioned her to write the libretto for an opera (*The King's Henchman*, music by Deems Taylor). After her marriage in 1923, she and her husband, Eugen Boissevain, lived principally in their Berkshire Hills farm, which she left only for occasional travel and public readings from her works. She won *Poetry* magazine's Helen Haire Levinson Prize in 1931. Miss Millay wrote less and less in later life; her poetry after 1940 was largely occupied with political and social themes. She died of a heart attack in 1950. Principal works: *Renascence and Other Poems* (1917); *A Few Figs from Thistles* (1920); *The Buck in the Snow and Other Poems* (1928); *Fatal Interview* (1931); *Collected Lyrics* (1943); *Collected Sonnets* (1941); *Collected Poems* (1956)

MARIANNE (CRAIG) MOORE was born in 1887 in St. Louis, Missouri, and was educated at the Metzger Institute, Carlisle, Pa., and at Bryn Mawr College, from which she received the A.B. degree in 1909. The next year she studied at the Carlisle Commercial College and from 1911 to 1915 was in charge of the commercial department of the U.S. Indian School at Carlisle. Her verse began appearing in the English periodical, *The Egoist*, and her first volume of poems, published without her knowledge by friends in England, appeared in 1921. At this time, and for four years thereafter, Miss Moore was an assistant in the New York Public Library. Her first American book, *Observations*, appeared in 1924 and subsequently won the Dial Award. She became acting editor of the *Dial* in 1925 and remained with that magazine until it ceased publication in 1929. Since that time Miss Moore has continued writing poetry and occasional criticism and has been given numerous honors, including *Poetry*'s Helen Haire Levinson Prize (1953); the Ernest Hartsock Memorial Prize (1935); the Shelley Memorial Award (1940); the Harriet Monroe Poetry Award (1944). She received a Guggenheim Fellowship in 1945 and a year later was given an award from the National Institute of Arts and Letters, of which she is a member. Her *Collected Poems* (1951) brought added recognition in the form of the Bollingen Prize in Poetry, the National Book Award and the Pulitzer Prize. She lives in Brooklyn. Principal works: *Observations* (1924); *Selected Poems* (intro. by T. S. Eliot, 1935); *What Are Years* (1941); *Nevertheless* (1944); *Collected Poems* (1951); translation: *Fables of La Fontaine* (1954); criticism: *Predilections* (1955); *Like a Bulwark* (1956).

HOWARD NEMEROV comes from New York City, where he was born in 1920. Educated at the Fieldston School and Harvard University, from which he received the B.A. in 1941, he served during the war of 1939–45 as a pilot with the RCAF and USAAF. He taught for several years at Hamilton College and has been at Bennington College since 1948. He was awarded *The Kenyon Review* Fellowship in Fiction for 1955. Principal works: *The Image and the Law* (1947); novel: *The*

Melodramatists (1949); *Guide to the Ruins* (1950); novel: *Federigo, or the Power of Love* (1954); *The Salt Garden* (1955).

JOHN FREDERICK NIMS was born in 1913 in Muskegon, Michigan. He received his early schooling there and in Chicago. After attending the University of Notre Dame, he did graduate work in comparative literature at the University of Chicago. Nims is now Associate Professor of English at Notre Dame, where he has taught since 1940, except for a year at St. Michael's College. University of Toronto, and two years (1952–4) as Fulbright Professor of American Literature in Milan and Florence. His verse has appeared in many of the "little magazines", particularly in *Poetry*, of whose editorial board he was a member from 1945 to 1948. During the period 1942–4 he won three of *Poetry*'s annual awards.

Nims is the author of *The Iron Pastoral* (1947) and *A Fountain in Kentucky* (1950).

EZRA (LOOMIS) POUND was born in Hailey, Idaho in 1885, of New England stock. He spent his early years in the Eastern United States and attended Hamilton College, Clinton, N.Y., from which he received the Ph.B. degree in 1905. From 1905 to 1907 he was a Fellow in Romance Languages and Literatures at the University of Pennsylvania (M.A., 1906). He spent the next year in travel abroad and, after four months of teaching at Wabash College, Crawfordsville, Ind., he returned to Europe and settled in London. Pound's first book of verse–*A Lume Spento*–appeared in 1908 and was followed by *Exultations* and *Personae*, both published in 1909. A leading figure in the London literary world, he strengthened the new *Poetry* magazine by contributing his own verse and serving as its European correspondent until 1919. A founder and leader of the Imagist group, he later (1914) founded and edited *Blast*, the Vorticist review. As unofficial literary executor for Ernest Fenollosa, Pound helped create an audience for Japanese drama and Chinese poetry in England and America. The most influential man of letters of his generation, he furthered the careers and reputations of Joyce, Eliot, Tagore, the composer George Antheil, the sculptor Gaudier-Brzeska and others. From 1917 to 1919 he was London editor of *The Little Review*, and during the next four years he was Paris correspondent for *The Dial*. Emigrating to Italy in 1923, he founded the short-lived magazine, *Exile*. During this period he was given the Dial Award for distinguished service to American letters. Pound continued publishing poetry–primarily the *Cantos*–literary criticism, biographies, and translations. His growing identification with the Mussolini régime in Italy was clearly established during his brief visit to the United States in 1939. Two years later he began broadcasting fascist propaganda to the U.S. from Rome. Pound was taken prisoner by United States forces in Italy in May 1945 and was brought back to this country in November. Charged with treason, he was adjudged "insane and mentally unfit for trial" by a commission of psychiatrists. He was committed in December 1945 to St. Elizabeth's Hospital, a government mental institution in Washington, D.C., but was released in 1955. In 1949 he was awarded the Bollingen

Prize for his *Pisan Cantos*, written while he was in an American prison in Pisa. Pound is a member of the American Academy of Arts and Letters. Principal works: criticism: *The Spirit of Romance* (1910; rev. ed., 1953); translation: *The Sonnets and Ballate of Guido Cavalcanti* (1912); *Canzoni* (1911) and *Ripostes* (1912); biography: *Gaudier-Brzeska* (1916); ed.: *Ernest Fenollosa: Certain Noble Plays of Japan* (1916); *Personae: Collected Poems* (1926, new and enlarged edition 1950); *Selected Poems* (ed. with introduction by T. S. Eliot, London, 1928); criticism: *How to Read* (1931); *Homage to Sextus Propertius* (London, 1934); essays: *Make It New* (1934); *A Selection of Poems* (London, 1940); *Pisan Cantos* (1948); *Cantos* (1948); *Selected Poems* (1957); *Letters of Ezra Pound* (ed. by D. D. Paige, 1950); *Translations* (1953); *Literary Essays of Ezra Pound* (ed. with an introduction by T. S. Eliot, 1954); translation: *The Classical Anthology Defined by Confucius* (1954); *Section: Rock Drill* (part of the *Cantos*); translation: *The Women of Trochis* (1957).

(HOWARD) PHELPS PUTNAM (1894–1948) was a native of Boston, Massachusetts. He attended Phillips Exeter Academy and Yale University, from which he was graduated in 1916 with a group that included Stephen Vincent Benét, MacLeish, and Thornton Wilder. He spent the year 1920 in Provence and a year in Italy on a Guggenheim Fellowship in 1933. He published two books of verse between 1927 and 1948. The second of these–*The Five Seasons* (1931)–was intended as part of a larger work, never completed, which would attempt to create an American mythology through an integrated group of poems. Putnam died in 1948 of a stroke brought on by asthma.

Putnam was the author of *Trinc* (1927) and *The Five Seasons* (1931), both books of verse.

JOHN CROWE RANSOM was born in 1888 in Pulaski, Tennessee, the son of a minister. He received his B.A. from Vanderbilt University in 1909 and spent three years as a Rhodes Scholar at Christ Church College, Oxford, where he received a bachelor's degree in humane letters in 1913. Returning to the United States, Ransom joined the English faculty of Vanderbilt, and, except for a two-year period in the field artillery during the war of 1914–18, he remained there until 1937. It was in Nashville that he helped found and edit *The Fugitive* from 1922 to 1925 and later contributed to the symposia *I'll Take My Stand* and *Who Owns America?* In 1931–2 he went to England on a Guggenheim Fellowship. Since 1937, Ransom has been Carnegie Professor of Poetry at Kenyon College where he founded and since 1939 has edited *The Kenyon Review*. He has lectured at a number of colleges and universities and has been a senior fellow at the Kenyon School of English, now the Indiana University School of Letters. In 1951 he received the Bollingen Prize and the Russell Loines Award. Principal works: *Chills and Fever* (1924); *Two Gentlemen in Bonds* (1927); prose: *God without Thunder: An Unorthodox Defense of Orthodoxy* (1930); criticism: *The World's Body* (1938); criticism: *The New Criticism* (1941); *Selected Poems* (1945); ed.: *The Kenyon Critics* (1951).

KENNETH REXROTH was born at South Bend, Indiana, in 1905. His childhood was spent in various parts of the Midwest; his adolescence, in Chicago. Having left high school before graduation, he supported himself from the age of thirteen in such diverse occupations as harvest hand, forest packer, factory laborer, fruit picker, and insane-asylum attendant. Alternating between Chicago and New York during the 'twenties and 'thirties, he was active in radical politics (particularly the I.W.W.) and knew many of the leaders in the Chicago underworld, the 'New Negro,' the world of jazz. An abstract painter, as well as poet, Rexroth lives in San Francisco and makes frequent trips skiing and mountain-climbing into the High Sierras. Principal works: *The Phoenix and the Tortoise* (1944); *The Signature of All Things* (1949); *The Dragon and the Unicorn* (1952); *100 Poems from the Japanese* (1955); *In Defense of the Earth* (1956).

EDWIN ARLINGTON ROBINSON (1869–1935) was born in Head Tide, Maine. He spent his youth in Gardiner, Me., prototype of the "Tilbury Town" of his poems. A precocious child, he read Shakespeare at seven and wrote verse at eleven, translating in his teens the *Antigone* of Sophocles and selections from Virgil. He attended Harvard University from 1891 to 1892, but was forced by the death of his father to give up his schooling. His first volume of poetry, *The Torrent and the Night Before* (1896), was privately printed in an edition of only 300 copies, but its favorable critical reception encouraged him to pursue the career of a writer. He moved to New York City and, to support himself there while *The Children of the Night* (1897) and *Captain Craig* (1902) were being published, he worked as an inspector of subway construction. President Theodore Roosevelt, impressed by what he had seen of Robinson's poetry, offered him in 1904 a clerkship in the New York customs house. Robinson held this job until 1910. From that time on he devoted himself entirely to earning a living by his pen and spent his summers at the MacDowell Colony, Peterborough, N.H., where he was the acknowledged "presiding genius." His reputation was fully established with *The Man Against the Sky* (1916), and in 1922 his *Collected Poems* won the first Pulitzer Prize to be given for poetry. He won the Pulitzer Prize again in 1925 for *The Man Who Died Twice* and in 1928 for *Tristram*. This long poem, part of his Arthurian trilogy (with *Merlin* and *Lancelot*), was a popular success. A year later the American Academy of Arts and Letters conferred upon him its gold medal. A man of extreme reticence, Robinson gave no lectures or public readings from his works. He died in 1935 at the age of sixty-five. Principal works: *Collected Poems* (1921; completed edition, with additional poems, 1937); *Letters of Edwin Arlington Robinson to Howard George Schmitt* (ed. by C. J. Weber, 1943).

THEODORE ROETHKE was born in Saginaw, Michigan, in 1908, and received his education at the University of Michigan and Harvard University. He has taught at Lafayette College, Pennsylvania State University, and Bennington College, and he is now Professor of English at the University of Washington. He has received two Guggenheim Fellowships, the Levinson Prize from *Poetry* for 1951, an award from the National Institute of Arts and Letters of which he is now a member, and the Pulitzer Prize in 1954.

Roethke is the author of four books of verse: *Open House* (1941); *The Lost Son and Other Poems* (1948); *Praise to the End!* (1951); *The Waking, Poems 1933–1953* (1953).

CARL SANDBURG was born in 1878 in Galesburg, Illinois. He left school at thirteen and worked at harvesting, bricklaying, dishwashing, and other odd jobs throughout the West. During the Spanish-American War he served eight months in Puerto Rico with the Sixth Illinois Infantry. After four years at Lombard College, he left without a degree. Sandburg held a newspaper job in Milwaukee and was secretary to the mayor of that city from 1910 to 1912. His first recognition was the Helen Haire Levinson Prize awarded him by *Poetry* in 1914. His six-volume life of Lincoln won the Pulitzer Prize in History in 1940. During the war of 1939–45 Sandburg wrote the commentary for a U.S. government film and made foreign broadcasts for the Office of War Information. A member of the National Institute of Arts and Letters, he won the Pulitzer Prize for Poetry in 1951, the gold medal for history of the American Academy of Arts and Letters, and the Poetry Society of America medal in 1953. Principal works: *Chicago Poems* (1916); *Cornhuskers* (1918); *Selected Poems* (ed. by Rebecca West, 1926); *Good Morning, America* (1928); *Abraham Lincoln: The Prairie Years* (1929); *The People, Yes* (1936); *Smoke and Steel* (1920) and *Slabs of the Sunburnt West* (1922); *Abraham Lincoln: The War Years* (1939); *Remembrance Rock* (1948); *Complete Poems* (1950); autobiography: *Always the Young Strangers* (1953).

DELMORE SCHWARTZ was born in Brooklyn, New York, in 1913. He received his B.A. from New York University in 1935 and studied at Columbia University, the University of Wisconsin, and Harvard University. After receiving a Guggenheim Fellowship in 1939, he taught English at Harvard from 1940 to 1947; he is a Fellow of the Indiana School of Letters. In addition to writing verse, fiction, and criticism, he is an associate editor of *Partisan Review*, a position he has held since 1943. Principal works: *In Dreams Begin Responsibilities* (1938); *Shenandoah* (1941); stories: *The World is a Wedding* (1948); *Vaudeville for a Princess* (1950).

KARL SHAPIRO was born in Baltimore, Maryland, in 1913, and was educated at the University of Virginia and at Johns Hopkins University. When his first book of verse was published in 1942 he was with the Army in the South Pacific, where he remained until the spring of 1945. During the following year he was appointed Consultant in Poetry at the Library of Congress, after which he taught writing courses at Johns Hopkins University until 1950. Since 1950 he has been editor of *Poetry: A Magazine of Verse*. Winner of the Levinson Prize and the Contemporary Poetry Prize in 1943 and an American Academy of Arts and Letters Grant in 1944, Shapiro was awarded the Pulitzer Prize in 1945 for his *V-Letter and Other Poems*. Principal works: *Person, Place and Thing* (1942); *V-Letter and Other Poems* (1944); *Essay on Rime* (1945); *Trial of a Poet* (1947); *Poems 1942–1953* (1953).

WILLIAM JAY SMITH was born in 1918 in Winnfield, Louisiana. Educated at Washington University in St. Louis, he later studied at

Columbia University, at Oxford (on a Rhodes Scholarship), and in France and Italy. Winner of *Poetry* magazine's Young Poets Prize in 1945, Smith has taught at Washington University, Columbia University, and Williams College.

Smith has written two volumes of verse: *Poems* (1947) and *Celebration at Dark* (1950). Most recent of his books are *Laughing Times*, a collection of children's poems, and *Selected Writings of Laforgue* (both 1955).

WALLACE STEVENS (1879–1955) was born in Reading, Pennsylvania. After attending Harvard University and the New York Law School, he was admitted to the bar in 1904 and for some years practised law in New York City. His association with the Hartford (Connecticut) Accident and Indemnity Company began in 1916, when he entered its legal department; from 1934 he was vice-president of the firm.

Although several of his poems appeared in *The Harvard Advocate* while he was an undergraduate, it was not until 1914 that he received recognition for his verse. So impressed with his work was editor Harriet Monroe that she revised a special wartime number of *Poetry* to make room for four of Stevens's entries. For these he won the *Poetry* prize in 1914, and a year later the magazine awarded him a similar prize for a one-act play in free verse.

His first book, *Harmonium*, was published in 1923, when Stevens was forty-four years old; before his death he wrote more than seven other volumes of verse. He received the Bollingen Prize in Poetry from the Yale University Library in 1949 and the National Book Award for *The Auroras of Autumn* in 1951 and again for his *Collected Poems* in 1955. Stevens was a member of the American Academy of Arts and Letters. He died from a cerebral hemorrhage in 1955. Principal works: *Harmonium* (1923); *Ideas of Order* (1935); *The Man with the Blue Guitar* (1937); *Parts of a World* (1942); *Notes Toward a Supreme Fiction* (1942); *Transport to Summer* (1947); *The Auroras of Autumn* (1950); essays: *The Necessary Angel* (1951); *Collected Poems* (1954); essays and uncollected poetry: *Opus Posthumous* (1957).

(JOSEPH) TRUMBULL STICKNEY (1874–1904) was born in Geneva, Switzerland, and lived abroad during the greater part of his childhood. Until he entered Harvard University his sole teacher was his father, Austin Stickney, head of the Latin department at Trinity College. After receiving his B.A. from Harvard in 1895, Stickney spent seven years in Paris studying Greek and Sanskrit at the Sorbonne and was the first American to be awarded its *D. ès L.* degree (1903). Having already published one volume of poetry, he was working on another when he became an instructor in Greek at Harvard. His plans for completing this book and for translating the *Persians* of Aeschylus were cut short by his death from a brain tumor at the age of thirty in 1904.

Only two volumes bear Stickney's name: *Dramatic Verses* (1902) and *The Poems of Trumbull Stickney* (edited by William Vaughan Moody, George Cabot Lodge, and J. E. Lodge, 1905).

ALLEN TATE was born in Winchester, Kentucky, in 1899; B.A. Vanderbilt, 1922. As an undergraduate at Vanderbilt University he was a founder and editor of *The Fugitive*. He married the novelist Caroline Gordon in 1924, and spent the years 1925–28 in New York, writing poetry and criticism. A Guggenheim Fellowship took him abroad during 1928–30. After teaching at several universities, he held the Chair of Poetry at the Library of Congress in 1943–44. After editing *The Sewanee Review* for two years, he was an editor at a New York publishing house, and taught for four years at New York University. Since 1951 he has been Professor of English at the University of Minnesota, on leave during 1953–54 as Fulbright Lecturer at the University of Rome. Tate is a member of the National Institute of Arts and Letters and a Senior Fellow of the Indiana University School of Letters. Awarded the Bollingen Prize of Yale University, 1957. Principal works: *Selected Poems* (1937); criticism: *On the Limits of Poetry: Selected Essays 1928–1948* (1948); criticism: *The Hovering Fly and Other Essays* (1949); *Poems 1922–1947* (1949); ed. with Caroline Gordon: *The House of Fiction* (1950); criticism: *The Forlorn Demon* (1953); *The Man of Letters in the Modern World* (1955).

Mark Van Doren was born in 1894 in Hope, Illinois. He received his A.B. from the University of Illinois in 1914 and his M.A. a year later. After two years in the infantry in the war of 1914–18, he spent a year in England and France on a travelling fellowship. He received his Ph.D. from Columbia in 1920 (his thesis on Dryden being published as a book that same year) and has been on the Columbia faculty ever since. Van Doren was *The Nation's* literary editor from 1924 to 1928 and its motion picture reviewer from 1935 to 1938. He won the Pulitzer Prize in 1940 for his *Collected Poems*. In addition to poetry, fiction, and children's books, Van Doren has written numerous critical studies and has edited a long list of anthologies and readers. He is a member of the American Academy of Arts and Letters. Principal works: criticism: *Edwin Arlington Robinson* (1927); ed.: *American Poets 1630–1930* (1932); criticism: *Shakespeare* (1939); *Collected Poems 1922–1938* (1939); *The Mayfield Deer* (1941); *The Seven Sleepers, and Other Poems* (1944); *New Poems* (1948); *Short Stories* (1950); *Spring Birth and Other Poems* (1953); *Selected Poems* (1954); and short stories: *Home with Hazel* (1957).

Robert Penn Warren was born in 1905 in Guthrie, Kentucky. He received his B.A. in 1925 from Vanderbilt University, where he was a member of *The Fugitive* group of poets. After graduate study at the University of California (M.A. 1927) and at Yale University, he went in 1928 to Oxford as a Rhodes Scholar, being awarded a B. Litt. degree in 1930. Back in the United States, he taught briefly at Southwestern University and from 1931 to 1934 at Vanderbilt. From there he went to Louisiana State where he taught for eight years and edited, with Cleanth Brooks, *The Southern Review*. In 1936 he won a Houghton Mifflin Literary Fellowship and *Poetry's* Levinson Prize, and in 1942, the Shelley Memorial Award. Warren came to the University of Minnesota in 1942 and remained there until 1950, except for one year (1944–45) as incumbent of the Chair of Poetry, Library of Congress, and one year (1947–8) abroad on a Guggenheim Fellowship. His novel, *All the King's Men*, won the Pulitzer Prize for Fiction in 1947. From 1950 to 1951 he was Professor of the Yale University School of Drama. He is married to the writer Eleanor Clark. He is a Fellow in American Letters of the Library of Congress and a member of the National Institute of Arts and Letters. Principal works: ed.: *A Southern Harvest: Short Stories by Southern Writers* (1937); ed., with Cleanth Brooks: *Understanding Poetry* (1938; rev. ed. 1950); novel: *Night Rider* (1939); novel: *At Heaven's Gate* (1943); *Selected Poems 1923–43* (1944); ed., with Cleanth Brooks: *Understanding Fiction* (1943); novel: *All the King's Men* (1946); *The Circus in the Attic and Other Stories* (1948); novel: *World Enough and Time* (1950); *Brother to Dragons* (1953); novel: *Band of Angels* (1955); *Promises Poems 1954–1956*.

JOHN HALL WHEELOCK was born in 1886 on Long Island, New York, and wrote poetry from an early age. At Harvard University he published with Van Wyck Brooks *Verses by Two Undergraduates*. He was graduated from Harvard in 1908 and spent two years studying for the Ph.D. degree in German universities. He brought out *The Human Fantasy*, his first book of verse, in 1911, and that same year he began his association with the publishing house of Charles Scribner's Sons, of which he is now editor and assistant treasurer. His volume of collected poems was given the New England Poetry Society's annual award for 1936. Principal works: *The Black Panther* (1922); *The Bright Doom* (1927); *Poems, 1911–1936* (1936); *Poems Old and New* (1956).

JOHN (BROOKS) WHEELWRIGHT (1897–1940) was born in Boston, Massachusetts, and was graduated from Harvard University. A political and religious nonconformist in the New England tradition, he practised architecture in Boston and published several volumes of verse, most of which were privately printed. Wheelwright died an accidental death in 1940. Principal works: *Forty Days* (1929); *Rock and Shell: Poems 1923–1933* (1933); *Mirrors of Venus: A Novel in Sonnets, 1914–1933* (1938); *Selected Poems* (1941).

REED WHITTEMORE was born in New Haven, Connecticut, in 1919. He attended Phillips Academy at Andover and Yale University, from which he was graduated in 1941. Two years before that he started with James J. Angleton the magazine *Furioso*, which he later revived and continued to publish until 1953. The years 1941–45 found Whittemore in the Army and Air Force, primarily in the Mediterranean area. Following a year of graduate study in history at Princeton University, Whittemore came to Carleton College, where he teaches English.

Whittemore is the author of *Heroes and Heroines* (1946) and *An American Takes a Walk* (1956).

RICHARD WILBUR was born in New York City in 1921 and was graduated from Amherst College in 1942. After serving several years with the 36th Infantry Division, he took his M.A. at Harvard University in 1947. At Harvard from 1947 until 1954, Wilbur was first a Junior Fellow of the Harvard Society of Fellows, then an Assistant Professor of English. He received a Guggenheim Fellowship in 1952 and was awarded the Prix de Rome of the American Academy of Arts and Letters in 1954. He is now Associate Professor of English at Wellesley College. Wilbur has written *The Beautiful Changes and Other Poems* (1947), and *Ceremony and Other Poems* (1950); *Things of this World* (1956), for which he was given the National Book Award and the Pulitzer Prize, a translation of *The Misanthrope* (1955); and lyrics for a musical version of *Candide* (1957).

WILLIAM CARLOS WILLIAMS was born in 1883 in Rutherford, New Jersey. He was educated at the Horace Mann High School, N.Y.; at Château de Lancy, near Geneva, Switzerland; and at the University of Pennsylvania, where he received the M.D. degree in 1906. Two years as an interne in New York were followed by a year of graduate study in Leipzig. Williams returned in 1910 to Rutherford, N.J., where he has lived and practised medicine ever since. His first book, *Poems*, appeared in 1909. In 1913 his *The Tempers* showed the influence of the Imagists. Since that date Williams has written more than a dozen volumes of poetry and a considerable number of novels, short stories, and prose essays. A member of the American Academy of Arts and Letters, he has won the *Dial* Award for distinguished service to American literature; *Poetry*'s Guarantors Prize; the Loines Award in 1948; the National Book Award for Poetry, 1949; and the Bollingen Prize, 1953. Principal works: essays: *In the American Grain* (1925); novel: *White Mule* (1937); *The Complete Collected Poems . . . 1906–1938* (1938); novel: *In the Money* (*White Mule*, part II, 1940); *Paterson* (Books I–IV, 1946–51); *Selected Poems* (ed. by Randall Jarrell. 1949); *Collected Later Poems* (1950); stories: *Make Light of It* (1950); *Collected Earlier Poems* (1951); *Autobiography of William Carlos Williams* (1951); *Selected Essays* (1954); *Desert Music and Other Poems* (1954); *Selected Letters* (1957).

YVOR WINTERS was born in Chicago in 1900 and attended schools in California, Washington, and Illinois. His first book of poetry, *The Immobile Wind*, appeared in 1921. For two years thereafter he taught elementary and secondary school in the coal camps near Santa Fe. In 1925 he received both his B.A. and M.A. in romance languages at the University of Colorado, and for two years he taught French and Spanish at the University of Idaho. After marrying the writer Janet Lewis, he came to Stanford University in 1927 as an instructor and graduate student. Winters helped found and edit *The Gyroscope* and was western editor of *The Hound and Horn* from 1932 to 1934. Continuing to write poetry and criticism, he has remained at Stanford, from which he received the Ph.D. in 1934, and is now Professor of English. Winters is a Fellow of the Indiana School of Letters, and in 1952 he was awarded a grant from the American Academy of Arts and Letters, of which he is now a member. Principal works: *The Bare Hills* (1927); criticism: *Primitivism and Decadence: A Study of American Experimental Poetry* (1937); criticism: *Maule's Curse: Seven Studies in the History of American Obscurantism* (1938); *Poems* (1940); *The Giant Weapon* (1943); criticism: *The Anatomy of Nonsense* (1943); criticism: *In Defense of Reason* (1947); *Collected Poems* (1952); criticism: *The Function of Criticism* (1957).

ELINOR WYLIE (1885–1928) was born Elinor Hoyt in Somerville, New Jersey. She spent her childhood and youth near Philadelphia and in Washington, D.C. After a season in Paris and London, she married Philip Hichborn; soon afterwards she eloped to Europe with Horace Wylie, whom she later married. They returned to the United States in 1916, and Mrs. Wylie continued to write the poetry she had been producing secretly for years. In 1921 her *Nets to Catch the Wind* won the Julia Ellsworth Ford Prize of the Poetry Society of America. By 1924 she had written another volume of verse, a first novel, and had married William Rose Benét. Principal works: *Nets to Catch the Wind* (1921); *Black Armour* (1923); *Angels and Earthly Creatures* (1929); *Collected Poems of Elinor Wylie* (1932); *Collected Prose of Elinor Wylie* (1933); *Last Poems of Elinor Wylie* (1943).

INDEX OF BRITISH POETS

INDEX OF AMERICAN POETS

INDEX OF FIRST LINES